KU-794-631

8

8

02

398 003

198

8

2 FEB 00
21 MAY 99

Leeds Metropolitan University

17 0088434 3

TRANSFORMING THE COMPANY

'A thought-provoking and refreshingly broad look at achieving corporate change.'

Personnel Today

'This book is essential reading for all managing directors and management consultants.'

Management Consultancy

'One of the most stimulating and refreshing books on corporate transformation available. Coulson-Thomas's approach is both pragmatic and inspirational.'

Vern Zelmer, Managing Director, Rank Xerox (UK) Ltd

'An authoritative, convincing and realistic guide. Colin Coulson-Thomas's invaluable and encouraging book reveals that fundamental change can be achieved if a practical and holistic approach is adopted.'

Martin Bartholomew, Director, Mercury Communications Mobile Services

'*Transforming the Company* is the ultimate "handbook" for top management. It is powerful, readable, prescriptive, and available now, when so much needs to be done to reshape organisations to compete in the marketplace.'

Harvey Parr, Managing Director, ACT Logsys Ltd

TRANSFORMING THE COMPANY

Bridging the Gap Between Management Myth and Corporate Reality

Colin Coulson-Thomas

KOGAN
PAGE

Dedication

To Yvette, Vivien and Trystan

LEEDS METROPOLITAN
UNIVERSITY LIBRARY

1700884343
B31 BV
7045   16 2·94
10·5·94
658.406 COU

First published in 1992
Reprinted 1993

Apart from any fair dealing for the purposes of research or private study, or criticism or review, as permitted under the Copyright, Designs and Patents Act, 1988, this publication may only be reproduced, stored or transmitted, in any form or by any means, with the prior permission in writing of the publishers, or in the case of reprographic reproduction in accordance with the terms of licences issued by the Copyright Licensing Agency. Enquiries concerning reproduction outside those terms should be sent to the publishers at the undermentioned address:

Kogan Page Limited
120 Pentonville Road
London N1 9JN

© Colin Coulson-Thomas, 1992

British Library Cataloguing in Publication Data

A CIP record for this book is available from the British Library.

ISBN 0 7494 0671 2

Typeset by Saxon Graphics Ltd, Derby
Printed in England by Clays Ltd, St Ives plc

Disclaimer
The masculine pronoun has been used throughout this book. This stems from a desire to avoid ugly and cumbersome language, and no discrimination, prejudice or bias is intended.

Contents

ACKNOWLEDGEMENTS

This book represents a distillation of some themes which have emerged from a programme of questionnaire and interview surveys that have been undertaken over a period of five years. Particular projects have been supported or sponsored by the Association of Project Managers, the British Institute of Management, Granada Business Services, the Institute of Directors, the Institute of Personnel Management, ODI International, Rank Xerox (UK) Ltd, Surrey European Management School and the Training Agency. The volume of material that has been collected, especially notes of interview discussions, is so extensive that I have had to be highly selective with the presentation of evidence. Most chapters could easily have been extended to book length, so the message to those who might question the conclusions is that there is more of the same!

I would like to thank Richard Brown, Alan Wakelam, Trudy Coe and Susan Coulson-Thomas who have worked with me on certain surveys; Peter Benton, formerly director general of the British Institute of Management, for encouraging me to bring the results of certain BIM surveys to the attention of a wider audience; John Nicholas, John Harper and other Institute of Directors colleagues who share a commitment to director development; and Vern Zelmer and the team of Rank Xerox (UK) Ltd for their collaboration in the field of implementing corporate transformation. Finally, I have fond memories of a visit some years ago to Xerox PARC which first alerted me to the extent to which we are surrounded by latent and unrecognised talent that is just waiting to be released and tapped.

Colin Coulson-Thomas, 1992

1

THEORY AND REALITY

THE OPPORTUNITY

There is an unprecedented and historic opportunity to transform the capacity of companies to serve customers. A revolution could occur in the working relationships between people, and the extent to which their individual talents could be harnessed and their personal requirements satisfied. In the process of generating the value sought by customers, managerial productivity could increase by a factor of ten or more.

This is not wild speculation, but a tantalising prospect. Many people, in different roles in a variety of organisations, have glimpsed the potential to break free of a range of traditional constraints. Most of those that remain are self-imposed and susceptible to appropriate action.

All the individual elements, from attitudes to processes, that are necessary to achieve the transition have been identified. These are already in place in leading-edge companies. The secrets of the individual and collective release of capacity, and the fulfilment of personal aspirations and corporate ambitions, are no longer hidden. Their use has been demonstrated and documented, and their utility is clear.

It can be done. However, it is not clear that it will be done. For too many companies the failure to question, anticipate and 'think things through' means that frustration is being snatched from the jaws of success. There is disappointment where there should be elation.

THE FRUSTRATION

If so much is known, why is the new Jerusalem not with us today? Why has so much aspiration, intention and vision had such apparently limited impact upon reality? Why has the talk and hype been accompanied by so little action? Why are we not 'getting it together'?

Senior managers in many companies are maintaining a stoic attachment to the public line that 'it will come out right'. However, in private many are experiencing a mixture of anguish and despair. Too many outcomes and events are different from expectations. It is not happening, and they believe something is missing.

Corporate management is not lacking in plans, programmes or initiatives. Major companies such as BP with its 'Project 1990', BT with its 'Operation Sovereign', and ICL and IBM, have 'gone public' with announcements of fundamental corporate transformation programmes.

The lives of many thousands of people are being significantly affected by these 'flagship' programmes. Their experiences are shared by those in a wide variety of smaller companies that are quietly, and sometimes painfully, seeking to bring about change.

Directors and senior managers feel they know what they want. Their desires are being reflected in corporate activity. Organisations are actively seeking a transition to more flexible and responsive forms, based upon teamwork and trust. Networks are being established that embrace customers, suppliers and business partners.

In the case of companies such as Data General and Philips, the extent to which corporate survival is dependent upon successful transformation is both clear and quite explicit. However, the widespread desire for change is not always matched by an awareness of how to bring it about. The issue is not whether to change, but *how* to change.

Corporate transformation is taking longer to achieve than was first thought. Momentum is being lost, and attitudes and behaviour are proving stubbornly resistant to change. In many organisations a wide gulf has emerged between expectation and achievement.

Not all is gloom, however. Leading-edge companies are clocking up examples of progress that make them 'targets' for writers of case studies and enthusiasts of 'benchmarking'. All too often, though, they are 'stumbling across' success rather than consciously creating or planning it.

Those who copy the pioneers, and emulate their initiatives, tend to accumulate 'examples', prototypes, experiments, individual innovations, islands of potential, that do not 'come together' to have a significant impact upon the total corporation. They collect some 'lovely pieces', but not enough of them to play a new game successfully.

In general, senior managers, most of whom have a genuine desire to achieve results, are disappointed. They are failing to spot inter-relationships, make connections, think ahead, 'manage through' the obstacles and 'line up' all the elements needed to 'make it happen'.

THE ANGUISHED MANAGER

The extent of frustration felt by senior decision makers was evident in the comments of many of those interviewed in the course of the surveys upon which this book is based. Consider the following selection.

'We say one thing and do another. People are not fools, they look for results. They look at what we do.'

'So far it's just words on paper. Nothing has happened out there.'

'Our actions undermine our words. Until top managers start acting as role models things won't begin to happen. People need to see that it is for real.'

'After a time you get totally immune to concepts, theories, and the blandishments of consultants and gurus. What is the point if you cannot put it into effect?'

'Too many visions remain as blue sky hidden by a layer of fog. Even if a few of them attract your attention, they do not reach your wallet because they have not been translated into products and services.'

'Why do we put so much stress upon packaging programmes that have little chance of ever being put into effect?'

'I assume you also have a credibility and delivery problem. What have you ever done to escape from the mire that traps the rest of us?'

'All over the world politicians say whatever is necessary to 'hang on in there', and once re-elected they do what they can in sometimes difficult circumstances. Why should it be different for corporate politicians facing employees, shareholders and customers? You have to say things to hang on to these people.'

'Never before has so much commitment and effort resulted in such disappointing outcomes. Something must be missing, something obvious that we haven't seen.'

'Would you believe someone who turned up with half a roof and a few bricks to make a house? People know what it takes, and they know it is not going to happen.'

Many of those who have expressed frustration are, or claim to be, 'victims' of the failure of colleagues to deliver. Others feel powerless because they have not been empowered or equipped to do what they feel is necessary. Some believe that, individually or collectively, they are responsible for what should have happened but has not yet come about.

DAWNING REALISATIONS

As organisations begin to flatten, and growth projections have been revised downwards, more managers are having to seek satisfaction in current roles rather than in future prospects. They can no longer move on before 'adverse consequences' or a lack of results 'catch them up'.

Management teams are having to confront reality, and live with the outcomes of their own decisions, initiatives and advocacy. Where it matters, many of them know they face a gap between aspiration and achievement. As awareness of this spreads, they are also conscious that they themselves will be held responsible for bringing outcomes more in line with both desires and claims.

In some cases, there have been premature celebrations of success. The false dawn makes continuing darkness even more unbearable. The following comments illustrate the extent of the anguish:

> 'Our internal journals have made the most of isolated successes, but we don't know how to apply the lessons to the whole company. People in different areas want to follow. We don't know how to handle it, or what the outcomes might be.'

> 'Everyone knows about our one team that is doing great things with the latest of everything. They produce all sorts of amazing projections of what would happen if we all worked the same way. What they don't know is the cost and management time involved. To do the same everywhere would kill us.'

> 'Past initiatives have been like forest clearings. They're great, but when you move on the old habits and ways of doing things grow back again. We thought we had made a permanent change, but in some areas what we congratulated ourselves on no longer exists.'

> 'If you achieve a breakthrough, it's best to keep quiet about it. Tell the centre and they will want it everywhere. They are desperate for results, but you can't replicate what we've done that easily. There are so many things that need to be got right.'

Many companies are in the position described by one director: 'We are in it up to our necks, and we need a way out. Our reputations are on the line, so we need it fast.'

THE DANGERS IN AN AGE OF HYPE

Economic recession and slow-down has had a sobering impact. As one chief executive officer (CEO) put it: 'We can't rely on economic growth to solve the problem. This one is not going to come right without us, or in spite of us.' Those who are in a pit are seeking a way out and adversity has made them more desperate for a 'handle' or a 'life-line'.

The situation is ripe for exploitation by the plausible, and the assault of the packaged. Instant solutions and the quick fix abound. Never has there been such an age for hype. The limiting factor is cynicism, fed by a continuing stream of disillusionment with the results of past panaceas. The safeguard is, paradoxically, a failure to implement, which protects some of the naïve from their own gullibility.

It is an age of temptation. There are more people alive today than have died throughout all eternity. And, given some forethought, most of them can be reached in seconds by one means or another. The technology of communications allows the deepest recesses of the most remote regions to be reached by a variety of media.

Industry sectors have grown up that are hungry for new messages to spread. Creative talent can turn the banal into an 'appeal' or a 'proposition' that lures with its appearance of profundity and insight. The 'management audience' has been a lucrative target for many years.

Never before has it been so easy to spread the latest fad. Never before has the organised peddling of simplistic notions offered such returns. The palate for the new and the catchy seems never to jade. The time of self-deception, group-think and the contagion of myth has surely come.

THE SEARCH FOR SOLUTIONS

If directors and managers are to turn their backs on hype, to whom should they look for the 'real solutions'? The answer is 'To themselves'.

Handing the problem to someone else, while continuing as before, does not work. Like people, organisations can die even when almost all their individual elements are in satisfactory, if not perfect, working order. No amount of external help of the highest quality that is devoted to honing parts of the body corporate to perfection can grant life if the will to go on is lacking, if a vital organ fails or if a crucial flow is blocked.

In most cases devoting more resources to the problem will not help. A superior technology of itself may not have a significant impact. People without direction, motivation and relevant skills may add more to costs than to output.

Well thought-out programmes, even a variety of distinct initiatives that in themselves are worthy, may not be enough. Their introduction, along with changes of structure, may fail to influence attitudes and behaviour. Their combination may not be sufficient to 'make it happen' in the unique context of a particular company.

A more holistic approach is required. One that involves:

- an emphasis upon vision, goals, values and objectives;
- establishing and nurturing relationships;
- empowerment and motivation, and the harnessing of potential;
- tolerance and encouragement of diversity, and a culture of learning;
- the introduction of a range of new skills and approaches;
- the appropriate use of a comprehensive and complementary armoury of accessible tools, techniques and processes;
- a focus upon attitudes and behaviour, and obstacles and barriers; and
- the identification and delivery of key priorities.

If progress is to be made, all the elements need to be in place. When they are, the results can be dramatic. Given a holistic approach to the achievement of corporate transformation, getting it right may turn out to be easier than doing it wrong.

THE LATENT REVOLUTION

The extent of frustration and concern should be viewed as a source of hope. Change emerges slowly and reluctantly from the soil of complacency.

Thomas Kuhn, following a study of the history of scientific discovery, concluded that revolutions in thought or a 'paradigm shift' tend to occur when, increasingly, what has been regarded as 'normal science' no longer appears to 'fit' or explain a growing number of observed situations and circumstances.[1] Prior to each watershed, individuals in different locations tend separately to challenge the *status quo*.

There is a parallel with the contemporary management world. Too many management theories appear no longer to match reality. In many cases, promising ideas have been crudely and unthinkingly applied. Our perceptions of them derive from their use and application in a world that is rapidly passing into folklore. President of Philips, Jan Timmer, has recognised that in order to achieve corporate transformation a 'mental transformation' must first occur.

There has been a succession of challenges to management orthodoxy and behaviour over a period of years, but the revolution in thought has not yet occurred. Prophets exist with perception and insight, but their various ideas are not being brought together in the form of workable corporate change programmes.

There has been much analysis of what is wrong, and there is a broad consensus concerning the general shape of what needs to be done. However, little progress has been made.

CORPORATE ASPIRATION

The desire for change, and for particular changes, is genuine enough. Chief executives, directors and senior managers consistently rank general organisational capabilities such as adaptability, flexibility, responsiveness and the ability to learn above 'single issues' in terms of importance. As one CEO put it: 'Without these qualities in our organisation, and in our people, how can we hope to achieve any of our other objectives and survive in a changing environment?'

The continuing importance attached to building more flexible and responsive organisations is confirmed by a series of three related questionnaire surveys carried out in 1989, 1990 and 1991.[2,3,4] Collectively, these surveys cover over 200 different organisations, most of which are among the 'market leaders' in their fields.

The 1991 survey reveals that 'creating a more flexible and responsive organisation' is the number one issue concerning the management of people, and this was also the case in the 1989 and the 1990 surveys.

Participants in the 1991 survey were asked to rank, in terms of their importance, 13 personnel issues.[4] The issues selected were similar to, and based upon, 14 'human resource challenges' presented in the 1989 survey,[2] and 12 'human resource issues' listed in the 1990 survey.[3]

The responses to the 1990 survey [3] are shown in Table 1.1. Over three-quarters of the respondents considered 'creating a more flexible and responsive organisation' to be 'very important', while every one of them regarded it as either 'important' or 'very important'.

Table 1.1 *Human Resource Issues*

Ranked in order of 'very important' replies (%)	
Creating a more flexible and responsive organisation	77
Quality and teamwork	58
Continuing updating and development of knowledge and skills	40
Succession	32
Building broader and more mobile managers	30
Internationalisation: preparation for the globalisation of business	28
Changing the corporate culture	28
Individual assessment replacing standard terms and conditions	27
Remuneration	21
Europeanisation: preparation for 1992	17
Preparation for appointment to the board	15
Alternative patterns of work, eg teleworking	1

Ranked when 'very important' and 'important' replies are added together (%)

Creating a more flexible and responsive organisation	100
Continuing updating and development of knowledge and skills	97
Remuneration	95
Building broader and more mobile managers	93
Succession	92
Quality and teamwork	88
Changing the corporate culture	80
Europeanisation: preparation for 1992	77
Individual assessment replacing standard terms and conditions	72
Internationalisation: preparation for the globalisation of business	70
Preparation for appointment to the board	58
Alternative patterns of work, eg teleworking	41

Source: C Coulson-Thomas, *Human Resource Development for International Operation*, 1990

Those interviewed in all three surveys did not rank very highly the prospect of corporate survival, unless their organisations could achieve a 'transition' or 'transformation'. Many of those from the largest companies considered these giants to be the most vulnerable. Sheer scale is perceived as a source of weakness when it is not accompanied by flexibility.

CHALLENGES

Why this strong and continuing desire for corporate transformation? Flexibility and responsiveness is not being sought for its own sake, but in order to cope with the realities of the business and market environment.

According to Sir John Harvey-Jones in a commentary to the 'responsive organisation' report based upon the 1989 survey:[2]

Organisational flexibility is essential. Rates of change have speeded up. The hierarchical organisation is slow to respond. Decisions taken at the centre are too far away from the coal face. While the centre seeks local and relevant understanding, delays in decision making result.

In today's turbulent business environment speed of decision making is critically important. Windows of opportunity quickly open and close. Adaptability and change must be continuous. The organisation that learns to learn will survive. To do this its people must also learn to learn.

In an ever-changing, at times bewildering and generally demanding business environment, companies are facing multiple challenges and opportunities. For example:

- international markets are becoming more open as deregulation and privatisation become global phenomena;
- more intense competition is strengthening the bargaining position of consumers *vis-à-vis* suppliers, and there is pressure upon prices and margins;
- demanding customers now expect quality and reliability. There is a need to find new sources of differentiation to avoid falling into the 'commodity products' trap.

These bracing and competitive market conditions give the advantage to companies that empower those who are closest to the customer; are alert, astute and act quickly; and operate with limited 'overheads'. Those whose thoughts, activities and various elements are co-ordinated and in harmony seize the opportunities.

The slow, cost-heavy bureaucracy is a threatened species. Size, reputation and track-records of past achievements are no guarantee of future success. Without the flexibility and responsiveness that comes from different values, attitudes, behaviour and processes, all may be lost. To freeze in the glare of the headlights of external challenge is to court the risk of calamity.

In response to both longer-term trends and short-term economic pressures, CEOs are seeking to create more flexible, responsive and adaptable organisations. As one chairman put it:

> 'I used to boast about our size, the number of people we employed, and how many buildings we had. I now see these as a source of weakness. We lumber forward under the burden of a capability we cannot use flexibly in order to quickly serve our customers. The central issue is the transformation of the company.'

The scale of readjustment that may be needed to adapt to changed market realities can be dramatic. For example:

- Olivetti has reduced its workforce by a quarter over a two-year period;
- already Philips has reduced its worldwide workforce by a sixth, and the process of rationalisation and restructuring continues.

CHANGE IMPERATIVES

Companies do not seek to turn the worlds of their people upside down without good reason. The imperatives of change vary from company to company. The following small selection of comments identifies the concerns that led particular companies to seek fundamental change.

> 'We were not moving quickly enough. Our competitors were beating us to the punch.'

> 'Customers are wanting things tailored to their particular needs. We have to be able to treat them all as individuals.'

> 'The underlying technology is entering a digital revolution. The impacts will be felt throughout the organisation.'

> 'My people are imprisoned in self-contained functional boxes. I cannot get at them. We can't use them more widely.'

> 'It's not coming together. Different parts of the company seem to have their own agendas.'

> 'How do you best prepare for the unknown? We don't know that much about what may happen tomorrow.'

Recognition of the stark nature of reality can stiffen the resolve. There is little point in attempting corporate transformation unless there is a strong change imperative.

Many organisations find it difficult to summon up the collective energy needed to succeed unless 'backs are to the wall'. In a world in which time can be spent listening to the rustle of the leaves in the trees, it does not make sense to cause disruption, anguish and frustration, or to nourish false hopes that are doomed to disappointment when there is not a realistic prospect of success.

INCREMENTAL OR RADICAL CHANGE?

In the past many companies have coped with changes in the business environment by responding and adjusting incrementally, as and when particular challenges arose. There are those who take the view of one interviewee: 'So what's new? We've always been faced with changes, from great crashes to world wars, and we are still here. History is full of social and economic revolutions. Every generation thinks it's facing unprecedented challenges.'

The bureaucratic organisation adjusts to discrete changes by taking relatively small, self-contained and incremental steps.[5] Over a period of time this can lead to a better accommodation with a slowly changing environment. As more portraits of past chairmen appear on the panelled walls of the boardroom, a warm glow of pride in a heritage of achievement can lead to complacency.

An incremental approach is unlikely to cope with a sudden rush of multiple challenges. Many of the pressures faced in the past were not 'life-threatening', and in the case of those that were, many people felt they had more time to make whatever adjustments were necessary. There was the security of 'protection against foreign suppliers', the cartel and the cabal. With hindsight, competition appeared less intense. As one director put it: 'We did not have a pack of wolves snapping at our heels.'

Today the perception is different. Directors and senior managers are aware of a multiplicity of changes in the business environment that could have far-reaching consequences for their companies (Table 1.2). Many of the changes represent a discontinuity, a break from the past. Their number and nature has led the management teams of many companies to conclude that incremental adjustment to change is no longer enough. A 'first principles' transformation is required.

Table 1.2 *The Changing Business Environment*

Old	New
Confidence and rigidity	Insecurity and openness
Permanence and certainty	Turbulence and uncertainty
Incremental change	Revolutionary change
Opinions and theories	Facts and values
Logic	Intuition
Boundaries and disciplines	Interests, issues and problems
Constraints	Priorities
Organisation	Adaptation
Attitudes	Feelings
Personalities and vested interests	Principles and business philosophy
Quantity	Quality and post-quality
Getting ahead	Achieving balance and harmony
Drives	Needs
Producer centred	Customer centred
Focus on activity	Focus on output
Conflict and rivalry	Co-operation and consensus
Command and control	Two-way communication and sharing
Direction and management	Facilitation and support
Power	Empowerment
Resources	Enablers
Bureaucratic hierarchy	Horizontal relationships
Absolutes	Solutions relative to context
Simplicity	Diversity and relative complexity
One-dimension maximisation	Multi-dimensional trade-offs
Answers	Questions
Solutions	Temporary accommodations
Authority	Consent
Sanctions	Encouragement
Departmentalism and procedures	Business processes
Sequential activities	Parallel activities

Discrete problems	Holistic issues
Uninformed customers	Demanding customers
Homogeneous customers	Diverse customers
Standard products and services	Tailored products and services
Local customers	International customers
Established relationships	Integration and fragmentation
Sales	Account management
Individuals	Teams
The self and the company	The group and the environment
The 'here and now'	The consequences and the future
Unsupported	Facilitating processes and technology
'Hoarding' by the few	Empowerment of the many
Protected information	Ubiquitous information
Single discipline	Multi-disciplinary
Diversification	Focus
Generalisation	Segmentation
Knowledge	Competence
Teaching	Learning
Specialist teaching institutions	Integration of learning and working
Initial qualification	Continual updating
Lifetime practice	Functional mobility
Job descriptions	Roles
Career ladders	Succession of projects
Standard employment	Various patterns of work
Commodity products	Search for differentiation
Limited competition and barriers to entry	Open competition and diversity of supply
Cartels and oligopolies	Competition and choice
Zero-sum relationships	Positive-sum collaboration
Independence and dependence	Interdependence and partnership

TRENDS

What avenues are being explored by those who are seeking to transform their organisations? A number of 'organisational' trends have been identified by two BIM surveys.[2,6]

- Externally, priority is being given to building closer relationships with customers in order better to understand their requirements, while internally the focus is upon harnessing human talent in order to deliver greater customer satisfaction.
- There is recognition of the importance of the 'people factor' and the need for both individuals and organisations to learn. In particular, there is a strong desire to integrate working and learning.[3]
- Responsibility is being devolved and delegated to groups and teams, and, as a result of roles and responsibilities and other exercises, these are being given specific tasks. The focus is shifting from 'input' to 'output', and the organisation is becoming a portfolio of projects.
- The membership of teams is being drawn from a wider spread of functions, locations, nationalities and organisations. It is becoming more widely recognised that heterogeneous groups are generally more creative than those which are homogeneous.
- Awareness is growing of the importance of access to the approaches, skills, processes and supporting technology that can facilitate team working.

- Companies are increasingly thought to be competing on the basis of their processes, attitudes and values rather than their products and services, or their technology, all of which can be copied. Money, information and other resources are 'there' in the environment, ready to be 'picked up' by the companies with the processes, attitudes and values to make the best use of them in terms of generating value for individual customers.
- The management of corporate transformation is becoming recognised as a strategic management challenge in its own right, requiring a distinct perspective and a special kind of awareness.
- Successful transformation is increasingly seen as dependent upon securing changes of attitudes and behaviour, and the co-ordinated bringing together of those 'transformation elements' that are particularly relevant to the change needs and barriers of each organisation.

Transformation cannot be achieved without fundamental change. Within organisations, interest in rules and procedures is waning, but a desire for new processes for generating and delivering value for customers, and achieving adaptation and change, is growing. In particular, companies are becoming conscious of the need for processes for continuing learning, adaptation and change.

Many people in transitioning organisations are being confronted with new terms such as 'empowerment' or 'process'. Familiar concepts that were once the foundation stones of management courses are no longer used. This should not have come as a surprise. In what Drucker described over 20 years ago as 'the age of discontinuity,'[7] we should expect that many traditional approaches will be challenged and many assumptions may no longer apply.

THE NETWORK ORGANISATION

The shape of the 'emerging organisation' that is desired, and to which managements aspire, is becoming clearer. CEOs are describing and defining their organisational goals in network terms.[2,6,8] Their jottings and doodlings are summarised in Figure 1.1.

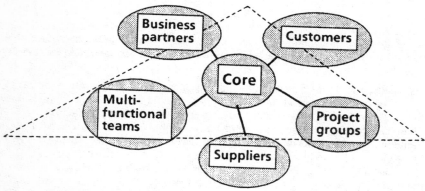

Source: Beyond Quality, BIM, 1990

Figure 1.1 *The Network Organisation*

There is a fair degree of consensus as regards the 'end point' of transition, or the nature of the transformed organisation.

- A high priority is being given to creating network organisations that are more adaptable and responsive to the changing needs of their customers and employees.

Organisations are becoming more fluid, facilitating networks rather than bureaucracies (Figure 1.1).

- As fewer companies are able by themselves to deliver 'total value' to customers, increasingly they are creating networks of relationships, with electronic links forward into customers, backwards to suppliers and sideways to business partners.
- The boundary of the organisation is becoming blurred. It is no longer a 'hard shell' surrounding all that which is owned or all those who are employed. Members of the network community are colleagues, peers, participants and partners, their membership being negotiated and a matter of choice.
- Networks and supply chains are becoming global, bringing together all those who share a common vision or a particular mission.[8] The network community resembles a cooperative collective or confederation of entrepreneurial teams and of groups with a particular focus.
- As a consequence, the formulation and implementation of information technology (IT) and other strategies increasingly involves co-operation and collaboration across organisational and national boundaries. These links, common access to ubiquitous information, and shared vision and values, hold together a constellation of entities of diverse natures, nationalities, shapes and sizes.
- Departmental barriers are fading as more work is done by groups, teams and project groups. The corporation is emerging as flatter, leaner and tighter. Processes are replacing procedures and, increasingly, organisation is by key process rather than by function.
- Within the network an internal market operates, groups and teams buying and selling services to and from each other. Some members of the network might be both collaborators and competitors.
- There is delegation, devolution and decentralisation, and greater accountability and responsibility. Remuneration is being increasingly linked to outputs that result in value for customers or the achievement of business objectives.

These changes and developments are ongoing. While start-up companies may have the option of going straight to the network form of organisation, most enterprises have a past. The organisational heritage from which escape is sought may be complex, and the bonds of corporate culture can be difficult to break. For example, Hewlett-Packard has been endeavouring to free itself from the constraints of an entrenched matrix form of organisation. These can confuse, bind and entrap like a spider's web.

Across companies in general, some progress is being made in such diverse areas as defining competency requirements, identifying empowerment methodologies, experimenting with self-managed work groups and installing facilitating processes. However, the relative significance of these various change elements, and how they should be brought together within the framework of an overall change programme, is rarely understood.

In the main, the 'end point' has not been reached. The network organisation remains an aspiration.

AREAS OF UNCERTAINTY

While there is some agreement as to the general shape of the organisational 'end point', there is little consensus as to how best to get there. The extent of the uncertainty is illustrated by the following selection of comments.

'Should we go straight to our end goal, or establish intermediate forms of organisation? Will this help or confuse?'

'We drew the conventional pyramid, but couldn't agree what to do with it. Turning it upside down with the customer on top put us [the board] in our place in terms of helping others to

serve the customer. But to show cross-functional processes we needed the customer over to one side. We ended up rotating the triangle, twisting it, looking at it this way, looking at it that way … it went on and on.'

'I worry about what new sets of problems are likely to emerge. None of us know anything about running the sort of organisation we are trying so hard to create.'

'We have our innovations, but how do we spread them through the organisation? What happens when we let go? Will revolution and chaos break out all over the place?'

'No one knows who the experts are. People make claims, but as these organisations we are all seeking don't yet exist, how do they know? Who knows what we might find?'

'I do try to benchmark, but it is difficult to judge who is ahead, or how much might be applicable to our situation. Will today's benchmark be tomorrow's disaster?'

It is beginning to dawn upon a number of advocates and agents of change that, for all the fanfares and bravado, many organisations are setting out on an uncertain journey with little in the way of experience, or the equivalent of a compass, to guide them. They do not know what the effect of a certain combination of change elements might be, and may not be in a position to know until these have actually been brought together.

The degree of acceptability of the individual elements of a change programme in different national and cultural contexts is also not easy to determine. For example, an organisation with aspirations to become an international network must recognise that while flexibility may be valued in some cultures, it is frowned upon in others.[8] A willingness to change may be interpreted as a lack of consistency and 'backbone'. Reliability and predictability may be highly valued qualities. Those thought to move according to whatever way the wind blows are not respected.

Pursuing the analogy with a journey, people are aware that there are winds and currents, and that choppy patches and occasional storms may well be encountered. The hope is that a degree of organisational unity and common purpose will allow the storms to be ridden out. However, the various possible effects of different combinations of wind and current make the drift and destination problematic.

ATTITUDES AND VALUES

More progress has been made in shaping the intended structure of the network organisation than in building the attitudes and values, and in encouraging and rewarding the behaviour, that will allow its full potential to be achieved. Few organisations reward on the basis of contribution to customer satisfaction, let alone role model behaviour or commitment to learning.

Wherever there is uncertainty, a common vision and shared values can allow commitment and unity to be sustained for longer than might otherwise be the case. The vision or purpose of a network, and its values, will become key sources of differentiation. Much effort will need to be put into articulating a distinct, shared and compelling vision that can hold a network together.

The bureaucracy was held together by a mixture of power, fear and guile, buttressed by the voluminous procedures manual. Gatekeepers hoarded information. There were those who played the power game like medieval bishops, willingly abetted by supine bootlickers and supplicating crawlers.

Given its potential for dispersing power and loosening many of the traditional forms of control, the evolving and moving network organisation could fragment without the gravitational pull of a common vision and shared values. As one CEO put it: 'Unless we all have the same end point vision, I can see us rushing off in all directions. Unless managed in new ways, the network and all these teams are a recipe for disaster.'

Michael Porter has summarised the traditional sources of competitive advantage such as relative bargaining power.[9] Credibility, the extent to which people will believe that an organisation can deliver, is emerging as an important differentiator. In a commodity product marketplace, the opportunity will go to those who can 'make it happen'. This demands that the process of corporate transformation be successfully managed.

THE AIM AND FOCUS OF THE BOOK

The aim of this book is to help facilitate the process of corporate transformation by sharing selected insights. The focus and subject matter of the book is not what should be in an ideal state, but what is, and what could be in the reality of the marketplace.

The individual chapters are all based upon the findings and implications of questionnaire and interview surveys undertaken by the author (see Appendix 1 for details of the principal surveys). In selecting tables for presentation in this book, preference has been given to the results of those surveys that are less accessible than, say, those published by the British Institute of Management (BIM).

At various points in the course of the text there will be discussion and analysis of:

- what should be the case, in terms of 'the words', myth or expectation;
- what the situation actually is, ie typical problems and difficulties; and
- what needs to be, and can be, done to bridge the gap between vision and reality.

When considering the many gaps between aspiration and perception, and corporate reality, value judgements should be avoided. Misperception and misunderstanding should not be regarded as an aberration. They should be assumed in complex and changing contexts, when there is uncertainty and there are other players in a competitive game.[10]

AN OVERVIEW PERSPECTIVE

Wherever possible, points will be made through actual quotes from a selection of the CEOs, directors and managers who were interviewed during the survey programme. These are not attributed, as openness and frankness was encouraged by a guarantee of confidentiality. Given the volume of available interview notes it has only been possible to include enough comment and elaboration to 'make a point' or give the reader a 'feel' for an issue.

The perspective of this book is that of the organisation as a whole. A considerable degree of self-discipline has been required to avoid going in great detail into particular aspects of corporate transformation in order to ensure the reader is presented with an 'overview' and a holistic approach. Senge has pointed out that in order to bring about fundamental change it is necessary to set about: 'destroying the illusion that the world is created of separate, unrelated forces'.[11]

No attempt has been made to sound catchy or to serve up a new set of buzz-words. There is little value in concepts that cannot be used. Ideas, however interesting, have been weeded out if they are not thought to be of practical value. In the main, the views expressed are those of real and 'hard-nosed' people who are running real companies.

THE PURPOSE

Every company is unique. It would be presumptuous to suggest what precise steps an individual company should take. How the reader should apply the lessons of this book will depend upon the situation and circumstances of his or her own company. Rather than present a detailed guide, key points are made, and questions are raised which could be posed in the context of a particular company.

It is hoped that the reader will gain a more balanced perspective on what is involved in transforming a company, and some guidance concerning how to manage the transformation process. No attempt has been made to hide the areas which are proving difficult, or to 'play down' likely obstacles and barriers. These must be recognised, confronted and tackled if success is to be achieved.

It is not the purpose of this book to debunk the work of particular management thinkers. Those who have developed individual approaches and tools are not generally responsible for the extent to which these may have been misapplied.

The utility of many individual concepts is apparent in the behaviour of companies. For example, Kenichi Ohmae has stressed the value of a strong presence and insider standing in each element of the 'triad', Europe, Japan and the UK, as a means of becoming globally competitive.[12] A good example of such an arrangement was the conclusion of a memorandum of understanding concerning global co-operation in 1991 between Fiat of Italy, Hitachi Construction Machinery of Japan and John Deere of the USA.

The concern of the author is that single and simplistic solutions should not be sought to a challenge as fundamental as transforming a company. Outdated ideas that can be dangerous when unthinkingly applied to the current context persist, while other approaches of greater relevance are grudgingly accepted or misused. An example is the instinctive tendency to adopt the Taylor concept of a division of labour,[13] when a better solution might result from involving more people and encouraging overlapping contributions. It all depends upon the task and the context.

THE EVIDENCE

The author's own confidence in the findings of the book stems not just from the number and seniority of those who have participated in the various surveys (see Appendix 1), but from the fact that the findings of different surveys support and complement each other so well. A remarkably consistent set of responses has emerged.

Many companies have participated in more than one survey. In some cases this provided an opportunity to cross-check perceptions, or to reinterview the same people one or two years later, using the same or similar questions in order to assess what progress had been made. Overall, in excess of 1000 separate companies have participated in the ongoing survey programme. In the case of over six out of ten of these, the participation has, at some point, involved the chairman or chief executive.

The organisations involved represent a broad mix of European, US, Japanese and international companies.

There is no substitute for examining what is happening in practice. Many years ago, while a student at the London Business School, the author paid the first of several visits to Brazil, which eventually resulted in a published report on the country's prospects.[14] Publication was held up for some months because certain views that were subsequently proved to be correct did not accord with those of the desk-bound experts at home.

The main findings of this book have been presented to a number of board-level seminars with which the author is involved. One series of seminars co-hosted by the author and held at Wokefield Park, the Rank Xerox UK national training centre, has been specifically concerned with corporate transformation. Directors from a broad cross-section of companies have recognised the reality portrayed and have endorsed the conclusions.

Finally, the lessons that emerge have been checked against the successful experience of one corporation that has achieved a documented reversal of fortunes – Xerox and Rank Xerox (Chapter 18). Xerox Corporation has adopted a holistic approach, avoids 'single solutions', and its transformation programme is influencing attitudes and behaviour.

Vern Zelmer, managing director of Rank Xerox UK, believes a variety of approaches to change are needed to achieve corporate transformation. He advocates the use of policy deployment, one such framework that can enable 'an organisation that acknowledges the need for change to actually make it happen'. It is the vehicle that 'turns intention into reality, it influences both thought and behaviour'.

Jacobson and Hillkirk subtitled their study of the Xerox turnaround 'The behind-the-scenes story of how a corporate giant beat the Japanese at their own game'.[15] The author has lived through the 'Xerox experience' for approaching ten years, initially as an employee, subsequently as an adviser, and more recently as a business partner. Knowing an organisation 'as it is' enables it to be seen 'warts and all'.

THE AUDIENCE

The point has already been made that this book is primarily based upon the experiences of those who occupy key roles in actual companies. Hence, its messages are rooted in reality and are not contrived. It should be of value and interest to all those practitioners, whether directors, managers or consultants, who are seriously trying to bring about change.

Because it is based upon a comprehensive programme of questionnaire and interview surveys, the book should also be suitable for those undertaking executive and MBA programmes who are seeking a contemporary overview of what is happening in the business environment that represents their 'marketplace'.

Organisational transformation is affecting the public sector as well as the private. In the UK, for example, there has been an extensive programme of 'privatisation', the growing use of 'contracting out', and the introduction of executive agencies and internal markets.[16] These changes are now occurring in many countries around the world. Hence, the book should also be of benefit to those in the public sector.

The implementation of initiatives such as the UK Citizens' Charter offers considerable scope for the use within governmental bodies of a range of techniques and approaches for 'making it happen'. What can and should be promised to the citizen in terms of outcomes and expectations will depend critically upon what it is felt could, with reasonable certainty, be delivered.

WARNING BELLS

It is clear from the survey evidence (see Appendix 1) that the successful implementation of a transformation programme depends critically upon the relevance of the selection, combination and application of change elements to the requirements of the situation at each stage of the change process. The experience of benchmark companies is that certain combinations and applications of change elements do work, and can 'bear fruit' when they are correctly applied.

In spite of the evidence that a carefully-selected combination of complementary change elements is needed, many organisations adopt a simplistic approach to the achievement of change within organisations. Too often people continue to believe in the general applicability of standard solutions, even though warning signals have been issued. For example, one study a decade ago of 64 organisation development applications concluded that: 'no one change technique or class of techniques works well in all situations'.[17]

Prahalad has concluded:[18]

No longer can top managers accept and impose on the organisation a single concept or methodology (eg BCG and PIMS) or bet on a single organisational

CHECKLIST 1

▶ Does your company have a compelling reason for existing?

▶ What would the world lose if it ceased to exist tomorrow?

▶ Does your company have clear and agreed vision, goals and values?

▶ Who within the company has thought through what the vision and these goals and values mean for its relationships with people, whether as customers, suppliers or business partners?

▶ Is there an overview of what the company is trying to achieve in terms of its various objectives?

▶ Are all the objectives expressed in terms of measurable outputs?

▶ To what extent are you and management colleagues frustrated with what has been achieved in the area of corporate transformation?

▶ What are the symptoms of non-achievement?

▶ Is there a process in place within your company to root out the underlying causes of gaps between aspiration and achievement?

▶ Is the complex nature, and full extent, of the corporate transformation challenge fully appreciated?

▶ Has thought been given to whether particular change elements are missing from the transformation jigsaw puzzle?

▶ How genuine is the desire to change in each functional component and business element of your organisation?

▶ Is there an agreed vision of a more flexible and responsive 'end point' organisation?

▶ To what extent have the changes which have been introduced into your company to date influenced attitudes, values and behaviour?

▶ Have the cross-functional and inter-organisational processes that are necessary to achieve desired outcomes been identified?

▶ Have relevant roles and responsibilities been allocated, and the required resources been lined up?

▶ Are people equipped, empowered and motivated to do what is expected of them?

REFERENCES

1 Kuhn, T S (1970) *The Structure of Scientific Revolutions* (2nd edn), The University of Chicago Press, Chicago and London.

2 Coulson-Thomas, C and Brown, R (1989) *The Responsive Organisation, People Management: the Challenge of the 1990s*, BIM, Corby.

3 Coulson-Thomas, C (1990) *Human Resource Development for International Operation*, Survey Report for Surrey European Management School, Adaptation Ltd, London.

4 Coulson-Thomas, C (1991) *The Role and Development of the Personnel Director*, an Adaptation Ltd Interim Survey undertaken in conjunction with the Institute of Personnel Management Research Group, Wimbledon.

5 Halperin, M H (1974) *Bureaucratic Politics and Foreign Policy*, Brookings Institution, Washington DC.

6 Coulson-Thomas, C and Brown, R (1990) *Beyond Quality: Managing the Relationship with the Customer*, BIM, Corby.

7 Drucker, P F (1969) *The Age of Discontinuity*, Heinemann, London.

8   Coulson-Thomas, C (1992) *Creating the Global Company: Successful Internationalisation*, McGraw-Hill, London.

9   Porter, M E (1980) *Competitive Strategy: Techniques for Analysing Industries and Competitors*, Free Press, New York, and (1985) *Competitive Advantage*, Free Press, New York.

10 Jervis, R (1976) *Perception and Misperception in International Politics*, Princeton University Press, Princeton, New Jersey.

11 Senge, P (1990) *The Fifth Discipline: The Art and Practice of the Learning Organisation*, Doubleday/Currency, New York, p. 3.

12 Ohmae, K (1985) *Triad Power: The Coming Shape of Global Competition*, The Free Press, New York.

13 Taylor, F W (1947) *Scientific Management*, Harper & Row, New York.

14 Coulson-Thomas, C (Metra Consulting and International Joint Ventures) (1980) *Brazil: Business Opportunities in the 1980s*, Metra Consulting Group, London.

15 Jacobson, G and Hillkirk, J (1986) *Xerox: American Samurai, the behind-the-scenes story of how a corporate giant beat the Japanese at their own game*, Macmillan Publishing Company, New York.

16 McDonald, O (1992) *The Future of Whitehall*, Weidenfeld & Nicolson, London.

17 Nicholas, J (1982) 'The Comparative Impact of Organisation Development Interventions on Hard Criteria Measures', *Academy of Management Review*, vol 9, pp 531–43.

18 Prahalad, C K (1983) 'Developing Strategic Capability: An Agenda for Top Management', *Human Resource Management*, fall, vol 22, no 3, pp 237–54.

19 Coulson-Thomas, C and Coe, T (1991) *The Flat Organisation: Philosophy and Practice*, BIM, Corby.

20 Coulson-Thomas, C and Coulson-Thomas, S (1991) *Quality: The Next Steps*, an Adaptation Ltd Survey for ODI International, Adaptation, London and (Executive Summary) ODI, Wimbledon, London.

21 Coulson-Thomas, C and Coulson-Thomas, S (1991) *Communicating for Change*, an Adaptation Survey for Granada Business Services, London.

2

ASPIRATION AND ACHIEVEMENT

CORPORATE ASPIRATION

A company is a community of people who have come together in order to increase their collective capability to turn aspiration into achievement. If the network organisation is to hold together, its members must share a feeling that the prospects of 'making it happen' are enhanced when they work as a group rather than separately.

While a company transitions to a more responsive and flexible form, other activities will be ongoing. Corporate transformation may be but one of a number of strategic programmes, such as internationalisation or federalisation, that are under way. Each of these initiatives, and the teams behind them, will have aspirations. Corporate transformation needs to facilitate, enable and support these other developments.

Many companies have set ambitious objectives for their change programmes. Here are some examples.

- Alcoa, a US corporation, is seeking to invert the organisational pyramid in order to put the front-line business units that serve the customer 'on top'. Such a change, when followed through, can have a traumatic impact upon how many people view their contribution and worth.
- Deere and Co, a US construction equipment company, is transitioning from a functional to a product-line form of organisation. The resources of the organisation are being focused upon the support of the product delivery processes that deliver products to customer requirements.
- The aspiration can be international. BP is encouraging networking across national borders in order that groups and teams can be brought together, independently of location, to tackle particular tasks.
- Within Europe the sales operations of Digital Equipment are being restructured from country-based units to some 50 pan-European units known as 'entreprises' which will serve particular vertical markets. DEC country managers will act as chairmen of groups of 'entreprises'.

The more profound the change, and the further its reach, the greater the number of barriers and obstacles that may be encountered. On the other hand, a certain level of scale, and perceived urgency and importance can increase the prospect that senior management attention will be secured and sufficient resources might be obtained to 'break through'.

CORPORATE REALITY

In view of the uncertainties involved in transforming companies to more flexible forms, it is not surprising that achievement generally lags behind aspiration. A family of surveys of CEOs, directors, and managers undertaken by the author over a period of five years (see Appendix 1) has revealed these factors about companies that are struggling to change:

- There is a growing gap between management theory and corporate experience, between expectation and achievement, and between rhetoric and reality.
- As a result of the achievement or delivery gap a number of arenas of confrontation are emerging. Perspectives are in conflict. People cannot agree the sources or root causes of problems being encountered, or the next steps to be taken.
- Patience and goodwill are not inexhaustible. In some companies there already appears to be a search for scalps and scapegoats.
- Many well-intended actions of boards and management teams are having unforeseen and counter-productive consequences. These are a source of angst, recrimination and division.
- The phenomenon of the 'herd instinct' or 'groupthink' is widespread. Groups are 'going automatic'.
- While there remains a desire for corporate transformation, its achievement is generally taking longer than expected and is often fraught with difficulties.
- The single-minded pursuit of particular panaceas appears to be driving some companies into the ground. A sense of balance is being lost, as a desire for outcomes results in management teams putting excessive, and sometimes blind, faith in 'solutions' such as 'quality' or 're-engineering'.
- As a result of unforeseen delays, some transformation programmes are being overtaken by events. The requirement is substantially changed before the outcomes or results that were initially agreed can be achieved.
- As a consequence of the above, there is widespread disillusion, cynicism and despair.
- People in many companies are beginning to lose faith in the 'vision', and are critical of the 'standard' solutions and simplistic generalisations of consultants, business schools and gurus.
- In general, many people within companies that are being subjected to fundamental change need both reassurance and practical help.

In many companies considerable effort is being devoted to initiatives that are doomed to failure. Reputations and much goodwill are being squandered upon approaches that are likely to lead to unintended consequences and disappointment.
One survey[1] concluded that:

> *'Many managers have 'had enough' of forever 'doing more with less', when the reality of the vision they are offered is corporate survival for another few months. … The life of the manager has become a tough one. … It was almost impossible to interview … without feeling both respect and sympathy for many hardworking and 'unsung heroes'. Realistic and dedicated, open and frank, they 'battle on' until they are 'dropped'.*

These findings are consistent with other work which has suggested that activities such as delayering and downsizing are often undertaken with little thought as to the consequences or concern for how people should be equipped to operate in changed circumstances. Scase and Goffee suggest that many managers feel themselves caught in a treadmill from which they cannot escape.[2] Subjected to a range of pressures and increasing demands, many derive little satisfaction from their work.
The problems that are beginning to emerge are sometimes embarrassingly visible. Organisational change is increasing the awareness of failure.

- The bureaucratic organisation protected some people from their own deficiencies. Departmental barriers and a penchant for secrecy prevented damage and knowledge of failure from spreading, inadequate implementation reduced the adverse consequences of bad decisions.
- In the more open corporation, the emphasis given to corporate communications ranging from videos to posters, and new-found enthusiasms for sharing visions,

have seen to it that expectations have been raised and hopes are high. When gaps between words and deeds arise, more people know about it.

One chairman summed up a new challenge faced by many companies:

'I rue the day we decided to invest so much in hype. We have so wound them up that many of those in the field are rushing about mouthing slogans and thinking we're on the way to great things. How do we get them to understand that it's just not working without totally disillusioning them? Imagine the reactions, for us and them.'

ACKNOWLEDGING THE EXISTENCE OF GAPS

A necessary first step is to recognise that there is a gap between aspiration and achievement. Its existence may be concealed by another gap between perception and reality. The point was made in Chapter 1 that misperceptions are likely to occur when people have to confront new situations armed with memories, experiences, attitudes and prejudices derived from a different reality[3].

People seek meaning and predictability in order to cope with a confusing and challenging environment such as that found in transforming organisations. They tend to ignore, 'screen out' or rationalise evidence that does not accord with their deeply-held views of reality.[4] A battery of psychological devices are deployed by individuals to avoid recognition and acceptance of failure.

People who are 'in the thick of it' also fail to spot signs and signals that with hindsight, or to a third party, might appear obvious. The members of a transformation team may not be able to agree the meaning or source of what is observed. When success is a matter of changes of attitude, or the internalisation of values, interpretation and assessment of what is happening is sometimes fraught with difficulties.

Even politicians, whose professional concern is understanding and working with public opinion in order to obtain and hold on to power, may misread how people actually feel. Reactions across Europe in June 1992 to the Danish vote on the Maastricht Agreement illustrate how governments can lose touch with their people.

Not all of those involved in the management of change will agree on the extent to which there is a gap. Much will depend upon expectations. Corporate transformation is a process, and in a turbulent and ever-changing world it is one that is ongoing. Some will be more pleased than others with the rate at which progress is being made. One person's shortfall in achievement could be another's excuse for a celebration.

AVOIDANCE AND CONCEALMENT

In the case of some gaps between programme objectives and actual outcomes, there will be those who do not know about the shortfalls. Others may be reluctant to tell them, or perhaps calculated concealment is taking place.

Bad news is generally regarded as a problem rather than as an opportunity to learn. In many companies, some managers will go to great lengths to conceal reality from others in the corporate organisation. This is especially likely when they feel it is in their best interests to do so.

The extent of deception can range from an emphasis, a biased slant or selective reporting with a view to portraying an individual in a more favourable light, to outright distortion. People also report what they believe those above them might wish to hear. As anxiety mounts, executives long visibly for good news.

To find out what is really happening, a senior or programme manager may need to be astute and engage in subterfuge. Some chief executives operate informal intelligence networks to uncover a 'different' version of reality. Others have 'listening posts' scattered around the corporate organisation, people who are pleased to have a degree of access to the CEO in return for 'telling it as it is'.

Avoidance and concealment involve risk. For example, when the 'truth is out', people may feel deceived and duped. No one other than the masochist likes to feel 'had'. A manager may feel bitter and angry at the betrayal of trust involved.

Given the risks and uncertainties, and the temptation to avoid, distort or conceal reality, it is not unreasonable to ask: why should anyone assume that a corporate transformation programme will succeed? Many years ago the author was asked to prepare a checklist on new product development.[5] All the evidence examined suggested that the overwhelming majority of new products fail. How much more difficult it is likely to be to bring about radical change throughout a corporate organisation.

APPEARANCE APPEAL

Appearance, rather than the reality of achievement, has great appeal for many managers. Dealing with symptoms can result in short-term payoffs, and may be less wearing than grappling with underlying problems.

In the case of some companies appearance is the product. Disneyland does not have employees, but cast members. Image may be the essence of the appeal of the rock band, and may add millions to the value of a brand.

Appearance and image can be important, and in some sectors are the crucial differentiators. However, a management team should not become so 'wrapped up' with the world of appearance as to lose touch with reality. The cocktails and bow-ties of the agency reception, and the atmosphere on set when the commercial is shot may have greater appeal than the engineer's report, but the latter may focus on an issue that needs to be addressed.

THE TEMPTATION OF THE VISIBLE

Both management training and the observance of supposed 'role-model' behaviour may encourage a focus upon the quick fix. According to one managing director: 'The temptation is to stick or tie, rather than reach for the toolkit.'

Activity, announcements, instant impacts and new initiatives are immediate, visible and relatively easy to associate with individuals. They earn 'brownie points', they help people to become noticed, and they can build a reputation for being the 'right stuff'.

Advancement, reward and remuneration may all be influenced by appearance. How the manager looks, presents and behaves in social situations can be significant factors in promotion and selection decisions. When senior executives pride themselves on being able to judge a person in 30 seconds, or on the basis of a firm handshake, it is little wonder that image consultants are having a field day. Packaging is often all-important.

Activity and hype can also be fun. Rushing about gets the adrenalin flowing and makes you feel good. In contrast, some find that thinking can be hard work. Others get bored very quickly. They may be reluctant to spend the time needed to really get to the heart of an issue.

Appearance can be talked about. It can be used to impress, flatter and beguile. Individually and collectively it can give rise to self-deception and delusion. People may cling to appearance in order to avoid reality.

REALITY RESISTANCE

Compared with appearance, reality is sometimes rather like the dull brother whom everyone wished had stayed at home. It can be uncomfortable, just as honesty may be unwelcome. The reality of achievement is hard work, and people may not wish to be reminded of this.

Achievement takes time, and may require the collective efforts of many people. It may not be easy for individuals to claim the credit when others are involved. Those who beaver away in unglamorous, but from a customer perspective important, activities may be hidden from view.

Some people will not want to commit to roles that are concerned with 'making it happen'. While they have their 'heads down' in the far reaches of the company close to the customer, they may be passed over in favour of the sly courtiers who are slinking and prowling head office corridors close to the centre of power.

Besides, reality is not so easy to 'fix' as appearances. What happens if it goes wrong? A focus upon reality, and a commitment to achievement, has been the graveyard of many careers. The achieving individual in a culture that does not encourage 'role model' behaviour, or reward achievement, may fail as a result of a lack of support from others. Favours may win over results.

Change and reality may be avoided for reasons of self-interest. In a classic article over a generation ago Bachrach and Baratz identified the 'non-decision' as both a demonstration and a source of power.[6]

The achievement of a significant change of attitudes and perspective within a management team tends to be associated with a change of leadership at the top.[7] This prospect is enough to encourage some to avoid the radical solution. How much more difficult it often is to achieve change through an unchanged team!

APPEARANCE AS POLICY

There are occasions when managers set out consciously to build an image, erect a façade or create an appearance that does not accord with reality. They may not have any intention of translating a public vision into corporate reality, or of closing what may be perceived as a gap between aspiration and achievement. Rhetoric may not have represented true aspiration.

In the field of environmental action a company might perceive that it has a vested interest in rhetoric. By articulating strategies, issuing protestations of concern and generally cultivating an appearance of activity, a company may feel it might be able to stave off the introduction of costly regulation.

The gap between myth and reality may reach such proportions as to threaten the existence of a whole country, let alone an individual enterprise.[8] The challenge in such circumstances is to make people aware of the 'realities' without causing disillusion and despair, and to reconcile the desire to be honest with the requirement to maintain confidence and positive leadership. Winners are sometimes those who choose to overlook 'realities' that cause their competitors to give up.

There may be occasions when a management team has to address both rhetoric and reality, and respond in both arenas. For example, stakeholders may say one thing and do another, just as members of the public may vote one way through the ballot box, and behave differently when spending the money in their purses and pockets.

JUDGING MANAGERS BY THEIR GAPS

A gap between aspiration and achievement is not something that is abnormal. Nor should it be a source of shame. The existence of gaps should not shock or be the cause of embarrassment. The likely existence of gaps should be assumed in the case of a wide-ranging and demanding change programme.

Deficiencies cannot be addressed unless they are first identified and their causes understood. Those without gaps may be the ignorant, those who have not set clear objectives or those who do not measure the extent of their achievement.

People who do not aspire do not have a gap between aspiration and achievement. In some competitive markets it may not be possible to achieve world-class performance without moving close to the limit of the capacity of the organisation and its people to deliver.

Some people will not know they have a gap until their annual review of strategy takes place, or the annual results are announced. These events could be scheduled to take place some months in the future. By then it may be too late to take corrective action.

Managers can and should be judged by the gaps they have identified, their understanding of them and what action they propose to take to deal with them. What is the root cause of the gap which has developed, and who is responsible for delivering the agreed response?

Many gaps occur as a result of external changes and developments. These may be beyond the control of the company. Things sometimes just happen, and may not be the fault of anyone in particular. 'Witch hunts' should be avoided if it is desired that people should be open about their mistakes, and prepared to learn from them and share what they have learned.

THE ROLE OF THE MANAGER

The role of the manager is to manage change. Once a direction has been set, objectives agreed, and roles and responsibilities allocated, the manager should establish frameworks within which gaps between intentions and outcomes can be identified, and subsequently assessed as they emerge or monitored as they are closed.

People should be motivated to actively seek out and manage gaps. A company could build its philosophy of management upon the identification and closing of gaps between aspiration and achievement. A company that encourages every group to carry out regular 'gap', 'barrier' or 'helps and hinders' analyses is involving all of its people in a process of steering towards its corporate goals.

Many managers are reluctant to think through the implications of change programmes and the likely consequences of their own actions. Some company cultures actually discourage this sort of behaviour. Consider the comments of three directors, one of whom has recently retired.

> 'If you see too many problems you get labelled as negative, a "wet blanket" or a pain. You might be taken as someone who is not a team player, or perhaps you are too thick to understand.'

> 'People are reluctant to raise things in case they might have missed the point. People don't like to look stupid in front of others. There were many times when the obvious questions were not being asked.'

> 'It really was the chief executive's baby. I looked around the room. Everyone knew that it wasn't working, but no one was prepared to say anything.'

So pervasive are gaps between aspiration and achievement, and so determined are so many managers to move rather than solve problems, that there appears to be the managerial equivalent of the doctrine of original sin. Even where progress is made in closing some gaps, others seem to open up. Perhaps, like the poor, they will always be with us.

MANAGING THE GAPS

More important than the scale of a gap, is the question: gap from what? A small gap may reveal a lack of ambition rather than limited management accomplishment. Those without visions, and those who do not dream, may be the satisfied and the content. It tends to be those who are restless and dissatisfied who move organisations forward.

A judgement may also need to be made (Figure 2.1) as to whether the source of a deficiency lies in the direction or speed of change.

- The gap that is perceived could be between a 'right' and a 'wrong' direction. A company could pursue the wrong (eg circuitous or tortuous) route towards an agreed goal or objective.
- Alternatively, the gap could exist between where a company thinks it is and where it is thought it ought to be. The movement could be in the right direction, and along the intended route, but at a slower speed than had been anticipated or hoped.

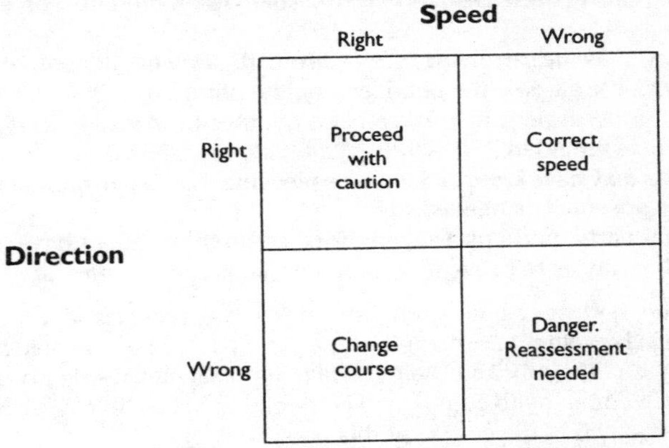

Speed

	Right	Wrong
Right	Proceed with caution	Correct speed
Wrong	Change course	Danger. Reassessment needed

Direction

Figure 2.1 *Speed and Direction of Change*

The route to be followed will depend upon the obstacles and barriers between where the company is and where it wishes to be. The desired speed of transformation will reflect the extent to which internal capability, attitudes and behaviour need to adapt to match the requirements for the achievement of corporate goals in the context of evolving opportunities and challenges in a changing external environment.

UNDERSTANDING THE SOURCE AND NATURE OF GAPS

There could be many reasons for the existence of a gap between aspiration and achievement. Here are some examples.

- The leadership of a company could be inadequate. There could be a lack of vision, will and unity at the top.
- The failure could be 'intellectual'. Corporate strategies could be inappropriate or wrong.
- What needs to be done, and what is necessary for its achievement, may not have been thought through.
- A company could be failing to understand and respond to the changing requirements of its customers.
- People may not be in a position as a result of the lack of skills, freedom to act, or resources, to do what they would like to do.
- They may be working on activities that do not add value for customers, or in ways that do not allow them to give of their best.
- They may lack clear priorities as a result of confused messages, or be perplexed by actions that do not match words.

- Initial expectations may have been unrealistic or overambitious.
- Some slippage might have occured with 'follow-through' consequences, or perhaps the results have yet to work their way through.
- Too much faith may have been placed in panaceas, instant answers, particular and self-contained initiatives, or simplistic approaches.
- The necessary potential might well exist within the company, but it may be unrecognised, or it might not be tapped.
- The company may have the desired capability, but it might be in the wrong place and cannot be reached when needed.
- A reassessment might have led to the conclusion that it would now be too expensive to do what was originally desired.
- Progress may have been held up by internal disagreements, or sabotaged by opponents.
- The company may be receiving advice from those who do not see the 'whole picture', a possible case of 'the blind leading the blind'.
- Some areas of investment may have been counter-productive, leading to results other than those intended.
- Problem areas may have been tackled on a piecemeal or departmental basis, when a more holistic approach is needed.
- Some external party, perhaps a regulator or competitor, might have stepped in or acted in such a way as to prevent certain outcomes from occurring.

One could go on and speculate endlessly about the reasons for a gap between expectation and achievement. Perhaps there are no particular reasons, but instead a combination of them, the mix and their relative importance varying from situation to situation, and from company to company. The selection of possible reasons above, and others, will be examined in the course of this book.

CLOSING GAPS

A gap between expectation and achievement could be reduced by lowering aspiration or raising achievement (Figure 2.2):

- Aspiration could be reduced by a conscious effort to lower expectations. Rhetoric could be toned down and more modest claims made. A company could claim some credit for realism and honesty, and differentiate itself from the hype of others by stressing the responsible nature of its own statements.
- Achievement could be boosted by such means as clarifying objectives, increasing motivation, or by enabling and empowering. 'Helps and hinders' analysis could be used to indentify strengths that could be built upon, and barriers and obstacles that could be tackled. The capability to deliver could be raised by a programme of improvements, and 'missing elements' could be put in place.

In some situations it may not be easy to lower expectations. People may want to believe something else and may resist. If anything, raising achievement may be easier than reducing aspirations. Consider the following selection of views:

'Once people have tasted something, how can you take it away?'

'Not all the expectations arise from within. We are not alone in the marketplace, and there is a lot going on out there that is raising expectations.'

'If we reduce by one jot, a competitor will be in there like a shot.'

'It took a long time, much creativity and quite a bit of money to raise those expectations. You can't turn them off like a tap.'

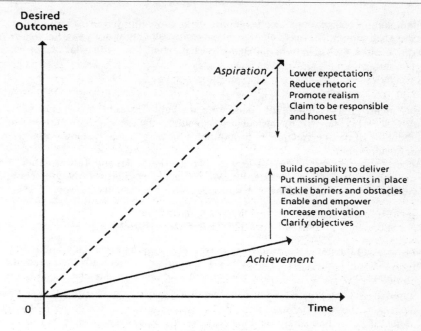

Figure 2.2 *The rhetoric/reality gap*

A sophisticated management would understand the need to manage both expectation and achievement. Expectation has to be at a level to 'interest', while delivery needs to be sufficient to hold or retain allegiance. A healthy balance needs to be maintained between them. Any gap must be wide enough to stimulate greater achievement, but not so large as to disappoint and alienate.

MISGUIDED ATTEMPTS

Some attempts to bridge the gap between aspiration and achievement may be misguided. For example:

- working harder may only mean sinking deeper into the mire, or moving further off course;
- spending more money may not be the answer if the activity in question is inconsistent with corporate objectives, or not adding value for customers;
- forcing dissent out of the boardroom may achieve unity at the cost of objectivity and balance;
- searching for a new panacea, or embracing an additional palliative, may result in the further postponement of necessary action;
- the use of common tools may help communication and integration, but if imposed in the face of cultural and other differences could achieve these benefits at the cost of a loss of diversity and involvement;
- relocating may demonstrate action, but may shift the site of the symptoms rather than deal with the underlying problems.

Often the source of unintended consequences will lie not in an individual change element itself, but in a lack of balance in its use. Some enthusiasts of particular tools and approaches do not know when to stop. As with most things, after a time, diminishing, and eventually negative, returns may result from additional use.

Also, some combinations of change elements may work better in certain circumstances than others. The art of change management is to know not just what to use, but also to consider such questions as: where, to what extent, how, with what, and by whom?

THE TIME FOR DECISION

The crunch time is coming. With economic 'daylight' around the corner it becomes more difficult to claim that the lack of visible results is the consequence of recession, or that benefits of change and quality programmes have been 'lost' among 'cutbacks' and other developments.

According to one chairman: 'The jury is still out. What will really show whether or not we are going to make it is the extent to which our business grows when the economy moves out of recession, and the global prospects for our industry improve.'

THE LURE OF THE FAST RESULT

Doing the right thing may not be easy when there is pressure for change, and a pressing desire for some evidence of rapid results. For example, consider the bringing together of a cross-functional team to consider a wider range of different aspects of a problem.

- Compared with just 'taking a view' on the basis of 'information to hand', this approach might appear to prolong decision making. Before any of the 'real work' is done the participants may need to be trained in how to operate effectively in such a team.
- However, as a result of the discussion, it may be both easier and faster to move through the subsequent delivery of what is required to an end customer. Potential pitfalls may be identified and thus avoided. Those involved in a 'first experience' may acquire skills that could be used in other groups to good effect. Thus wider benefits might accrue.

A desire for early and tangible results could lead to the avoidance of the team approach, but at the cost of later problems during the implementation phase. It sometimes takes a strong personality to remain underground while digging deeper foundations as others are already visibly piling the bricks on top of each other. For a time the risks inherent in shallow foundations may not be apparent.

THE POTENTIAL FOR STRATEGIC MISUNDERSTANDING

A further reason for 'putting out' a strong warning signal is that a number of companies appear to be considering a change of strategic direction for the wrong reasons, and at the worst possible time:

- Not realising the extent to which the failure to achieve corporate goals is the result of inadequate implementation, they assume an original strategy was at fault or, as one interviewee put it, they have been 'barking up the wrong tree'. With this perspective, and the need for change becoming daily more urgent, they are engaged in a frantic search for a new panacea or source of hope.
- Some companies appear to be contemplating moving off in a new direction and abandoning initiatives that in themselves may be valuable just at a time when the identification of the remaining elements required for successful transformation and the elimination of certain barriers could bring them within sight of their destination. They are losing heart when so much of what needs to be done has already been accomplished.

- The desire to slim down and reduce overheads is leading to the negativism of cost cutting when the focus should be upon what additional steps should now be taken to derive the latent benefits of past expenditure. Assembling the final pieces of the jigsaw puzzle might yet result in past costs turning out to have been strategic investments.

A fundamental reason for the gap between rhetoric and reality is the tendency to 'go automatic' on implementation. There is too often a reluctance to challenge basic assumptions and explore other alternatives.

For a generation Edward De Bono has argued the case for the use of lateral thinking to break out of established patterns in order to view challenges and opportunities in a new light.[9] Too many managers cling like limpets to old ways. Accustomed to living for so long in a murky world of avoidance and rationalisation, some find it difficult to adjust to the prospect of a reality that might consist of favourable outcomes.

CHECKLIST

▶ Have the aspirations of your company's corporate change programme been clearly articulated?

▶ Have they been agreed by the board?

▶ Have they been expressed in operational and measurable terms?

▶ Who within your company shares these aspirations?

▶ How aware is the top management of your company of gaps between aspiration and achievement?

▶ How willing are they to confront reality?

▶ Is there agreement on the nature and extent of the gaps that have been identified?

▶ To what extent have any gaps between aspiration and achievement been publicly acknowledged and shared with the people of the company and other 'stakeholders'?

▶ Does the culture and reward system of the company encourage openness and trust, or avoidance and concealment?

▶ Are there areas in which the company has a conscious, if unstated, policy of rhetoric or concealment?

▶ Have the dangers and possible implications of such policies been thought through?

▶ Are the general and specific reasons for the existence of a gap between aspiration and achievement understood?

▶ How tolerant is your organisation of mistakes?

▶ Has a 'helps and hinders' analysis been undertaken to identify the specific barriers and obstacles to progress, and what needs to be done about them?

▶ Has your company's management team thought through how it should divide its effort between managing expectations and managing achievement?

▶ Who balances the make-up of the various elements in your company's corporate transformation programme?

▶ Does your company fall prey to the lure of the fast result?

▶ Is your company considering a fundamental reassessment of its corporate transformation programme?

▶ Is this being undertaken for appropriate and valid reasons?

REFERENCES

1   Coulson-Thomas, C and Coe, T (1991) *The Flat Organisation: Philosophy and Practice*, BIM, Corby.
2   Scase, R and Goffee, R (1989) *Reluctant Managers: Their Work and Lifestyles*, Unwin Hyman, London.
3   Jervis, R (1976) *Perception and Misperception in International Politics*, Princeton University Press, Princeton, New Jersey.
4   Festinger, L (1962) *A Theory of Cognitive Dissonance*, Stanford University Press, Stanford.
5   Coulson-Thomas, C J (1978) 'New product development checklist', *Accountants Digest No 60*, Institute of Chartered Accountants in England and Wales, London.
6   Bachrach, P and Baratz, M (1962) 'Two faces of power', *American Political Science Review*, vol 56, pp 947–52.
7   Tushman, M L, Newman, W H, and Nadler, D A (1988) 'Executive leadership and organisational evolution: managing incremental and discontinuous change', in Kilman, R and Covey, T J (eds), *Corporate Transformation*, Jossey-Bass, San Francisco.
8   Ponting, C (1990) *1940: Myth and Reality*, Hamish Hamilton, London.
9   De Bono, E (1967) *The Use of Lateral Thinking*, McGraw-Hill, Maidenhead, and (1971) *Lateral Thinking for Management*, McGraw-Hill, Maidenhead.

3

Myths and Realities in the Boardroom

The hidden factor

Read through the latest bestselling 'guru book' and count the number of references to company directors and corporate boards. In some of the most popular management titles there is not a single reference to the board. It is as if the board does not exist.

Much of the advice in the management literature on what to do to achieve all sorts of desirable changes within a corporate organisation does not mention the group that should determine the purpose, vision, goals, values, objectives, strategy and policies of the company. Is this because boards have been overlooked, or is it because they are not discharging their responsibilities to the extent that they can be ignored?

What is the role of the board in relation to corporate transformation? Are boards catalysts, enablers, engineers and instigators of change? Or are they at best bystanders, and at worst obstacles to the change process, and a burden upon the body corporate?

Corporate drive and purpose

The board should provide the heart and soul of a company. It should be the source of its will, ambition and drive. Without a sense of purpose, and the will to achieve, the most well-endowed corporation can wither and die.

Members of the senior management team are likely to take their cue from the attitudes, behaviour and commitment of the members of the board, both individually and collectively. The conduct of the directors as 'role models' can inspire and motivate, or stunt and sap the management spirit.

As one managing director put it: 'If we don't "walk the talk", why should we expect anyone else to?'

A united directorial team that visibly displays a common and sustained commitment to corporate transformation can be a powerful force for change. A divided board can spread a canker of destructive forces throughout the corporate organisation, undermining morale and resolve. Inconsistencies between words and deeds can result in a climate of cynicism, despair and distrust.

Successful corporate transformation is very dependent upon the quality of the board, and its commitment to the achievement of change. It can thrive where there is an effective board composed of competent directors. So important is commitment at this level, that if it cannot be obtained, an executive team would be ill-advised to initiate a fundamental transformation.

The function of the board

Whether or not the board is perceived as an overhead cost or a source of focus and inspiration, and regarded as an obstacle or an enabler, will reflect its own view of its role. Too many boards concentrate upon 'staying alive', and responding to good or bad news, rather than proactively guiding their organisations towards the achievement of corporate goals.

How do company chairmen see the function of the board? Seven out of ten describe the function of their boards in terms of establishing policy, objectives, strategy or vision, and monitoring and reviewing the extent of their achievement.[1] The implementation of strategy is usually undertaken by a management team that is accountable to the board.

The focus of most boards is very much upon crafting strategy and monitoring the work of management. The term 'corporate governance' reflects the primary role of the board which is to govern. Governance generally involves:

- examining challenges and opportunities in the business environment;
- determining a purpose for the company, a reason for its continued existence, and articulating a vision that can be communicated;
- establishing achievable objectives derived from the vision;
- formulating a strategy for the achievement of the defined objectives;
- ensuring that the company has adequate finance, people, organisation, supporting technology and management processes to implement the agreed strategy;
- in particular, appointing a management team and establishing the policies and values that define the framework within which management operates;
- agreeing and reviewing plans, and monitoring performance against agreed targets, taking corrective action where appropriate;
- reporting performance to the various stakeholders in the company, and particularly to those with 'ownership rights' and a legal entitlement to certain information.

THE BOARD AND THE MANAGEMENT TEAM

While assuming the ultimate responsibility for a company, directors usually delegate responsibility for operational implementation to members of the management team. The key members of the executive team may be appointed by the board. The organisational framework, including accountabilities, processes and values within which the executive team operates, is usually established by the board.

Too often in strategic management there is a stark separation between: (i) the role of the board in creating the vision; and (ii) the role of management in delivering the vision. As gaps emerge between aspiration and achievement, and it becomes clear that management is finding it difficult to deliver, a number of boards are recognising that more effort needs to be devoted to motivating, empowering and equipping the people of the organisation to 'make it happen'.

Successful transformation requires an interactive parnership of management and board. While advocating 'relationship management', many boards are failing in their relationship with their own management.

Robert Waterman stresses the need for a corporation to renew itself.[2] To achieve this, the focus of the board needs to shift from command and control to empowerment, sharing, enabling, building trust and commitment, and the shaping of attitudes and values. Directors are being required to move into areas with which they are unfamiliar, and which many fear.

THE ACCOUNTABILITY OF THE BOARD

To whom is the board accountable? Much of the corporate governance debate revolves around the accountability of the board to various stakeholders in the company such as the owners or shareholders, the employees, customers, the government and the community at large. The obligations of the board to certain stakeholders are covered by legal and other requirements. The prime 'legal' accountability of the board is to the owners of the company – the shareholders.

A traditional view has been that the interests of certain stakeholders may be in conflict. The role of the board in such circumstances is to arbitrate between them. In the more predictable world of the past, some boards got into the habit of approaching this task as if 'dividing up the cake'. Benefits such as dividends or pay increases were determined, and pricing decisions taken, on the basis of what could be afforded, or what the board thought it could 'get away with'.

In the world of emerging network organisations this 'static' view of the directors sitting around the boardroom table and allocating a determined pot needs to be replaced by a more flexible approach that focuses on flows and the process of generating value for customers. Various stakeholders provide inputs to, and receive outputs from, the process.

SHAREHOLDER AND CUSTOMER INTERESTS: HARMONY OR CONFLICT?

Most boards emphasise their obligations to shareholders in speeches at AGMs and words in annual reports. However, actual shareholder returns in the form of the dividend cheque that arrives through the post are rarely the product of rhetoric. They are the net result of a number of factors. Some of these are 'helps', and others are 'hinders'.

A board that focuses upon the process of delivering enhanced value to shareholders may find that its priorities need to change. In particular, 'profit' may come to be seen as the consequence of initiating and undertaking a combination of activities that collectively result in satisfied customers.

Those who aim straight for 'profit', or 'return on net assets', without much thought as to the implications of their actions for customers, often find that what they are seeking turns out to be as elusive as the end of the rainbow. Companies like Xerox now put customer satisfaction at the top of their list of business objectives.

Dixons Group plc undertook a 'value-based strategic management' (VSM) exercise and identified a number of 'value destroyers'. The company's strategy for creating shareholder value now concentrates upon a number of long-term programmes and investments to build customer satisfaction and customer loyalty.[3]

The focus of the board should be upon the customers. These are the people who are ultimately the source of all value. Financial returns to shareholders should be seen as the product of satisfied customers, and the consequence of involved and satisfied employees and partners who are empowered and equipped to deliver the value sought by customers.

The words and deeds of the board will reflect the depth and extent of its commitment to the customer. Table 3.1 identifies some of the positive and negative symptoms that may be evident in the boardroom agenda and the conduct of board business.

If the interests of customers are sacrificed to achieve a short-term accommodation with other stakeholders, the company in a competitive market may prejudice its longer-term capacity to serve all stakeholders. The wise investor prefers the reality of commitment to the customer to the rhetoric of 'investor relations'.

CURRENT CONCERNS AND PUBLIC DEBATE

There has been much recent criticism of the performance and conduct of boards. In practice, in a world of 'strong chief executives' and dependence upon information supplied by management, boards are often not as powerful as the legal situation might suggest. Lorsch and MacIver have suggested that many of those sitting on US boards are pawns rather than potentates.[4]

Table 3.1 *The Boardroom Agenda: Positive and Negative Symptoms*

Positive symptoms	Negative symptoms
Breakout/transformation	Spiral of descent to marginal commodity supplier status
Long-term focus	Short-term orientation
Redeploy to activities that add value for customers	Headcount reduction
Concern with customer satisfaction	Concern with financial numbers
Investment approach to quality, training and IT	Preoccupation with costs of training, IT etc
Build added-value opportunities	Lower price/price competitively
Securing commitment	Wordsmithing
Speed up service to customers to increase customer satisfaction and generate cash	'Screw customers' to increase margins and generate cash
Emphasis on building relationships	Bargaining and negotiation orientation
Empowering and sharing culture	Control culture
Focus on fact, reality and intention	Expressions of opinion, surmise and hope
Holistic approach	'Line-by-line' approach

While some boards and institutional investors do flex their muscles, others seem powerless in the face of circumstances such as those surrounding the demise of the Bank of Credit and Commerce International or following the death of Robert Maxwell. In such cases, and there are many others, people ask: 'Where was the board?' Advocates of change, such as Monks and Minow, have catalogued various abuses and excesses.[5]

Corporate governance has become a subject of public debate and focused scrutiny on both sides of the Atlantic.

- In the UK the 'Cadbury Committee' has been reviewing the financial aspects of corporate governance. The committee produced its first draft report in May 1992.[6]
- In the USA, a more wide-ranging review is being undertaken by the Subcouncil on Corporate Governance and Financial Markets as part of a review of 'competitiveness policy' by a presidential council. The corporate governance group is examining: 'if, and to what extent [the] current system of corporate governance and the nature of financial markets constrain US corporations' ability to fully realise their strategic plans and to compete in world markets'.

ASSESSING WHAT NEEDS TO BE DONE

To determine what needs to be done to improve the effectiveness of boards it is necessary to understand the current situation. Our expectations regarding boards of directors derive from those boards we read about, and our personal experience of particular boards.

The companies selected by journalists tend to be 'names' that are likely to be familiar to readers. Hence they tend to be large, or of some special significance. The great majority of companies, however, are 'small businesses' and little known beyond the ranks of their employees, customers and suppliers. All of these companies have directors, and all of these directors assume particular legal duties and responsibilities.

What constitutes a competent director and an effective board? How are directors selected? What do they consider the function of the board to be? How do boards in general operate in practice as compared with assumptions drawn from what is known about the boards of larger companies?

These and other questions have been considered in a continuing series of related questionnaire and interview surveys with which Adaptation Ltd has been involved (see Appendix 1).

- Over 800 individual directors have participated in the programme, and over two-thirds of these are the chairman, CEO or managing director of their company.
- As a consequence of the findings, nine distinct categories of services have been developed to improve the performance of individual directors and boardroom teams. These are available from selected professional associations and other specialist organisations.

The boards covered by the survey programme are representative of the total population of companies. The replies to most of the particular questions that have been posed do not appear to be significantly influenced by company size or status.

GAPS BETWEEN REQUIREMENTS AND REALITY

What emerges is that the reality of the boardroom is often very different from the requirements for successful corporate governance. The very people who should be the fount of corporate drive and purpose are frequently plagued by insecurity and doubt.

The actual operation of boards is clouded by myth, uncertainty and misunderstanding.[7] These are some examples.

- Many directors are uncertain as to their directorial duties and responsibilities. Others experience a conflict between the different roles which they may have. An executive director could be a director, a manager and an owner, and in each role might be expected to have a distinct perspective on certain issues.
- In many companies, the allocation of responsibilities between the board and management is unclear. This can lead to confusion, both in the boardroom and throughout the senior management team.
- New members of a board are typically selected on account of being thought to possess directorial qualities. Once appointed, however, if executive directors are assessed at all, they are likely to be evaluated in terms of their managerial performance in running a functional department rather than their directorial contributions to the business of the board.
- In very few companies is there a clear path to the boardroom. The qualities sought in new directors are rarely made explicit. Hence, many managers with directorial ambitions find it very difficult to prepare for membership of the board.

When roles and responsibilities are unclear, the energy that is devoted to sorting out confusions and uncertainties in and around the boardroom is not available for the task of achieving corporate transformation.

EXPECTATIONS REGARDING THE CONTRIBUTIONS OF DIRECTORS

There is little consensus among chairmen concerning the contribution that is expected from members of boards. Only one in eight companies operates any form of periodic and formal appraisal of personal effectiveness in the boardroom.[1] As a result there is little to guide those seeking to improve the quality of directorial contributions.

- The evaluation of the effectiveness of individual members of boards is over-whelmingly informal, and little attempt appears to be made to link performance assessments with the contributions sought from directors.
- When and where boards are assessed, this tends to be in terms of the overall performance of the business, rather than the dynamics of the boardroom and the distinct 'value-added' contribution of the board.

Perhaps because many chairmen find it difficult to define the 'outputs' of a board, their expectations regarding director contributions largely concern 'input' factors such as expertise and personal qualities.

Personal qualities that are important in securing access to a board do not appear to be so relevant to continuing membership, although about one-fifth of chairmen evaluate directorial effectiveness in terms of the demonstration of personal qualities and competencies[1].

DIRECTOR EXPECTATIONS AND DIRECTORIAL FRUSTRATIONS

For the individual director, the gap between prior expectations and the realities of boardroom life can be a source of personal dissatisfaction. The following comments are representative of the disappointment with the directorial role felt by many directors.

'I was originally selected because I had worked abroad and was thought to have an understanding of global issues. I'm now judged as a manager, by how I run my bit, not on the basis of my contribution to the whole.'

'My expectations were unrealistic. What I had expected to be doing just isn't done.'

'I had anticipated much more freedom, but the board is dominated by the CEO with the aid of a bunch of cronies.'

'I should have known, but I expected more discretion. The tentacles of corporate bureaucracy reach across the sea into the boardroom. That's the penalty of being a subsidiary. To the head office bureaucrats we are local managers not directors.'

'I sometimes wonder what value we really add. It is difficult to assess our contribution. Our role seems intangible.'

'The papers set out what individual directors want to put on record. We all know the reality is different.'

'When you are struggling to keep your own end up, you don't have the time to go through everything with a fine-tooth comb. A lot of rubber stamping goes on.'

'We are both judge and jury. As an executive director I decide on my own performance. We set our own remuneration and run the AGM on proxies. In a way I felt more under pressure as a manager.'

'In law I am directly accountable. If things go wrong I am one of those who will suffer the legal penalties. I feel I could be penalised for things I cannot really influence.'

EXPECTATIONS AND THE REALITY OF BOARD PERFORMANCE

There is little satisfaction with the performance of boards. Three-quarters of chairmen believe the effectiveness of their companies' boards could be improved.[1] Given this background, perhaps the presumption should be against any particular board being effective.

There are those who have been concerned about the performance of boards for many years. Twenty years ago Mace identified a considerable gap between myth and reality when observing the actual conduct of US boards, many of whom did not question management or have a major role in the formulation of objectives, strategies or policies.[8]

Following his retirement from ITT Harold Geneen has estimated that among the boards of Fortune 500 companies: '95 per cent are not fully doing what they are legally, morally and ethically supposed to do. And they couldn't, even if they wanted to.'[9]

In theory, directors of public companies are in exposed positions. On occasion the penalties of disappointing corporate performance can be swift and severe. Mergers and acquisitions can also decimate boards, and the 'golden goodbye' will not always compensate for the damage done to a public reputation or to personal pride. In the case of the great majority of companies, however, it is difficult to foresee (other than the case of retirement) circumstances that might lead to a termination of a board appointment.

THE GAPS BETWEEN ACTIONS AND WORDS

The board itself, in terms of its own role-model behaviour, may be partly to blame for the disillusionment that is found in many companies [1,7] as a result of the growing gap between initial expectations of corporate change programmes and what is actually being achieved. The failure of 'actions to match words' is the source of much misunderstanding and distrust, as follows.

- Under pressure to perform and survive, the focus of many (particularly UK and US) boards has become visibly internal and short term, while the messages that have been communicated to managers have encouraged them to develop longer-term relationships with external customers.
- While the directors advocate the transition to a team-based form of organisation, the effectiveness of many boards is being limited by poor teamwork. Improved communication, open discussion, regular meetings and a shared or common purpose were all cited in one survey[1] as ways of ensuring that a board works effectively as a team.
- Few of the boards that call for a 'focus upon the customer' have initiated activities to identify the key business processes that deliver customer satisfaction. Boards are defining goals without ensuring that the mechanisms are in place to achieve them.
- While the rhetoric of many boards stresses the need to put the customer first, their ordering of business objectives and the reward systems of their companies generally result in managers concentrating upon other priorities.
- Boards talk about 'continuous improvement' and the need to develop people, while failing to identify and address their own deficiencies. Many boards do not even recognise the need for improvement. Dissatisfaction is accepted simply because of an inability to determine how it might be addressed.
- Among those who advocate 'benchmarking' and the merits of the 'learning organisation', there is little evidence of experimentation with new ways of organising boards. Alternative models exist, as is evidenced by the different approaches to corporate governance taken within the various Member States of the EC. Peer reviews by other boards, or the benchmarking of other boards, is rarely undertaken.

BRIDGING THE GAP BETWEEN REQUIREMENT AND PERFORMANCE

Reality suggests that one should not expect either directors to be competent or boards to be effective.[1,7] In many companies:

- no one is consciously focusing upon the competence of the directors and the effectiveness of the board; and

- no initiatives are in place to bridge the significant gaps that often exist between directorial responsibilities, expectations and aspirations, and the capacity of the board to deliver.

Where action is taken, it is often inappropriate. For example:

- such 'development' as is provided may fail to take account of the distinction between direction and management;
- a new board structure might not match the situation and circumstances of the company, while the way the business of the board is conducted may frustrate contributions and inhibit the effectiveness of the team;
- new appointments may ignore the fact that every board is composed of a unique group of personalities. An 'impressive' individual who is effective on one board may be of little value on another. The competence and contribution of individual directors can be very dependent upon the boardroom context.

So far as the implementation of corporate transformation is concerned, some boards do not acknowledge a role for themselves in closing the gaps that are emerging between expectations and achievement. In interview discussions, chairmen drew a distinction between formulating and implementing strategy. It is recognised that the 'right' strategies can be inadequately implemented. However, many boards do not apply 'output' measures to themselves as implementation is generally regarded as a managerial rather than a directorial responsibility.

THE QUALITY OF BOARD DECISIONS

The obstacles and barriers that are giving rise to gaps between aspiration and achievement cannot be addressed without confronting reality. Many boards appear to operate upon the basis of opinion rather than fact. The information they receive, and the ways in which they conduct their business, does not allow them to penetrate the façade of appearance in order to identify root causes.

The pressure of events, and a concern with the lack of real progress, is resulting in an excessive focus upon 'the decision'. Many boards devote insufficient attention to understanding the true nature of the situation they are in. Having determined what it is that they wish to do, they are also giving too little consideration to making it happen.

Many boards perceive their field of action in terms of discrete events rather than ongoing flows. Thus, a decision is taken to introduce a quality programme or establish a strategic relationship. What happens thereafter is a matter for the management team.

Within the network organisation, greater emphasis needs to be put upon the dynamics of situations, flows and processes. For example:

- quality is an ongoing process of changing attitudes, expectations and behaviour, which should not be dropped from the boardroom agenda once a programme has been set up or a quality standard has been obtained;
- relationships need to be nurtured and sustained. There are boards that establish relationships with aplomb, and subsequently devote far too little effort to consolidating them and learning from them.

Taking discrete decisions can demand a high level of analytical skill in the boardroom. The information is presented and a conclusion is reached. Once documented it becomes a matter of record. The building of relationships and the steering of processes that have the in-built capacity to learn and evolve may require greater sensitivity, and a heightened awareness of feelings and values.

In the case of corporate transformation, individual decisions of high quality may not add up to successful outcomes where crucial 'change element' building blocks are missing. It is the accumulation and sequencing of key decisions that closes the gap between aspiration and achievement (Figure 3.1). This requires a holistic approach in the boardroom.

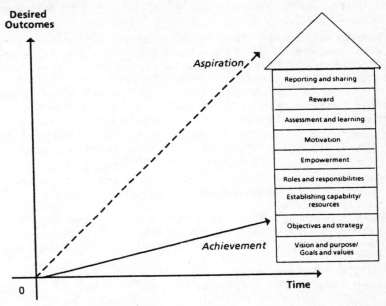

Figure 3.1 *Assembling the Building Blocks*

FOCUSING ON FACT RATHER THAN OPINION

Reference has already been made in Chapter 2 to the 'lure of appearance', and the tendency to focus on symptoms and cosmetics rather than causes and fundamentals. The following comments illustrate the frustration experienced by many chairmen.

'I respect their opinions, but would prefer some facts.'

'Everyone has views and opinions, and we are not short of background information. What we need is more understanding.'

'Too often I get played back something that was read or seen. This tells me something about the board members but very little about the problem.'

'We need a framework for structuring problems and sharing understanding.'

Structured discussion, the sharing of information and the application of understanding does not just happen. The board and its members may need to be equipped with the processes and tools to focus upon fact and reality, in place of opinion and assumption.

AVOIDING REALITY

Reality is not always welcomed with open arms into the boardroom. The failure of a key corporate programme to generate the hoped-for results can be painful to confront. People within a boardroom team may react to reality in different ways, as follows.

- There are those who do not like to be told there is a gap between aspiration and achievement. Some directors, and particularly CEOs, exhibit a tendency to 'shoot the messenger'.
- Others may 'play up' the value of encouraging sources of information and use 'selectively' the uncomfortable signals. When all, or a majority, of the directors adopt this ploy, the board as a whole may be not only deceived but also cocooned in a world of fantasy.

Within an organisation, as Janis warns, 'groupthink' and the collective denial by a group of key decision makers of what is happening in practice can distort their decision making.[10] In the boardroom 'groupthink' can have severe consequences from which many directors are only saved by their inability to implement.

During a period of corporate transformation, the presence of non-executive or independent directors on a board can introduce a much-needed sense of objectivity, balance and perspective into a directorial team. Transformation can become an unhealthy obsession. In particular, the pursuit of the single solution can lead to introversion and the instinctive denial of any hint that so much emotional and physical commitment may not be leading to the hoped-for results.

PEOPLE AND NUMBERS

A board intent on changing attitudes and values needs itself to relate to them. It must be sensitive to feelings and values, and recognise the extent to which attitudes are healthy and supportive, and behaviour is appropriate. To do this the directors must look beyond the numbers.

It is easy to become mesmerised by numbers, especially after they have been carefully selected and packaged in the form of 'board papers'. Behind the customer and employee satisfaction ratings, the response rates and the involvement ratios, are real people. How do they feel? What do they believe or expect?

A board should carefully consider what 'the figures' mean. Here are two examples.

- As many as 80 per cent of employees may be satisfied, and this might represent an increase over the previous quarter. But why are one in five not satisfied? How many hundreds or thousands of people does this represent?
- An error rate may only be a fraction of one in a thousand components, but what might happen to an aeroplane in the event of just one failure? What are the 'worse-case' consequences, and are crisis processes in place to enable the company to respond in the event of a disaster?

Just relying upon numbers may enable a board to track some of the consequences of past decisions without necessarily being able to influence future events.

The very numbers used by a board can influence its own attitudes and perspective. For example, when investment decisions are made:

- the use of a measure such as return upon net assets can result in options being considered from the point of view of the company, and decisions could be taken that might, unwittingly, have adverse consequences upon customers;
- relating options to improvements in customer satisfaction may increase the prospect of them being assessed in relation to impact upon the customer.

The use of particular measures by the 'core' team to monitor and control the activities of a network organisation can influence the thinking of all the members of the network. Others are likely to take a cue from, reflect or follow the approach of the board.

Changing the attitudes and values that make up the culture of a company can represent a major challenge. It also presents the board and senior management with a number of dilemmas. For example, certain of the attitudes and values that are not compatible with 'the vision' may need to be preserved for a while as others are changed. Some sense of continuity and shared values may be needed to hold the corporate team together.

DECISION MAKING IN CRISIS SITUATIONS

Corporate transformations often occur in situations of crisis. Classic studies of crisis decision making have highlighted the tendency to focus on the short term, and to concentrate upon fewer options, when the 'going gets tough'.[11] There is a danger that a sense of balance and perspective might be lost just when it is most needed.

Members of boards can experience a tension between the requirement to become more deeply involved in order to demonstrate commitment, and the desirability of maintaining a distance in order to preserve a degree of independence and objectivity. A corporate change or quality programme can increase this schizophrenic pressure upon the individual director.

One director summed up the dilemma:

'We are under tremendous pressure to maintain a façade of unity. People out there are beginning to question whether we will succeed. The views of analysts can't be ignored. They have a direct impact upon the share price. I'm being asked to "bang the drum" and to go out there and "sell the programme". This puts off the day when we will have to "grasp the nettle" and make some changes. To do this now could lead to a loss of confidence.'

In situations of crisis there is a tendency to cut out information and people who do not 'fit', and to concentrate power in the hands of a smaller group of people.[11] This prospect can pose problems for some directors who have genuine reservations which they feel duty bound to express.

A chairman should think twice before 'wielding the knife'. It is important to probe the reasons for hesitancy. Enthusiasm could be the product of sycophancy, and caution the result of thought. One chairman acknowledged: 'Team players are not those who just go along without thinking. Some of my colleagues are cautious. They are not obstructive. They are realistic.'

LETTING GO

Given the many challenges facing companies which we considered in Chapter 1, and the pressures upon central decision makers, it makes sense for a board to delegate. As bureaucracies make the transition to more flexible and responsive network organisations, boards are having to let go.

- In the bureaucratic company a very high proportion of significant decisions used to be taken by individual directors, if not the board as a whole. Corporate procedures existed to ensure this was the case.
- In a growing number of companies the board is sharing rather than hoarding power. Decision-making discretion is being devolved closer to customers, many of whom are increasingly demanding tailored products and services, and to those managing networks of relationships with customers and suppliers.[12,13]

One no longer needs to be a director in order to take significant decisions. Decision-making skills are now perceived by many as 'management' rather than 'directorial' competencies. Decision-making skills *per se* do not rank in the 'top ten' qualities that chairmen seek in directors.[1]

INVOLVING AND EMPOWERING

A majority of boards meet on a monthly basis. Directorial duties tend to be intermittent.

An executive director will typically spend a quarter of his or her time on directorial duties and devote the remainder to managerial responsibilities. Hence the need to involve members of the management team in transformation roles that require continuous attention.

Executives are increasingly required to establish 'output' objectives for the business units and teams for which they are responsible and, subsequently, to monitor their achievement. Objectives of business units to which considerable discretion may have been devolved are negotiated with the board rather than imposed by the board.

Involvement does not just happen as a consequence of what is recorded in the minutes of a board meeting. The consequences of board decisions need to be thought through, as follows.

- Past attitudes can have a continuing impact. A board should not be surprised if some people are reluctant to accept responsibility and risk. For many years a focus upon order and predictability may have discouraged initiative. One director commented in the context of a reluctance to 'accept empowerment': 'We used to decide everything. We didn't particularly want people around us to think. Their job was to implement and to do it "by the book".'
- People also need to be equipped to handle extra responsibilities. They themselves may need to be encouraged to prioritise and delegate if they are not to be swamped. As one director put it: 'We've cleared our plate, but out there they need help.' To become an operational reality, empowerment should go hand in hand with appropriate learning and development.

Involvement can have significant consequences for the board itself. In place of decisions concerning individual products, sales or investments, boards are considering framework issues such as whether the company has adequate processes for ongoing learning and change. The establishment and monitoring of frameworks, relationships, values and processes, and arbitrating and negotiating, are growing in importance as agenda items at the expense of 'one-off' or discrete considerations.

LEADERSHIP FOR CORPORATE TRANSFORMATION

So how are boards performing as enablers and facilitators of corporate change? The findings of a number of the surveys upon which this book is based suggest that many boards are not prepared or equipped to bring about corporate transformations.[14,15,16]

The great majority of boards are not systematically assembling the building blocks shown in Figure 3.1. There are some, as we have seen, who deny that their role is to 'make it happen', achievement being regarded as the responsibility of the management team. The board establishes the vision and wrings its hands as the gap between aspiration and achievement grows wider.

According to one chairman: 'The role of the board is the formulation and implementation of strategy. We put our backs into the former, but when it comes to implementation we hand it over to management and hope for the best.'

In one survey concerning the implementation of total quality[14] 'top management commitment' emerged as overwhelmingly the number one barrier to change. It is thought to be essential in view of the complex nature of the change task in many organisations, and the number of individuals and groups that must be involved.

To many directors the widespread perception of a lack of commitment in the boardroom is understandable. As one quality director put it: 'How can they believe we are committed when we have not put in place all the actions that are necessary to make it happen?'

Many boards are abdicating their responsibility for leading the process of corporate transformation. In one survey, leadership appears seventh in a list of 'other qualities' which are sought in company directors[1]:

- determining vision, mission and strategy appears to be perceived as 'direction' rather than as an aspect of 'leadership';
- the term 'leadership' tended to be applied by chairmen to the 'management' process of motivating people to understand and achieve vision, mission and strategy, once these have been defined by the board.

'Leadership' appears to be seen by the chairmen of many boards as a management responsibility rather than a boardroom competence. It is not surprising that many management teams perceive a lack of commitment on the part of the boards of their companies.

THE EFFECTIVE BOARD

A collection of outstanding individuals will not necessarily 'gel together' in the context of a particular boardroom. The effective board is composed of a united team of competent directors who are willing to assume responsibility for bringing about corporate transformation. The first step in formulating, communicating and sharing a vision of a different form of organisation, and a transformation strategy, is for the chairman to ask the the following questions.

- Do the members of the board share a common vision of a more flexible and responsive form of organisation? If fundamental change is to occur there must be an agreed vision of a better way of operating and relating to various groups of stakeholders.
- Has the board identified what represents value for customers, and the processes that deliver this value? Are there hidden barriers to improved customer satisfaction that fall between departmental responsibilities?
- Are the directors committed to an agreed transformation strategy? The directors should be commited to both a clear and compelling vision, and a common and realistic strategy for its achievement.
- How effective are members of the board at communicating with customers, employees and business partners? A clear and compelling vision has to be communicated and understood if it is to be shared, and if it is to motivate.

The board that is a facilitator of change, rather than its victim, and an active enabler of the transition towards the network organisation, understands the inter-relationships between strategy, structure, people, process and technology.[17] The views of the author as to how these and other factors should be brought together are set out in *Creating Excellence in the Boardroom*.[7]

AVOIDING GENERALISATION

Those who are intent on restructuring their board should bear in mind that there is no such thing as a standard board in terms of size and composition, and perceived roles and responsibilities.[1] There is a variety of both boards and directors:

- the various types of board include unitary and supervisory boards, subsidiary and holding company boards, and boards of private and public companies;
- a board could contain different types of director, for example, executive and non-executive directors, and owner-directors or alternate directors;

- corporate transformation is resulting in new portfolios and job titles. Within the boardroom team there could now be facilitating directors, or directors of change, transformation, involvement, empowerment, thinking or learning.

This diversity should be a warning to those who are tempted to reach for a 'standard board package'. The right approach to adopt will depend upon the situation and circumstances of the individual company, and may need to evolve and adapt during the course of a transformation programme.

According to Bob Tricker:[18]

> *'the fact that boards and directors can be so different ... means that generalisations about how directors operate, or suggestions for change to the legal requirements on how they should operate, may well be useless, and lead to guidelines that are relevant and useful in one situation, yet irrelevant and unhelpful in another.'*

BOARD SIZE AND COMPOSITION

The size and composition of a board should reflect what is necessary to develop a particular business and achieve a transformation from where a company is to where it aspires to be. Many boards are quite small. The most common size of board in one survey, accounting for a quarter of the respondents, consisted of six members.[1] To achieve corporate transformation a board will need to share, involve and empower.

Company size can have an influence upon the composition of a board. For example:

- in the case of many smaller companies there is an allocation of roles and responsibilities among members of the boardroom team, according to inclination and availability of time;
- in smaller companies there may be fewer 'vacancies' as there is less pressure to have a certain number of people on the board, and owner-directors of smaller companies are also sometimes inhibited by the cost of bringing extra people on to a board;
- as company size increases there is a greater tendency to take the view that certain directors ought to have particular and exclusive responsibilities. Only in such larger companies is there clear evidence of a conscious search to appoint a director to a functional portfolio because of a 'vacancy'.[1]

Board size and composition should not be taken for granted. The advantages and disadvantages of having more, or fewer, directors will depend upon a company's business opportunity and its transformation challenge.

APPOINTING DIRECTORS

An obvious way to increase board size is by means of new appointments. In corporate mythology there is tough competition for boardroom appointments. Every so often the chairman opens the door to the boardroom just long enough to let in some new blood before shutting it again in the faces of a jostling mass of ambitious managers. In reality, many chairmen appear to find it difficult to identify individuals with directorial attributes.

Overwhelmingly, directors are appointed as a result of their personal qualities. Language skills and academic, professional and technical qualifications are only of secondary significance in boardroom appointments, and expert opinion tends to be treated with some caution and scepticism. Qualities sought in new appointees to the board include judgement, objectivity, balance, perspective and individuality.

Many chairmen are 'supply constrained' when it comes to making new appointments to the board, and would consider bringing extra directors on to their boards if individuals with the appropriate qualities could be found. When seeking additional members of the boardroom team:

- the key requirement of chairmen and CEOs is for individuals who are able to develop a perspective of the organisation as a whole, and facilitate corporate development and change;
- there also needs to be an understanding of the distinguishing characteristics of the network organisation, such as the relationships between its members, and the processes by which value is generated and delivered to customers.

Above all, the attributes and qualities of new board members should complement and support those of the existing members of the directorial team. New appointments should be used to remedy deficiencies within the group and plug any awareness or perspective gaps that might emerge.

ATTRACTING CONTRIBUTORS RATHER THAN COURTIERS

The overwhelming majority of boards limit their search for potential directors to those who happen to be a member of a company's senior executive team. The perceived 'supply constraint' of potential directors could be a result of this practice of confining recruitment to the board to those holding senior management positions or acquaintances of the chairman or chief executive.

A more open approach would be to recognise that some individuals with 'direction' qualities might well be found elsewhere.

- As greater numbers of managers, as a result of quality and other programmes, focus on external customer requirements, acquire general facilitating competencies, and become involved in company-wide task forces and international projects, more of them may have an opportunity to acquire a sense of the 'company as a whole'.
- In contrast, a senior manager in a 'head office' environment may have little direct customer contact, and could well be immersed in the relatively narrow concerns of a particular functional department. Such an individual may possess the qualities and characteristics of the bureaucratic past rather than the network future.

The people who reach the top of organisations are often those who have been adept at climbing the corporate bureaucracy, rather than those who can bring about change in the future. They are courtiers rather than contributors. Some of those who can influence, get along with others, create a good impression, and who appear to be good team players, have been found by one study to lack the capability to deliver results in the context of cross-functional teams.[19]

Relationships with other organisations in supply chains, and individuals who are colleagues or partners rather than employees or subordinates, are assuming greater importance. Paying attention to the needs of both internal and external customers is now a requirement for effective operation at all levels in a company. The development paths of both directors and managers must now take account of this new reality.

In the case of the emerging 'network organisation' the route to the boardroom is likely to consist of a movement around the network in order to gain some understanding of its various processes and components, rather than a series of steps up, or movement between, functional ladders (Figure 3.2)

Potential board members appear to be increasingly aware of the legal liabilities which directors can incur. Some evidence emerged in interviews of highly qualified and sought-after individuals preferring to avoid or limit board appointments in favour of working upon *ad hoc* projects for negotiated fees.

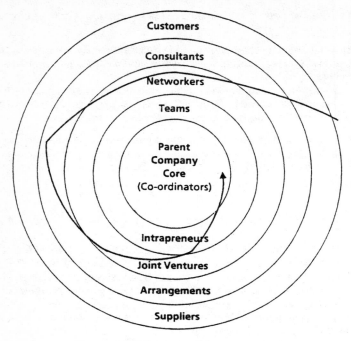

Figure 3.2 *The Network Organisation*

DIRECTORIAL QUALITIES

The qualities that distinguish directors from managers derive from: (i) their different legal duties and responsibilities; and (ii) the role of the board. Directors require strategic awareness, the ability to see a company as a whole and understand the context within which it operates. Formulating a distinctive vision and a realistic strategy requires objectivity, and the ability to look ahead.

Not surprisingly, strategic awareness, objectivity, communication skills and the willingness to assume individual and collective responsibility rank high among the qualities sought in new appointees to the board.[1] A degree of self-discipline may also be needed to be an effective member of a boardroom team.

There are particular roles in the boardroom such as chairman, chief executive or non-executive director that may require 'additional' skills beyond those possessed by other directors. For example, independence and a willingness to probe and ask questions which executive directors may feel inhibited from raising, are desirable qualities in non-executive directors.

At minimum, directors should be aware of their legal duties and responsibilities. As well as having similar accountabilities, it would appear from recent research by Demb and Neubauer that directors from a wide range of boards face a similar set of issues and problems.[20] Some awareness of these is also desirable.

Matters relating to the operation of the board itself of concern to many directors include:[20]

- the need to balance delegation of responsibility to management with the maintenance of control;
- the need to reconcile involvement and commitment with the value of detachment and objectivity; and

- how to establish an effective team without inhibiting the contributions of individuals.

Many boards face a chicken-and-egg dilemma. The perspective of a board, its perception of issues and how it analyses problems, are likely to be significantly influenced, even determined by the organisational context.[21] Yet many directors are expected to possess the attitudes and approaches associated with the flexible network organisation if they are to bring it about, while they are acting within the context of a traditional bureaucracy.

Hardly any corporate organisations make explicit the qualities they are seeking in new directors or have open routes to the boardroom. This makes it difficult for those with 'different' qualities or characteristics to break in. Women are grossly under-represented in the boardroom, and even more so among CEOs, a single female appearing in one study of 802 corporate leaders.[22]

INTERNATIONALISING THE BOARD

The board of an international network organisation requires a global perspective. There are various ways in which a board could be internationalised, as follows.

- Membership could be internationalised. ICL and Rank Xerox are among companies with an international board composed of a mix of nationalities.
- Responsibilities, function or scope could be internationalised. Unilever established Lever Europe with a European board as part of its Europeanisation strategy.
- Some companies such as Motorola and Xerox hold board meetings abroad. Such a practice can enable board members to meet local partners, government representatives and major customers.

When a main board is composed entirely of nationals of an ultimate holding company, and local operating company boards are largely made up of local nationals, a 'cultural divide' can exacerbate various arenas of conflict. We will examine this area in Chapter 12.

DEVELOPING DIRECTORS

Companies and their chairmen may like to think they 'groom' their directors. In some larger companies there appears, at least on paper, to be a management development and succession planning route from graduate recruit to the boardroom. So far as companies in general are concerned, however, there does not appear to be a generally practised route to a boardroom appointment.

Few companies appear to operate an effective 'induction' process for newly-appointed directors. Unlike the effort devoted to briefing and inducting new members of staff, directors are required to 'pick things up' as they go along.

Nine out of ten of those surveyed did not receive any preparation for their role as a company director prior to their appointment.[23] Over two-thirds did not receive any formal help after their appointment.[24]

Four-fifths of those surveyed remain 'up to date' by means of informal discussion with colleagues and reading appropriate journals.[24] It would appear that such formal training as is received is largely concerned with management rather than direction skills. While there are many management programmes 'on the market', relatively few of these appear to focus on the distinct competencies required by company directors.

A significant proportion of directors are thought to lack business acumen and a strategic perspective.[25] Few of those interviewed felt their experience prior to their first boardroom appointment had equipped them with the perspective needed to be an effective director. 'Stategic awareness' and 'strategic business understanding' are the two director development priorities.[23,25]

RESPONDING TO THE NEED FOR DIRECTOR DEVELOPMENT

Few companies acknowledge the need for investment in professional development in the boardroom. Some have 'burnt their fingers' with 'board-level' programmes that have turned out to be management modules 'retreaded' and 'repackaged' as courses for directors.

A danger of integrating the development of director competencies into regular management programmes such as MBA courses, is that students undertaking them may not fully appreciate the distinction between direction and management. A focus upon boardroom qualities, and the roles and responsibilities of the company director, might be more appropriate in the run-up to, and just after, a boardroom appointment.

Given the extent to which directors are able to learn from each other in informal discussion, there is a particular need for effective facilitators rather than subject teachers. Facilitators are required to guide the development of individual directors, and to work with boards to develop their skills as a team.

A chairman could use such opportunities as boardroom discussion for informal learning. Chairmen should be encouraged to act as catalysts in assessing boardroom development needs and ensuring that appropriate action is taken.

FACILITATING DIRECTORS

A challenge for many boards is to bring about change, while keeping an existing 'show on the road'. Chris Argyris and Donald Schon have recognised that achieving change, and maintaining an existing status and capability, can appear to be contradictory goals.[26]

One may see further appointments of facilitating directors to supplement or replace 'traditional' functional directors in order to enhance the ability of boards to cope with change. Rank Xerox (UK) Ltd has adopted this approach. The 'end points' of this trend, so far as executive directors are concerned, are boards composed largely of the owners of 'horizontal' or cross-functional processes, rather than the heads of 'vertical' or functional departments.

Many directors do not have the qualities, attitudes and perspectives, or the enabling and empowering skills, to undertake a facilitating role. Such places within the boardroom team will be occupied by those who can direct and manage change, and work with others, those who understand how to re-engineer and support key management and business processes, harness skills and build external relationships.

Facilitating directors with longer-term responsibilities relating to reshaping the organisation to meet strategic business development opportunities, and establishing and supporting its business systems requirements, may assist a company to achieve longer-term change, without losing a grip on the need to deliver current business objectives.

Individual members of a board may feel threatened by the prospect of fundamental change. The successful management of change may require the introduction of 'new blood' without loyalties, attachments and associations with the past.[27] On the other hand, there is little point in importing new directorial or managerial talent if the circumstances are not created for it to be effective.

HARMONY, UNITY AND EFFECTIVENESS

A long period of success can result in a complacent management team.[28] Those who have known 'hard times' may be more flexible and resilient than those who have had it 'cushy'. Too often appointments to boards are made on the basis of a past record of success which may have done little to prepare those concerned for future challenges.

The chairman is the most appropriate person to monitor and evaluate how effectively the board works together as a team. Teamworking in a situation of collective responsibility in the boardroom can demand skills that may be different from those required when working in a management group on an assigned task, either as a subordinate or project leader.

The danger of a comfortable group of people who are unwilling to challenge each other should be avoided. However, following full and frank discussion there needs to be some respect for a collective decision.

A group cannot effectively plan for change without assuming a degree of resistance and addressing how this should be tackled.[29] It is arrogant of a board to assume that its decisions represent the end of the matter, and to automatically label any future dissent as a case of disloyalty or evidence that someone does not fit in.

Training and changing the composition of a board are the two most commonly cited means of improving the effectiveness of a board.[1] Improved communication, open discussion, regular meetings and a shared or common purpose are all given as ways of ensuring a board works effectively as a team.

THE ROLE OF THE CHAIRMAN

The chairman is the single most under-used person who is associated with most companies. While all eyes are on the CEO, the role of the chairman tends to be overlooked.

During an era of corporate transformation it is especially important that the distinct roles of chairman and chief executive are both addressed, particularly when they are combined in one person. Ideally, and in most situations, the roles should be separated and two individuals should be involved:

- the CEO should have the prime responsibility for bringing about the transformation of the corporate organisation and achieving business objectives.
- the chairman should ensure that the process of transformation is understood by the external stakeholders in the company, and that the board is effective in initiating, facilitating, supporting and sustaining it.

The chairman has a particularly important role to play in improving board effectiveness.[1] Reference has already been made to the need for company chairmen to assume responsibility for ensuring that all directors are properly prepared, and that their boards operate effectively as a team.

The chairman should:

- monitor the effectiveness of the board, and that of individual directors, on an ongoing basis;
- periodically review the size, composition and operation of the board;
- ensure that all candidates for boardroom appointments are made aware of the qualities sought in directors, and of the distinct legal duties and responsibilities of the company director;
- assess annually the personal effectiveness in the boardroom, and contribution to the board of all directors. Where appropriate, such an assessment of executive directors could draw upon the views of non-executive directors.

SELF-ASSESSMENT

A chairman should encourage the board as a whole to take greater responsibility for its own effectiveness and performance. At least once a year all boards should carry out an objective assessment of their function and purpose, their individual and collective roles and responsibilities, and their overall effectiveness as a board. To ensure objectivity, some boards might seek external assistance in facilitating their reviews. 'Non-competing' company boards could carry out a 'peer review' or audit of each other's performance.

Particular attention should be given to the appointment of non-executive directors, and whether the search for candidates for executive director appointments might be extended beyond the senior management team. Boardroom appointments could be rotated to give more members of a senior management team or network partners experience of board service.

Few boards seek to compare themselves with and to learn from others. According to Sir John Harvey-Jones: 'unless a board continuously criticises the way it is working, is clear as to what it should be seeking to achieve, and its members ... learn from each other, it is extraordinarily difficult for it to improve its performance'.[30]

THE BOARD AND CORPORATE TRANSFORMATION

All boards tend to develop their own approach to corporate transformation. The role of a board in bringing about change could vary from a benign or hands-off approach, through encouragement by means of guidelines, more active planning, co-ordination and control, to active involvement in a number of initiatives to 'make it happen'.

If significant change is to occur, sustained and shared board and top management commitment is of crucial importance. Many boards would benefit from undertaking a review process along the lines of that shown in Figure 3.3. This incorporates the traditional view of the function of the board we examined earlier in this chapter. A systematic approach increases the prospects of identifying all the various 'change elements' that need to be brought together to achieve a successful transformation.[7]

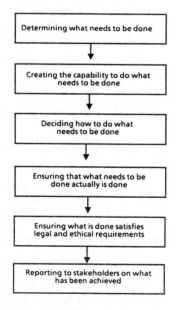

Figure 3.3 *Board Review Process*

To ensure that it fully confronts the transformation challenge a board must do the following.

DETERMINE WHAT NEEDS TO BE DONE

The board should determine a purpose for the company, a reason for its continued existence and articulate a vision that can be communicated. It should establish achievable and measurable objectives derived from the vision, and formulate a strategy for the achievement of the defined objectives.

CREATE THE CAPABILITY TO DO WHAT NEEDS TO BE DONE

The board should ensure that the company has adequate finance, people, organisation, supporting technology and management processes to implement the agreed strategy. In particular, it should appoint a management team, and establish the policies and values that define the framework within which management operates.

DECIDE HOW TO DO WHAT NEEDS TO BE DONE

The board should agree and review plans, and allocate roles and responsibilities. In particular, it should identify the key processes that will deliver business objectives, and especially value to customers.

ENSURE THAT WHAT NEEDS TO BE DONE ACTUALLY IS DONE

The board should monitor performance against agreed targets, taking corrective action where appropriate. Gaps between expectation and achievement need to be identified and subjected to 'barrier', or 'helps' and 'hinders' analysis. Particular attention should be paid to the operation of processes, changes of attitudes and behaviour, and to ensuring that the necessary empowerments are in place.

ENSURE THAT WHAT IS DONE SATISFIES LEGAL AND ETHICAL REQUIREMENTS

The board should pay particular attention to its own conduct, and to ensuring that corporate codes of conduct and statements of corporate values are not regarded as 'nice sentiments' or 'words on paper'.

REPORT TO STAKEHOLDERS ON WHAT HAS BEEN ACHIEVED

Performance should be reported to the various stakeholders in the company. Particular attention should be given to those with 'ownership rights' and a legal entitlement to certain information.

The review process that links these responsibilities is that illustrated in Figure 3.3.

The board has to forge a balance between its vision, corporate capability and the demands of the external business environment.[31] Moving too far ahead of capability may disturb an established position and result in demoralisation. Where corporate transformation is occurring, balance has to be maintained in a dynamic situation.

EMERGING BOARD PRIORITIES

A focus upon activities that identify and deliver the value sought by customers can increase the pressure upon a board to reassess its own role and the extent to which it is adding value or could contribute more to satisfying customers. We have seen that the search for a more customer-related role could lead it away from ordering and deciding to supporting and facilitating type activities.

Discussions with company chairmen[7] suggest that in future the following will happen.

- Boards will spend less time establishing and monitoring procedures, and will devote more time to initiating and facilitating processes for delivering customer value and satisfaction, and achieving ongoing adaptation and change.
- Boards will devote significantly greater effort to 'making it happen', or ensuring that measurable objectives are both set and achieved. There is little point in crafting a superb strategy that remains as 'words on paper'.
- Boards will pay more attention to attitudes, values and behaviour. Increasingly, companies are competing upon the extent to which their management and business processes enable them to cope with a changing business environment.[32]

DIFFERENT NATIONAL PERSPECTIVES ON BOARDS

The author, brought up in a UK context, happens to believe that boards are important. However, a word of caution is needed:[33]

> *A company negotiating with others should remember that the role and purpose of the board can vary greatly across countries. In some countries the board determines strategy and may act in a general supervisory capacity. In others its main purpose could be legal, to technically approve accounts or to appoint a chief executive to whom wide powers are delegated. Some boards exist to tap expert advice, to lend prestige or authority by drawing upon big names or to give the appearance that certain interests are represented.*

Those seeking to build international network organisations should remember that: ' The degree of influence exerted by a board and the importance of its individual members may not be easy to determine ... the main board may be but one decision making forum within a company.'[33]

All sorts and conditions of boards may be encountered by those intent upon building international network organisations.

CHECKLIST

▶ Who is responsible for ensuring that the board is effective and composed of directors that individually and collectively are competent?

▶ Does the board evaluate its own effectiveness at least once a year?

▶ What does the board do to benchmark itself against other boards?

▶ Is the nature of the board and how it conducts its operations appropriate to the situation and circumstances of the company?

▶ Is the board aware of its accountabilities to various stakeholders?

▶ Does the board fully understand the requirements of the various stakeholders in the company?

▶ Have the cross-functional and inter-organisational processes that deliver these requirements been identified?

▶ Are the individual members of the board aware of their legal duties and responsibilities as directors?

▶ Has the board identified a distinctive purpose for the company, and agreed and shared a compelling vision?

▶ Has the board agreed and shared clear goals and values, and established measurable objectives?

▶ Have the 'vital few' actions that must be done been identified, and roles and responsibilities relating to their achievement been allocated?

▶ Does the board pay sufficient attention to the implementation of objectives and policies?

▶ Are the resource requirements for implementation in place?

▶ Are the people of the organisation motivated, empowered and equipped with the necessary skills to make it happen?

REFERENCES

1 Coulson-Thomas, C and Wakelam, A (1991) *The Effective Board, Current Practice, Myths and Realities*, an Institute of Directors Discussion Document, London.
2 Waterman, R H Jnr (1987) *The Renewal Factor*, Bantam, New York.
3 Handler, S (1992) 'The Emphasis on Value-based Strategic Management in UK Companies' *Journal of Strategic Change*, vol 1, no 1, January–February, pp 19–37
4 Lorsch, J and MacIver, E (1989) *Pawns or Potentates: The Reality of America's Corporate Boards*, Harvard Business School Press, Harvard.
5 Monks, R and Minow, N (1991) *Power and Responsibility*, Harper Business Books, New York.
6 Committee on the Financial Aspects of Corporate Governance (chairman, Sir Adrian Cadbury) (1992) Draft Report issued for public comment, London, 27 May.
7 Coulson-Thomas, C (1993) *Creating Excellence in the Boardroom*, McGraw-Hill, London.
8 Mace, M (1971) *Directors: Myth and Reality*, Division of Research, Graduate School of Business Administration, Harvard University, Boston.
9 Geneen H S (1984) 'Why Directors Can't Protect the Shareholders', *Fortune*, 17 September, p 28.
10 Janis, I L (1972) *Victims of Groupthink*, Houghton-Mifflin, Boston.
11 Allison, G T (1971) *Essence of Decision*, Little Brown, Boston; and Steinbruner, J D (1974) *The Cybernetic Theory of Decision*, Princeton University Press, Princeton, New Jersey.

12 Coulson-Thomas, C and Brown, R (1989) *The Responsive Organisation, People Management: the Challenge of the 1990s*, BIM, Corby.
13 Coulson-Thomas, C and Brown, R (1989) *Beyond Quality, Managing the Relationship with the Customer*, BIM, Corby.
14 Coulson-Thomas, C and Coulson-Thomas, S (1991) *Quality: The Next Steps*, an Adaptation Survey for ODI International, Adaptation, London and (Executive Summary) ODI, Wimbledon, London.
15 Coulson-Thomas, C and Coe, T (1991) *The Flat Organisation: Philosophy and Practice*, BIM, Corby.
16 Coulson-Thomas, C and Coulson-Thomas, S (1991) *Communicating for Change*, an Adaptation Survey for Granada Business Services, London.
17 Benjamin, R I and Scott Morton, M (1988) 'Information Technology, Integration, and Organisational Change', *Interfaces*, 18, May–June, pp 86–98.
18 Tricker, R I (1978) *The Independent Director: A Study of the Non-executive Director and of the Audit Committee*, Tolley Publishing Company Limited, Croydon, p 35.
19 Miller, A and Hanson, M (1991) 'The Smile on the Face of a Leadership Tiger?', *Personnel Management*, October, pp 54–57.
20 Demb, A and Neubauer, F-F (1992) *The Corporate Board: Confronting The Paradoxes*, Oxford University Press, New York and Oxford.
21 Quinn, B (1980) *Strategies for Change: Logical Incrementalism*, Richard D Irwin, Homewood, Ill.
22 Boone, L E and Johnson, J C (1980) 'Profiles of the 801 Men and One Woman at the Top' *Business Horizons*, February, pp 47–52.
23 Coulson-Thomas, C (1990) *Professional Development of and for the Board*, Institute of Directors, London.
24 Wakelam, A (1989) *The Training and Development of Company Directors*, a report on a questionnaire survey undertaken by the Centre for Management Studies, University of Exeter for the Training Agency, December.
25 Coulson-Thomas, C (1991) *The role and development of the personnel director*, an interim questionnaire and interview survey undertaken by Adaptation Ltd in conjunction with the Institute of Personnel Management Research Group.
26 Argyris, C and Schon, D (1978) *Organisational Learning: A Theory of Action Perspective*, Addison-Wesley, Wokingham.
27 Hambrick, D and Mason, P (1984) 'Upper Echelons: The Organisation as a Reflection of Its Top Management', *Academy of Management Review*, Vol 9, no 2, pp 193–206.
28 Schon, D (1967) *Technology and Change*, Delacorte Press, New York.
29 Bennis, W, Benne, R and Chin, R (eds) (1970) *The Planning of Change*, Holt, Rinehart and Winston, New York.
30 Harvey-Jones, Sir J (1988) *Making it Happen*, Collins, London, p 162.
31 Ansoff, H I (1984, updated 1990) *Implanting Strategic Management*, Prentice-Hall, New Jersey.
32 Tushman, M and Anderson, P (1986) 'Technological Discontinuities and Organisation Environments' *Administrative Science Quarterly*, Vol 31, pp 439–65.
33 Coulson-Thomas, C (1992) *Creating the Global Company, Successful Internationalisation*, McGraw-Hill, London, p 325.

4

CORPORATE STRATEGY: CLEAR VISION OR CORPORATE CON?

DOING THE VISION THING

Most executives assume the value of a compelling corporate vision that 'grabs the attention' of customers and 'turns on' employees. The annual report is considered naked without its statement of vision, and helping companies to formulate visions and missions has become a lucrative area of practice for consultants.

A clear vision is of value internally and externally.

- internally, it motivates people to achieve and focuses their efforts;
- externally, the vision differentiates a company from its competitors;
- internally and externally, the common and shared vision is a unifying factor in holding the network organisation together and providing it with a sense of common purpose.

The people of some organisations are held together by a relatively simple common purpose such as the 'Kill Kodak' slogan of Fuji Film's enthusiasts. The Federal Express approach to the customer, 'absolutely, positively and overnight', and the Golden Corral mission of making pleasurable dining affordable both act as guides to what the organisation is all about.

Chief executives consider themselves negligent if their companies are without a mission statement that is generally available to all employees. Major companies have devoted considerable effort to communicating corporate visions and missions through-out their corporate organisations. The evidence is all around, in the posters on the walls of corporate offices and the 'mission cards' carried by employees.

VISION AND REALITY

Has all this activity been worthwhile? A vision can inspire, but it can also result in disillusionment if it is incomplete or incapable of achievement. Like an idea, it may have little value outside of an organisation with the capability to give it a tangible reality.

Three recent reports,[1,2,3] all based on questionnaire and interview surveys completed in 1991, suggest that much of the effort associated with visions and missions has been counter-productive.

Many attempts to formulate and implement visions and missions have been naïve, and in some cases destructive. A wide gulf has emerged between rhetoric and reality, and between aspiration and achievement. Instead of inspiration and motivation, there is disillusionment and distrust.

In too many boardrooms the agreement of a vision is perceived as the 'output', rather than as an initial step on what may prove to be a long process of implementation. Warren Bennis has defined leadership in terms of not only creating a compelling vision, but also translating it into action and sustaining it.[4]

This chapter examines what has gone wrong, and the longer-term and sometimes hidden consequences of the short-term reactions of corporate boards to economic pressures. It emphasises that changing attitudes and perspective generally takes longer than is first thought. We will see in Chapter 12 that arenas of confrontation have arisen between directors and managers, head offices and business units, holding companies and their subsidiaries, and between specialists and generalists.

The evidence we considered in the last chapter suggests that more competent directors and more effective boards are needed. In particular, greater unity and commitment is needed in the boardroom.

The lack of top management commitment and of communication skills are major barriers to change. To share a compelling vision requires new attitudes and approaches to communication. In this chapter we will also further examine the respective roles of the chairman and the CEO in relation to corporate transformation.

THE NEED FOR CLEAR VISION AND STRATEGY

The *Flat Organisation*[1] survey is the third of a series of annual BIM surveys. We saw in Chapter 1 that the 1989 and 1990 surveys revealed that in order to survive in the face of multiple challenges and opportunities, companies are having to: (i) differentiate themselves from competitors; and (ii) become more flexible, responsive and adaptable.[5,6]

The notion of the flexible and responsive network organisation is far from being a quaint concept that 'sounds nice'. Hard-nosed chief executives are seeking to bring it about. The 1991 survey[1] reveals the extent to which changes are now occurring within organisations: 'Approaching nine out of ten of the participating organisations are becoming slimmer and flatter, while in some eight out of ten more work is being undertaken in teams, and a more responsive network organisation is being created.'

In such circumstances, involving change and uncertainty, a clear vision and strategy is essential. Without it, organisations can fragment as devolution and delegation occur during the transition from the bureaucratic to the emerging network organisation. One CEO confessed: 'We almost lost control. People went off in all directions. I've had to put the old restrictions back on. They will have to stay until we can communicate or share the vision of what we are trying to do.'

THE IMPORTANCE OF VISION

The 1991 survey evidence reveals a consensus on the central importance of a clear vision.

- In the *Flat Organisation*[1] survey: 'Every respondent assessing it believes clear vision and mission to be important, and about three-quarters of them consider it "very important"' (Table 4.1).
- The desired focus of the 'network organisation' vision is clear from the importance attached by respondents to 'customer focus' and 'harnessing human potential' (Table 4.1), while the importance attached to 'attitudes, values and behaviour' suggests what needs to be changed to achieve the required focus.
- The *Quality: The Next Steps*[2] survey concludes that: 'A clear and shared quality vision and top management commitment are essential.'
- In the *Communicating for Change* survey,[3] 'clear vision and strategy' and 'top management commitment' are jointly ranked as the most important requirements for the successful management of change. Interviewees saw both as inter-related.
- The *Communicating for Change* survey[3] concludes that: 'Clear vision and strategy, and top management commitment are of crucial importance in the management of

change. The vision must be shared, the purpose of change communicated, and employee involvement and commitment secured.'

Table 4.1 *Factors for Creating a New Philosophy of Management In order of 'very important' replies (%)*

Clear vision and mission	74
Customer focus	66
Harnessing human potential	66
Attitudes, values and behaviour	52
Personal integrity and ethics	40
Individual learning and development	29
Process for ongoing adaptation and change	29
Turbulence and uncertainty	19
Organisational learning	14
Management techniques	5
Others	3

Source: The Flat Organisation: Philosophy and Practice, BIM, 1991

THE DISTINCTIVE VISION

A vision should be distinctive. It should differentiate, and answer the question: 'What's so special about your organisation?' Consider the following typical comments.

'We have not given the company a distinctive purpose. We are in a commodity marketplace and are difficult to distinguish from our competitors.'

'Yes, like almost everyone else our vision is to be the best or number one – however it is phrased. But doesn't everyone want to be important? Wouldn't we all like to be number one?'

'Lop off the branches of a tree and it sprouts again, it has a sense of purpose, a drive for life. Too many companies give up at the first challenge, because their plans are not rooted in anything substantial.'

Sir John Harvey-Jones believes a vision should present 'an attractive and clear view of the future which can be shared. It must motivate, be ambitious, and should stretch people to achieve more than they might ever have thought possible.'[1]

The visions established by many boards fall far short of this ideal. Quite simply, what is presented does not suggest any reason why a potential customer or possible employee should have any interest in whether or not the companies concerned live or die. No indication is given of what might be lost to the world in the event of their demise, or why anyone should care that they succeed.

THE FAILURE OF IMPLEMENTATION

Given the extent of agreement on the importance of vision, why is there thought to be a problem? Our family of three surveys[1,2,3] suggests that, in the case of the vision of the flexible and responsive network organisation, aspiration is not being translated into achievement.

The *Flat Organisation*[1] survey reveals a widespread failure of implementation.

● 'There is an emerging consensus concerning what is sought. The uncertainty is about how it might be achieved.' According to one chairman: 'Almost every day I build a more complete picture of what we are aiming at. However, at the same time its achievement .... appears ever more remote.'

- Managers are not being equipped or empowered to handle the new demands that are being placed upon them. One chairman confided, 'I worry that every change, every extra demand, may turn out to be the last straw'.
- The short-term responses of many boards to economic recession are not always consistent with either a company's vision or the building of long-term relationships with its customers. The 'gap' between rhetoric and reality suggests to many people that there is 'a lack of top management commitment'.
- Reference has already been made in Chapter 1 to the extent of disillusionment felt by: 'many managers [who] appear to have "had enough" of forever "doing more with less", when the reality of the vision they are offered is corporate survival for another few months.'
- The anguish of many managers is real and needs to be addressed as a matter of urgency. As one manager put it: 'our treatment makes a mockery of all that has been said about the importance of people.'

The BIM *Flat Organisation* report[1] concluded that: 'While clear vision and mission are thought to be essential, in many companies both are regarded as just words on paper and they do not act as a guide to action.' As one director put it, 'A document is dead'. A vision needs to live in the hearts and minds of all employees.[7]

THE ELUSIVE BENEFITS OF QUALITY

These findings are not 'out of step with other results'. Other studies have confirmed that the good intentions that can lead groups to craft a mission statement do not always follow through into successful implementation.[8]

They are also supported by the author's second 1991 survey, *Quality: The Next Steps*,[2] which reveals the following.

- The people of many organisations lack both a common understanding of what quality is, and a shared 'quality vision' of what it ought to be. One quality manager complained that 'quality is now all things to all people.'
- The quality message is not being effectively communicated. Over seven out of ten respondents agree that 'quality too often consists of "motherhood" statements'. Interviewees used words such as 'general', 'bland', 'mushy', 'not actionable' and 'unfocused' to describe their companies' quality messages.
- Quality in many organisations is largely a matter of rhetoric. One general manager described it as 'a communication device, an umbrella, an adjective, a label or a slogan'. A quality manager talked about 'a wish list of things we don't really understand and don't know how to bring about'.
- Short termism, and the perceived constraints upon directors and boards to focus excessively upon financial ratios, has become a significant issue. We considered in the last chapter the desirability of focusing on customer-related objectives. A CEO summed up a dilemma common to many of those interviewed: 'I face a real conflict of interests, between the long-term demands of the vision and a short-term imperative to survive. I don't want the vision to become an epitaph.'
- The main quality barrier, by a large margin, in terms of 'very significant' replies is 'top management commitment'. We noted in the last chapter that over nine out of ten respondents consider this to be a 'very significant' barrier to the successful implementation of a quality process.

Overall, the results of the programme of interviews suggest that as many as four out of five quality programmes are having little, if any, impact upon attitudes, values and behaviour. What is worse is that many are unlikely to unless additional 'change elements' are put in place. By this litmus test most companies are failing at quality.

In general, too many barriers are speculated upon, reported and discussed without actually being tackled. As one chairman put it: ' Ambitious, even exciting objectives, do not constitute a strategy if you have not thought through how to put it into effect.'

We will be examining the many frustrations of those weary people who are struggling to implement total quality in greater detail in Chapter 9.

THE FAILURE TO COMMUNICATE AND SHARE

The author's *Communicating for Change* survey[3] provides further support for these disappointing conclusions.

- 'There is widespread awareness of the need to change. However, a commitment to significant change is rarely matched by a confident understanding of how to bring it about.' Insecurity and uncertainty is the result of sensing that 'something is missing'.
- 'Simple and superficial changes, such as shifting priorities, or those involving the use of words, can and sometimes do occur overnight. Fundamental changes of attitudes, values, approach and perspective usually take a longer time to achieve. The timescale to achieve such changes may extend beyond the lifetime of the change requirement.'
- 'Most companies believe the communication and sharing of vision and strategy throughout their organisation could be much improved.' Top management commitment emerges as a significant barrier to effective internal and external communication.
- 'In many companies there is a feeling that visions and missions are just words on paper. Directors and senior managers are not always thought to be committed to their implementation.' Even when they are, they are thought not to be.
- 'The recession has increased the extent of cynicism and mistrust, as boards have felt it necessary to take short term actions that conflict with longer-term objectives.' A managing director confided in despair, 'I know I'm doing things that will weaken us in the long term. What's worse, almost everyone else knows as well. I'm surviving, but one day when the recession is over what we have done will come back to haunt us'.

Beckhard and Harris have described a vision as a 'picture of the future'.[9] A picture not a plan, not just words on paper but something which can be seen as a whole, and which can reach the emotions as well as the intellect.

If a vision is to be shared by employees and understood by customers it must be seen by them as relevant. It must relate to their needs and interests. As one frustrated corporate communicator exclaimed: 'We have a vision and a strategy, but I don't see why anyone else should be interested. It is all about us.'

We will return to the important area of corporate communications in Chapter 7.

CORPORATE TRANSFORMATION OR CORPORATE BUTCHERY?

The gap between vision and reality is particularly evident in the arena of corporate transformation. We have seen that a widespread desire for corporate transformation is not matched by any real understanding of how to bring it about.

Many corporate transformation programmes are carried out with the subtlety of the crazed butcher wielding a chain-saw. The blind pursuit of 'flattening the hierarchy' or 'overhead reduction' can have unexpected consequences, as follows.

- The section that is cut out might be a vital component of a key cross-functional process. Many companies settle down to the task of amputation without first identifying the key processes that deliver the value sought by customers. These are the nerves and arteries without which the organisation is dead meat.

- Areas and activities that 'lose money' may still generate a contribution. Cutting them out, without reducing activity elsewhere that does not add value for customers, could result in a heavier burden upon other units. Further activities may appear 'unprofitable' in the light of the reallocated costs.

Much of the damage results from the application of approaches that were accepted with some reluctance, practised and regarded as legitimate in the bureaucratic organisation. In the network organisation, however, they can be dangerous, and may also be regarded as being in direct conflict with its articulated values.

MOVING FROM MACHINE TO ORGANISM

The bureaucracy may have been perceived as a machine, with parts that can be replaced. But the network organisation is a living organism made up of flows and relationships. Organisms are sensitive, and crude approaches to transformation can be as indiscriminate in their impact as the plague.

To set out with an objective defined in terms of cost savings, or headcount or management layer reduction, can be a recipe for disaster. Instead, the focus should be upon identifying and strengthening those areas, activities and processes that deliver value and satisfaction to customers, and contribute to corporate objectives, while eliminating those which do not.

Unwanted fat may be distributed throughout the corporate organism. Removing it can result in a leaner and fitter organisation. However, many areas of fat lie close to vital organs, and uninformed and misguided butchery can result in a mutilated cripple that is left to die by its more nimble competitors.

MECHANICAL AND INTUITIVE APPROACHES

Viewing the corporate organisation as a machine can lead to a mechanical approach to planning. There has been a general reaction against many of the analytical approaches to strategy formulation that were used in many companies during the 1970s.[10] Advocates of excessively quantitative and mechanical approaches who have been 'shown the door' of planning departments should not be allowed to 'settle' in corporate transformation teams.

To implement a vision it may be necessary to reach the emotions and change attitudes, feelings and values. In a world in which establishing and sustaining relationships and partnerships with a range of stakeholders is of crucial importance, sensitivity to a diversity of values and cultures is becoming essential.

The writing is on the wall. Management thinkers have issued warnings and guidance. For example:

- Kenichi Ohmae has stressed the need to mix analysis and intuition;[11]
- Mintzberg has expressed the view that the process of formulating of strategy in many companies is excessively analytical and insufficiently intuitive[12].

According to the 1990 BIM report *Beyond Quality*:[6]

'Many companies encourage their managers to distrust their emotions. Feelings it is believed should be hidden. There is no room for emotion in the executive suite.'

'Now it is being recognised that as feelings influence purchase decisions and working preferences, there is value in the ability to identify, understand and relate to feelings.'

The *Beyond Quality* report concluded: 'Reason is no longer enough. Managers must understand feelings, emotions and values.'

VISION AND THE NETWORK ORGANISATION

The vision of an organisation should represent a strategic intent to bring about a desired state of affairs. Many companies also have mission statements which set out the values, principles and priorities of the organisation.

A living organism is in a continual state of flux as it evolves and adapts. Flexibility has been identified as a key requirement for the successful introduction of a change strategy. David Apter has defined modernisation and development in terms of the ability to be flexible.[13] The flexibility of execution may be as important as the approriateness of the direction that has been established if success is to be achieved.

Flexibility requires the freedom to think and the empowerment to act. The reality of the workplace is often far removed from the concept of the reflective feeling organisation. As one manager put it: 'Stop to think about anything around here and you become a headcount reduction opportunity.'

The compelling vision needs to secure the commitment of, and hold together, the diverse members of the network organisation. To do this may require the skills of the politician in holding together a coalition of interests. In the event of failure the network may fragment.

A global vision can bring about a degree of common focus and harmony of purpose, but at the same time care needs to be taken to ensure that responsiveness to local needs is encouraged.[14] A transformation strategy may need to set out consciously to create both unity and diversity.

TURNING VISION INTO REALITY

Many carefully crafted strategies remain on 'wish lists', or as 'monuments' in the form of dead documents gathering dust on shelves. They are not alive in the hearts and minds of people engaged in the task of implementation. Very often this is because of missing elements. For example:

- the strategy has not been converted into action programmes;
- roles and responsibilities relating to these programmes have not been allocated;
- measures of success have not been identified; and
- target levels of achievement have not been set.

Goals need to be translated into objectives that can be measured in terms of tangible outputs. Otherwise they are not a basis for action. They will not pass the 'So what?' test.

Even when responsibilities have been allocated and targets set, the desired action may not occur where:

- the reward and remuneration system encourages people to do something else; and
- they are not empowered or equipped with the skills to do what is necessary.

Very often visioning activities are hermetically-sealed exercises, that are carried on in isolation from the other elements of a corporate change programme. They happen at locations such as country house hotels that are as far removed as can be imagined from the world of work, and the little that is done afterwards to translate flip-chart scribblings into implementable initiatives ensures that they will never intrude upon it.

Too many strategic activities are self-contained rather than carried on as an integral component of an overall management process. It has been recognised for many years that failure in strategic planning is often the result of deficiencies in a company's overall strategic management process, rather than in just the planning component.[15]

DIRECTION AND MANAGEMENT

Respondents in all three of our 'family' of 1991 surveys[1,2,3] emphasise the need for 'top management commitment'. We saw in the last chapter that the key responsibilities of the board include:

- determining a purpose for the company, a reason for its continued existence and articulating a vision that can be communicated;
- establishing achievable objectives derived from the vision, and formulating a strategy for their achievement.

Both vision and strategy have to be communicated and shared.[1,2,3] The results of communication should be monitored to ensure that it leads to understanding. One managerial interviewee pulled a mission statement out of his wallet: 'Here it is. They put it on a piece of card. I couldn't tell you what it says. It's one of those things that doesn't stick, but we've all got one.'

A board and its directors need to be persistent. The *Quality: The Next Steps* survey[2] concludes: 'commitment needs to be sustained if barriers to full implementation are to be identified and overcome.'

We saw in the last chapter that many boards spend far too much time 'crafting strategy', and far too little time 'making it happen'. In terms of the functions of leadership identified by John Adair,[16] there is often a fair degree of planning and initiating and a certain amount of controlling and evaluating. What tends to be missing is the supporting and informing.

ROOTING THE VISION IN REALITY

In formulating strategy, a high degree of intuition and judgement is needed to identify and assess relevant developments in the social, economic, political, technological, physical and competitive environments. Carrying out an analysis of corporate strengths and weaknesses, and of external challenges and opportunities requires sensitivity, and the capacity to select and prioritise.

Not all developments can be foreseen, let alone quantified. Some tolerance of uncertainty and understanding of risk is required. In many cases it may be worth tracing through the impacts of alternative sets of assumption. For example, one could examine the impacts of a high, medium or low rate of market growth.

We saw in the last chapter that directors require strategic awareness, and the ability to see a company as a whole and understand the context within which it operates.[17] Formulating a distinctive vision and a realistic strategy requires objectivity and the ability to look ahead. Not surprisingly, strategic awareness, objectivity, and communication skills rank high among the qualities sought in new appointees to the board.[17]

FOCUS AND HORIZON

A 'traditional' view has been that: 'directors [focus] on the external business environment ... and are concerned with long-term questions of strategy and policy', while 'in comparison the great mass of employees are thought to concentrate upon short-term questions of implementation'.[17] 'In reality' both directors and managers 'concentrate upon both the outside world and the company, and also the inter-relationship between the two' (Figure 4.1), although the perspective of the manager may be that of a particular function or business unit.

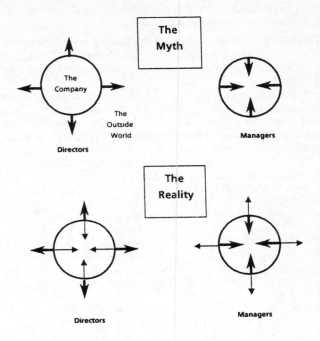

Source: The Effective Board, 1991

Figure 4.1 *The Roles of Directors and Managers*

Managers, particularly those in larger and international companies, also need strategic awareness, communication and team skills, and an understanding of the business environment.[18] In the *Flat Organisation*[1] survey the only 'management quality' assessed as of importance by every respondent is 'understanding the business environment'.

Corporate visions and strategy have encouraged managers to 'think long term' and to develop more of an external focus. The efforts of companies to articulate and communicate a longer-term and customer-focused vision has shifted the focus of many managers to the extent that distinctions of perspective between many directors and managers may have become a matter of emphasis or degree.

This should be a matter for celebration. Instead it has become a reason for concern. The following comments illustrate the dilemma.

> 'For the first time people out there believe in all sorts of good things that we will have to ask them to stop doing for a while. We can't afford it.'

> 'We've wound them up and now we've got to wind them down again. Due to a temporary blip, [some] things are going to be put on hold.'

> 'They give us a hard time now. They have their own perspective and challenge us about impacts on their customers. In theory that's healthy. In practice it makes it tough for us.'

The efforts of many boards to 'share a vision' has increased the potential for conflict where vision and conduct are perceived to be incompatible[1,2,3]

Figure 4.2 illustrates the conflicting pressures at the heart of the relationship between directors and managers, head offices and business units, and holding companies and their subsidiaries or national operating companies.

- Business unit managers and the directors of operating or subsidiary companies are striving: (i) to build longer-term relationships with customers, and in many cases also with suppliers; and (ii) to focus externally on the customer and relationships within supply chains.
- At the same time, those occupying head office and main board positions feel under pressure from analysts to maintain short-term performance. They are also putting more emphasis upon internal headcount reductions, 'delayering', and corporate transformation, as they strive to contain operating costs, and create more flexible and responsive organisations.

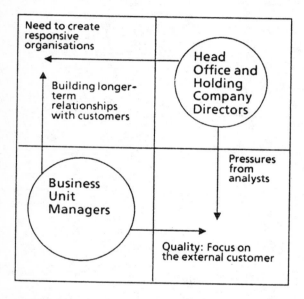

Source: *The Effective Board, 1991 and Quality: The Next Steps,* 1991

Figure 4.2 *Focus and Horizon*

In chapter 12 we will examine a number of arenas of confrontation that can arise as a result of the clash of different perspectives within corporate organisations, and how potential conflicts can be avoided and actual conflicts resolved.

THE INTERNATIONAL DIMENSION

A significant justification of the network form of organisation is its potential for internationalisation. An international vision is relatively easy to articulate, as readers of annual reports and accounts will be aware, but difficult to achieve in practice. There are various cross-cultural issues, sensitivities and barriers.

The need for internationalisation may be clear, and the priorities will vary from company to company. The author's book on 'creating the global company' focuses upon the desire to serve the customer better, irrespective of barriers of place, time and national culture,[19] but for some companies survival is the spur. For example:

- an Olivetti may seek to increase overseas sales in order to spread the burden of excessive and stubborn overheads;
- a McDonnell Douglas may seek overseas partners in order to spread the costs of developing the next generation of aerospace technology.

However, the international dimension may compound the problem of translating a corporate vision into a working reality. Here are some examples.

- A proposed relationship based upon commercial logic between companies such as that sought towards the end of 1991 between British Airways and the Dutch airline KLM may trigger sensitivities, and the interests of regulators and other parties at local, regional and international level.
- An overseas market may prove difficult to penetrate, while an arrangement or joint venture is just as likely to fail as it is to succeed. In 1991 both Peugeot of France and Rover of the UK announced that they were pulling out of the US car market following a period of significant losses, while in the same year Fiat and Chrysler terminated a distribution arrangement.
- It may take many years and sustained commitment both to penetrate a particular market such as that of Japan, and to develop the capability and forge the relationships needed to implement an internationalisation strategy. In the mean time there will be frustrations and disappointments.

Resources on the scale of a British Telecom (BT) will not shield a company from making costly mistakes such as BT's acquisition of Mitel in Canada. Five years into an internationalisation programme informed opinion was not convinced that BT would succeed. According to Stephen MacRae of the Scottish investment house Murray Johnstone: 'It is a wonderful strategy on paper, but they may have difficulty putting it into action.'[20]

In Chapter 11 we will be looking in some detail at many of the challenges that face the network organisation with international ambitions. Later, in Chapters 16 and 17, we will see how the network form of organisation can fulfil its full potential in the global arena.

BEGINNING IN THE BOARDROOM

So what needs to be done to make the corporate vision come about? The whole of this book sets out to address this question. But first, let us consider the articulation of, and commitment to, a common vision in the boardroom.

The board should be seen to be the source of the vision to be communicated. The board is in the best position to communicate with all the various stakeholders in the company. External, as well as internal, interests will be looking for evidence that a vision has the authority and support of the board behind it.

To formulate and agree an operational vision[7] may require more than the board 'away-day'.

- The vision should 'paint a picture' of a desired future that is preferable to the present, but rooted in marketplace reality. Underlying it should be an opportunity to generate and deliver value.
- The vision should be distinctive, and must command attention, and be both credible and memorable. It must create interest and be a catalyst of action. It should inspire and liberate. People must want to join the network and strive to bring it about.
- A vision should be succinct. It needs to be understood in a variety of contexts. To be shared and owned by a great many people, to live and spread across the barriers of culture, space and time the vision should stir the emotions, engender feelings and effect attitudes.
- The vision may be ambitious, but it should be achievable. It could stretch to, but not beyond, the limit. It must fuel an ambition to become better than the best.

In contrast to the compelling vision, many corporate mission statements are too long, unfocused, too detailed and bland. They are pale, anaemic shadows, mere verbiage that stirs little interest. Few represent a guide to action, most are instantly forgettable. The vision should be not only agreed and shared, but should also ooze through every pore. Directors and managers should act as vision role models. Explanations should be provided for any departures from the vision.

There should be a clear link between vision, values, goals and objectives, and all the elements needed, from empowerments to processes, to implement the strategy for the achievement of the vision, must be seen to be in place. People must believe that it is going to happen. Each of them needs to know what they can and must do to help bring it about.

ROLES AND RESPONSIBILITIES

Within the boardroom there are two distinct and key roles and responsibilities (even if both roles are occupied by one person) which will largely determine the extent to which a compelling vision is articulated, agreed, communicated and shared.

THE CHAIRMAN

The chairman is generally the individual who is best equipped to form an overview of the board and its operations, and hence should be responsible for ensuring the board is equipped to play its part in formulating, agreeing, sharing and implementing the vision. In the last chapter it was suggested that the chairman should reflect upon the following questions.

- Are your directors committed to a common vision and an agreed strategy? Which of them are 'paying lip-service' or are 'just along for the ride'?
- How effective are the members of your board at sharing the vision, and communicating with customers, employees and business partners? Is anything happening out there?

The chairman should assume responsibility for ensuring that external stakeholders understand the vision.

THE CHIEF EXECUTIVE

The chief executive should take a lead in: (i) securing the commitment of the people of the organisation; and (ii) communicating and sharing the vision with them. The CEO can also play a key role in preventing the occurrence of 'perspective gaps' and 'arenas of confrontation'.

Almost all those interviewed during the course of the three 1991 surveys[1,2,3], and who were not CEOs, referred to the importance of CEO commitment. CEOs themselves acknowledged the importance of their 'lead', as fellow directors and many senior managers tend to base their own level of commitment upon the priority being given to 'change' or 'quality' by the CEO.

One CEO summed up the dilemma of the 'fellow traveller' director: 'I lived for too long with directors who did not really believe in what we were trying to do. They didn't raise objections in the boardroom. What's worse, they sometimes said yes, and then went away and did nothing. They didn't implement the changes in their divisions, and everyone knew it.'

THE NEED FOR MORE EFFECTIVE COMMUNICATION

Once agreed by a competent and committed board, a vision has to be communicated and shared. Sir John Harvey-Jones believes that: 'effective communication requires effort, commitment, time and courage. Full commitment is the result of integrity, openness and real two-way communication.'[1]

Visible commitment is crucial. Vern Zelmer, managing director of Rank Xerox (UK) believes that : 'the role of the manager must change from one of managing the *status quo* in a command and control environment to one of managing change through active teaching, coaching, and facilitating in a participative work group.'[1]

Participants in the *Flat Organisation* survey[1] were asked to rank in importance the management qualities which will enable their organisations to respond more effectively to challenges and opportunities within the business environment. When these are ranked in order of 'very important' replies, the 'ability to communicate' comes top. Two-thirds of the respondents consider it to be 'very important'.

The *Quality: The Next Steps*[2] survey also emphasises the need for more effective communication.

- A broader view of quality needs to be communicated. Nine out of ten respondents consider 'too narrow an understanding of quality' to be either 'very significant' or 'significant' as a quality barrier.
- Managers need to be better equipped to manage change. The 'quality of management', followed closely by 'quality behaviour, attitudes and values', are the top quality priorities. Over eight out of ten respondents expect to give them a 'higher priority' over the next five years. Communication is necessary if behaviour, attitudes and values are to change.

Further confirmation of the need for the more effective communication of a shared vision comes from the *Communicating for Change*[3] survey:

- Communicating or 'sharing the vision' is considered 'very important' by over seven out of ten respondents, followed by 'communicating the purpose of change' and 'employee involvement and commitment' – both considered 'very important' by two-thirds of the respondents.
- 'Communication skills' are felt by respondents to be the top barrier to both internal and external communication. A third of the respondents consider 'communication skills' to be a 'very significant' barrier to internal communication. The deficiency is largely one of attitudes and approaches.

Whatever their boards might think or hope is the case, in reality many companies are finding it difficult to articulate and communicate a compelling vision. Words and slogans are passed on without being fully understood.

THE EFFECTIVE COMMUNICATOR

The effective communicator needs to think through what is being communicated, to whom and why. As David O'Brien, chief executive of the National and Provincial Building Society has pointed out: 'Often people will pick up and use the words associated with change, but without really thinking through what they mean.'[1]

Messages must be straightforward, and related to the needs and interests of the audience if they are to 'come alive'.[21] The communicator must be open, determined to build relationships and willing to learn. The communicator must share the vision, must feel the vision and must be visibly committed to it.

Customers and employees are attracted to those organisations whose principles they share. The 'vision message' must empathise with people's feelings and values, and it must be believed. Sir John Harvey-Jones stresses the importance of both integrity and commitment if communication is to be based upon trust and mutual respect. He believes that 'the manager should not be afraid to show emotion'.[1]

Honesty is even more important in an era of recession and retrenchment, when there is bad news to communicate. There are also, as we have seen, many gaps between rhetoric and reality, and aspiration and achievement, some of which are straining patience and credibility. The *Flat Organisation* report[1] concludes: 'In a few companies urgent action is needed to re-establish an atmosphere of trust.'

DANGER AREAS

Where implementation requires the co-operation of many people, and various groups are responsible for delivering aspects of what is needed, commitment may be withheld until all the elements needed to achieve success are seen to be in place. Achievement then becomes a self-fulfilling prophecy. Because people believe it will happen, it actually does start to happen.

At the same time, a 'common vision' and 'shared values' should not be driven through the network organisation to the extent that thinking is discouraged. The strength and vitality of the network may lie in the richness of its diversity. There will be differences of perspective and viewpoint, and these will need to be accommodated if co-operation is not to turn to conflict.

Thinking should not be regarded as an exceptional activity to be reserved for the occasional 'away-day' workshop or an annual corporate planning exercise. Nor is it something to be delegated to consultants or advisers. Thinking should be an essential component of daily management activity.

Too clear a public articulation of a vision and strategy can allow competitors to put blocking actions into place. As one interviewee ruefully put it: 'As a result of telling everyone at enormous cost, it now won't happen. The competitors are as smart as us, and in our game countering an initiative is a darn sight cheaper than launching it in the first place.'

VISION AND COMMUNICATION

Vision and communication are like cup and saucer or knife and fork. Each is of little use without the other. Vision without communication could be a private day-dream. Communication without vision could be background noise. Vision and communication together can 'move mountains'.

So far as corporate transformation is concerned, therefore, the following should be noted.

- The vision of the flexible and responsive network organisation must be compelling. It must be shared, the purpose of transformation communicated, and employee involvement and commitment secured. The chief executive should assume responsibility for communicating and sharing the transformation vision. Sharing can only be said to have taken place when people both understand and feel the vision.
- The ability to change and communicate about change, in the context of change, is an essential directorial and management quality. The focus needs to be upon changing attitudes and approaches to communication. Significant change will not occur in many organisations, unless managers are equipped with the skills to bring it about.

The three 1991 surveys[1,2,3] which we have examined in this chapter all reveal that clear vision and strategy, top management commitment and communication skills are of crucial importance in the management of change. Yet all of these are lacking in many companies. Hence all of them need to be addressed

CHECKLIST

▶ Does the company have a distinctive vision that is rooted in the reality of customer requirements?

▶ Has the vision been agreed by the board, and communicated and shared with the people of the company, and with its customers, suppliers and business partners?

▶ Do people remember the vision? What does it mean to them?

▶ What would you do differently if you had not heard of the vision?

▶ Is there a clear, comprehensive and realistic strategy for implementing the vision?

▶ Is the strategy a document in a filing cabinet or a working process?

▶ Is it to be implemented through quantifiable objectives that are consistent with the goals and values of the company?

▶ Do all those with the responsibility for delivering each objective know what is expected of them?

▶ Have they the motivation, skills and necessary discretion to 'make it happen'?

▶ Have the resources and other implications of implementation been thought through?

▶ Have the implementation 'helps and hinders' been identified?

▶ In particular, have all the necessary management and business processes been established?

▶ What is being done to identify all those activities within the organisation that are either not compatible with, or not contributing to, the objectives of the organisation?

REFERENCES

1   Coulson-Thomas, C and Coe, T (1991) *The Flat Organisation: Philosophy and Practice*, BIM, Corby.
2   Coulson-Thomas, C and Coulson-Thomas, S (1991) *Quality:The Next Steps*, an Adaptation Survey for ODI International, Adaptation, London and (Executive Summary) ODI, Wimbledon, London.
3   Coulson-Thomas, C and Coulson-Thomas, S (1991) *Communicating for Change*, an Adaptation Survey for Granada Business Services, London.
4   Bennis, W (1976) *The Unconscious Conspiracy*, Amacon Press, New York.
5   Coulson-Thomas, C and Brown, R (1989) *The Responsive Organisation, People Management: the Challenge of the 1990s*, BIM, Corby.
6   Coulson-Thomas, C and Brown, R (1990) *Beyond Quality, Managing the Relationship with the Customer*, BIM, Corby.
7   Coulson-Thomas, C and Didacticus Video Productions Ltd (1991) *The Change Makers, Vision and Communication*, booklet to accompany integrated audio and video-tape training programme by Sir John Harvey-Jones. Available from Video Arts, London.
8   Campbell, A, Devine M and Young, D (1990) *A Sense of Mission*, Hutchinson and *The Economist*, London; and Campbell, A and Tawadey, K (1990) *Mission and Business Philosophy*, Heinemann, Oxford.
9   Beckhard, R and Harris, R T (1977) *Organisational Transitions: Managing Complex Change*, Addison-Wesley, Reading, Mass.
10 Kiechel, W, III (1982) 'Corporate Strategists Under Fire' *Fortune*, 27, December, pp 34–41.
11 Ohmae, K (1982) *The Mind of the Strategist*, McGraw-Hill, New York.
12 Mintzberg, H (1989) *Mintzberg on Management*, The Free Press, New York and Collier Macmillan, London.
13 Apter, D (1968) *Some Conceptual Approaches to the Study of Modernisation*, Prentice Hall, Englewood Cliffs, NJ.
14 Bartlett, C A and Goshal, S (1989) *Managing Across Borders*, Harvard Business School Press, Cambridge, Mass.

15 Ansoff H I, Declerck, P and Hayes, R L (joint eds) (1976) *From Strategic Planning to Strategic Management*, John Wiley & Sons, London.

16 Adair, J (1990), *Understanding Motivation*, Talbot Adair, Guildford.

17 Coulson-Thomas, C and Wakelam, A (1991) *The Effective Board, Current Practice, Myths and Realities*, an Institute of Directors Discussion Document, London.

18 Coulson-Thomas, C (1990) *Human Resource Development for International Operation*, a survey sponsored by Surrey European Management School, Adaptation Ltd, London.

19 Coulson-Thomas, C (1992) *Creating the Global Company, Successful Internationalisation*, McGraw-Hill, London.

20 Dixon, H (1992) 'BT Makes Connections Overseas' *Financial Times*, 29 November, p 21.

21 Bartram, P and Coulson-Thomas, C (1991) *The Complete Spokesperson*, Kogan Page, London.

5

THE CUSTOMER: COLLEAGUE OR TARGET?

CORPORATE TRANSFORMATION AND THE CUSTOMER

Corporate organisations are aspiring to become more flexible and responsive in order to better deliver value to customers. The vision is of networks of longer-term relationships embracing customers, suppliers and business partners. But, as we have already seen, the desire for change is not always matched by an awareness of how to bring it about.

Customers are the source of all value. In a market economy, the revenue of a company derives from its customers through voluntary exchanges in the marketplace. The first CEO of Xerox Corporation, Joseph Wilson, emphasised the importance of the customer: 'It is the customer and the customer alone who will ultimately determine whether we succeed or fail as a company.'

Many of the fundamental changes that are occurring within individual companies are driven by a desire to better serve the customer. Here are some examples:

- Major corporations such as Chrysler and IBM are restructuring to match their expectations regarding the future evolution of customer requirements. Hoechst is pulling together group-wide teams, irrespective of location, to meet customer needs. Deere and Company has also adopted a team-based approach in order to achieve a faster response to demanding customers.
- Sharp and other major Japanese companies are moving R & D and market research activities into local communities in order to identify opportunities to adapt products to particular lifestyle trends. Ricoh and Sony have a localisation policy, encouraging managers to put themselves in the shoes of local customers and employees. Matsushita has established 'lifestyle centres' in major cities.

THE CHALLENGE OF IMPLEMENTATION

Most companies claim to be dedicated to customer service, even British Rail, an organisation that would be overwhelmed by protest if it transported animals in the conditions taken for granted by resigned and stoic commuters. The value of a mission statement that proclaims concern for the customer is assumed. Customer focus is referred to on posters and handouts, in videos and house journals, and in speeches at annual general meetings.

However, in a growing number of organisations there is disillusion, and a considerable gulf between expectation and achievement. For example, in many companies the following can be observed.

- Visions, values, goals and objectives reflect the requirements of the company rather than those of its customers. Roles and responsibilities, and specific tasks to deliver improvements in customer satisfaction, have not been allocated.
- People have not been equipped with the skills, or empowered, to bring about a transformation in the relationship with customers. Neither does the reward and remuneration system encourage a priority upon delivering value to customers.

- Cross-functional account teams and partnerships, and account management processes that give the customer a single point of contact, have not been introduced. The customer is confused and frustrated when trying to tap the potential and capability of the corporation.
- The processes that actually deliver customer satisfaction and dissatisfaction have not been documented, and no one is specifically responsible for them or has been trained to operate them. IT is also rarely applied to them, past investment being largely devoted to departmental activities which may or may not add value for customers.

One could go on. This chapter identifies the skills and processes that are sought, and suggests that new attitudes and approaches are needed.

SOMETHING IS WRONG

We saw in the last chapter that the efforts of many companies to 'share' visions, including customer-focused and customer-related visions, have been counter-productive. At a time when companies have given a higher priority to employee communication and employee involvement, a barrier of suspicion and misunderstanding has grown up between many boards and their companies' management teams. While some customers may be bemused or confused, many employees have been 'turned off'.

The following selection of interview quotations illustrates the extent to which there is perceived to be a gap between rhetoric and reality.

'We still regard the customers as targets. We bombard them with direct mail.'

'Our approach to customers is a question of what we can get away with, not what we can do for them'.

'Our short-term requirements for survival are taking priority over the long-term interests of customers.'

'Every contact revolves around selling or persuading. There is not much listening or sharing going on.'

'Ask people about themselves at a party and you are surrounded in no time. When we meet customers we talk about ourselves and wonder why they are not interested.'

'Most of our products and services revolve around the things we can do, rather than customer requirements.'

Paradoxically the desire, and resultant drive, of many CEOs and boards to communicate and emphasise the need to focus upon the customer is the source of much of the frustration that is evident. As a result of a perception that their actions do not match their words, they are hoist with their own petards.

Asea Brown Boveri is an example of a company that is endeavouring to make a focus upon the needs of the customer more than rhetoric. According to Percy Barnevik, the president and CEO: 'Our performance measures define success from the customer's point of view. ... Customer satisfaction is not just another improvement programme, but an effort to permanently change our value system and to orient the entire [group] in the direction of the customer.'

THE EVIDENCE

The primary sources of evidence for this chapter are organisational studies published in 1989[1] and 1990[2] and the three complementary 1991 surveys, [3,4,5] that were referred to in the last chapter. Details of all these, and other surveys cited which were undertaken by the author, are given in Appendix 1.

The BIM report, *Beyond Quality*,[2] was specifically concerned with 'managing the relationship with the customer'. Together with the 1989 *Responsive Organisation* report[1] it suggests that the company is becoming a network of relationships as 'electronic' and other links are being developed with customers, suppliers and business partners.

The focus of the three 1991 surveys is as follows.

- the BIM *Flat Organisation* report[3] considers the management of the transition from bureaucratic to flexible organisation;
- the survey, *Quality: The Next Steps*,[4] is concerned with quality priorities and barriers;
- the survey, *Communicating for Change*,[5] examines the role of communications in the management of change.

REACTIONS TO A CHANGING BUSINESS ENVIRONMENT

We saw in Chapter 1 that corporate transformation is increasingly seen as a necessity rather than as a choice. There are environmental, social, economic and technological pressures to contend with. Markets have become more open, competitive and international; customers are more demanding.

Priority should be given to creating an organisation that is adaptable and responsive to the changing needs of its customers. Those in the front line should be empowered and enabled to become facilitators, harnessing relevant expertise and resource by all available means, and irrespective of function and location, in order to add and deliver value for customers. The organisation lies between customer requirement and customer satisfaction, and needs to be a 'help' rather than a 'hinder'.

Where the transition is occurring, elation is replacing frustration as people find they can 'do things' for customers. According to one enthusiastic interviewee: 'Account teams are now where the action is. They're the fast jet jocks. What's left of the hierarchy is for the desk-bound who are past it.'

An ability to deliver can change the opinions of existing customers and attract new ones. Just as people are sometimes judged by the company they keep, so companies can be judged by how demanding their customers are. Without expectations they will not demand, and demanding customers keep companies on their toes. Porter has identified the discriminating customer as an important stimulant to international competitiveness.[6]

THE CUSTOMER IN RHETORIC

The customer appears to be king in thought if not in deed. According to the BIM report *Beyond Quality*, building longer-term relationships with customers, and introducing a more customer-oriented culture are the most important management issues; while the top three customer issues are customer satisfaction, quality and identifying what constitutes value to the customer.[2]

Among those interviewed there has been an overwhelming consensus on the following.

- The essence, purpose and vision of a company ought to derive from the customer. Initiatives, activities, organisation and corporate culture should result from what is necessary to deliver value and satisfaction to customers. None of these has any meaning apart from customer requirements.
- The customer needs to be better understood, and closer and longer-term relationships with customers are desirable. Mission, values, goals, objectives,

strategy and processes should be defined and implemented in the context of customer understanding. Organisations need to be flexible, adaptable and responsive in learning from customers, and sustaining relationships with them as their requirements change.

It is difficult to fault the rhetoric, although it is surprising that so many of its elements are regarded as 'insights' or 'discoveries'. Few of the strands which are apparent should have been the focus of innovation in the late 1980s. The key requirements were formulated a generation ago. Here are two examples:

- For over 20 years Levitt has stressed that the essence and purpose of a business derives from the customer.[7] A generation of students familiar with the Levitt message emerged from business schools and worked their way through the hierarchies of many corporations before these bureaucracies took their first steps to measure customer satisfaction.
- Alfred Chandler established a link between strategy and structure[8] a generation ago. If a strategy of continuous and flexible adjustment to changing customer requirements is to be implemented, the structure of an organisation needs to be sufficiently adaptable to accommodate them.

Why does it always take so long to translate insight based upon analysis and thought into implementable action?

THE CUSTOMER IN REALITY

The customer should be seen as a partner and colleague, an integral and the central element of the network organisation. The participation and contribution of customers should be encouraged and managed. Yet the reality is that customers continue to be treated as outsiders who should be 'kept at a distance'.

There is a fundamental 'mismatch' in the way different members of the network organisation are treated. For example:

- the self-seeking organisational bureaucrat that costs the company a great deal of money is trusted with access to 'privileged information', even while keeping in touch with headhunters just in case there may be opportunities to 'get more money' from a competitor;
- in contrast, the customers who provide the company's revenues are treated with suspicion in case they might want or learn something. Without some knowledge of corporate capability, how can the customer judge the potential benefits of a deeper relationship?

In too many companies the focus on the customer is little more than rhetoric. While the people of the company are asked to 'put the customer first', the organisation itself, in terms of its business goals, and reward and remuneration practice, puts the priority upon 'return on net assets' or 'market share'.

Short termism, and the perceived constraints upon directors and boards to focus excessively upon financial ratios, is killing many customer relationships. The pressures are particularly strong in the case of public or quoted companies, and tend to be more apparent during periods of economic slowdown and recession.

While distracted with 'balancing the books', key executives may have little time to devise action programmes derived from 'wish lists' and slogans that might have an impact upon reality. One senior manager was introduced to the 'twin pillars of customer satisfaction and employee involvement' by a European director who had just returned from an international meeting with the president of the corporation.

'He just burst into my room one day. He was full of it. He told me they were the latest thing. He had spoken to the other directors, and we were to drop 'team work'. He wanted 'employee involvement' on everything we put out, posters on the walls, internal stationery – the lot. He then asked for a couple of lines on what it was in case anyone should ask.'

With such an approach it is hardly surprising that 'top management commitment' is sometimes thought to be lacking.

The very concept of the company is the result of a Victorian preoccupation with developing safeguards and creating a structure to protect the interests of investors and creditors. It does not reflect contemporary views of the importance of customers and employees as stakeholders in a business.

THE BUREAUCRATIC ORGANISATION AND THE CUSTOMER

The bureaucratic organisation is doomed. Given its cost and inefficiency, it would be more expensive to preserve than opera.

Giant corporations are wide open to plunder, and are being 'taken apart'. We saw in Chapter 1 that developments in the marketplace are increasing the bargaining power of customers *vis-à-vis* suppliers. The availability of the skills and technology of communication enables competitors to 'come from nowhere and walk off with the best customers'.

The 'new companies on the block' can afford to be selective, and the best advice in the world is generally available for a fee. As one jaundiced director emphasised: 'They are not interested in the rubbish. They target and work on the prizes, the ones that are keeping us alive.' Incisive competitors are like smart ticks feasting upon the blood of dumb beasts.

Established duopolies are not free of challenge, as the entry of Mars into the ice-cream snack market has demonstrated. The existence of networks and network organisations makes it easier for 'newcomers' to secure direct access to targeted groups. This can be done by avoiding channels and outlets that may be controlled or dominated by the 'established players'.

In struggling to respond, executives in the megaliths are 'running with lead boots on'. Operating units with market and customer responsibilities are often organisationally quite separate from manufacturing units. Each reports upwards to a group board, with little or no direct contact or lateral communication. Sales targets may be given to marketing operations based upon what manufacturing can produce.

Manufacturing companies are reorienting towards putting more emphasis upon meeting market needs and less on such considerations as available capacity. Flexibility and responsiveness is becoming more important than optimisation of aspects of the production process. A director of one manufacturing multinational expressed the view that 'meeting customers' needs will become even more important to the whole organisation. All parts of the organisation will need to think from a marketing perspective.'

A company can be constrained by its past. The larger and more complex the bureaucracy, the greater the danger of being sucked into the internal operations of the company, the endless round of asset and headcount reduction programmes, as smaller and more nimble competitors 'cream' off the more lucrative business.

SIZE AND RESPONSIVENESS

The desire of larger companies to focus on those things which they do well and hive off or subcontract non-core activities creates new opportunities for the smaller company. In the knowledge society there is more open access to insight, information, skill and funding. Scale is less significant as a source of competitive advantage compared with flexibility and responsiveness.

Opportunities that suddenly arise are new for all, large and small company alike. Relevant expertise may not be found in either the small or the larger company. The rate of change erodes existing understanding and established capability. A larger workforce increases the requirement for continuing learning and updating.

The small company does not need to develop large overheads if flexible access to appropriate skill and expertise is available as and when required. There is no reason why an alert and astute competitor should not tap the most relevant expertise and 'out-think' and out-perform a larger bureaucracy that feels compelled to make use of less relevant resources and procedures just because they happen to be 'on the books'.

Different parts of the corporation should be allowed to evolve distinct forms of organisation and management processes that meet their own particular requirements. Tied together, all the business units may drown. Empowered and set free, some may survive.

PEOPLE AND THE NETWORK ORGANISATION

The evolving company is becoming a network of those who share a common vision and have compatible interests. We have seen that it is a network including within its membership customers, suppliers and business partners. It is also increasingly a network that is international; a network that matches the most relevant expertise to the greatest opportunities to add value.

Networks need not be permanent, but may be called together to achieve a particular task. The larger projects could be handled by a network brought together for the specific purpose. People and organisations could belong simultaneously to a number of networks. Networks could resemble consortia of venturers coming together to stage an event or to undertake a voyage.

People could also have more than one role within a network. For example, many employees are also customers. Nick Kane of BT points out that 'every one of our employees is a customer, or potential customer. So they can put themselves into other people's shoes and imagine what it must feel like to receive poor services, and how rewarding it is to have a job well done.'[2]

As companies focus upon core areas in which they have a strong comparative advantage, a growing range of tasks will be subcontracted to individuals and networks with specialist expertise in the activities concerned. Another BIM study by the author[9] has shown that a greater distinction is likely to emerge between those who commit themselves to a managerial role within a single organisation and 'new professionals' who develop a distinct skill or competence which they are willing to make available on a fee basis to multiple clients.

TECHNOLOGY AND THE NETWORK ORGANISATION

The people of the network organisation need to be supported by a communications network that can facilitate the delivery of value to its customers. Supporting technology needs itself to be flexible and adaptable in allowing multifunctional, multilocation, multiorganisational and multinational teams to work together.

According to David O'Brien, chief executive of the National Provincial Building Society: 'the process of working effectively in a team involves more than just sharing data. It must also be possible to share thoughts, insights and concepts.' Technology should allow thoughts, insights and concepts to be refined and amended. It should facilitate learning and development, and itself be capable of learning and development.

Technology can create opportunities for new relationships with customers, as follows.

- Purchasing, in the case of a consortium or 'Euro-enterprise', could be located at a single point for the whole of the Single Market. Companies marketing to emerging Euro-enterprises will need to find new ways of bringing together relevant expertise from across the Community in order to focus it upon a particular opportunity.
- Customers of DHL, an international courier company, can opt to join a global network. An electronic link enables them to secure access to their account details, and initiate certain activities and transactions.
- BT uses its own services to achieve a link with customers. Nick Kane, director, marketing and sales, BT UK, explains that in using a computerised customer service system 'front office staff can get lines reinstated, test for basic faults, and allocate new telephone numbers – all while the customer is actually on the phone'.[2]
- In 1992 the early US presidential campaign of H Ross Perot demonstrated how an entrenched, two-party establishment could be bypassed through intelligent use of alternative networks. Using teleconferencing and phone banks to stage electronic meetings, Perot established direct and spontaneous links with individual members of the electorate in the place of the more traditional use of the bland and pre-packaged broadcast commercial.

More continuous, intimate and intense relationships with customers are becoming possible. Developments in personal communications are allowing freer access to global networks. Converging technology enables 'multimedia' screens to be used for home banking, home shopping, home working and home learning. Portable and disposable technology options will mean that individuals can work in a variety of locations, and use alternative technology environments, according to how appropriate they are felt to be to particular activities, tasks or projects.

We will be examining various aspects of the technology of the network organisation in Chapters 15, 16 and 17.

VALUES AND THE NETWORK ORGANISATION

Networks will become global, bringing together all those who share certain values and goals, and who wish to contribute a proportion of their time to the pursuit of a particular vision. We saw in the last chapter that the vision, purpose and values of a network are key differentiators. Much effort needs to be put into articulating and propounding those that are distinct and compelling.

Values may need to be put up on hoardings in order to differentiate one network from another. As one manager complained: 'Technology is boring. One modem or switch is rather like another. We need something different to attract attention.'

When technology, information and knowledge become commodities, equally available to all, competition between networks may be on the basis of values, rather than such factors as price. Customers may choose between producers, all of which have access to state-of-the-art technology and up-to-date knowledge according to the underlying values of the producing or converting network. One value network, for example, may be chosen rather than another, because it is more environmentally conscious.

People who can learn and empathise with the changing values, emotions and desires of customers are of critical importance when competitors can copy more tangible products and services. Increasingly, intangibles will be the basis of sustained competitive advantage.

THE CUSTOMER AND CORPORATE TRANSFORMATION

Not all customers are prepared to wait. Some will use their purchasing power to prise open a bureaucratic shell in order to get at what is within. The more confident and assertive customers are catalysts of corporate transformation.

According to Renato Riverso, president-directeur general, IBM Europe:[10]

> *'... we recognise that our customers require specialist, not generalist support. This has led us to start redefining IBM worldwide into smaller, more autonomous units that can react more rapidly to customer needs. The effects of these changes will be profound and far-reaching.'*

The smart company actively learns from its customers. The awkward customers may be 'trying it on', or they may be useful sources of new product ideas.[11] The demanding customer can be used as an agent of change. External customers can be used to help shift internal attitudes and change expectations.

LEARNING FROM THE CUSTOMER

Value is created by the customer. All commercial activity derives from the requirements and aspirations of customers. They must be not only understood but involved. A higher priority is being attached to learning from customers. Customers are being asked about their requirements. Sometimes the questions are asked by independent third parties, or the name of the supplier is withheld in order to obtain a fair comparison with competitors.

Yesterdays findings and assumptions may be different from the reality of tomorrow's need. Deming has suggested that suppliers should do more than satisfy the *ad hoc* requirements of customers. They should aim to establish and build an ongoing relationship with them.[12]

Customer feedback does not automatically occur, it needs to be managed. Customers must be actively encouraged to give their views. As one interviewee put it: 'We've never listened. We always thought we knew best. Customers have never had any reason to be open with us.'

The learning loop process shown diagrammatically in Figure 5.1 illustrates how an organisation's vision and capability should be matched to customer requirements. Distinct subprocesses are involved.

- An issue monitoring and management process, and customer satisfaction surveys should be used to review and refine the vision in order to ensure that the purpose of the company remains focused on the customer. It is worth reassessing the vision even though the temptation may be to jump straight from survey findings to organisational capability.
- The process used to deploy the vision and resulting values, goals and objectives must reach through to all the people and elements that collectively make up the capability of the company to deliver value to its customers.
- When matching organisational capability to customer requirements, particular attention should be paid to the processes that identify and deliver the value sought by customers, those that harness the potential and capability that this requires, and those that enable and facilitate continuous learning and improvement.

BUILDING RELATIONSHIPS WITH CUSTOMERS

Some companies, operating through intermediaries or channels of distribution may be surrounded by concentric rings of 'customer' until a final consumer is reached. In such cases relationships may need to be established with all of the concentric rings. Each will have its own concerns and requirements.

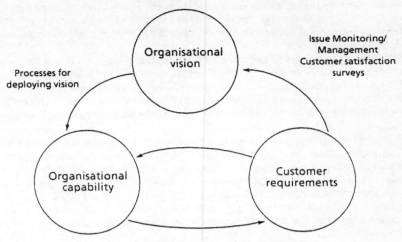

Issue Monitoring/
Management
Customer satisfaction
surveys

Processes for
deploying vision

Processes for focusing on delivery of value to customers
Processes for harnessing talents of groups and teams to add value for customers
Processes for continuous learning and improvement

Figure 5.1 *The Learning Loop*

There appears to be growing awareness of the margin and profitability advantages of emphasising higher added-value considerations and the wider benefits of products and services (Figure 5.2). A closer relationship with customers can enable a company to spring the commodity products trap. In some sectors this can involve working with customers to develop their understanding of what can be achieved and enhance their expectations.

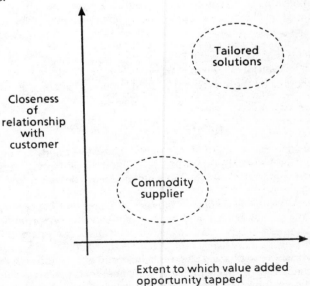

Figure 5.2 *Breaking Out of the Commodity Product Trap*

Customers are becoming collaborators and partners. Hilary Cropper, chief executive, FI Group plc, believes 'as for future trends, we have seen an increasing number of alliances between suppliers and customers – for example in those situations where the customer sells on a developed system.'[2]

The growing heterogeneity of customer requirements suggests that if they are to be addressed, and a greater variety of relationships sustained, we will need to tap into and build upon the differences inherent in us. More attention should be paid to the recognition, identification and development of diversity. The need to ensure that the dogged drive for transformation does not destroy diversity is a recurring theme of this book.

Relationships with groups of customers can be established by acquiring rather than competing with other companies that supply them. Such a strategy is particularly suited to sectors in which there are brand and other loyalties. Thus in 1988 the Swiss company Nestlé acquired the UK company Rowntree, while in 1990 another Swiss company Jacobs Suchard was acquired by Philip Morris of the USA. BSN of France has pursued an aggressive expansion strategy through the acquisition of strong brands in other European countries. The quality of the customer relationship is itself a source of value.

RECONCILING INTEGRATION AND FOCUS

Traditionally companies have integrated forwards and backwards in order to control more of the opportunity to generate the ultimate value that is sought by customers. This approach continues, as in the case of the purchase of CBS Records and Columbia Pictures by Japan's Sony Corporation. In the self-contained bureaucratic organisation the desire to slim down and focus upon core strengths can run counter to an integration strategy.

The network organisation that embraces a range of business partners is able to reconcile integration and focus. Integration may be achieved by bringing new members into the network, while the existing members concentrate upon those things which they do best.

Building relationships with customers may require a significant change of attitudes on the part of those involved. A career lifetime of bargaining and negotiation, and the 'zero-sum' perspective that regards the gain of one party as the loss of the other, needs to be replaced by different and co-operative patterns of behaviour.

Joint teams from the customer and supplier organisations need to work together in the 'positive-sum' search for outcomes that offer benefits to all players. This is often best achieved by encouraging those involved to focus upon an outcome to which all can aspire.[13]

THINKING IT THROUGH

Network membership can enable individuals and companies both to contribute and benefit. The balance between putting in and taking out will vary according to the member. One interviewee said ruefully: 'Rather than access a flexible resource we ended up being milked.'

In some sectors a wide gulf appears between the desires of suppliers with their rhetoric of 'building relationships' and 'tapping added-value opportunities', and the intentions of customers to buy at the lowest price. It takes two compatible and like-minded parties to form a mutually advantageous relationship.

The consequences of establishing electronic links and putting the customer 'on line' can be unexpected. What, to the supplier, is a channel to 'broaden' and deliver more value, may, to the customer, be seen as a means of sending out tender details in an attempt to 'commoditise' a product.

An organisation may be both a customer and a competitor. Even IBM has started to sell semi-conductor products to competitors. The people of the network organisation need to be equipped to handle different and parallel sets of relationships with the same network partners.

BARRIER ANALYSIS

In order to close the gap between where it is and where it would like to be, a company needs a realistic appreciation of its current state and a detailed assessment of its desired state. Too often companies are unrealistic in their understanding of a current situation, and a desired state is not translated into sufficient detail to allow important implications and requirements to be identified.

If corrective and appropriate action is to be taken, barriers and gaps between a current and desired state have to be identified. Out of this analysis of the situation will emerge a set of priorities regarding the actions that will need to be taken to close a gap between aspiration and achievement that exists or might emerge. These are the 'vital vitals' or 'vital few'. They are the 'crucial deciders' which will determine the extent to which the company will 'make it'.

Figure 5.3 illustrates a summary of the barrier analysis undertaken by one company seeking to 'improve' its relationships with customers. In this case many of the 'hinders' represented outcomes that were perceived as desirable by customers. Hence, it was decided to stress the extent to which the 'helps' would benefit both customer and supplier.

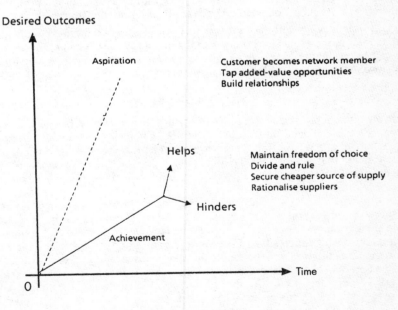

Figure 5.3 *Helps and Hinders*

Another message of the case illustrated in Figure 5.3 is that, in the absence of management action, the 'hinders' that 'are in the hands of external parties' and over which the company does not have complete control may combine to widen the gap between aspiration and achievement. The company that treads water gets taken backwards by the current.

SPEED OF RESPONSE

For many companies speed of response has become a major barrier and the focus of competition. Speed of reaction or delivery to customers is becoming a more significant benchmark test for many companies in a variety of sectors, as follows.

- Many Japanese companies, such as Casio, have based their competitive strategy upon the speed with which a new product concept can be turned into an offering in the hands of the customer. Xerox and Canon, 'facing off' in a field characterised by continuing technological innovation, are competing on the processes that put new features into the hands of customers.
- Hyundai of Korea has moved the management of its worldwide personal computer operations to California in order to be closer to, and more responsive to, both customers and the creators of future generations of technology. The move to the USA is expected to significantly reduce the time it takes to bring new products to the marketplace. Being closer to customers also makes it easier for products to be tailored to their individual requirements.
- Ford of Europe is reducing its product range, giving greater discretion to those responsible for each product line, and introducing new project management techniques in an attempt to halve the time it takes to develop new models.
- Sun Alliance has recognised the need to consider intermediaries as integral elements of the international network organisation. Sun Alliance International has established electronic mail (or E-mail) links with brokers and other 'third-party' members of its supply chain in order to build closer relationships with them.

Companies such as Hewlett-Packard and Xerox have achieved dramatic reductions in the time required to bring new products to the marketplace.[14] Such improvements are achieved by asking 'first principles' questions about every aspect of activities and operations that have for long been taken for granted.

SOURCES OF DELAY

Within the bureaucratic form of organisation, a high proportion of the delays and costs of non-conformance occur at the cross-over points between functional departments. Those companies that have traced customer-related processes through their organisations often find that as much as 90 per cent of the elapsed 'time to respond' occurs at these handover points. During this period of 'waiting in in-trays', nothing is being done to progress or add value.

One director describes what appears to be a normal experience within the bureaucratic corporation that is organised by function rather than by process: 'My people kill themselves, working flat out with the latest technology to tackle something within minutes which then sits around for days in an in-tray in the next department.'

With the transition to the network organisation there is an opportunity to organise along the flow of work that generates the value that is sought by customers instead of by function. The first step is to identify and document what these cross-functional and inter-organisational processes are. The next stage is to simplify or re-engineer them. While this is being done, activities that do not add value may be discontinued and organisational boundaries redrawn.

PROCESS SIMPLIFICATION AND RE-ENGINEERING

In essence, process simplification involves putting a time stamp upon activities and cutting out those which do not deliver value to customers. It may be possible to save three-quarters or more of waiting time by simple empowerment, giving people the discretion to act on their own initiative without seeking authority, unless in exceptional circumstances.

The boundary around what is exceptional can be drawn ever more tightly according to the extent to which people share corporate vision, goals and values and understand what they as individuals need to do to deliver value to customers or to contribute to specific corporate objectives.

Tom Peters has argued that the horizontal approach, with its emphasis upon cross-functional co-operation, is the more likely to lead to flexible and fast responses in an increasingly chaotic business environment.[15]

There are those who thrive within bureaucracies, and who 'know their way around' and can work the bureaucracy to their own advantage. Those intent on changing bureaucracies should examine how they work in practice, how people get things done and the internal politics – the world portrayed by Downs in a seminal study of behaviour in organisations.[16]

Examining how the 'streetwise' salesperson uses an informal network to cut a path through the bureaucracy in order to meet a 'rush order' and win a place on the 'Performance Club' trip to Kenya may yield vital clues as to the cross-functional processes that work. Looking at what shouldn't happen may be more useful than examining what should.

Schonberger has suggested that elements or departments within a company should develop customer-supplier relationships with each other.[17] Those contributing to a cross-functional process could negotiate their contributions with a process owner. The prices offered should reflect the relative value of the various contributions, and thus would help to align personal, work group and process objectives.

CAN YOU DO TOO MUCH FOR THE CUSTOMER?

So impressive have been the improvements in speed of response achieved by one US financial services company, as a result of process re-engineering supported by the introduction of new technology, that delays have been built back into the tail end of the delivery process. According to one manager:

> 'We were responding too quickly. Customers were saying "You couldn't have spent much time thinking about it" or "why should I pay that much when it only took you a couple of minutes?" By delaying, people feel happier, they imagine we must have at least spent a few days working on their problem.'

The speed with which new products can be introduced to the marketplace can result in product proliferation. Hitachi is seeking to slow down the pace at which new models, types and varieties of product are introduced.

A company has to decide when enough is enough, and what is enough may depend upon economic circumstances. Many Japanese companies have pursued a policy of continuous innovation which has resulted in a flow of new products to the marketplace. The result, in an era of economic slowdown, has been an excessively wide range of products. Brother is seeking to drastically reduce the number of items in its product range.[18]

REWARD AND REMUNERATION

A company that does not properly understand its customer requirements may devote a lot of effort to improvements which are not significant from the point of view of the customer. In many companies people are not provided with an incentive to either learn from the customer or deliver what the customer wants.

Nine out of ten of the respondents to the *Beyond Quality* survey consider it important to link remuneration to customer satisfaction as a method of making management more customer oriented. David O'Brien is one of the few to move from aspiration to action. He believes that: 'With many of the traditional short-term measures and targets, there is the danger of an incompatibility between supplier and customer objectives.'[2]

If remuneration is to be linked to customer satisfaction a company needs to make absolutely certain that it has really uncovered what represents value to the customer. Otherwise, as one managing director pointed out: 'We will be paying people to bark up the wrong tree.'

Wherever possible, performance assessment and remuneration should be MACRO, (ie Measured According to Customer-Related Outputs) and not MICRO (or, Measured in Terms of Internal Company-Related Outputs). There are companies such as IBM (UK) and Rank Xerox that relate a proportion of remuneration to customer assessments of performance.

Management by objectives[19] may come back into favour when the focus shifts to customer-related objectives. Barrier analysis can be used to identify the various 'helps' and 'hinders' relating to the achievement of objectives.

SEGMENTATION, PRIORITISATION AND DIFFERENTIATION

A company, even the most extensive network, cannot be all things to all people. Segmentation, prioritisation and differentiation are important, inter-related and inter-dependent (see Figure 5.4). Because of the inter-dependence team working becomes more important. A segment could be a single customer, and all stages of the review process could be undertaken within an account team.

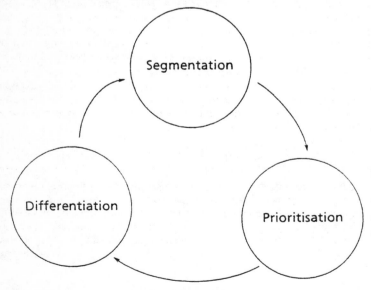

Source: Beyond Quality, 1990

Figure 5.4 *The Customer Review Process*

Segmentation, prioritisation and differentiation decisions increasingly require a knowledge of the customer and business environment, and of the company and its strategy beyond the product or business unit.

- Segmentation requires an awareness and understanding of the particular advantages an organisation has *vis-à-vis* the alternatives available in satisfying decisive customer requirements. Such particular comparative advantages must be sustainable over the period of time necessary profitably to develop and supply whatever is needed to meet the selected needs.
- Prioritisation of selected segments reflects current views of what the organisation does best. Effective differentiation can require disciplined prioritisation in order to focus effort and concentrate resources upon the requirements of particular sectors and segments.
- Differentiation further sharpens those areas in which an organisation can add the greatest value and this awareness is reflected in the further review of chosen segments. With each iteration of the review process groups and teams should have a sharper and more developed understanding of their comparative advantage.

Segmentation, prioritisation and differentiation are ongoing processes that themselves need to be reviewed from time to time to ensure that they are capable of responding to significant and fundamental, as well as incremental, change. All those who deliver value sought by customers should be involved.

WHO IS RESPONSIBLE FOR THE CUSTOMER?

We have seen that the vision of many CEOs is of a network that embraces both customers and suppliers. It is realised that in many sectors an individual company cannot deliver the whole of the value-added sought by customers without working closely with other companies in the total supply chain.

The *Quality: The Next Steps*[4] survey suggests that more attention will be given to joint quality approaches, working with business partners and along value chains. We will see in Chapter 9 that a natural progression is envisaged from quality product to quality organisation, and then on to quality network. Implementation within the network will depend even more upon relationships, the agreement of equal partners rather than 'cascading from above'. Network quality is a mutual and joint responsibility.

CEOs have been slow to recognise that within their own companies the contributions and co-operation of several departments may be needed to deliver the value that is sought by customers. Those functions, departments and groups that are not working within a value-generating process may be surplus to requirements.

The experience of those benchmark companies which have examined their business processes suggests that the perceptions senior management have of relative worth and contribution may bear little relationship with reality from a customer point of view:

- as many as one in four of those in a 'slimmed down' organisation may not be generating value for customers;
- whole groups of highly-paid staff may be preoccupied with tasks that have no direct link with customer satisfaction, while the activities of obscure and overlooked areas can suddenly assume considerable significance;
- in some cases up to one in five have been found to be engaged on activities that are directly counter to current business goals and priority objectives.

The respondents in the *Beyond Quality* survey[2] consider 'customer satisfaction' to be primarily the responsibility of line management. Over three-quarters of the respondents believed line management would be devoting more time to customer issues within five years. The service and quality functions are expected to assume greater responsibilities

/mers as the emphasis shifts from winning isolated orders to building and
onger-term relationships.

rgies of a wider range of people, account groups and project teams are to be
co-operative and customer-related activities, greater empowerment will be
ne   As we saw in Chapter 3, the board has to let go. However, Brooke has found that,
in practice, organisation in terms of project groups tends to be associated with a
relatively high level of centralisation.[20]

WHO SPEAKS FOR THE CUSTOMER IN THE BOARDROOM?

Departmentalism and professionalism are curses upon those trying to develop network
organisations. We have seen that vertical departmental barriers are generally the prime
source of delay in delivering the value sought by customers.

The consequences of departmentalism, and a functional division of duties and
responsibilities are painfully apparent in boardrooms. The view of many 'generalist'
CEOs, especially those trying to implement a vision, is that 'specialist' directors in the
boardroom are often obstacles to, rather than facilitators of, change.

Surveys undertaken by the author of personnel,[1] marketing,[2] IT[21] and quality[4] issues
have all revealed a gap of perspective and understanding between CEOs and the heads
of specialist functions.

- Functional heads are perceived by CEOs as lacking in strategic perspective and
other 'directorial' qualities, and many of them have not been given a seat on the
main board. Their self-identity and the 'pulls' of past and profession encourage them
to think in a functional rather than holistic way.
- Many of those with 'director' job titles are perceived as technical specialists who
lack 'people skills', and are unlikely to hold main board appointments. They cannot
see the wood for the trees, and when the cross-functional challenge or opportunity
arises, many seek security and lurk in the undergrowth, cultivating 'busyness' with
technical matters.
- Chairmen and CEOs feel that most functional directors need to become more
involved in the strategy of the business as a whole. Few of the key issues on the
boardroom agenda can be neatly packaged into functional boxes. They are not
'someone else's responsibility', but holistic business issues that frequently require a
total response and absolute commitment.
- Functional heads are seen as excessively territorial and over-protective of their
departmental boundaries. The phrase 'warring barons' was used by several
interviewees. One chairman grumbled: 'I get asked: whose departmental budget will
it go on? The question should be what can we do collectively for the customer?'

The differences of perspective in some boardrooms appear to have widened as a
consequence of differing interpretations of, and commitment to, a corporate vision. A
corporate transformation programme can bring matters 'to a head'.

Kotler has concluded[22] that while:

> *'In principle, business functions should mesh harmoniously to achieve the firm's overall*
> *objectives, in practice, departmental relations are often characterised by deep rivalries and*
> *misunderstandings. The problem remains: getting all the departments to think 'customer', to*
> *look at their activities through the customer's eyes.'*

The *Beyond Quality* survey[2] revealed some particular criticism of marketing professionals. In the view of one chairman: 'Customers have been treated by our marketing
people as cannon fodder for generalised ads and direct mail shots. Other people in the
company, including personnel, are telling me we've got to start treating customers as
individuals.'

THE FATE OF THE FUNCTIONAL DIRECTOR

Whether or not the head of a functional department, such as personnel or IT, should be on a board depends upon both the individual and the context. The general consensus is that an individual lacking in directorial qualities should not be put on a board just to 'fill a particular slot'. Very often there could be a seat on the board for a person thought to have the necessary personal qualities and when it is felt the individual could 'contribute'.

Spurious and questionable arguments may be put up by 'functionals' seeking to bask in the glory of a boardroom slot. Each case should be considered on its own merits. The following viewpoints could be 'reasonable', or applicable, according to the corporate context.

- People, customers etc are too important to be 'left' to one director; they are the responsibility of the whole board.
- The chairman or chief executive, or the board as a whole, rather than one director should be seen to give a lead.
- The important thing is being respected, contributing, having the 'ear' of the chairman etc, whether or not this is linked with a seat on the board.
- Being on the board can be largely 'cosmetic'; what really counts is being among the 'inner circle' of directors who 'call the shots'.
- The status associated with being a director should be played down. People should be remunerated according to value generated for customers rather than organisational position.
- Unless there is a dedicated functional director on the board, a group, and the issues with which it is concerned, will not get the attention they deserve.
- Good people will either leave or will not be attracted to a department if it is not perceived to be a 'boardroom function'.
- The whole board must debate the issues, but 'implementation' is helped when there is a dedicated director on the board.

THE CROSS-FUNCTIONAL VIEW

We saw in Chapter 3 that the perspective of a director should be that of the business as a whole. A theme of many interviews with CEOs across a succession of surveys (see Appendix 1) has been the extent to which many issues on the boardroom agenda transcend traditional functional divisions. Here are examples.

- Customers are too important to be left to sales and marketing. We have seen that a number of other functions are now being expected to add value for customers.
- No single department or group can 'deliver quality' by itself, which raises the question of the role of, and justification for, a quality specialism.
- Corporate transformation requires the total commitment of all the people of the organisation. There is a need for everyone to be involved in 'the change process'.
- IT is regarded in many companies as an integral part of the subject matter of many disciplines, and of the processes of many functions. It cannot be left to technical specialists, and it must be in the hands of users, as the focus shifts from technology to its application.
- There is a requirement in many boardrooms for facilitating roles such as directors of learning or thinking.
- Companies which are focusing upon the cross-functional and inter-organisational processes that deliver the value sought by customers are allocating process owner roles at board level.

Ultimately the executive members of the board may consist of facilitators and key process owners.[23] The cross-functional view will come to predominate and departmentalism will wither away. In the meantime, functional directors will 'fight their corner'. The chairman or chief executive who genuinely wants to transform a company cannot afford to overlook their machinations.

CHECKLIST

▶ Is the vision of the company, and are its goals and values, rooted in the customer?

▶ How differentiated is the company from its competitors in the marketplace?

▶ How bothered or inconvenienced would the company's customers be if the company ceased to exist?

▶ How customer-focused is the board? Where do the customers rank in relation to other stakeholders?

▶ What steps does the company take to identify customer requirements and measure customer satisfaction?

▶ How much of the value sought by the ultimate customer is delivered by your company, and how much by other members of the supply chain?

▶ What do the customers of your company really think about it?

▶ Is customer satisfaction at the top of the list of key management priorities?

▶ Is reward and remuneration linked to the delivery of value and satisfaction to customers?

▶ Has the company identified those key management and business processes that deliver the value sought by customers?

▶ How effective is the company at harnessing and applying its resources to meet the needs of the individual customer?

▶ Who is, and who is not, adding value for customers?

▶ Are customers regarded as 'outsiders', or as colleagues and business partners?

▶ What processes are in place to learn from customers?

▶ How much effort is put into building close working relationships with customers, and other members of the supply chain?

REFERENCES

1 Coulson-Thomas, C and Brown, R (1989) *The Responsive Organisation, People Management: the Challenge of the 1990s*, BIM, Corby.
2 Coulson-Thomas, C and Brown, R (1990) *Beyond Quality, Managing the Relationship with the Customer*, BIM, Corby.
3 Coulson-Thomas, C and Coe, T (1991) *The Flat Organisation: Philosophy and Practice*, BIM, Corby.
4 Coulson-Thomas, C and Coulson-Thomas, S (1991) *Quality: The Next Steps*, an Adaptation Survey for ODI International, Adaptation, London and (Executive Summary) ODI, Wimbledon, London.
5 Coulson-Thomas, C and Coulson-Thomas, S (1991) *Communicating for Change*, an Adaptation Survey for Granada Business Services, London.
6 Porter, M E (1990) *The Competitive Advantage of Nations*, Macmillan, London.
7 Levitt, T (1962) *Innovation in Marketing*, McGraw-Hill, New York; and (1983) *The Marketing Imagination*, The Free Press, New York.

8 Chandler, A (1962) *Strategy and Structure*, The MIT Press, Massachusetts.
9 Coulson-Thomas, C (1988), *The New Professionals*, BIM, Corby.
10 Riverso, R (1992) 'IBM Serves you Better' *1999 Now: A European Review*, Spring, p 3
11 Von Hippel, E (1978) 'Successful Industrial Products from Customer Ideas', *Journal of Marketing*, vol 42, no 1, pp 39–46
12 Deming, W E (1986) *Out of Crisis*, The MIT Centre for Advanced Engineering Study, Massachusetts.
13 Burton, J W (1968) *Systems, States, Diplomacy and Rules*, Cambridge University Press, Cambridge.
14 Smith, P and Reinertsen, D (1991) *Developing Products in Half the Time*, Chapman & Hall, London.
15 Peters, T (1987) *Thriving on Chaos*, Alfred A Knopf, New York.
16 Downs, A (1967) *Inside Bureaucracy*, Little, Brown, Boston.
17 Schonberger, R J (1990) *Building a Chain of Customers*, The Free Press, New York; Business Books, London.
18 Thompson, R (1992) 'Brother Slims Down Bloated Product Range' *Financial Times* 22 June, p 19.
19 Humble, J (1971), *Management by Objectives*, McGraw-Hill, Maidenhead.
20 Brooke, M Z (1984) *Centralisation and Autonomy: A study in organisation behaviour*, Holt, Rinehart and Winston, New York.
21 Coulson-Thomas, C (1990) *Developing IT Directors*, an Adaptation Ltd report to the Department of Computing Science, Surrey University, London.
22 Kotler, P (1983) *Principles of Marketing*, 2nd edn, Prentice-Hall, Englewood Cliffs, NJ.
23 Coulson-Thomas, C (1993) *Creating Excellence in the Boardroom*, McGraw-Hill, London.

6

CORPORATE TRANSFORMATION: INTENTION AND REALITY

ASPIRATION

Intention is not in doubt. We have seen that corporate organisations are seeking to make the transition to more flexible and responsive networks embracing customers, suppliers and business partners. However, companies are finding the translation of intention into reality intractable and elusive. The desire for change is not always matched by an awareness of how to bring it about, and corporate transformation is taking longer to achieve than was first thought.

Recent surveys of larger organisations highlight the need for clear vision and sustained top management commitment. In particular, many managers are not being equipped with the skills, attitudes and approaches that are needed to bring about corporate transformation. In this chapter, we will review the current status of transformation.

The picture that emerges is of a growing gap in many companies between aspirations and achievement. Expectations have not been fulfilled, and intentions have been 'blown off course' by the swirling winds of economic adversity.

TRANSFORMATION: NECESSITY OR CHOICE?

Acceptance of the need for transformation is becoming universal. As the forces of international competition erode national barriers, the national champion company may find that past protection and dominance in one market has led to complacency. For example:

- in Italy companies such as Fiat and Olivetti have belatedly recognised that without global alliances the local giant may be an international dwarf;
- in the case of Pan American reality was grasped too late to prevent the demise of a corporation that had once been a national 'flag carrier' and market leader.

The drive to 'slim down' and consolidate activities around core businesses is a widespread phenomenon. Unilever's plan to dispose of its agribusiness activities in order to concentrate upon food and consumer products, affected 4000 of its employees.

In other sectors 'downsizing' is the consequence of structural change or a slowdown in economic growth. In the USA, companies as varied as Bethlehem Steel, Tenneco, Union Pacific and Citicorp have experienced losses on a scale sufficient to trigger restructuring programmes. Service companies, such as accounting firm Peat Marwick and American Express, have not escaped the need to reshape and sharpen up.

It is now over 30 years since Burns and Stalker concluded that to survive in a turbulent business environment companies need to be flexible and adaptable.[1] Many of those companies that remained unaware of their findings, or chose to ignore them, no longer exist. They have died and we are not able to learn of the mistakes of their managements through their participation in surveys!

While the lecture circuit fawns upon gung-ho enthusiasts who may be 'riding for a fall', those whose warnings should be listened to hide away and lick their wounds.

HOW MUCH TRANSFORMATION?

How much transformation is required, the form it should take, and its pace, will depend upon customer requirements, the opportunities, pressures of circumstances, and views and assumptions of what can be accomplished.

- Attempt too much and the programme may fail. People and resources may be stretched to breaking point. Companies, like individuals, can over-reach themselves by behaving recklessly, or with an excess of ambition.
- Move too slowly and the company may miss the strategic opportunity, or be 'beaten to the draw' and 'taken out' by a faster competitor. Move with speed but without sufficient weight and commitment, and the momentum may not be enough to 'break through'.
- The fleeting prospect may not be recognised by the self-centred or the preoccupied. On the other hand, while waiting for the 'main chance', necessary action may be postponed. A company can spend so much time looking over its shoulder at other corporations that it neglects to put its own house in order.

The transformation process requirement can be broadly scoped by examining what needs to be done to achieve a matching overlap of customer requirement, organisational vision and organisational capability (Figure 6.1). The final stage, currently 'out of the frame' in the case of most companies, would be a single circle indicating a perfect alignment of requirement, vision and capability.

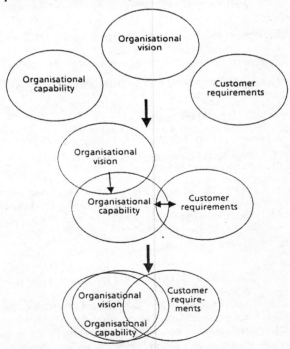

Figure 6.1 *The Transformation Process*

Each of the elements can be assessed using the 'learning loop' process of Chapter 5 (Figure 5.1). The minds of managers should be continually travelling around the loop, and short cuts should be avoided.

Lord Butler entitled his political memoirs *The Art of the Possible*.[2] The politician recognises that people have a choice, and while their attention and allegiance have to be won and retained, a balance should be kept between what is promised and what is delivered. Customers, employees and business partners are like the electorate in that they become bored, can take things for granted and may transfer their support elsewhere when they feel it is in their interests to do so.

INCREMENTAL OR FUNDAMENTAL CHANGE

There is an evident and strong desire for corporate transformation. With all the smoke there has to be some fire. We saw in Chapter 1 that against the background of multiple and profound changes and challenges in the business environment, many managements are coming to the conclusion that incremental change is no longer enough.

How fundamental the transformation should be will depend upon the situation and circumstances of the individual company. As one chairman put it: '*You don't transform for the hell of it.*' There are easier ways of getting directorial and managerial 'kicks'.

Circumstances might allow a gradual transition and incremental adjustment. For example:

- the pressure could be rather like the gentle but nagging pain that suggests some action now might avoid a toothache later.
- the penalty of failure could be mild, perhaps a marginal loss of market share.

Alternatively, a crisis situation might require radical, even revolutionary change. For example:

- the crisis could be more like a heart attack that demands an immediate change of lifestyle;
- the penalty of failure could be severe, even receivership or liquidation.

Whole industries face painful structural change. For example:

- suppliers of IT hardware may not for some years experience rates of growth that were in the past taken for granted;
- the 'peace dividend' has created a transformed market environment for defence industries;
- consumer electronics stands on the threshold of new technologies that have yet to be fully tested.

In the case of many large and traditionally bureaucratic organisations, what is sought amounts to little less than revolutionary change. Do managers fully understand the profound nature of the distinction between evolutionary and revolutionary change, and the requirements for bringing about a revolution in thought?[3] If not, they need to learn from radicals rather than administrators.

TRANSFORMING THE LEVIATHAN

The past experience of sectors such as electronics and aerospace has not equipped them to cope with a transformed market environment. They face the twin tasks of dismantling a past form of structure and pattern of operation they can no longer afford, while at the same time creating a new form of organisation to cope with a world they do not understand.

A company the size of General Motors can be more, rather than less, vulnerable than smaller rivals. Protected from reality by a flow of profit resulting from past decisions, the Detroit bureaucracy was slow to recognise and react to changing circumstances. When the corporation experienced losses in 1990 it was confronted with the need to undertake drastic surgery and bear heavy restructuring costs in the struggle to become more flexible.

Restructuring a company the size of General Motors is rather like stopping an oil tanker. It takes a long time. Restructuring can also be expensive. In 1991 the corporation's losses were the highest ever suffered by a US company.

Many large corporations have clung for too long to the characteristics described by Mintzberg in his portrayal of the 'machine bureaucracy', due to the vested interests of the functional experts composing their 'technostructures'.[4] As a consequence these many-layered organisations were too slow to adjust incrementally to change.

THE SCALE OF THE CHALLENGE

The recent experience of IBM illustrates the range of responses required to transform the bureaucratic corporation in the face of various challenges in the business environment. In recent years, approaching $8 billion has been expended on corporate reorganisations and over 50,000 jobs have been shed.

The search for flexibility and responsiveness continues. For example, under IBM's transformation programme:

- a monolithic corporation is to become a federated network of increasingly independent businesses;
- business units are being encouraged to focus upon particular market segments;
- the corporation is to assume greater responsibility and risk in broadening and deepening its relationship with the customer;
- the focus is shifting away from products to services in order to tap greater added-value opportunities;
- a growing number of joint ventures and arrangements are being concluded to create a comprehensive global network of relationships;
- a uniform corporate culture is to be replaced by planned diversity;
- the culture is becoming less paternalistic, and managers are being required to assume extra responsibilities;
- certain central and service functions are to become separate businesses;
- a programme of disposals will spin off businesses that do not fit the thrust of the new IBM;
- worldwide units will be formed to pull together certain areas of expertise and capability;
- new co-ordinating mechanisms and processes are being established to manage the evolving organisation;
- the internal bureaucracy is being more sharply cut back;
- layers are being taken out of the corporate organisation and spans of control widened;
- new independent but wholly-owned subsidiaries are being set up to compete with the mainstream business.

Many of the programmes and initiatives that are being introduced into IBM are coming on top of others that are already under way or in the pipeline.[5] The transformation war against a bureaucracy that has always prided itself on being the biggest and the best needs to be waged simultaneously on a number of fronts.

In recognition of the problems involved in achieving significant changes of attitude and behaviour, the emphasis in management writing is shifting from establishing the need for corporate transformation to its achievement.[6] But what is happening in practice? How much has actually been achieved? If 'barriers' exist, what are they, and what needs to be done about them?

THE EVIDENCE

To answer these and other related questions, let us return to the family of three complementary questionnaire and interview surveys that were undertaken during 1990 and 1991 (see Appendix 1).

- The 1991 BIM report *The Flat Organisation: Philosophy and Practice*[7] is specifically concerned with the management of corporate transformation from bureaucracy to flexible 'network organisation'.
- The *Quality: The Next Steps* survey[8] is concerned with quality priorities and barriers, and the introduction of the 'total quality culture'.
- The *Communicating for Change* survey[9] examines communication priorities and barriers in the context of the management of change.

RHETORIC AND ASPIRATIONS

Attempts, on occasion valiant but usually incomplete, are being made to turn aspiration into achievement. Corporate transformation is not just being discussed, it is being actively sought (see Table 6.1) by participants in the *Flat Organisation* survey:[7]

- approaching nine out of ten of the participating organisations are becoming slimmer and flatter;
- in some eight out of ten participating organisations, more work is being undertaken in teams, and a more responsive network organisation is being created;
- over two-thirds of participants acknowledge that functions are becoming more inter-dependent, and procedures and permanency are giving way to flexibility and temporary arrangements. Over half consider that organisations are becoming more inter-dependent.

Table 6.1 *What Organisations are Doing to Better Respond to Challenges and Opportunities Within the Business Environment (%)*

Creating a slimmer and flatter organisation	88
More work is being undertaken in teams	79
Creating a more responsive network organisation	78
Functions are becoming more inter-dependent	71
Procedures and permanency are giving way to flexibility and temporary arrangements	67
Organisations are becoming more inter-dependent	55

Source: The Flat Organisation, BIM, 1991

Turning to what respondents feel their organisations should be doing:

- some eight out of ten respondents agree that more work should be undertaken in teams, that their organisation should become slimmer, flatter and more responsive and that procedures and permanency should give way to flexibility and temporary arrangements;
- over three-quarters agree that functions should become more inter-dependent, and over two-thirds agree that organisations should become more inter-dependent.

THE NETWORK ORGANISATION

Something must result from all the activity to build more flexible and responsive organisations. Certain companies and other institutions are 'making it'. Varieties and elements of network organisation exist. Here are some examples.

- The US company Lewis Galoob Toys subcontracts to a network of suppliers a range of management activities that are traditionally undertaken in-house. Only such key tasks as strategy formulation and co-ordination of the network are performed by the core team.
- Apple has used an international network of subcontract and temporary staff to speed up the introduction of tailored products.
- Sherwood Computer Services operates a flexible network form of organisation based upon client service teams and market co-ordination groups. All the staff were involved in the process of reviewing the form of organisation and method of operation which would best enable the company to meet the requirements of its customers.
- Aspects of the network organisation are being introduced into large and mature companies. Within BP, networking across national borders is encouraged to bring together groups and teams to handle particular tasks.
- Rank Xerox, a pioneer of the use of independent contractors in the UK through its 'networking programme', has introduced a range of corporate transformation services through the route of a joint venture framework with Adaptation Ltd and a network of associates. The Partners Association Ltd has been established as a network of 'third parties' with whom Rank Xerox has concluded various arrangements.
- Various European networks are emerging. Networks such as the Tenders Electronic Daily (TED) can be used to secure daily access to EC business opportunities. Possible business partners can be identified by means of the EC Business Co-operation Network (BC–NET).
- Co-operative networks of suppliers share marketing and other costs. This form of organisation is very popular in Italy. The agricultural co-operative that enables separate private businesses to share common services has been the normal form of operation for generations in many parts of the world.
- Purchasing networks enable member companies to secure the benefits of bulk buying. Retail networks such as Eurogroupe and the European Retailing Alliance are buying at the European level.
- Whole markets are becoming electronic. Globex has been launched by Chicago's Mercantile Exchange and Board of Trade to offer a 24-hour-a-day trading network. Lloyd's of London is developing an integrated computer network embracing hundreds of independent brokers and underwriters.
- The global network of Daiwa Securities allows management responsibilities to be reallocated to different locations around the network according to the pattern of trading that develops. The organisation never sleeps, as some markets come on stream while others close down as the earth spins relentlessly on its axis.
- Computer-based networks for individuals with common interests and characteristics are springing into existence. SeniorNet, which is aimed at those aged 55 and over, attracted over 15,000 members in its first 6 years of existence. Members can secure access to a range of services, and the system supports the establishment of subnetworks of those with particular interests in common.
- New areas of operation have come into existence using IT to overcome problems that customers have in securing access to particular physical locations. Home

banking, for example, allows customers to obtain account information and undertake transactions outside of normal banking hours.

One could multiply the number of examples. It can be done. In some knowledge-based sectors, and in certain types of start-up situation, the network form of organisation has become the norm. However, the major corporation that has comprehensively adopted and implemented the many different dimensions of network operation is a rare animal. As the endangered herd tramps through the bleak desert of trial and tribulation only a few are 'sensing the presence of water'.

NATIONALITY AND THE NETWORK ORGANISATION

Managers can expect to spend more time working in teams, and with colleagues from other functions and organisations.[7] Yet, in many companies, few managers are being prepared either for effective team working, or to build working relationships with network partners.

In an international context, there are areas of the world in which the transition from bureaucratic to network organisation may be seen as a move 'with the grain'. In parts of Asia the issuing of commands in the hierarchical organisation represented an unfamiliar and 'western' form of behaviour for many new MNC recruits. These people may instantly empathise with the network approach, and breathe passion and life into it. Outsiders could suddenly become insiders.

When multinational groups are formed, or people are introduced into international teams, account may need to be taken of distinct national approaches. For example:

- a German may be inclined to be more formal, and such formality should not be mistaken for a lack of 'team spirit' or commitment to the group;
- whereas a Japanese manager may feel bound to observe a consensus outcome because of the 'legitimacy of the process', a French colleague may not feel obligated to implement a decision with which he or she personally disagrees.

NATIONALITY AND NETWORK MEMBERSHIP

Within the network organisation the attitudes of certain members or partners may reflect national characteristics.

- A US or UK company may pursue short-term self-interest. Equity ownership by institutions that compare and trade stocks according to changes in relative performance may encourage such behaviour.
- In contrast, much of the equity of a Japanese company may be held by other companies with which it trades, or by supply chain partners. The Japanese company could well be a loyal member of a network, and may exhibit concern for the good of the network as a whole.

We will return to considerations of national culture in Chapter 11.

THE IMPLICATIONS OF CHANGE

Physical manifestations of the network are already visible. The consequences of decentralisation, devolution and delegation are beginning to work their way through to IT and other support requirements. For example:

- Glaxo Pharmaceuticals and other companies now operate without a mainframe system;

- Pilkington and the Sedgwick insurance group were among the first to replace central mainframe computing with personal computers distributed around a corporate network.

Attitudinal and behavioural evidence of change can be more difficult to identify and interpret. Rationalisation, uncertainty, concealment, perceived self-interest and deception can so muddy the waters that it is not easy to uncover the reality of what people are feeling and thinking. While achieving the transition, a careful watch should be kept for certain telltale successful and unsuccessful change symptoms, such as those shown in Table 6.2.

Table 6.2 *Achieving the Transition*

Unsuccessful Symptoms	Successful Symptoms
Working harder for longer hours	Working smarter in a more focused way
Change seen as headcount reduction and cost cutting	Change seen as improving service to customers
Insecurity and uncertainty	Confidence and commitment
Internal politics, competition and power struggles	Common customer focus
Keeping head down and playing it safe	Assuming responsibility and getting it right
Frantic search for instant and final solution	Frank discussion to build understanding of what is required
Repetition of slogans and production of motherhood videos and brochures	Each group responding according to context
Directed or instructed change	Shared desire to change

Change is not neutral in its impact and may adversely affect certain senior staff and many middle managers, thus encouraging them to block initiatives.[10] In order to contain the intrigue and infighting that can result, mechanisms and processes that are perceived as objective and neutral may be required. An 'internal market' is one example. Some companies adopt the approach of retaining only those staff functions which business units are prepared to fund.

A certain degree of bureaucracy may well be the result of a caring culture, a range of specialists being retained to watch over the various interests and concerns of the people of the organisation. When this support is suddenly taken away, and people are required to do more with less and assume extra responsibility, not all will react in the same way. While some may thrive, others may experience stress. Process and technique may appear a poor substitute for 'love and kindness'.

The tenacity with which critics of bureaucracy, as well as its supporters, cling to bureaucratic positions is evident in the experiences of the countries of the former Soviet bloc while endeavouring to make the transition from command to market economies. One Eastern European economist has observed: 'This is the paradox in the fight for suppressing bureaucracy: in spite of the general anti-bureaucratic feeling, great powers are fighting for the preservation of every single bureaucratic position.'[11]

MOVING FROM THE PARTICULAR TO THE GENERAL

Having got some movement, the next problem may be to hang on. The advice of one interviewee is simply: 'Hold tight. You could be stuck fast at one moment and into a roller-coaster ride the next.'

Transformation has a tendency to get out of control. When momentum appears to be building, the wagon may suddenly slip off the rails. The result can be the sudden appearance of a gap between assumed and actual outcomes. Here are some examples.

- Initial quality improvement projects may focus upon carefully chosen topics and where there is a reasonable prospect of success. As enthusiasm spreads and greater numbers of people acquire the desire 'to be seen to be doing something' groups may be set up all over the place. Chaos can result, with groups tackling everything bar the key priorities of the business.
- The first process re-engineering project may be carefully selected, and all available expertise and a fair amount of senior management time may be devoted to it. These conditions may not apply to follow-on projects, and when processes under examination appear to overlap, or be in conflict, confusion can reign.
- A prototype micro-business unit or self-managed workgroup may require and receive extensive support from a number of central centres of competence. Those involved may receive extensive and monitored preparation. Once the pilot is up and running, subsequent groups may be left to fend for themselves. Senior managers may assume that later groups will learn from the pioneers, without putting in place a process to enable this to happen.

Why are the short-term results that sometimes appear to follow initial bursts of change activity so difficult to translate into more lasting changes of attitudes and behaviour? Beer and Walton suggest that changes in part of an organisation are difficult to consolidate when the culture as a whole, and particularly top management, is not supportive and the general structure and management processes of an organisation are unchanged.[12]

Once a number of cross-functional or 'horizontal' processes are in place, the process owners may need to negotiate the boundaries between processes. In some companies process owners enter into contracts to provide each other with services.

THE TIMING OF CHANGE

Western defence contractors have faced a sharply diminished demand for their products following the greatly reduced threat as a consequence of the break-up of the former Soviet Union. The need for fundamental transformation arose with dramatic suddenness. General Dynamics has responded with a programme of disposals, contraction and focus upon core businesses.

A corporate change programme may need to cope with a variety of economic situations from boom to bust. Both the extremes present problems.

- At the peaks the people may be running flat out to meet orders and unwilling to be distracted from 'making hay while the good weather lasts'. The most typical response may be: 'Let's talk about it later.'
- During the troughs there is pressure on budgets, and a preoccupation with cutbacks, laying people off and 'keeping the creditors at bay'. This is not the best time to interest people in long-term commitments that may be perceived as requiring up-front investments.

For some it will never be the right time to initiate a transformation programme. Sooner or later the nettle needs to be grasped if a transition is to be voluntary, rather than an imposed consequence of adversity and crisis.

In some cases, it may not be desirable or feasible to move directly to a desired goal. An interim stage or intermediate initiative might be advisable, prior to the introduction of a main programme.

For example, it could be thought that in order to achieve the attitudes that are required for the eventual internalisation and consolidation of change, it might be advisable to alter patterns of behaviour. Thus 'groupware', or the software that encourages improved co-operation within a group, might be introduced in order to develop a more direct and proactive approach to the use of information.

THE NEED FOR NEW ATTITUDES

Transformation is not a state, but a combination of changing attitudes and expectations. These are expressed through the use of concepts such as 'empowerment', and models such as the 'network organisation', so that people can share a common understanding of what is desired and the means by which it might be achieved.

People need to understand that their role is to manage change, and not to operate a procedure. Their perspective should extend to the total process with which they are concerned so that they can assess their own priorities in terms of the purpose of the process and their own role in it.

Table 6.3 *The Bureaucratic Machine v The Organic Network*

Company as Machine	Company as Organism
Self-contained and independent	Interdependent
Hard shell	Porous skin
Separate departments	Communicative groups
Objectives to maximise sales and profits	Objectives reflect society and interests of stakeholders and customers
Focus on maximisation	Focus on satisfaction
Efficiency	Adaptation
Insider/outsider distinction	Information flows
Assemble resources	Establish relationships
Closed organisation	Open, flexible and receptive
Directive	Negotiative
Ideas judged by source	Ideas judged by quality
Innovation seen as a threat	Ideas considered important
Avoids risks	Encourages innovation
Fosters myths	Frank and honest
Conceals weaknesses	Tackles deficiencies
Hidebound by tradition	Dynamic
Competitive	Co-operative
Deals	Obligations
Orders and instructions	Bargaining and negotiation
Authority and direction	Consensus and compromise
Vertical communication	All channel communication
Task centred	People centred
Understand through parts	Understand through the whole
Machine Manager	**Network Member**
Technician or driver	Communicator
Defined skills	Intuition and sensitivity
Functional specialisation	Holistic perspective
Keeps machine running effectively	Organism lives and spreads
Conscious of position/status/authority	Aware of when adding value
Talks	Listens

There are still managers who appear to have a fixation with the contents of their in-tray. There are also management programmes that include in-tray exercises, as if documents have a significance in themselves and quite apart from any process that delivers value to customers.

The network organisation is an organism rather than a machine. The extent of the need for new attitudes is illustrated by comparative features of the bureaucratic machine organisation and the organic network identified by the author over a decade ago.[13] These are shown in Table 6.3.

The network is dynamic, and an organic whole. The 'health of an individual department or "organ" will influence the general health of the whole organisation and vice versa ... the communications system is rather like its nervous system'. If flows and processes are blocked, 'organs will go to sleep and then gangrene will set in'.[13]

The author concluded as follows.[13]

> *Organic management is concerned with flows rather than stocks, dynamic rather than static situations, change and development rather than order, effectiveness and adaptability rather than efficiency. ... Organic growth is evolutionary. Survival is a question of balance between capacity and capability, and problems and opportunities. ... Success is a matter of coping with change and uncertainty .... an ability to objectively assess relative strengths and weaknesses and to learn and keep on learning. 'Organic' managers are sensitive, subtle and aware.*

Adaptability, the ability to communicate, flexibility and a balanced perspective are considered by almost all respondents in the *Flat Organisation* survey[7] to be important. The one quality assessed as being of importance on every returned questionnaire is 'understanding the business environment'.

Participants in the *Flat Organisation* survey[7] were also asked to indicate the extent of their agreement with a number of statements concerning broadening the horizons of their managers. Over 19 out of 20 respondents agree that 'reward should reflect output and added value'. Over a half of them 'strongly agree' with this statement, and no one among the participants strongly agrees with the view that 'reward should reflect position and rank'.

Talcott Parsons has drawn attention to the fact that power is a relational attribute, as much as a consequence of position and status.[14] Relative power can be very dependent upon the context and issues involved. A move away from the bureaucratic organisation undermines those who are dependent upon situational power. Within the network organisation power can ebb and flow around the network as new relationships are formed and situations change. This can be disturbing for those who like to know where they stand.

NETWORK RELATIONSHIPS

The model of the network organisation offers more hope than the self-contained bureaucracy that environmental improvements and better quality can be delivered. In each area there is only so much that one organisation can do. Sooner or later incremental, and very often substantial, progress can only be made when there is co-operation along a supply chain.

In some sectors, co-operation rather than competition is the preoccupation of many senior management teams that have hitherto not had to enter an arena in which power is shared, rather than exercised, and the focus is upon common interests and mutual strengths that can be built upon, rather than individual weaknesses that should be exploited:

- relationships are being forged within countries between historic competitors, such as between the German steel and engineering companies Krupp and Hoesch;

- partnership links are also extending across national borders, as with the joint venture in the automobile industry between Volvo of Sweden and Renault of France.

Rosabeth Moss Kanter has described her vision of an organisation that combines strength and agility in network terms, with the notion of the company as a 'switchboard', co-ordinating the activities of various organisations.[15]

FORMAL AND INFORMAL ORGANISATION

The organisation to 'work on' is the one which operates in practice as opposed to what ought to or is thought to happen. The official or formal view, as set out in the organisational chart, may not reflect what happens on the ground. In view of the inefficiencies of the bureaucracy, various people find 'informal' ways to cut corners.

One quick and crude way of determining what the flow of work ought to be is to create a series of open environments, in which there is relatively free access to information and most departmental constraints are removed, and then watch and wait. When left to themselves, people that have been focused upon the customer are likely to establish whatever network linkages and relationships, and to follow whatever paths, best enable them to respond to customer requirements. The informal organisation that emerges could become the basis for redesigning the formal organisation.

Plodding through the existing organisation in terms of seeking to determine what happens next can be a soul-destroying occupation. Reading the reports is rather like listening to a confessional.

In many corporate bureaucracies a high proportion of document flows terminate in dead ends. Paper in files may do little to boost customer satisfaction. The individual trying to reach the goal of a satisfied customer may find the corporate game has many snakes and few ladders.

NEW PROBLEMS FOR OLD

Change for the right reasons, but with the wrong attitudes and values, can create new problems as rapidly as older ones are tackled. For example, layers of bureaucracy may need to be cut out, as previous levels of 'overhead' can no longer be afforded as margins are squeezed. While passionate advocates of change may view all bureaucrats as incompetent, or a burden, some of those who are squeezed or eased out may have added value, others may see certain contributions as of value.

New models of organisations also have their problems. For example, the following views were expressed by a few of the early exponents of process re-engineering.

'While the processes have changed, the people remain the same. The process owners cling to their processes – they see them as their processes, and they talk about their group – and run them as if they were running another department.'

'The first was a sweat, but now we have overlapping processes, even boundary problems between processes. It's becoming a bit of a mess.'

'How do you explain an organisation that's all processes? The whole becomes too complex. People put their heads down and tend to just concentrate upon a bit of one process – they are already compartmentalising.'

'Try to draw our processes and it comes out like a ball of wool that the cat has been at.'

'I worry that we may replace a set of "vertical" problems with another set of "horizontal" problems. We've turned the organisation around, but not ourselves.'

The need for clear roles and responsibilities is stressed by Jaques, following his workplace observations during the early 1950s.[16] They have to be created anew in the very different operating context of the network organisation.

THE IMPORTANCE OF VISION AND COMMITMENT

We have already identified the central importance of vision and commitment in an environment and situation of change.

- The *Flat Organisation* report[7] reveals that: 'Every respondent assessing it believes clear vision and mission to be important; and about three-quarters of them consider it "very important".'
- The *Communicating for Change* survey[9] also confirms the importance of articulating and communicating a clear vision: 'clear vision and strategy' and 'top management commitment' are jointly ranked as the most important requirements for the successful management of change.
- In the *Quality: The Next Steps* survey[8] the main barrier, by a large margin, to the successful implementation of a quality process is 'top management commitment'. Over nine out of ten respondents consider it 'very important' as a barrier.

We have also seen that the 'gap' between vision and conduct, and rhetoric and reality, which appears to have emerged,[7,8,9] suggests 'a lack of top management commitment' in many companies. In the case of some corporate transformation programmes the commitment to change has been quite explicit and sustained. For example:

- in April of 1991 BP ran one-page advertisements in newspapers outlining its intentions and progress to date;
- ICI has made a sustained commitment to change through the chairmanships of both Sir John Harvey-Jones and Sir Denys Henderson.

THE CLARITY OF THE TRANSFORMATION VISION

A transformation vision may represent a picture of a 'new world'. It needs to give some idea of the sorts of beings that inhabit it. How will they operate and inter-relate? What constitutes acceptable and exemplary conduct? Without knowledge of what may be encountered, it is difficult to prepare for the journey.

Another common question is: 'Where is this new world?' Is it just around the corner, or separated from present reality by what may appear to be an unbridgeable chasm? Some transformation visions appear to 'float in space'. Others are rather like a negative. As one director explained: 'We are not too sure what it will be like. At times we are more conscious of what is missing.'

A diagrammatic vision of the journey from bureaucratic to network organisation is set out in Figure 6.2. The first stage is to obtain a realistic appreciation of the nature of the challenge by ensuring that the attitudes, values and behaviours of both are understood. During the transition stage, the attitudes, values and behaviour of the network organisation will slowly replace those of the bureaucratic machine. This will occur more rapidly and painlessly for some than for others. During this stage there is the ever-present risk of confusion, if not chaos.

Eventually when, and if, the transition is achieved, a new set of attitudes, values and behaviours will emerge. The outcome is likely to be a fusion or synthesis rather than a replacement. Some aspects, particularly distinctive strengths and relevant qualities, will live on through the organic network.

THE TRANSFORMATION JIGSAW PUZZLE

The efforts of many companies to define and communicate a transformation vision are turning out to be counter-productive. Some of those who 'believed', or who 'tried', now

Stage I : The Challenge

Stage 2 : Risk of Confusion

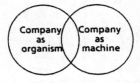

Stage 3 : Changed Attitudes and Behaviour

Figure 6.2 *The Organic Eclipse*

feel betrayed. The investment that has been made in communicating visions and missions, has led to an unprecedented degree of cynicism in many companies. There is insecurity and widespread disbelief, particularly among the ranks of middle managers.

One of the reasons why so many people question either the commitment of senior management to change, or the feasibility of transformation, is that they perceive that all the change elements that are necessary for successful transformation are not in place. Consider the following selection of comments.

> *'For many years not much happened. Then we stumbled upon a few things we hadn't done. It broke the log jam.'*

> *'It won't happen unless it is believed. What you believe in influences what you do. People did not believe our strategy, it was just words.'*

> *'For far too long we just assumed it had to come good because of the amount of money we were spending and the amount of talking we were doing. We didn't deem it necessary to identify and address the few things that were getting in the way.'*

> *'It's what you are not doing that tends to be the problem, not the things that you are doing. We overlooked a couple of things that were absolutely crucial to making it happen.'*

> *'We asked people to do one thing, and then we paid them for doing something else.'*

> *'There is no point asking or expecting people to work in new ways if you do not give them the skills, resources or discretion to succeed.'*

THE UNRECOGNISED BUSINESS

The document is the currency of a business, the signals that pass through the nerves of the organic network and trigger intelligent reactions. It is the means by which most of the activities that build the value delivered to customers are made to happen.

Many organisations are unaware of how many of their people are working on an unrecognised area of business, the production and distribution of documents. Publishing is a hidden enterprise that consumes the resources of corporate organisations. Within bureaucracies, it feeds upon bureaucracy and in turn nourishes it.

When a distinction is made between processing and generating data, and the production and handling of documents, whether electronic or paper, many companies discover that as much as 70 per cent of the costs of administrative activities relate to documents, while only 30 per cent relate to data.

In spite of the importance of documents, the bulk of 'infrastructure investment' goes into IT to generate data rather than document systems to handle documents. While great difficulty is experienced in demonstrating that there is a positive return from expenditure on IT, little effort is devoted to document flows and processes.

Companies that continue to search for 'hypothetical' or 'speculative' benefits appear to be turning their backs upon positive returns in terms of time saved or management productivity of 10 per cent from marginal improvements in document flows, through 100 per cent from business process simplification, to 1000 per cent from business process re-engineering.

LEADERSHIP FOR CORPORATE TRANSFORMATION

There is some consensus concerning what is important, and what needs to be done, to bridge the gap between transformation expectation and transformation achievement that is found in many companies.

- A clear and compelling vision and strategy is essential for both differentiation and transformation. The vision should embrace both the transformation 'end state' and the transformation process.
- Top management commitment is of crucial importance in the management of change. It needs to be communicated and sustained. A practical and necessary demonstration of commitment is to ensure that all the pieces of the transformation jigsaw puzzle are in place.
- People need to be empowered and equipped to manage change, and to handle the extra responsibilities that are being placed upon them. This requires a holistic perspective, new attitudes, fresh approaches and additional techniques. In particular, there is a need for the qualities associated with the 'organic manager'.
- Within corporations there are hidden businesses. Management and business processes will often need to be re-engineered in order that energies and resources are focused upon those people and activities that make the greatest contribution to delivering the value sought by customers.

It has been suggested that many companies are over-managed and under-led[17]. New champions of corporate transformation are needed. In terms of Max Weber's classic study of behaviour within bureaucracies, as the shift to a network organisation occurs 'legal-rational' sources of authority may be replaced by the 'charismatic'.[18]

All forms of organisation attract the adventurers and the opportunists. The organic network is unlikely to be an exception. New breeds of people will emerge that are especially adept at 'playing' the network organisation. Temperamentally, they may be very different from the traditional organisational bureaucrat. Rather than 'toadie' upwards, there will be horizontal relationships for the network politician to forge.

CHECKLIST

▶ Does your company have a vision of a flatter and more flexible form of organisation?

▶ Is there a corporate-wide transformation programme in place to bring it about?

▶ Does the programme embrace facilitating skills, enabling processes and supporting technology?

▶ Is it designed to influence attitudes by changing behaviour?

▶ How disruptive will it be of short-term customer relationships?

▶ What will be done to retain the commitment of those who may be disadvantaged at a particular stage in the change process?

▶ How committed is top management to achieving the transformation?

▶ Has this commitment been communicated?

▶ Do the managers of the organisation, and particularly the senior managers, behave as role models?

▶ Have all the requirements for a successful transformation been identified?

▶ What 'building blocks' or 'pieces of the jigsaw puzzle' might be missing?

▶ In particular, are the necessary empowerments in place, and have skill requirements been addressed?

▶ Is it clear to the people of the organisation that the programme has been thought through?

▶ Is the reward and remuneration system compatible with the changes that are being sought?

▶ Have likely obstacles and barriers been identified, and are programmes in place to deal with them?

REFERENCES

1 Burns, T, and Stalker, G M (1961) *The Management of Innovation*, Tavistock, London.

2 Butler, R A (1971) *The Art of the Possible: The Memoirs of Lord Butler KG CH*, Hamish Hamilton, London.

3 Johnson, C (1966) *Revolutionary Change*, Little, Brown, Boston, Mass; and Kuhn, T S (1970) *The Structure of Scientific Revolutions*, University of Chicago Press, Chicago.

4 Mintzberg, H (1979) *The Structuring of Organisations*, Prentice-Hall, New Jersey and (1983) *Structures in Fives: Designing Effective Organisations*, Prentice-Hall, New Jersey.

5 Sobel R (1981, 1984) *IBM: Colossus in Transition*, Truman Talley Books-Times Books, New York; and Sidgwick & Jackson, London.

6 for example, Kanter, R M, Stein, B A and Jick, T D (1992) *The Challenge of Organisational Change: How People Experience It and Manage It*, The Free Press, New York.

7 Coulson-Thomas, C and Coe, T (1991) *The Flat Organisation: Philosophy and Practice*, BIM, Corby.

8 Coulson-Thomas, C and Coulson-Thomas, S (1991) *Quality: The Next Steps*, an Adaptation Survey for ODI International, Adaptation, London and (Executive Summary) ODI, Wimbledon, London.

9 Coulson-Thomas, C and Coulson-Thomas, S (1991) *Communicating for Change*, an Adaptation Survey for Granada Business Services, London.

10 Passmore, W A (1982) 'Overcoming the Roadblocks in Work Restructuring Efforts' *Organizational Dynamics*, 10, pp 54–67.

11 Kornai, J (1990) *Vision and Reality, Market and State*, Harvester/Wheatsheaf, Hemel Hempstead, Herts, p 10.

12 Beer, M and Walton, E (1987) 'Organisational Change and Development', in Rosenzweig, M and Porter, L (eds), *Annual Review of Psychology*, Annual Reviews, Palo Alto, Calif.

13   Coulson-Thomas, C (1981) *Public Relations is Your Business: a guide for every manager*, Business Books, London.

14   Parsons, T (1969) *Politics and Social Structure*, The Free Press, New York.

15   Kanter, R M (1989) *When Giants Learn to Dance*, Simon and Schuster, London and New York.

16   Jaques, E (1951) *The Changing Culture of a Factory*, Tavistock, London and (1956) *The Measurement of Responsibility*, Tavistock, London.

17   Kotter, J P (1990) *A Force for Change, How Leadership Differs from Management*, The Free Press, New York.

18   Weber, M (1966) *The Theory of Social and Economic Organisation* (1st edn 1925), The Free Press, New York.

7

RHETORIC VERSUS COMMUNICATION

COMMUNICATIONS ACTIVITY

Communication is regarded as an integral element of management. In many companies it is almost impossible to find a manager who has not been on a communication skills course. Corporate speeches extol the importance and virtues of communication, and statements of corporate values highlight the need for openness, integrity and trust.

Never before has so much been invested in the technology of communications. Companies are spending large amounts on corporate videos and other channels of internal communications. They are advised by some of the brightest minds of the younger generation, who have flocked to join corporate communications consultancies.

Executive desks are groaning under the weight of a myriad of publications, print-outs and general corporate bumpf. Even those who would never dream of buying a periodical are zapped by controlled circulation magazines.

COMMUNICATIONS RESULTS

Yet, what is the result of all this communications activity? Too often energy and resources appear to have been consumed to little effect.

- Where there should be understanding there is confusion. As one chief executive who was interviewed explained in frustration: 'I am the target of a hundred and one presentations, and half the world seems to be trying to impress me. But whenever I want an answer [to] something I'm really interested in, no one seems to know.'
- In place of trust there is suspicion. One director confided during a discussion of his company's approach to internal communications: 'Given our track record, if anyone believed this they would be either naïve or a bunch of crawlers.'
- Rather than motivation there is insecurity. One personnel director explained: 'Our latest corporate initiative ends up as disruption, intrigue, disappointment and a host of other things to those further down the organisation.'
- People are lured into complacency just when they need to be alert and on guard. Spending on hype is best avoided as it can make it more difficult to get people to confront reality.

Some years back, in the process of writing a basic marketing textbook,[1] the author was struck by how little evidence there was of the effectiveness of such activities as advertising, although a substantial industry had arisen with a vested interest in demonstrating a direct contribution to corporate objectives.

In the area of corporate communications, the gulf between rhetoric and reality appears to be especially large. In some companies the gap between expectation and achievement is narrowing as managers reduce their sights regarding what can be achieved using the traditional channels of communications.

TRANSFORMATION AND COMMUNICATION

Communication is especially important in a revolutionary context. The first move of any insurgent group is to control the means of communication. The presses and the airwaves are used to encourage dissatisfaction with what is, and support for a suggested alternative.

According to Vern Zelmer, managing director of Rank Xerox UK: 'People move in the way they think and believe. This determines what happens, not what you say and want, which may or may not lead to changes in perception and behaviour. The management of change is all about influencing the way people think and believe.'

The legitimacy of change and the extent to which the network organisation is accepted, will largely depend upon the process of communication, and the extent to which it is supportive or undermining of the values and ethos of the network. Communicators in a situation of change may be 'playing with fire'.

Chester Barnard recognised that the extent to which people accept organisation depends upon their understanding and participation in the communication process.[2] Barnard saw the essence of the managerial role in terms of building co-operative activity through communication, motivation and sharing of values.

We have already seen that there is a widespread failure to communicate and share a clear transformation vision and strategy. In many companies, a perceived lack of director and top management unity and commitment is the most significant barrier to change management.

In this chapter we will examine internal communications. We will see that the prevailing pattern of communications is that of the bureaucratic rather than the network organisation, and that managers are deficient in their approaches and attitudes to communication.

THE EVIDENCE

The primary source we will draw upon is the Adaptation survey report *Communicating for Change*.[3] As its name suggests, this report is specifically concerned with the role of communications in bringing about organisational change, and communication problems and priorities.

This chapter also draws upon the findings of various other surveys by the author which are listed in Appendix 1. Collectively, these suggest a widespread failure of communication.

- The 'director' surveys reveal inadequate communications within the boardroom, and the need of directors to improve their communications skills.[4]
- The picture that emerges from the study of such functions as personnel,[5] IT[6], and marketing[7] is of professional specialists who find it difficult to communicate with management colleagues. In particular, many professionals appear not to share the network organisation vision of their CEOs.
- Surveys concerning the management of people,[8] customer relationships,[9] quality[10] and the management of corporate transformation[11] conclude that in all these areas changes in attitudes and approaches to communication are the key to improved relationships.

Increasingly, the author has argued, those appointed to the key positions within companies should be selected according to their communication skills rather than their professional or technical understanding of the field in question.[12] For example:

- the best financial director may be the individual best equipped to share financial understanding, rather than the person most familiar with the intricacies of the latest statement of standard accounting practice;

- similarly, the best person on the marketing side may be the individual most attuned to the requirements of customers, and sensitive to what needs to be done to build relationships with them.

THE NEED FOR EFFECTIVE COMMUNICATION

Our surveys are clear about the need for the more effective communication of a shared vision. For example, in the *Communicating for Change*[3] survey, we saw the following.

- 'Clear vision and strategy' and 'top management commitment' (Table 7.1), are jointly ranked as the most important requirements for the successful management of change. Approaching nine out of ten of the respondents ranked these as 'very important'.
- Communicating or 'sharing the vision' is considered 'very important' by over seven out of ten respondents, followed by 'communicating the purpose of change' and 'employee involvement and commitment' – both considered 'very important' by two thirds of the respondents.

Table 7.1 *Change Requirements in Order of 'Very Important' Replies (%)*

Clear vision and strategy	86
Top management commitment	86
Sharing the vision	71
Employee involvement and commitment	65
Communicating the purpose of change	65
An effective communications network	54
Communicating the expected results of change	44
Understanding the contributions required to the achievement of change	42
Communicating the timing of change	38
Linking a company's systems strategy with its management of change	38
Project management of change	27
Ongoing management education and development programmes	23
One-off management education and development programmes	8

Source: Communicating for Change, Adaptation, 1991

Those at the core of the network organisation must create a culture of openness and trust, within which there is a willingness to obtain and share relevant information about the world as it is, rather than as it ought to be. Reality must be confronted if change is to occur. This requires listening, feedback and all-channel communication.

According to the author, following a comparison of open and closed approaches to communication over a decade ago:[12]

> *'Management is about information, communication. Without adequate information an organisation cannot adapt. Without any information the organisation becomes a corpse.*
>
> *'Receptiveness is the key to organic management. The healthy organism needs internal information about its own state of health and acute senses to detect and evaluate what is happening in the environment. A company needs to know what is going on around it, at many points of contact, and in good time if it is to cope. ...*
>
> *'The closed organisation can filter out a message that does not fit in with the conventional wisdom or which might rock the boat. The open organisation lives while the closed organisation rusts on the scrap heap.'*

Barriers and obstacles need to be actively sought out. If they are concealed, the 'helps' and 'hinders' type of analysis cannot be brought to bear on them. 'The grapevine may be more valuable as an information source than the formal information and reporting system. A pocket of information can represent a time bomb ticking away at the heart of an organisation.'[12]

THE REALITY OF CORPORATE COMMUNICATION

Corporate life is often far removed from the sharing, trusting and cross-functional communication of change programme rhetoric. The *Communicating for Change*[3] survey reveals that 'reality does not always match our aspirations and intentions'. A disturbing and disappointing picture emerges.

- There is little satisfaction with what is being achieved. 'Most companies believe the communication and sharing of vision and strategy throughout their organisation could be much improved.'
- The approaches to communication which companies are adopting tend to be those of the bureaucratic rather than network organisation.

  The priority channels of communication are vertical flows, or a cascade, down the hierarchy of the corporate organisation. Cross-functional and horizontal communications have yet to become ... widespread. ... While there is often a desire to create flatter and more flexible and responsive organisations, the patterns of communication being used to bring about major change are typically those which characterise the bureaucratic hierarchy, ie predominantly 'top down' and with inadequate 'feed-back'.

- There is a fundamental incompatibility between communication preferences and communication channels.

  Face to face meetings with teams and groups are the preferred channel of communication, but there is little confidence that middle and junior managers can communicate effectively with the employees as a whole. As a consequence the vision, strategy and commitment of the board is not reaching the 'coal-face' employee in a form which can be understood.

- Companies are uncertain about how to address the evident deficiencies.

  Many companies acknowledge that their middle and line managers are not able to communicate effectively, but do not know how to remedy the situation. The traditional 'technique-oriented' communication skills courses are thought to be inadequate when changes of attitude and approach are called for, and the insecurity of many managers has to be addressed.

- The lack of 'role-model' behaviour, and the perceived gap between rhetoric and reality, is a cause of disillusionment and despair. 'In many companies there is a feeling that visions and missions are just words on paper. ... The recession has increased the extent of cynicism and mistrust as boards have felt it necessary to take short-term actions that conflict with longer-term objectives.'
- 'Communications technology is not perceived as a significant barrier to communication.' The problem lies in its use and application. People are reaching for the video of the company broadcast rather than talking and listening.
- Corporate transformation and IT strategies appear to be unrelated in many companies. 'There is widespread awareness of the potential contribution of communications technology, but only in about one in six companies is a formal management of change programme linked with a systems strategy.' Systematic application of technology to support the cross-functional and inter-organisational processes that deliver value to customers is extremely rare.

These dismal findings are echoed in the 1991 BIM *Flat Organisation* report[11] which concludes: 'Senior management must discharge its responsibility for making choices, focusing and prioritising, and creating an environment of manageable tasks that add value for customers. In a few companies urgent action is needed to re-establish an atmosphere of trust'.

THE COMMUNICATIONS PARADOX

Of particular concern is the suggestion that the desire to achieve corporate transformation could actually give a new meaning and purpose to bureaucratic channels of communication.

According to the *Communicating for Change* survey[3]:

Companies face a paradox. Many are seeking to delegate, and to encourage greater co-operation across departmental barriers. There is a real desire to undertake more work in cross-functional and multi-location teams. The objective is often to replace 'top down' vertical communication with horizontal communication. However, in order to achieve the significant change of attitude and approach that is required, companies are using 'top down' cascade processes to drive change through their organisations.

Care should be taken to ensure that 'top down' approaches to communicating the need for, and nature of, change do not entrench the existing hierarchy and make it more difficult to bring change about.

Many boards face a communications dilemma when particular layers of management are perceived as a communications barrier between themselves and employees. Communicating direct with employees cuts through this barrier at the expense of reducing the authority of managers, many of whom are already feeling insecure. On the other hand, building the role of managers as communicators and investing in the development of their communication skills may take some time to be effective.

COMMUNICATING QUALITY

Total quality is being driven through most companies using a top down approach. Results to date suggest there has been little impact upon attitudes and behaviour. The *Quality: The Next Steps*[10] survey emphasises the need for action.

- Commitment is often lacking. Over nine out of ten respondents consider 'top management commitment' to be a 'very significant' barrier to the implementation of a quality process.
- A broader view of quality needs to be communicated. Nine out of ten respondents consider 'too narrow an understanding of quality' to be either 'very significant' or 'significant' as a quality barrier.
- As technical quality is assumed, the competitive focus is shifting to quality of process, quality of attitude, quality of understanding, quality of behaviour and quality of relationships.
- Managers need to be better equipped to manage change. The 'quality of management', followed closely by 'quality of behaviour, attitudes and values', are the top quality priorities. Over eight out of ten respondents expect to give them a 'higher priority' over the next five years.

The 'quality' survey[10] concludes that: 'Quality needs to influence attitudes, feelings and values.' It must 'go deep' and reach the 'core' or 'essence' of all employees. The quality priorities are the 'quality of management' and the 'quality of behaviour, attitudes and values', the means by which it is hoped more incremental and fundamental quality steps can be taken.

We will return to these and other findings concerning quality problems, barriers and priorities in Chapter 9.

COMMITMENT TO CHANGE

In general, the surveys reveal a genuine commitment to corporate transformation. A few management teams are reluctant to change, but in the main those interviewed see fundamental transformation as a necessity rather than as a matter of choice.

The desire to change makes the inability to 'make it happen' all the more frustrating. Consider the following two comments which highlight some of the frustrations that are encountered.

> 'This time it's for real, but we have been trying to appear committed for years to whatever was the flavour of the month. By now the immunity factor is quite high.'

> 'We have all been trained in public speaking, and spend a fortune on the videos. The problem is no one believes a word, even though we mean it. The packaging seems to get in the way.'

In order to bring about change, corporate leaders have to be able to communicate effectively with a variety of groups that have an interest in a company.

> 'The modern company is not a machine to be run or driven by its board but rather is a complex organism, a network of interests co-operating in some areas and conflicting in others. One of the jobs of the board is to arbitrate between the various interests in the company ... In essence this is a political activity. Its critical component is communication.'[12]

Walton identifies this ability to explain, persuade and arbitrate between many competing interests that arise as central to the 'enabling' role of an effective 'change leader'.[13] The experience of Robert Horton during his period as chairman and chief executive of BP illustrates that these requirements are far from academic. Even when a 'change leader' possesses drive, intelligence, vision and commitment, this may not be enough.[14]

COMMUNICATIONS AND THE NETWORK ORGANISATION

'In the case of the network organisation, the communications network is the organisation.' This is the emerging consensus view, although it tends to be expressed in general terms, more precise details being to some extent uncertain or 'moving targets' as circumstances change. However, in spite of a widespread vision of a responsive network organisation, we have seen that in many cases the approaches to communication that are being adopted appear to be closer to the bureaucratic past than the network future.

The members of the network organisation of the 'vision' are participants, collaborators and colleagues. Yet the reality is that members are too often treated as targets. Rather than use the technology of the network to involve, learn and encourage participation, it is being used to 'blast' people with the corporate message.

EXTERNAL COMMUNICATION AND THE NETWORK ORGANISATION

The focus of this chapter is upon internal communication. The bureaucracy makes such a distinction between 'insiders' and 'outsiders'. For the network organisation, communication with customers, suppliers and business partners could be said to be 'internal'.

However, in the *Communicating for Change* survey[3] it was described as 'external'. The second most significant barrier to effective 'external' communication (after communication skills) is the 'speed of communication'. Companies are becoming less tolerant of external communication delays as these may lead to a loss of business.

Customers with a choice can place their business with the supplier that responds the quickest. Facsimile transmission ranks relatively high as a means of rapid external communication among the participants in the *Communicating for Change* survey.[3] As supply chains and networks become still more important in delivering value to customers, and communications technology is of increasing significance in sustaining relationships among and between network members, a distinction between 'internal' and 'external' communication may cease to be made.

TECHNOLOGY AND SPEED OF COMMUNICATION

Satellite and broadcast technology allows almost instantaneous communication across a network organisation. One interviewee summed up an emerging area of concern: 'Business TV is the latest craze. The CEO loves it. You can directly reach your people all over the world. What we haven't done is thought through what the broadcast approach, and the simplification and packaging means for involvement and participation. Should we be listening more, and broadcasting less?'

The *Communicating for Change* survey[3] uncovered some anxiety that the technology of communication might discourage two-way communication.

Electronic communication encourages people to 'hide behind the technology'. Electronic messages are passed on without being interpreted. Managers can become lazy, and may not add value to information or test if it has been understood.

In contrast, face-to-face communication can allow a manager to explain or tailor a general message to the needs of a specific audience. The message can be put into a particular context, instant feedback can be obtained, and managers can demonstrate personal commitment to what is being communicated.

Enthusiasts of transformation need to take care that they do not run over those they want to empower and 'build' with a technological juggernaut, or seduce them into blind acceptance.

INVOLVING OR INHIBITING THROUGH TECHNOLOGY

There are dangers in the excessive use of technology that might be insidious in new ways. Paul Saffo has warned of the dangers of: 'an electronic cloak of darkness that candidates can use to distance themselves from constituencies even as they give the illusion of closeness.'[15]

Debates concerning the openness of communications tend to circle around incremental alterations to current practice. Change is discussed in terms of 'more of this or less of that'. Little thought appears to be given to the various possible and significant consequences of a transition to a network form of organisation, as follows.

- Could the technology of the network allow views to be expressed by means of 'electronic voting'? Would this allow a degree of corporate democracy, with alternative courses of action and assessments of their consequences being 'put' to the people and members of the network?
- How will the relationships with trade unions develop when both officials and union members are privy to more of the information traditionally reserved for senior management? Could the network be used, perhaps informally or unofficially, to organise opposition or to canvas support?
- Groupware along the lines of Lotus's Notes could be introduced to allow significantly more open access to information. When the equal availability of information can be assumed, what will the impact be upon the attitudes and behaviour of those working in groups? Where will the 'gatekeepers' go?

While managements drive or cascade quality through their corporate organisations, it is worth reflecting upon the stress which pioneers of quality such as Deming put upon active two-way communication.[16]

COUNTER-PRODUCTIVE COMMUNICATIONS

An approach to communications can itself be counter-productive. We have seen that in many companies there is a basic incompatibility between the means of communication used to increase awareness of corporate goals and objectives, and the communications requirements for translating these into relevant activities and resulting outcomes.

- The aspiration, or what needs to be done, is generally communicated by means of a 'vertical' or 'top down' approach to communication. This bureaucratic or 'one-way' approach views communication as a series of discrete activities (see Figure 7.1). As one managing director put it: 'When we have something to say, we tell them.'
- Managers adopting the discrete approach decide, inform, allocate, arrange, provide and determine according to their status, and what is set out in their job description. The techniques and channels of communication adopted are those which 'get the message across'.
- Achievement, or 'making it happen', depends upon 'horizontal' communication across departmental and functional boundaries. The cross-functional pattern of communication is that which is increasingly sought by the people of the organisation with the responsibility of making the flexible network organisation a working reality.
- Within the organic network, communication is seen as an ongoing responsibility (Figure 7.1). The emphasis is upon 'involvement' through visioning, sharing, empowering, enabling, facilitating and supporting. Attitude is important rather than technique. Managers need to be sensitive, intuitive and patient in order to learn, build relationships and establish mutual trust.

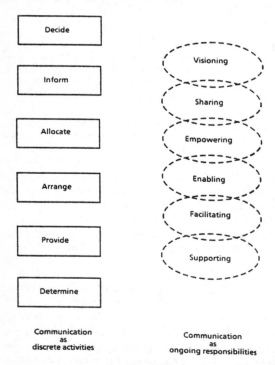

Figure 7.1 *Changing Approaches to Communication*

Likert's various studies from the early 1960s suggest that a participative style of management and a free flow of communications, up, down and across organisations are more likely to achieve results than more authoritarian approaches that involve top down communication.[17] This is especially true of the network organisation.

DIVIDING BY COMMUNICATION

Paradoxically, the very investments in the technology of communications, for example ever-slicker videos, that result from a desire to spread the 'change message' are making it more difficult to change. They are reinforcing the 'top down' approach, and are distancing top management from the rest of the organisation.

The slickness of the packaging results in the passive and disinterested acceptance of what is sought as a *fait accompli*, rather than as an aspiration that will only become a reality with the active participation of the people of the organisation. Little hint is given of the desire for involvement and the need for thinking, elaboration and refinement during the implementation process.

Psychological studies suggest that delegating communications activities to a group of specialists within an organisation will not result in a sustained change of attitudes and behaviour, unless top management behaviour and the structure and operation of the corporation as a whole is consistent with, and supportive of, what is being communicated.[18]

SYSTEMATIC COMMUNICATION

For three years from 1989–92 the author served as the judge for the internal communications category of the Institute of Public Relations' 'Sword of Excellence' Award. This experience suggests the following.

- While undertaking work of a high professional standard, too many communication professionals initiate activities without first analysing the situation, and thinking through what they need to communicate and to whom. They just open fire with the heaviest artillery they can get a boss or a client to pay for.
- Far too much communication is one way. There is often little attempt to encourage two-way communication, or establish a dialogue or relationship. Information, press releases and bumf are poured on to people, as if from an overflowing gutter in a tropical storm.
- There is little correlation between how much is spent on communication and the success of a campaign. In fact, the reverse is often the case. A little thought about objectives, and what people might be interested in, can go a long away.
- Overall, far too high a proportion of time is spent upon 'doing things', and too little attention is paid to analysis, thinking and planning. Being more focused early on in terms of objectives, and selective in respect of publics, can allow time to be saved, and a better use made of resources, later on.
- Many professional communicators operate in a departmental world of their own, applying their technical skills to individual jobs. They are not an integral element of a multifunctional team at the heart of a co-ordinated set of change processes that make up a comprehensive transformation programme.

The overall winner of the 1992 'Sword of Excellence' competition organised by the Institute of Public Relations, and the winner in the internal communications category, was Forte plc. In changing its name from Trusthouse Forte, the corporation employed an approach which encouraged people at all levels throughout the corporation to work in groups to better understand the thinking behind the change of name, and relate the underlying change of business philosophy to their own particular responsibilities and activities. A conscious attempt was made not just to pass on information, but also to get something to happen.

COMMUNICATION AND CORPORATE TRANSFORMATION

There is little point in communications activity that does not contribute to business goals and objectives. Figure 7.2 sets out a systematic approach to communication which has been developed by the author,[19] and identifies where the various steps relate to other vital corporate processes.

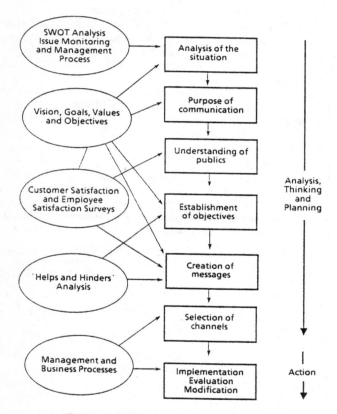

Figure 7.2 *Communication Process*

The communication process should be integrated with the other activities and processes that are being used to bring about corporate transformation. Here are some examples.

- A first step is to understand the situation in order to ensure that underlying or root causes are identified. Use should be made of relevant outputs from a SWOT (strengths, weaknesses, opportunities, threats), analysis or issue monitoring and management process.
- The analysis of the situation, establishing both the purpose of communication and specific communication objectives, and the creation of messages should all reflect the vision, goals, values and objectives of a company.

- The results of customer and employee surveys could be used to better understand those with whom it is desired to communicate. They could also be used when messages are crafted.
- Communications objectives and messages should also take account of the results of relevant 'helps' and 'hinders' analysis, if communications activity is to be focused upon specific barriers and obstacles to change.
- The selection of communication channels should take account of any work that is under way to identify, document and simplify or re-engineer business processes. If communication is undertaken along these cross-functional processes, communications activity will support the transformation process.

COMMUNICATION AND DIVERSITY

The cross-cultural aspects of communications should not be overlooked. Sony Corporation of Japan is increasing the proportion of its production outside of Japan by internationalising its manufacturing operations with the aid of a computerised global network. However, according to Nobuo Kanoi, the company's deputy president, human rather than technical factors are inhibiting the globalisation of production: 'the communication gap between people of different nations, different lifestyles and ways of thinking has become the key issue'.[20]

The reality is that we do not all see things the same way. Effective communication is built upon an understanding of underlying differences of perception, while communication that does not reflect them can exacerbate a situation by making people more aware of differences and bringing a latent conflict into the open.[21]

When communicating across national and cultural boundaries, it needs to be remembered that non-verbal clues, such as body language and the context within which communication occurs, may be as significant as the language used. Much may be lost when electronic forms of communication are used. Video-conferencing has certain advantages in this respect.

Problems for the grumbling many represent business opportunities for the astute few. NEC has seen cross-border communication as a market opportunity for telecommunications technologies that incorporate a range of automatic translation facilities. Other aspects of international communication will be examined in Chapter 11.

People and groups vary in terms of their receptiveness to new ideas. This needs to be understood by those driving communication and transformation programmes through organisations. Some groups will respond more quickly than others, and varying degrees of persistence and tailoring will be needed. Even within the same groups there may be 'open minds' and 'closed minds'.[22]

COMMUNICATION BY ROLE-MODEL EXAMPLE

One of the most potent channels of communication is the role-model behaviour of senior managers, and the extent to which they 'walk the talk'. Do managers themselves 'practise what they preach', or are their actions at variance with the carefully crafted messages that seep or blare from the official channels of communication?

The failure to 'walk the talk' is not confined to corporate presidents. Consider the following comments of the 'environment president', George Bush: 'We want to save the little furry feathery guy and all of that, but I don't want to see 40,000 loggers thrown out of work.'[23]

Role-model behaviour does not just happen. In the case of the 'hard nosed', conditions may need to be created within which they understand what 'role-model' behaviour is, and believe it is in their best interest to exude and practise it. In particular, the following should be noted.

- Standards of role-model behaviour should be defined. These could cover such matters as understanding, use and support of certain approaches and techniques; focus and orientation; attitudes, values and behaviour; and contribution to business goals and objectives.
- Decisions relating to promotion should be visibly linked to the extent to which people act as role models. Some will make an effort, but not succeed, while others may make no attempt to live up to what is required. Those seen to be rewarded should be the people who 'take on board' and practise role-model attitudes and values, while those who consistently and quite naturally act as role models and achieve results could be 'fast-tracked' for promotion.
- Remuneration could also be linked to role-model behaviour. A proportion of remuneration could be used in this way, or a range of incentive schemes could be introduced.
- Some companies encourage people to assess each other in terms of role-model behaviour. Subordinates could be given an opportunity to assess their managers, or teams could carry out peer reviews. An employee attitude survey could be used to assess the attitudes of departmental or divisional work groups. The results of all these activities could be used in various ways, ranging from remedial training to rewards.

Role-model behaviour should be demanded at all levels and, in terms of example, can be especially important at the senior level. There are those who believe the use of particular 'role-model' techniques is 'for the little people'. Not so, a tool such as the quality improvement process can be used at the micro level by a work group or at the macro level by the board.

Changing the role of the manager from command and control to that of counsellor, mentor, coach and facilitator has important consequences for communications. It is difficult for those who are incapable of listening to counsel and coach.

MANAGERS AS COMMUNICATORS

How are people living up to the standards of role-model conduct? The *Communicating for Change*[3] survey reveals little satisfaction with the communication skills of managers.

- Managers are struggling to communicate difficult concepts to people at various levels within an organisation. People listen to the words without being fully aware of their relevance to their own situation.
- Many managers are not comfortable at communicating 'face to face' in group situations. They find it difficult to achieve a rapport, openness and trust, and to hold attention, when they do not fully understand the purpose of various communications.
- Particular difficulties are being experienced by middle managers. Many of them feel their status has been eroded and they are insecure. Few companies have done enough to equip these anguished managers with the confidence, perspective and skills to be an effective element of the cascade process.
- Reference was made earlier in this chapter to the fact that most companies believe the communication skills of their managers could be greatly improved, but they are not finding this easy to do. Few of the courses available 'on the market', concerning communication techniques, are thought to have much impact upon deep-rooted attitudes and approaches to communication.
- 'Communication skills' are felt by respondents to be the top barrier to both internal (see Table 7.2) and external communication. Not a single respondent considered 'communication skills' to be 'insignificant' as a communication barrier. Those

interviewed described the deficiency in terms of attitudes, approaches and perspective. 'Employee attitudes' and 'lack of two-way communication' rank in Table 7.2 as equal third as an internal barrier to communication.

Table 7.2 *Barriers to effective internal communication*
Ranked in order of 'very significant' replies (%)

Communication skills	33
Top management commitment	27
Employee attitudes	19
Lack of two-way communication	19
Organisation structure	13
Ability to access people when needed	10
Management processes	8
Speed of communication	8
Organisational politics	8
Cost of communication	6
Communications technology	2

Source: *Communicating for Change,* 1991

Participants in the *Flat Organisation* survey[11] were asked to rank in importance the management qualities which will enable organisations to implement the changes that are desired, in order to respond more effectively to challenges and opportunities within the business environment. When these are ranked in order of 'very important' replies, the 'ability to communicate' comes top. Two-thirds of the respondents consider it to be 'very important'.

The following selection of quotes sums up the sense of frustration felt by those at the top of organisations.

> *'Passing something on is not communicating. Too many of our managers see the corporate message as an in-tray item. They get it out the other side without adding value to it.'*

> *'Communicating has become a substitute for thinking and understanding. There is a lot of traffic on the line, but what does it all mean?'*

> *'We talk about empowerment, but our managers hoard information. They are reluctant to share what they perceive is their source of power.'*

We have seen that 'face-to-face meetings with teams and groups are the preferred channel of communication'.[3] If managers are as dependent upon informal and verbal communications, rather than formal and written reports, as Mintzberg suggests,[24] then many organisations are paying a heavy price as a result of the failure of their managers to communicate with their workgroups.

THE EFFECTIVE COMMUNICATOR

Where are we going wrong? What is needed, according to Peter Bartram, co-author of *The Complete Spokesperson*,[25] is 'not technique but a change of approach, attitude and perspective. An excess of techniques, which results in people not being true to themselves, can actually inhibit effective communication.'

Bennis and Nanus have identified the 'managing of meaning' or the communication and sharing of vision as one of four key leadership abilities, the others relating to the initial articulation of the vision and the abilities to engender trust and sustain commitment.[26]

Messages must be straightforward, honest and related to the needs and interests of the audience if they are to 'come alive'.[27] The communicator must be open and willing to learn. The communicator must share the vision, must feel the vision and must be visibly committed to it.

Communication must be seen as an ongoing and key element of the role of the manager, and not as a discrete and intermittent activity (Figure 7.1). The ability to communicate is an essential management quality. Companies cannot afford to continue to acknowledge the deficiencies of their managers as communicators without taking concrete steps to improve their attitudes and approaches to communication.

More emphasis needs to be given to the role of the manager as a communicator within groups. Significant change will not occur in many organisations unless managers are equipped with the awareness and skills to bring it about. For example, to achieve greater two-way, and more lateral, communication, managers accustomed to communicating primarily within their own functions and departments may need to understand better the concerns, perspectives and terminologies of a wider range of colleagues.

RESPONSIBILITIES FOR COMMUNICATIONS

Putting corporate communications responsibility into the hands of communications or public relations specialists may encourage some managers to rely upon them, rather than take steps to improve their own communications skills. The delegation of communications to specialists, or a reliance upon 'house journals' and corporate videos, can send out 'negative signals'. Managers tend to do themselves the things they regard as really important.

If fundamental shifts of attitude and perspective are to occur, managers cannot abdicate their responsibility for communicating with people. Some of the communications professionals interviewed appeared to take the view that employee communications was a matter for them, rather than managers generally. Others adopted a more strategic view, and saw their own roles in terms of being advisers and facilitators. These were the people who were most concerned to build the management, and particularly the communication, skills of their colleagues.

ATTITUDES AND CHANGE TIMESCALES

Changing attitudes can take many years. Establishing the extent to which attitude changes are occurring is not easy when managers rapidly assimilate what they perceive to be the words that are in vogue, while retaining their previous views, opinions and perspective. This eagerness among managers to agree and conform, to appear supportive and a 'team player', and to use the 'right words', can make it difficult to judge the extent of internalisation or 'real understanding'.

Attitudes will not change if observed conduct, as opposed to the words, reinforces them. In many companies, there is considerable cynicism and not a little distrust. The economic downturn and recession have not helped. The apparent inconsistency between stated longer-term objectives and short-term actions has seriously damaged the credibility of many senior managements. One exasperated manager complained: 'They may have had good reasons, but we have not been told about them.'

Flexibility and responsiveness are perceived by many as a cover for overhead savings and headcount reductions. According to one divisional director: 'Corporate vision and top management commitment has been tested, and has been found wanting.' Honesty and openness in communication is even more important in an era of recession and retrenchment, when there is bad news to communicate, and at times of crisis communication.

Companies need to focus upon the reality of managerial attitudes, not the wishful thinking of the corporate video. In many companies there is an overwhelming sense of personal insecurity.[11] Individuals doubt that they or their organisations will ever 'arrive', or that their own efforts will result in more than temporary recognition and reward. People feel a loss of loyalty and mutual commitment when their value and relevance has to be demonstrated on an almost continuous basis, and they must fight daily for their jobs.

COMMUNICATION AND CARING

Economic recession and corporate change are sapping management morale and commitment at a time when greater flexibility is required. The battle for 'hearts and minds' is being lost in many companies.

A little caring and sympathy would go a long way. One chairman admitted: 'All too often, when heads are taken out of organisations, priorities are not reassessed and achievable objectives are not rematched to available resources. This comes across as callous, unfeeling ... as if we don't care.'

'Delayering' can cast a shadow over many lives. 'Flattening hierarchies' sends a chill up many spines. In contrast to the rhetoric of 'widening opportunities', the actual experience is too often of previous workloads and responsibilities being just reallocated to those that remain. People are required to do more with less, and are rarely equipped or helped to cope with the extra pressure.

This process of putting more upon the shoulders of managers who have 'lost the vision' can only go on for so long. After a time people can feel that they are on a treadmill, where the harder they work the more they attract extra tasks. As one manager appealed: 'Where is the joy? Where is the fun?' This is the reality of the world in which many attitudes are forged. Too many of the signs and symbols are negative.

THE IMPORTANCE OF SYMBOLS

When the reality, whether an actual situation, hidden motives or the thinking behind communication is hidden, people judge on the basis of appearance. Symbols can be of great importance in shaping behaviour. People do take account of what they see, and this visible evidence is the source of credibility gaps in many companies.

A new corporate jet, or redecorating the executive restaurant at a time of cutbacks, may appear trivial examples, but they happen, are noticed and get talked about. Events and images that do not appear to match stated priorities and objectives can result in a breakdown of trust. Hence the need for managers, especially senior managers, to act as role models.

REWARD AND ACHIEVEMENT

A wide range of management decisions communicate messages, many of which may be unintended. For example, as a symbol, money does talk. Reward and remuneration policy, rather than the corporate video, may be taken to represent what 'management' really means. The video may stress the need for satisfied customers and investment in training, while managers are rewarded for achieving short-term cost-savings which may be thought to have adverse longer-term consequences.

One of the most potent sets of symbols in any company derives from the factors that lead some people to visible success. Among the senior ranks of many companies are the 'whiz-kids' who move quickly around the corporate organisation, dazzling people with short-term activity and rhetoric. When the longer-term consequences of their incumbency of various roles catch up with their successors, these often seem to make their previous performance even more impressive.

If changes of attitude and behaviour are to occur, and cynicism is to give way to a focus upon the delivery of measurable objectives that add value for customers, reward and advancement must be seen to be related to achievement, to outcomes rather than to activity. The bias towards activity must be replaced with a focus upon results. Activity that does not contribute to customer satisfaction must be driven out.

THE BOARD AS A ROLE MODEL

People are not fools, but perceptive and astute. A lack of commitment among one or two directors who are 'going along' with colleagues can seriously undermine a change programme. People notice when directors and senior managers say one thing and do another.

Reference has already been made to the importance of role-model behaviour. The 'tone' is set by those at the top. Their deeds must match their words. They must exude visible commitment and consistent action, although consistency may need to be tempered with flexibility if it is not to constrict and constrain.

Divisions within the boardroom are usually difficult to hide. Time spent agreeing and sharing a transformation vision and a change strategy is rarely wasted. Unity, and a common and shared approach, along the corridors of the directorial suite is vital.

When chairmen and CEOs cannot carry their boardroom colleagues with them, ambivalent and confusing signals are sent out. Will and purpose may be thought to be lacking. The bureaucratic beast may be perceived as 'all muscle', but without a heart.

A board should never assume understanding and commitment. Even when people say 'Yes' or 'I agree', they may not fully understand, and their commitment may be lukewarm. People may 'go along with the drift' in order to keep in with a CEO or their boss. The slug sticks to a wall. The same words may mean different things to various people. Understanding should be tested, and some effort devoted to ensuring that there is a shared appreciation of the meanings of key words .

Many companies need to become more open. Boards and senior managers need to change their approach from one of 'disclosure' to an emphasis upon sharing. In some cases, a reassessment of the role of the board may be necessary. As we saw in Chapter 3, the board may need to become more of a facilitator and enabler, and less of a 'decider'.

CHECKLIST

► Is communication activity in your company an integral part of its management and business processes?

► Is communication regarded as a number of specialised activities, or is it the responsibility of every manager?

► Does communication activity follow an analysis of the situation?

► Do people think through why they are communicating, and what needs to be communicated to whom?

► Have customer and employee surveys been undertaken to determine the requirements and interests of those with whom the company wishes to communicate?

► Are the messages used compatible with the vision, goals and values of the organisation?

► Is the prevailing pattern of communication one way or two way?

► How genuine is the desire to involve, listen and learn?

► What is really happening out there? What do people think and feel?

► Have the barriers to communication been identified, and are action programmes in place to deal with them?

► What is done to monitor and assess the results of communication activity?

► Do the signs and symbols support or undercut change messages?

► Do key people in the organisation exhibit role-model behaviour?

► What incentive is there, in terms of reward and recognition, for people to act as role models and positive symbols?

REFERENCES

1   Coulson-Thomas, C (1983) *Marketing Communications*, Heinemann Professional Publishing, Oxford and London.
2   Barnard, C (1938) *The Functions of the Executive*, Harvard University Press, Cambridge, Mass.
3   Coulson-Thomas, C and Coulson-Thomas, S (1991), *Communicating for Change: Communications and the Management of Change*, an Adaptation Survey for Granada Business Services, London.
4   Coulson-Thomas, C (1993) *Creating Excellence in the Boardroom*, McGraw-Hill, London.
5   Coulson-Thomas, C (1992) *The Role and Development of the Personnel Director*, interim and final surveys undertaken by Adaptation Ltd in conjunction with the Institute of Personnel Management Research Group.
6   Coulson-Thomas, C (1990) *Developing IT Directors*, an Adaptation Ltd Report to the Department of Computing Science, Surrey University.
7   Coulson-Thomas, C (1991) 'Customers, Marketing and the Network Organisation', *Journal of Marketing Management*, 7, pp 237–55
8   Coulson-Thomas, C and Brown, R (1989) *The Responsive Organisation*, BIM, Corby.
9   Coulson-Thomas, C and Brown, R (1990) *Beyond Quality*, BIM, Corby.
10 Coulson-Thomas, C and Coulson-Thomas, S (1991) *Quality: The Next Steps*, an Adaptation Ltd Survey for ODI International, Adaptation, London and (Executive Summary) ODI, Wimbledon, London.
11 Coulson-Thomas, C and Coe, T (1991) *The Flat Organisation: Philosophy and Practice*, BIM, Corby.
12 Coulson-Thomas, C (1981) *Public Relations is Your Business: A guide for every manager*, Business Books, London.
13 Walton, R E (1987) *Innovating to Compete*, Jossey-Bass, San Francisco.
14 Lorenz, C (1992) 'Oil and Troubled Waters' *Financial Times*, 29 June, p 9.

15   Turque, W, Fineman, H and Bingham, C (1992) 'Wiring Up the Age of Technopolitics' *Newsweek*, 15 June, p 23.

16   Neave, H (1990) *The Deming Dimension*, SPC Press, Knoxville, Tenn.

17   Likert, R (1961) *New Patterns of Management*, McGraw-Hill, New York; and (1967) *The Human Organisation: Its Management and Value*, McGraw-Hill, New York.

18   Boss, W B (1983) 'Team Building and the Problem of Regression: The Personal Management Interview as an Intervention', *Journal of Applied Behavioral Science*, 19, pp 67–84; and Guzzo, R A, Jette, R D and Katzell, R A (1985) 'The Effects of Psychologically Based Intervention Programs on Worker Productivity: A meta-analysis' *Personnel Psychology*, 38, pp 275–292

19   Coulson-Thomas, C (1979) *Public Relations: A Practical Guide*, Macdonald and Evans, Plymouth.

20   Kanoi, N (1991) First International Manufacturing Lecture, Institution of Electrical Engineers, London, November.

21   Burton, J W (1969) *Conflict and Communication*, Macmillan, London.

22   Rokeach, M, (1960) *The Open and Closed Mind*, Basic Books, New York.

23   Dunne, N (1992) 'Complacency Breeds Contempt', Business and the Environment, *Financial Times*, 17 June, p 16.

24   Mintzberg, H (1973) *The Nature of Managerial Work*, Harper & Row, New York.

25   Bartram, P and Coulson-Thomas, C (1991) *The Complete Spokesperson: A workbook for managers who meet the media*, Kogan Page, London.

26   Bennis, W and Nanus, B (1985) *Leaders: the Strategies for Taking Charge*, Harper & Row, New York.

27   Coulson-Thomas, C and Didacticus Video Productions Ltd (1991), *The Change Makers, Vision and Communication*, booklet to accompany integrated audio and video-tape training programme by Sir John Harvey-Jones. Available from Video Arts, London.

8

MYTHS AND REALITIES RELATING TO WORK

WORK, FLEXIBILITY AND THE NETWORK ORGANISATION

It is almost impossible for a director or senior manager to communicate with employees without mentioning the importance of people, their skills and their commitment. The essence of business success lies in establishing and maintaining effective relationships with various groups of people; and harnessing the talents and potential of people in order to add value for customers.

It has become difficult to locate a recent article dealing with 'human resource' issues that does not use such words as involvement, empowerment and participation; or group working and team working. We saw in Chapter 1 that attitudes are changing.

- Individuals with skills that are in demand are becoming more conscious of the fact that they have a greater choice than any generation in history in terms of how, where, when, with whom and for whom they can work. A long-term trend, concealed by the insecurities of economic recession, is a greater desire for fulfilment, satisfaction and personal identification with outputs.
- Organisations are having to become more adaptable and responsive in order to cope with change, they are seeking more flexible access to skills and are expecting people to assume more responsibility. More attention is being given to harnessing individual contributions.

On the face of it, at a time when the technology exists to facilitate a wide range of patterns of work, the interests and requirements of both individuals and organisations appear to coincide on such matters as responsibility and flexibility. One might expect an explosion of innovation and experimentation.

What is happening in practice? Why is there despair and disappointment when there should be fulfilment? With the verbal emphasis that is given to employee empowerment and involvement, why are so many employees so dissatisfied? These are some of the questions that will be explored in this chapter.

THE UNLOVED BUREAUCRACY

Dissatisfaction with the bureaucratic form of organisation is overwhelming. Consider the evidence we examined in Chapter 1.

- 'Creating a more flexible and responsive organisation' is top of a list of 12 human resource issues according to a 1990 survey of 91 organisations employing over 2.7 million people.[1]
- In 1989 in another survey of 100 organisations employing over 2.97 million people 'making the organisation structure more flexible' came top of a list of 14 human resources challenges.[2]

In the interviews for both surveys, not one person favoured a continuation of the traditional pyramid form of bureaucratic organisation. All were seeking to create organisations that were both slimmer and flatter, and more flexible and adaptable. All those asked to draw or describe the form of organisation they were seeking, formulated a vision of a flexible and responsive network organisation.

Those interviewed were also in broad agreement over the distinguishing features of the transition from bureaucracy to network organisation (Figure 8.1).

- The transformation process begins with the functional bureaucracy. Within the 'hard-shelled' command and control corporation, compartmentalised by vertical functional divisions, early efforts are devoted to establishing cross-functional groups to undertake certain tasks.
- As the cross-functional teams become more established, the functional barriers begin to fade. This is the team-based organisation. Its shell is more porous, as it is willing to learn from others and is keen to establish a network of external relationships. During this transition phase a central but loosening grip may be kept upon the change process.
- Eventually, a network of empowered groups and project teams, including inter-organisational teams, that share a common purpose is created. The network organisation has arrived. The co-ordinating core concentrates upon the review and refinement of vision, values, goals, objectives, relationships and processes.

Functional Bureaucracy

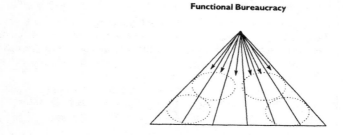

Team Based Organisation

The Network Organisation

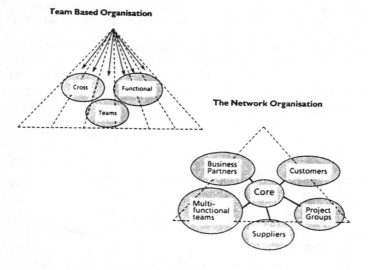

Figure 8.1 *The Transitioning Organisation*

SO WHAT'S NEW?

The transition to the network organisation tends to be 'sold' to its people in terms of the wider and richer range of opportunities it provides. Very much the same creative teams used to be at work in the now unloved bureaucracy, extolling its virtues to the employees.

In terms of how organisations treat people and vice versa, there has always been a wide gap between actions and words.

- Individuals pledge loyalty and commitment, but 'head hunters' would be out of business within weeks if most people did not perk up at the thought of obtaining something better. People mouth corporate slogans and 'play the corporate game', in between reading the situations vacant columns. Most will readily 'jump ship' and switch organisations, given the right opportunity.
- Company 'house magazines' and videos stress the commitment of organisations to their people. Yet, most larger organisations have corporate initiatives under way to 'delayer', 'slim down', 'reduce headcount' or 'tackle the cost base'. 'Brownie points' are given to those managers who achieve the greatest headcount reductions at the lowest cost.

It is almost as if there has been a joint conspiracy of both people and organisations to avoid confronting reality, and to encourage both self-deception and the collective deception of 'groupthink'.

In the traditional bureaucratic organisation myths abounded. For example, individuals motivated themselves with thoughts of 'getting on', while collectively management teams felt good about the 'prospects' which their organisations offered. However, career change and advancement for many plateaued managers was a dream rather than a practical reality.

- Towards the top of the pyramid, the corporate structure became too narrow for more than a few to achieve any significant advancement.
- Occupying a particular slot, or moving up the ladder, depended heavily upon the views of a handful of people. Many individuals became blocked for a variety of personal reasons, while others greased and slimed.
- Remuneration was tied to position in the bureaucratic hierarchy, so for the plateaued manager a substantial real increase in remuneration was also an unrealistic prospect.
- It was difficult for people to 'be themselves', as progress depended upon displaying the characteristics associated with the occupation of particular slots in the organisation structure.

In reality, the bureaucracy constrains rather than liberates enthusiasm, energy and initiative. It blinkers and strait-jackets. It forces people to put up with a great many inhibitors of the ways in which they would naturally work, think and learn, in return for the rewards which it provides in terms of material benefits and the reality or prospect of job titles and other trappings of status.

Too often, the hoped-for rewards prove illusory. When the curt 'early retirement' note arrives, many of those who have lived a dream are pole-axed by reality.

The roles that people occupy within bureaucratic structures inhibit the extent to which their contributions and talents can be tapped, and to break free they need to be empowered.[3] This should be easier to achieve in the context of the team-based network organisation.

THE NETWORK ORGANISATION

In theory, the team-based network organisation should satisfy the desires which people articulate for personal responsibility, growth, development and fulfilment. It should offer a rich environment of continuing opportunities for those who wish to learn and be themselves.

In the flatter team-based network organisation future challenges should become the norm.

- As projects are completed, groups are formed to undertake new ones.
- The individual with particular strengths, who stays up to date and delivers, might receive invitations to join a number of project teams. A relatively open market for skills might exist.
- Remuneration tends to be tied more to output, so there are prospects of varying rewards, according to individual and group performance in relation to corporate objectives. To a greater extent, people rather than the organisation establish ceilings and limits.
- As those with the responsibility for leading individual projects seek to assemble teams made up of people with complementary skills, so there is every advantage in focusing upon those things one is good at and does best.

Within the network organisation there are roles in relation to business objectives rather than job descriptions. Getting on is a question of growing, changing and enriching roles rather than 'climbing ladders'.

The values of the international network organisation may be more compatible with people of some cultures than those from others. The author has observed that 'those from other cultures may be more receptive to what a company is seeking to achieve':[4]

> *UK and US managers may persist in seeing life in terms of a series of steps up a career ladder to an eventual goal that will justify the hard work and commitment of the intervening years. The company, however, may be intent on replacing functional chains of command with a flatter organisation composed of teams and taskforces working on various projects. This may match the aspirations of those in other cultures who see life as a journey between situations, each of which should be handled and even enjoyed, but that do not inevitably lead.to a certain destination.*

TECHNOLOGY AND NETWORKING

Increasingly, the essence of the new 'network organisation', and the relationships that are sought, lies in its facilitating technology.[5] The network organisation is perceived and described as an IT network, embracing internal and external project groups, customers, suppliers and business partners. The network is increasingly international. It runs along supply chains, and is blurring the distinction between executive and consultant.

Once people in organisations start to work electronically, and in groups, it soon becomes clear that the source of value added often bears little relationship to position in the formal hierarchy. The chief executive no longer needs to give a verbal instruction to a director who will pass it to a manager, who may pass the task on down through the organisation until it reaches the person who will provide the answer. Instead, the CEO can go direct, via the terminal on his or her own desk.

The work of the network organisation can be undertaken from wherever it is possible to access the network. The log cabin in the hills or retreat in the forest might be the best location for a group engaged in a 'thought-intensive task'.

Caribbean islands such as Barbados, Jamaica and St Lucia are becoming 'off-shore' centres for a variety of information processing activities ranging from the processing of insurance claims to electronic publishing. AT&T, Cable and Wireless, and Telecommunications of Jamaica are co-operating in the construction of a 'teleport' offering voice, video, facsimile and data-communications services for those in the region wishing to undertake work for international companies.

Supporting technology can facilitate the creation of particular working and lifestyle environments. This is not a new concept to a generation reared on a diet of Toffler,[6] but it has become more achievable as a result of recent developments in IT. If human talent and creativity is the limiting constraint, then 'automation' needs to give way to facilitation and support.

THE EVIDENCE

While the precedents are not encouraging, the opportunity is extensive. Let us now consider some evidence of what is happening.

Reference has already been made to certain reports[1,2] from a programme of organisational surveys undertaken by the author which have charted the changing nature of organisations over a period of years (see Appendix 1).

Other studies undertaken by the author are also relevant to this chapter, especially the following.

- A doctoral study of the professions undertaken at Aston University,[7] the main findings of which are summarised in the 1988 BIM report *The New Professionals*.[8]
- An exploration of the myths, misunderstandings and prejudices concerning the widespread phenomenon of ageism. The results of this investigation are summarised in the 1989 BIM report *Too Old at 40?*[9]
- An examination of the practical problems that organisations appear to be experiencing in introducing new patterns of work. This led to the publication of a guide to the implementation of telecommuting.[10]

RHETORIC AND REALITY

Let us begin with the organisational surveys. For three years running, while the aspiration of a more flexible and responsive organisation has been at the head of a league table of human resource issues,[1,2,11] new patterns of work, which is both a means by which this might be achieved and a consequence of it, has been placed last.

Interview discussions suggest that new patterns of work, such as teleworking and telecommuting, as they relate to individuals, are perceived as matters for those concerned, and not as issues for the boardroom agenda.[2] The focus of the board is more on whether or not whole functions and activities should be contracted out or hived off. The preoccupation continues to be with the organisation rather than its people.

Many organisations make little attempt to assess the quality of working life from the perspective of their employees. If their concerns, preferences and priorities are not known, they cannot be addressed.

Overwhelmingly, changes in the way people work and their implications are considered in terms of impacts upon the ability of companies to survive, rather than consequences for those who work within them. Consider, for example, how the transition from bureaucratic to flexible network organisation could affect lifestyles and prospects.

THE POTENTIAL FOR FULFILMENT

A growing number of young professionals do not want to be pieces on someone else's chess-board.[8] They are seeking greater control of their lives and opportunities to build a portfolio of particular skills and competencies. They are strongly attracted by the concept of the network organisation.

Those with the sought-after expertise may make it available to those who are sufficiently responsive to offer a form of relationship that matches the way they prefer to work. Charles Handy has suggested that as more people become knowledge workers, companies may need to become membership organisations, with individuals belonging to them rather than being employed by them.[12]

There are many situations that affect millions of people, from the desire to start a family, through safeguarding school prospects, to supporting a partner's career, which can be addressed by more flexible patterns of working.[10] Too often, however, the solutions that would mean so much remain as pipe-dreams because of blinkered attitudes towards patterns of work. The frustration of those with a sense of what is possible is particularly intense.

THE AGE OF OPPORTUNITY

The gap between rhetoric and reality is particularly acute in the area of opening up opportunities for all. Here are some examples.

- Ageism is rife, even though in the UK half of all managers are over the age of 40, the point at which age discrimination begins to bite. As one interviewee said: 'It's like saying to half of your people: "the words are great, but in your case forget it".'
- Myths and prejudices abound concerning the general effects of the ageing process.[9] Most have little substance, yet they are generally accepted and rarely challenged.
- 'Equal opportunities' is more talked about than practised. A keen editor once subbed an article of the author based upon a survey of company chairmen to replace all references to 'chairman' by 'chairperson'. In reality, every one of the 218 participants was a man.[13]
- The concept of the network organisation matches the international vision of many companies. One survey has suggested that women are greatly under-represented and account for a minuscule proportion of internationally mobile managers, even though many may be more sensitive than male colleagues to cultural differences.[14]

Hertzberg and his colleagues recognised in the late 1950s the importance of an inner satisfaction with the activity of work, and a sense of progress, development and fulfilment, in sustaining motivation.[15] Various short-term actions taken in haste by companies in response to economic recession have cut away many of the traditional satisfiers. As one manager put it: 'All that is left is a bad taste in the mouth.'

FRUSTRATION RATHER THAN FULFILMENT

The evidence of these, and other, surveys suggests that in many companies frustration is more widespread than fulfilment. The reasons for this range from duplicity, through naïvety, to a failure to 'think things through'.

Consider the following selection of comments from some of those interviewed in the course of the above surveys.

> 'Helping people to realise their full potential is a credo of the company. That is so long as they are prepared to work in a way, and at a time or place that is compatible with our procedures, systems ... and just about every other impediment you could think of.'

> 'I read a lot, and hear a lot, about empowerment. What I want to know is where I can go out and buy some.'

> 'We focused so much upon the customer that we forgot our own people. When we started measuring their satisfaction we got a shock. External improvements in satisfaction had been achieved at a cost in terms of internal morale.'

> 'There is no point asking people to work in a new way if the process and technology [are] unchanged. Change the process and they may need to change the way they work to match.'

'It used to be simple, people followed the procedures and did what they were told. Now they are self-managed, managing projects, participating in processes, building relationships, practising quality – you name it and we are asking them to do it.'

'We had a working party on the "demographic time bomb". After a year of economic recession it was disbanded. The long-term problem is still there, but it is not today's priority.'

GROUPS AND TEAMS

Team work is expected to become more significant.[16] It is not brought about by talking about it, but by recognising its distinct requirements as an approach to harnessing the talents of people within organisations.[17]

The concept of teamwork is inseparable from the notion of the network organisation. Yet, there tends in most companies to be a wide gulf between what is and what should be:

- too frequently, groups and teams are departmental rather than cross-functional and inter-organisational;
- few of the companies that champion teamwork are taking sufficient steps to equip their people to work in groups and teams;[16]
- many groups and teams are not being given objectives that are expressed clearly in terms of measurable outputs;
- insufficient attention is paid to good team work in the allocation of reward and remuneration;
- those at the top of organisations who 'play politics' or 'defend their turf' are frequently perceived as poor role models of teamwork;
- very often, even where groups have clear objectives and are motivated, the neccessary empowerments and supporting technology are not in place to 'make it happen'.

Many groups and teams are MICRO managed, that is according to internal company-related objectives, rather than MACRO managed, that is according to customer-related objectives.[10] The preoccupation tends to be with internal quantitative measures rather than external customer requirements.[18]

A Warwick University study of the management of change in UK companies has stressed the need to translate strategic changes into operational reality.[19] The study identifies the importance of teams at all levels in an organisation, and the need to maintain a unity of purpose, while at the same time being alert to changes in the business environment.

PROJECT MANAGEMENT AND PROJECT MANAGERS

The network organisation is becoming a portfolio of projects, and competent project managers are in increasing demand. The good project manager is used to being accountable for delivering a defined output within a set timescale, and to agreed levels of cost and quality. As Tim Carter, the chairman of the Association of Project Managers, put it: 'When the going gets tough the project manager is the one left when all the others have slid under the table.'

However, a survey undertaken by the author[20] suggests that many project managers are slow to grasp the wider opportunities that are open to them outside of the 'traditional' areas of construction and computing projects, while companies seeking project managers are failing to understand the distinct nature of project management competency.

One 'human resource' issue for the organisation that is a portfolio of projects is how to handle those that finish projects. The ideal of a smooth transition from one project to another may not be easy to achieve, when both parties may have different views on the appropriateness of different project opportunities.

A traditional drawback of project management for those involved has been the prospect of periods of down-time between assignments.[21] Against this risk, which can be higher during periods of economic adversity, may be set various factors such as discretion, accountability, relative freedom in terms of 'how to do the work' and more of a chance to be oneself.

According to one interviewee: 'Project management is empowerment for real. If people are to feel a part of something it needs to be on a human scale.' In terms of harnessing commitment and encouraging involvement there is much to be said for Schumacher's argument that 'small is beautiful'.[22] The self-managed workgroup can evolve into an enterprise within an enterprise.

THE CURSE OF AGEISM

'Ageism' is a good example of a widespread set of prejudices based upon myth and misunderstanding. The population of the EC is ageing. In some respects, age and the experience that comes with it, can be positively beneficial. And yet age discrimination is overt and extensive.

One-half of all managers are over the age of 40. One interviewee admitted: 'I would be appalled if someone applied to me the prejudices we automatically apply to others.'

Many job advertisements specify an upper age limit of 40. Such limits can prevent women, who have left the labour market in order to raise families, from returning. Peter Naylor, vice-president of the Institute of Personnel Management, believes 'many women aged 35 plus find it difficult, and some find it impossible, to return to work, particularly at the same level of the job they left. Men aged 40 plus applying for jobs, or seeking promotion, face similar problems.'[9]

Many companies that are strong on people rhetoric are as singleminded as a terminator in weeding out 'over-aged' or 'plateaued' managers. Whose fault is it that the contributions of these people are not being fully tapped in the first place? When were they last empowered or equipped to undertake new challenges?

As some are forced into early retirement, others are encouraged to seek it. Those remaining may miss colleagues that have retired, and can feel left behind. As younger generations move into positions of power, older employees can experience a sense of 'isolation'.

Older people bear disproportionately the unemployment costs of economic change and structural adjustment. They tend to be over-represented in the long-established and declining industries, while in start-up and rapidly growing sectors there is a tendency to recruit younger employees. The motto for many 'caring companies' should perhaps be: 'Stay smart, keep in, play the game, give your all, but don't grow old.'

THE TERROR OF TERMINATION

Sudden retirement can have traumatic consequences for the physical, psychological and social health of an individual. For a company it can lead to a loss of access to knowledge and expertise that has been accumulated over a number of years. A more gradual transition for both parties, involving part-time or temporary work, could be less disruptive and increase the chances of successful adjustment.

The use of more flexible patterns of work could smooth the burden of adaptation to changing economic circumstances. An alternative to compulsory redundancy would be to phase in retirement for volunteers by offering a reduction of, say, one day in the working week each year for a period of five years.

Given the great range of motivation, energy and capabilities among older generations, it is not easy to identify an optimum or standard age of retirement. A more flexible approach would be to link the payment of levels of benefit to the number of years in which contributions have been paid. Individuals could be given the choice of opting to receive a higher level of payment, commencing at a later date.

AGE AND TRAINING

The amount of training received by employees declines with age.[9] Many employers are unwilling to invest in the training of those over 45. A higher proportion of older employees lack qualifications. Fewer of them are willing to consider or imagine future vocational education and training.

One manager observed: 'The promises about developing you ... appear to have a "cut-off" point. One day you are a non-person ... something that is not worth investing in any more. ... You just give up.'

The argument that older employees are not worth training, as there will be inadequate opportunity to secure 'a return upon the investment', has less force in a turbulent business environment:

- Innovation and change continually erode existing skills and demand new ones. Ongoing development and updating becomes a requirement for all. In this respect, the 'window of opportunity' to benefit from newly acquired technical or professional understanding may last no longer for the younger employee than for an older person.
- Also, companies such as B&Q that have gone out actively to recruit older staff find that very often they change employers less often than their younger colleagues. They tend to stay, customers have confidence in them and the enlightened employer benefits.

ROLE-MODEL COMPANIES

Ageism is being tackled by some companies. According to John Hougham, Ford Motor Company's executive director of personnel:

> 'Ford has now, as a general policy, dropped references to age in its recruitment advertising. Every effort is made when drafting job descriptions to ensure that anything which could be termed an experience requirement does not amount to unfair discrimination on the grounds of age. Competence and the ability to do the job should be the key issues in recruitment decisions.'[9]

It should also not be thought that more general innovation and experimentation in terms of new patterns of work is not occurring.

Not only has the Brazilian manufacturing company Semco become flatter and more flexible in structure, but empowerment is such that employees determine their own salaries and hours of work. Mutual respect and trust, and shared goals and commitment, have replaced traditional hierarchical authority.

New patterns of work are being introduced. Here are some examples within the UK.

- A variety of companies such as Rank Xerox, F International, ICL and IBM have introduced telecommuting networks.
- IBM has introduced a 'Space, Morale and Remote Technology' or 'Smart' initiative. Staff are equipped with mobile telephones and laptop computers, and are able to work at various locations, including at home and on client premises, accessing information from the IBM corporate network as required.

- Rank Xerox UK is introducing the concept of 'self-managed work groups'. These groups are given business objectives and plan themselves how to achieve them, monitoring and assessing their own performance, and determining matters such as hours of work, holidays, and the rewards and remuneration of individual members of the group.

WORK AND CORPORATE TRANSFORMATION

Innovation excites some and worries others. It should be remembered, as change programmes are cascaded through an organisation, that not all those likely to be affected may consider what is sought to be desirable from their point of view.[23] For example, consider the case of the company that is operating internationally.

- Companies such as BP have traditionally lavished care and attention upon their managers, particularly those that are internationally mobile. Where established relationships are disrupted by staff cutbacks and transformation programmes, a company may need to work hard to maintain, let alone increase, employee satisfaction ratings.
- The introduction of a greater number of multilocation and international project groups and teams can bring people into contact with each other who may be paid very different amounts in various parts of the world for work of a similar nature. Rather than enhanced satisfaction, a company may be faced with comparability complaints.
- The vision of the flat and flexible organisation may be received very differently according to local labour market conditions. According to one MNC manager with the responsibility for introducing changes into a German company: 'They are cynical and distrustful. There is such a large gap between what we say and what we do. Every move is seen by our social partners as a way of cutting costs.'

CHANGE AND SATISFACTION

Organisational change can be protracted and costly. For example, termination payments to people and penalties relating to changed property arrangements can both be expensive. In some companies it would appear that decisions regarding who should be kept or made redundant are governed more by accumulated rights in the event of termination than managerial merit or quality. Some assets are also difficult to dispose of in a recession.

Occasionally, companies become carried away with concepts and push their application to the extreme. Judgement is needed to decide how far to go in relation to the current situation and context of a company. Trade-offs may still exist. For example, Saab has found that giving groups of people greater added-value responsibilities improves their 'employee satisfaction', but at the cost of longer car production cycles.

For a period, and until the benefits appear to come through, corporate transformation may be accompanied by a slide in the employee satisfaction ratings. The trends need to be monitored, the causes identified and, where appropriate, remedial programmes put in place. IBM UK has made considerable use of opinion surveys to track attitudes to change in various parts of the corporate organisation.

Understanding the reasons for dissatisfaction could lead to a change in transformation priorities, if not in direction. For example, more emphasis could be given to cascading clear objectives, responsibilities and tasks through an organisation, while at the same time allowing greater discretion in terms of their accomplishment.

Sir John Harvey-Jones believes 'people must be dissatisfied in order to be motivated to do better'. Japanese companies such as Honda encourage their staff to be dissatisfied with whatever has been achieved in order that they will aspire to do even better.

ACCOMMODATING DIVERSITY

Those who advocate empowerment, and who challenge the reluctance of senior management to let go of more of the reigns of power, should reflect upon the persistence of the view that a degree of coercion is necessary to hold a social organisation together.[24] The risks have to be weighed. Would shared values hold the people of the organisation together, or would it fall apart?

Organisations composed primarily of knowledge workers have tended to assume a community of people of similar competence, working as individuals rather than in teams.[25] In bureaucracies, there is much emphasis upon co-ordination by standardisation of skills, and some resistance to innovation.

In the network organisation, the focus is upon teams, developing variety and facilitating change, and there is more emphasis upon the management of groups. Awareness has grown of the value of diversity within teams, and the extent to which professionals vary widely in their competence and attitudes, their market value, and their work, lifestyle and learning preferences.[8]

The imposition of standard approaches, and an appreciation of the value of common tools, should not be allowed to result in an organisation losing sight of the value of diversity. The recognition of individual differences can be important when roles are allocated to people within teams.

Harmony does not mean that we all have to be the same. The achievement of balance implies that differing forces are at work, and a degree of reconciliation or accommodation within a relationship has been achieved. People, whether employees, network members, colleagues or business partners, should be encouraged to play to their strengths.

DIVERSITY AND EQUAL OPPORTUNITY

Between now and the year 2000, if the labour force in the UK is to increase by a million, over eight out of ten of the new jobs created will need to be taken by women. To tap this resource, greater use will need to be made of child-care facilities, career break schemes and new patterns of work such as telecommuting.

The Rank Xerox approach to diversity is only to discriminate on ability. Equality of opportunity is a strategic element of Rank Xerox's business objectives and priorities. The company's vision of a workforce which reflects the talent that exists in the community, and various action programmes to make this a reality, resulted in Rank Xerox UK winning the 1992 Women in Business Award.

Vern Zelmer, managing director of Rank Xerox UK, believes that: 'By tapping into the widest pool of talent and most importantly creating a culture where individual differences are valued and respected, the quality and competitiveness of the workforce will be enhanced.'

NETWORK ACCESS TO SKILL

Citizens of the network organisation are increasingly reluctant to 'make do' with average professionals when a world expert may be a phone call or electronic mail message away. Access to skills is becoming more important than the particular means by which the skills are secured. The network organisation is a skill network.

The globalisation of business is giving rise to a new requirement to access and focus relevant expertise on an international basis. Skill shortages, exacerbated by demographic trends, are causing organisations to look further afield for sources of relevant expertise. To ensure that the processes and patterns of work are appropriate to what companies are seeking to achieve, a new approach to skill management strategy is required.

INTERNATIONAL SKILL MANAGEMENT STRATEGY

In general, companies require more effective skill management strategies.[9,26] Too many management teams begin with an existing organisation and look for new ways of keeping it alive. This 'old approach' tended to regard the structure of the organisation as a given. How one worked depended upon a standard contract of employment. In some cases, work would only be packaged when it was felt necessary to seek some external advice on a consultancy basis.

Under the new approach which is suggested (see Figure 8.2) a company should undertake the following steps.

1 It should begin by setting out a vision of what might be achieved to encourage people to offer or contribute their skills to 'make it happen'. The vision needs to be 'rooted in the customer' and compelling – bearing in mind that both customers and employees have a 'choice'. How far it is communicated and shared will depend upon the ambition and reach of the company.

2 The company should next determine what needs to be done in order to achieve the vision. Values and goals should be determined, and a strategy formulated to achieve the vision. Measurable objectives will need to be established. A roles and responsibilities exercise could be cascaded through the organisation.

3 The outcome of all this activity should be a list of specific tasks to be performed, and a set of project group and team requirements. These are the 'vital few' programmes that need to be undertaken to deliver value to customers and achieve corporate objectives.

4 Relevant skills have now to be identified. People, whether as individuals or in groups, will need to be 'profiled' to help locate those who have the skills necessary for the accomplishment of the identified tasks. Complementary sets of skills will need to be assembled. Where the key cross-functional and inter-organisational processes that deliver value to customers are known, these will also have an influence upon skill requirements – but customers, not processes, should come first.

5 Sources of skill will need next to be identified. The aim should be to find the most appropriate source of skill, whether 'internal' to, or employed by, the organisation, or 'external', eg, an independent contractor. Where particular skills do not exist, they will have to be developed.

6 The identified sources of skills will now need to be contracted to provide the services that are required. Process and technology support requirements will also need to be identified and agreed. The contracted arrangements will need to suit both the organisation and the individuals whose skills are sought.

7 Various patterns of work will emerge, according to what is required to meet the needs of, and suit the preferences of, skill suppliers. They will also need to reflect the requirements of customers. A form of organisation will evolve that best allows the co-ordination of the various network 'partners' in the achievement of the vision. Their talents and contributions will be harnessed and focused upon that which delivers value to customers.

THE REQUIREMENT FOR FLEXIBILITY

Needs can change while transition occurs. In some cases, a major change such as a relocation can take longer to achieve than the likely timescale of an operational requirement. Hence the interest in the more flexible forms of network organisation that can enable groups and teams to work together for particular purposes independently of location.

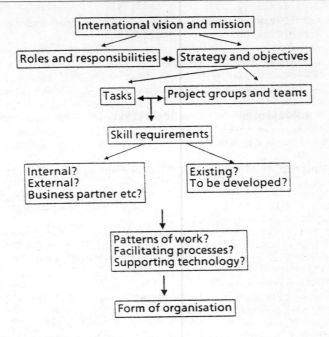

Source: *Creating the Global Company*, 1992

Figure 8.2 *International Skill Management Strategy*

Charles Handy has advocated greater flexibility in allowing individuals to work in ways that best allow them to play to their strengths and satisfy their particular preferences.[27] People should be allowed to work in whatever ways best allow them to achieve the objectives they have been set, particularly in terms of satisfying customers.

The effective network is sufficiently flexible to make use of whatever pattern of work is most appropriate for the task in hand. Individuals are able to work in a mode and at a location that best taps their competence and expertise. The response to those who wish to be different is 'No sweat' rather than 'No way'.

Paying on a flexible basis for tangible and agreed outputs can allow an organisation to secure access to a higher calibre of staff than would otherwise be the case.

By operating as a flexible network, accessing a range of relevant knowledge and facilitation skills, as and when required, organisations can become learning networks that devote a higher proportion of their resources to working and the facilitation of learning, and a lower proportion to 'overheads' such as land, buildings and permanent staff costs. We will consider learning networks in Chapter 17.

INTRODUCING NEW PATTERNS OF WORK

Telecommuting is but one of a number of possible patterns of work. It is also an aspect of a more general question, namely the extent to which IT can be used to support and facilitate the creation of more flexible and responsive organisations, which we will consider in Chapters 16 and 17.

If a new pattern of work, such as a telecommuting programme, is to be successfully introduced:[10]

- it must be appropriate for both the tasks to be performed and the people concerned;

- tasks should be defined in terms of supplying a specified 'output' with fixed parameters of cost and time;
- the people selected should be inner-directed, and able to apply their knowledge and skill independent of a particular location;
- those likely to be affected should be both prepared and involved;
- not only the programme participants, but those who work with them and manage them, should also be prepared;
- employees, or network members, should participate in the design and implementation of the programme.
- top management commitment should be secured and retained, and clear objectives and targets set;
- a respected member of staff should be appointed to lead the implementation programme;
- the programme itself should be voluntary, and allowed to evolve naturally;
- every effort should be made to communicate regularly with the programme participants during both the implementation and operational stages.

According to one guide: 'If the implementation of a telecommuting programme requires compulsion and needs to be forced, one should question whether it meets the needs and objectives of those concerned.'[10]

When considering the introduction of new patterns of work, the gimmicky solution that absorbs a disproportionate amount of management time, and attracts three researchers for every practitioner, should be avoided. 'The acid test for assessing the relevance and potential contribution of telecommuting and other patterns of work is the extent to which they facilitate a more effective response to customer requirements by securing flexible access to appropriate expertise.'[10]

MORALITY AND CHANGE

On occasion, moral and other arguments are deployed against transformation programmes on account of their impacts upon jobs, and the disruption and stress which they can cause. Such concern is certainly valid in respect of much reorganisation within a bureaucratic framework which moves problems rather than solves them, and deals with symptoms rather than underlying causes.

In reality, one could argue that work on activities that do not deliver value to customers, or which are incompatible with the objectives of a company, is ultimately not ethical. When, in their hearts, people either cannot perceive their contribution or doubt its value, they become prey to temptations to 'look busy' or to exaggerate the importance of their role. The uncertain may become 'easy meat' for the corporate butcher, even though their contribution may be real.

Knowing or believing that one does not contribute saps the management spirit. It can lead to deception and protectionism. Much of the communication and visible activity within the bureaucratic organisation consists of internal self-promotion and role justification. Bureaucracies breed corruption.

When roles and responsibilities relate to the achievement of corporate goals, and objectives are established in terms of measurable outputs, a transparent honesty is introduced into working relationships. People know that they and others are working on activities of importance and value, and they can measure the extent of their achievements. The scope for concealment and sophism that favours the smart rather than the sound is reduced.

The scope for discrimination on such grounds as sex, colour, religion, age or nationality is reduced when the focus is put upon the generation of agreed outputs, rather than subjective 'input' considerations such as 'appearance' or 'commitment'.

Reward and recognition can be more easily related to achievements. In the absence of measurable outputs, rewards and status tend to drift to those who possess certain characteristics, irrespective of what they actually do.

Network organisations with appropriate values and processes have the potential to become honest corporations. Expectations relating to role-model behaviour, shared values and a rigorous focus upon the generation of value, and customer and employee satisfaction, can represent the moral cement that holds the network organisation together.

CHECKLIST

▶ What importance does your company place upon employee involvement and participation?

▶ Does it measure employee satisfaction and views?

▶ Is there a business objective to achieve measurable improvements in employee satisfaction?

▶ What does your company actually do to empower employees?

▶ Do members of the management team understand what empowerment means?

▶ Are the processes that deliver value for customers identified and documented in order that opportunities can be found to speed them up through the empowerment of people?

▶ Do all the people of your organisation know what they are expected to contribute to corporate objectives?

▶ Does each person have a 'vital few' list of things to do?

▶ What use does your company make of self-managed workgroups?

▶ Does the skill management strategy of your company match the needs of its situation and circumstances?

▶ How flexible is your organisation in terms of access to skills?

▶ How tolerant is it of diversity in terms of both people and patterns of work?

▶ How moral is your company, and how might it be made more honest?

REFERENCES

1 Coulson-Thomas, C (1990) *Human Resource Development for International Operation*, a Survey sponsored by Surrey European Management School, Adaptation, London.
2 Coulson-Thomas, C and Brown, R (1989) *The Responsive Organisation, People Management: the Challenge of the 1990s*, BIM, Corby.
3 Kanter, R M (1983) *The Change Masters: Corporate Entrepreneurs at Work*, Simon and Schuster, New York.
4 Coulson-Thomas, C (1992) *Creating the Global Company, Successful Internationalisation*, McGraw-Hill, London, p 202.
5 Coulson-Thomas, C and Brown, R (1990) *Beyond Quality, Managing the Relationship with the Customer*, BIM, Corby.
6 Toffler, A (1970) *Future Shock*, The Bodley Head, London.
7 Coulson-Thomas, C (1988) 'Status and Professional Association Councils', (unpublished PhD thesis), University of Aston, Birmingham, January.
8 Coulson-Thomas, C (1988) *The New Professionals*, BIM, Corby.
9 Coulson-Thomas, C (1989) *Too Old at 40?*, BIM, Corby.
10 Coulson-Thomas, C and Coulson-Thomas, S (1990) *Implementing a Telecommuting Programme: A Rank Xerox guide for those considering the implementation of a telecommuting programme*, Adaptation Ltd, London.

11 Coulson-Thomas, C (1991) *The Role and Development of the Personnel Director*, an interim questionnaire and interview survey undertaken by Adaptation Ltd in conjunction with the Institute of Personnel Management Research Group.

12 Handy, C (1978) *Gods of Management, How they work and why they will fail*, Souvenir Press, London.

13 Coulson-Thomas, C (1990) *Professional Development of and for the Board*, Institute of Directors, London.

14 Scullian, H (1992) 'Attracting Management Globetrotters', *Personnel Management*, January, pp 28–32.

15 Hertzberg, F, Mausner, B and Snyderman, B (1959) *The Motivation to Work*, Wiley, New York.

16 Coulson-Thomas, C and Coe, T (1991) *The Flat Organisation: Philosophy and Practice*, BIM, Corby.

17 Petersen, D and Hillkirk, J (1991) *Teamwork: New Management Ideas for the 90s*, Victor Gollancz, London.

18 Hampden-Turner, C (1990) *Charting the Corporate Mind: from dilemma to strategy*, Blackwell, Oxford.

19 Pettigrew, A and Whipp, R (1991) *Managing Change for Competitive Success*, Basil Blackwell, Oxford.

20 Coulson-Thomas, C (1990) *The Role and Status of Project Management*, an Adaptation Survey for the Association of Project Managers, London.

21 Reeser, C (1969) 'Some Potential Human Problems of the Project Form of Organisation' *Academy of Management Journal*, p 463

22 Schumacher, E F (1973) *Small is Beautiful: A Study of Economics As if People Mattered*, Blond & Briggs, London.

23 Schlesinger, L A, and Oshry, B (1984) 'Quality of Work Life and the Supervisor: Muddle in the middle' *Organisational Dynamics* 13, pp 4–20.

24 Dahrendorf, R (1959) *Class and Class Conflict in Industrial Society*, Routledge & Kegan Paul, London.

25 Mintzberg, H (1989) *Mintzberg on Management, Inside our strange world of organisations*, The Free Press, New York.

26 Coulson-Thomas, C (1992) *Creating the Global Company, Successful Internationalisation*, McGraw-Hill, London.

27 Handy, C (1984) *The Future of Work*, Basil Blackwell, Oxford.

9

QUALITY: PROSPECTS AND PRIORITIES

QUALITY : PANACEA OR PLACEBO?

Quality gurus are jet-setting around the world and performing to packed houses at corporate conferences. Hardly a company of any significance is without its brochures and videos calling upon staff to 'get it right first time'. In larger companies there are hundreds, if not thousands, of quality improvement projects under way. For many companies, total quality is *the* route to corporate transformation.

UK industry minister Edward Leigh believes quality is not an 'optional extra' but 'vital' for the survival of his country's industrial base and its services sector. Leigh, in championing European Standard EN29000 (known in the UK as BS 5750, and internationally as ISO 9000), claims companies 'looking to supply customers in Europe and beyond must realise the benefits of achieving an internationally recognised standard of quality.'

Yet achieving standards, even awards for quality, can lead to complacency. It's tempting to satisfy a standard and then stand back and say, 'That's it, we've done it.' If the criteria for satisfying a standard are too narrow, and not updated, a gap can emerge between their achievement and customer expectations.

IS THERE A PROBLEM WITH QUALITY?

All may not be well. Many CEOs are concerned about quality according to a 1990 BIM report *Beyond Quality*.[1] The report, based upon a questionnaire and interview survey of 100 organisations employing over two million people, suggests the following.

- Customers increasingly assume quality and reliability. In some sectors all competitors now have quality programmes. As one CEO put it ,'Those who didn't supply quality are no longer trading.'
- Technical or product quality of itself may no longer differentiate between alternative suppliers. Many CEOs are looking beyond 'traditional' or 'internal' quality, that is concerned with products, and towards attitudes and values, less tangible factors such as 'look or feel', and the quality of external supply chain relationships.
- Companies relatively new to quality have significantly higher expectations about their potential benefits than those with some years of the 'quality approach' under their belt. Experience dampens ardour and reins-in expectations.
- Many quality programmes seem to be running out of steam. After some initial improvements 'diminishing returns' appear to set in. One chairman used the analogy with a drug: ' At first it works, but then the effect wears off. You get used to it, and have to take extra doses, or take something else to make an impact'.

In general, companies appear to be initiating quality programmes without thinking through what they are trying to achieve, or anticipating the various change elements that will need to be lined up to achieve a successful implementation. The BIM report *Beyond Quality*[1] concludes that 'in markets in which all suppliers have their quality programmes, managers need to consider what lies beyond quality'.

Other surveys have confirmed the dangers of rushing headlong into a quality programme without setting clear and realistic goals, and objectives that can be measured in terms of sought-after outcomes. For example, a survey undertaken by A T Kearney and *The TQM Magazine* has concluded that although nine out of ten chief executives plan to introduce total quality programmes, four out of five existing quality programmes do not produce any tangible benefit.[2]

A FAILURE OF CONCEPT OR OF IMPLEMENTATION?

So what is going wrong? Why are expectations not being achieved? Is the concept of quality itself at fault, or do the roots of failure lie in faulty and inadequate implementation?

According to Malcolm Graveling of A T Kearney:[3]

> *The problem with all new management concepts is their alarmingly high failure rate. ... It is because management fails to set challenging but achievable goals or target tangible benefits. ... Most companies focus on applying the technique, not on the benefits it provides ... jump on a bandwagon and you may get taken for a ride.*

Manrico Mincuzzi, president of ODI Italia, acknowledges that, while the basic concepts of quality are widely shared, 'some companies excel in customer satisfaction and others do not. Clearly it's a problem of implementation.'

The BIM survey[1] reveals that, in spite of the concerns, quality is still felt to be important. 'Customer satisfaction' and 'quality' are ranked as the top two 'customer issues'. Nine out of ten of the participants in the survey consider them to be 'very important'.

Critics of current approaches to quality are not saying 'quality is no longer important' – product quality is assumed by customers and has to be achieved. However, while quality may be a necessary condition for success, is it of itself sufficient?

The *Beyond Quality* report[1] raises some significant questions. Is a new approach to quality needed, or just greater commitment to total quality? What are the 'quality barriers' that are being encountered? What are the quality priorities?

THE EVIDENCE

The primary source of evidence for this chapter is the 1991 survey *Quality: The Next Steps*.[4] This is specifically concerned with quality priorities and barriers, and was undertaken to address the questions which have just been raised. It was carried out by Adaptation Ltd, and involved over 100 organisations with a combined turnover of some £85 billion and employing 1.6 million people. The survey was sponsored by ODI International.

Details of two other related and relevant 'organisational' surveys completed by the author in 1991 are given in Appendix 1. These are as follows.

- The BIM *Flat Organisation* report,[5] which is concerned with the management of the transition from bureaucratic to flexible organisation. The rhetoric of quality and the use of quality teams are prevalent features of transitioning companies.
- The 1991 survey, *Communicating for Change*,[6] which examines the role of communications in the management of change. A commitment to quality has to be communicated and shared if it is to take root and flourish.

THE RELEVANCE OF QUALITY

When quality was born, the business environment, or context, within which managers operated was less turbulent, and in many ways less demanding. It had many of the characteristics associated with the 'old' environment of bureaucracies which we examined in Chapter 1 (Table 1.2).

The business world has subsequently experienced profound change. There are the environmental, social, economic and technological pressures of the 'new' environment. Markets have become more open, competitive and international, and customers are more demanding.

To survive, we have seen that companies are having to become more flexible, responsive and adaptable.[7] The introduction of total quality is just one of a number of significant changes occurring within corporate organisations.[5]

Yet, quality is still perceived as relevant. In spite of the great difficulty that is being experienced in achieving significant changes of attitudes and behaviour, people are still 'keeping the faith'.

The participants in the *Quality: The Next Steps* survey[4] were asked to rank the relevance of quality to a number of selected 'management issues'.

- The priority management issue in terms of 'very important' replies is 'closer relationships with customers', followed by 'securing competitive advantage'. Over eight out of ten respondents consider the contribution of quality to be 'very relevant' to both creating 'closer relationships with customers' and 'securing competitive advantage' (Table 9.1).
- When the 'very relevant' and 'relevant' replies are added together, quality is considered to be relevant to all 15 of the management issues that are listed. Every respondent considers quality to be relevant to 'securing competitive advantage'.

Table 9.1 *The Relevance of Quality in Order of 'Very Relevant' Replies (%)*

Closer relationships with customers	82
Securing competitive advantage	81
Improved teamwork	65
Closer relationships with suppliers	60
Determination of strategy	51
Tailoring products and/or services	49
Facilitation of change	47
Creating a flexible, adaptable organisation	40
Greater focus upon priorities	37
Ongoing learning	33
Tapping new added-value opportunities	32
Linking remuneration to customer satisfaction	31
Delegation	29
Relationship between subsidiary and parent	21
Linking remuneration to tangible output	16

Overall, greater importance is attached to the contribution of quality to 'marketing type' management issues such as competition, customers, suppliers and added-value opportunities, and relatively less importance is attached to its contribution to human resource type management issues such as remuneration, and internal relationships and organisational considerations.

In the view of one newly appointed quality director: 'Too much of quality is internal .... it's all about us. We've been doing it for a couple of years, ... but its real relevance is in the external areas ... where we have not yet really started to apply it properly.' Customers and suppliers are too often told about it, and too rarely involved in it.

In general terms, quality is thought most relevant to those issues concerning desired outcomes (eg competitive advantage and closer relationships with customers and suppliers), and it is thought less relevant to the issues concerning how these outcomes might be achieved (eg remuneration issues).

The participants in the *Quality: The Next Steps* survey[4] were also asked to indicate the extent of their agreement with a number of quality issues. The responses suggest they have a positive view of quality. The statement most agreed with, in terms of 'strongly agree' replies, is that 'quality is a critical success factor', followed by 'quality is not a question of choice, it is a necessary requirement of being a supplier'.

QUALITY CONCERNS

The supportive responses of participants in the 1991 *Quality: The Next Steps* survey[4] do not negate the views expressed in the 1989 *Beyond Quality* report[1]. When the 'strongly agree' and 'agree' replies to the question concerning 'quality issue statements' are combined (Table 9.2), it is clear that some areas of concern remain.

Table 9.2 *Quality Issue Statements*
Ranked in order of 'strongly agree' and 'agree' replies combined (%)

An organisation should periodically reassess its approach to quality	97
Quality is a critical success factor	96
Quality is not a question of choice, it is a necessary requirement of being a supplier	96
A broader and more comprehensive approach to quality is needed	93
Quality has resulted in more demanding customers	88
Each organisation's approach to quality should reflect its own circumstances	87
Quality needs to embrace less tangible factors such as feelings or values	86
After a couple of years a quality programme can run out of steam	78
Quality too often consists of 'motherhood' statements	73
Customer satisfaction matters, not internal quality measures	64
Quality improvement projects can lead to people trying to find better ways of doing things that perhaps shouldn't be done in the first place	56
Customer satisfaction should be measured by an independent, objective third party	41
Quality has caused pressure upon prices	32
When all competitors have quality processes these cease to be a source of competitive advantage	27
Quality has increased operating costs	15

These areas of concern are as follows.

- The statement, 'an organisation should periodically reassess its approach to quality', is either strongly agreed with, or agreed with, by all those respondents answering this particular question (97 per cent). Six out of ten of the respondents answering a separate question, felt that their organisation should 'carry out a fundamental review of its quality process'.
- Over nine out of ten respondents believe 'a broader and more comprehensive approach to quality is needed', and almost as many believe 'quality needs to embrace less tangible factors such as feelings or values'.
- Some eight out of ten respondents also agree that 'after a couple of years a quality programme can run out of steam'. This is the phenomenon of the 'quality hump' (Figure 9.1). This interim state was described by one interviewee as: 'like travelling through the valley of the shadow.'

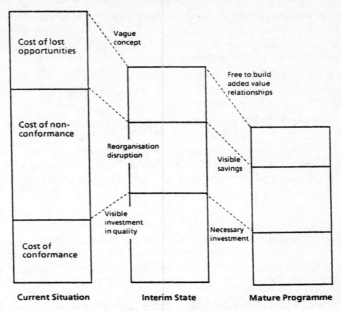

Figure 9.1 *The Quality Hump*

The 'quality hump' is a frequent occurrence. There is a visible investment in quality that requires 'real money', at a time when the 'cost of lost opportunities' can appear a vague concept, and squeezing out the 'cost of non-conformance' may involve the hassle of challenge and disruption. Tangible benefits and visible savings may appear to be few and far between. This is the time for review and recrimination. Like the 'wall' that confronts the long-distance runner, the 'quality hump' has to be overcome if the programme is to succeed.

It is apparent that a belief in quality as an aspiration is not matched by satisfaction with what is being achieved or confidence in the approach that has been adopted. According to one CEO: 'We are going to stay with it ... but the time for review has come. We just can't go on ploughing ahead.'

Overall, the responses reveal an awareness, and a consensus, that the successful implementation of a quality programme represents a significant management challenge. As one chairman reflected: 'You don't get quality out of the in-tray that quickly. I've got a feeling it will always be with us in one form or another.'

QUALITY FRUSTRATIONS

What is clear from interviews is that many of those 'keeping faith' with quality are frustrated by the continuing inability of their organisations to 'deliver'. Consider the following selection of comments.

'There are thousands of 'Quips' [Quality Improvement Projects] throughout the corporation, but we are only now identifying those things our customers want us to deliver.'

'We have a quality standard for documenting and operating our processes. I can't tell you whether they are the processes that deliver the value that is sought by customers.'

'You can't afford to be without quality – it's become the norm in our business. However, you would be naïve to think a standard approach to quality is of itself going to make you world class.'

'All our customers now assume quality. Their expectations are rising faster than our ability to deliver.'

'In spite of all the activity and investment, the programme is running out of steam. Basic attitudes have not changed. Something is missing.'

'However good we are, we cannot deliver more than a proportion of the value sought by customers. And yet each of our major customers and suppliers, all components in a supply chain, have their own quality programme.'

'Why should any of our thinking people show any enthusiasm for [our] TQM programme? How many programmes, when you look around you, have really delivered?'

That so many people are unhappy with their quality programmes should actually be a source of encouragement. As both Beer and Walton have pointed out, people need to be dissatisfied with what is if they are to be sufficiently motivated to bring about change.[8]

THE QUALITY VISION

So what should be done? Let us begin with the quality vision. At a number of points in this book the importance of a clear, distinctive and compelling vision has been stressed. The *Flat Organisation* report[5] reveals that: 'Every respondent assessing it believes clear vision and mission to be important; and about three quarters of them consider it "very important".'

Interviewees in the *Quality: The Next Steps* survey[4] stressed the importance of a compelling quality vision, one that 'turns people on' and motivates them to achieve. As one quality manager put it: 'Having a quality programme is not a vision ... saying quality is important is not a vision.'

The survey reveals the following.

- Many organisations do not have a 'quality vision'. There is a lack of both a common understanding of what quality is, and a shared 'quality vision' of what it ought to be.
- In general, the 'quality message' is not being effectively communicated. Approaching three-quarters of respondents agree that 'quality too often consists of "motherhood" statements'.

SHARING THE VISION

We saw in Chapter 7 that the *Communicating for Change* survey[6] also confirms the importance of articulating and communicating a clear vision. Let us now review the evidence (see Table 7.1):

- 'Clear vision and strategy' and 'top management commitment' are jointly ranked as the most important requirements for the successful management of change. Approaching nine out of ten respondents ranked these as 'very important'.
- 'Sharing the vision' is considered 'very important' by seven out of ten respondents, followed by 'communicating the purpose of change' and 'employee involvement and commitment' – both considered 'very important' by two-thirds of the respondents.
- Every respondent considers 'clear vision and strategy, sharing the vision, top management commitment, communicating the purpose of change, and employee involvement and commitment' to be either 'very important' or 'important' in the management of change.

The vision must be shared, the purpose of change communicated, and employee involvement and commitment secured. People need to understand why quality is needed and what it will do. As one director stressed: 'They need to feel good about it.'

In too many companies quality is just the latest of a series of initiatives that have come and gone. It has not been sufficiently differentiated.

THE 'VISION GAP'

Emphasis needs to be placed upon 'communicating the vision' because of the relatively common phenomenon of a gap between vision and reality.[5] We have seen that much communication appears to be counter-productive.

- In many companies 'the vision' is regarded as just 'words on paper'. According to one manager: 'It changes nothing.'
- Bland 'motherhood' statements suggest people have not thought through what needs to be done. As one manager put it: 'If they knew what to do, I wouldn't be fed a diet of slogans ... unless they think I'm a fool, which I don't think I am.'
- Many managers appear to be receiving conflicting signals. For example, while being pressured to improve customer satisfaction they may also be under pressure to achieve headcount reductions and cost savings in related areas. One reaction was: 'How can you hold back quality training at a time like this [and be] serious .... where are the priorities?'
- While the rhetoric stresses the need to improve the quality of management, individual managers are not being empowered or equipped to handle the new demands that are being placed upon them. When quality programmes are evidently incomplete, and crucial change elements are missing, the words can come across as a case of the pot calling the kettle black.
- There is an incompatibility between the objectives and the methods of communication. What is done often appears to reinforce rather than erode the bureaucracy. Talking heads on videos tell people to communicate personally in groups.
- Real business priorities do not seem to match the rhetoric. For example, remunerating people to 'go for' a measure such as return on net assets rather than customer satisfaction, speaks louder than the corporate audio-tape 'turned up high'.

Directors and senior managers are not acting as visible role models. They are not 'walking the talk'. They do not appear to be committed. Even those who believe that senior management are committed to change are not confident that they know how to bring it about.

QUALITY BARRIERS

The participants in the *Quality: The Next Steps* survey[4] were asked to attach varying degrees of significance to selected barriers to the successful implementation of a quality process. The overall ranking of the barriers in terms of 'very significant' replies is given in Table 9.3.

Table 9.3 *Quality Barriers*
Ranked in order of 'very significant' replies (%)

Top management commitment	92
Too narrow an understanding of quality	38
Horizontal boundaries between functions and specialisms	31
Vested interests	29
Organisational politics	28
Cynicism	28
Organisational structure	27
Customer expectations	26
Speed of corporate action	24
Too general an approach	18
Loss of momentum	17
Boredom	15
Gap between management expectation and process achievement	15
Vendors'/suppliers' capabilities	15
Subsidiary/parent relationships	9
Cost	6

The main barrier, by a large margin, in terms of 'very significant' replies is 'top management commitment'. Over nine out of ten respondents consider this to be a barrier to the successful implementation of a quality process.

Reference has already been made to the *Communicating for Change* survey[6] finding that 'clear vision and strategy' and 'top management commitment' are jointly ranked as the most important requirements for the successful management of change.

Quality is one aspect of corporate transformation. Barriers such as 'horizontal boundaries between functions and specialisms', 'vested interests', 'organisational politics', 'cynicism' and 'organisational structure' all reflect a general lack of progress in the transition from bureaucratic to flexible network organisation. Sustained top management commitment is needed to assemble the remaining change elements that must be put in place in order to 'make it happen'.

Some senior managers themselves are becoming restive, and a few seem desperate for results. There is recognition that action is needed before it is too late. One CEO used a 'coffee tree' analogy: 'The chances are that the tree will be hit by a frost before it has time to grow to maturity.'

UNDERSTANDING WHY COMMITMENT IS LACKING

Why do so many senior people appear hesitant and 'half-hearted'? Why are the communications concerning quality so anaemic, especially when coming from those who have little difficulty in putting their points across in other contexts?

We have to get at the roots of ambivalence. The reasons for concern, quiet dissent, and a reluctance to commit need to be probed.

- Apparent support may only mean that those concerned are crawlers, bootlickers and toadies. There is often a reluctance to accept the reality that all manner of loathsome and self-serving creatures inhabit the corridors of corporate bureaucracy. Their wiles, and the games they play, which are so transparent to outsiders, and destructive of external relationships built upon mutual trust and respect, go unnoticed or are ignored within.
- Those who appear 'difficult' may be the individuals with intellectual reservations. These could relate to the application of a programme in a particular area, or to an

initiative as a whole. The 'objectors' could be the ones who have thought it through and uncovered missing elements. An implementation process needs to incorporate a means of listening to, and learning from, those who have valid objections.

The *Communicating for Change* survey[6] identifies the lack of communication skills as a significant change barrier. Many senior managers are conscious of their inadequacies as communicators and are frustrated that they cannot 'put across' the commitment they feel. One general manager made the rhetorical observation: 'What's the point having it if you don't communicate it?'.

THE IMPORTANCE OF ROLE-MODEL BEHAVIOUR

People judge by what they see rather than on the basis of what is said. We saw in Chapter 7 that the informal messages, the examples and the symbols, can undercut formal communications.

Too often, the changes of attitudes that are sought are not reflected in the language used by managers, the anecdotes and 'war stories' that make up the mythology of a company, in symbols such as the allocation of parking spaces or use of exercise facilities, and in how a myriad of day-to-day matters are handled. Changing structures and processes may not be followed by attitudes where managers themselves, and particularly senior managers, refuse to act as role models.

IS IT POSSIBLE TO HAVE TOO MUCH QUALITY?

The pioneers of quality established a demanding regime for their followers. Deming's advocacy of the need to stay one step ahead of customer requirements[9] becomes ever more demanding in those sectors in which consumers have become accustomed to innovation and regular improvements in performance at a declining real cost. Could commitment to quality break a company?

There may come a time when customers become bemused and confused by the continuing flow of incremental improvements and additional refinements. Within the IT sector, there are those who hesitate to purchase because of uncertainty as to what 'new products' might lurk around the corner.

Also, not all customers have the same preferences. What is added value for one person may be regarded as an expensive luxury by another. Different attitudes and tastes can become even more apparent in the international arena.

The blind pursuit of innovation for the sake of it should be avoided. The goal of change is not progress *per se*, but sufficient progress to satisfy and retain customers, and achieve business objectives. Improvements in quality, even when the trend is in the right direction, may not be enough. Only very satisfied customers may stay. The gap to focus upon is that between customer expectation and corporate delivery.

REWARD FOR THE RIGHT ATTITUDES BUT WRONG RESULTS

Don't be fooled, or seduced into complacency, by external recognition. It may be possible for a company to acquire a recognised quality standard by demonstrating that various processes are in place, documented and observed. The business result, however, could be disastrous:

- The processes concerned may not be those most appropriate, or even relevant, to delivering value to customers or achieving business objectives.
- Having achieved a 'standard' and documented everything, managers may be reluctant to introduce changes, even when these may be desirable or necessary. The achievement of a standard can result in the 'freezing' of an organisation

when it needs to be fluid. It can lead to denial of the requirement for diversity. Supporting technology and mechanical approaches to the management of change can lead to an organisation becoming muscle bound when it needs to be flexible.

In the USA, the criteria of the Malcolm Baldrige National Quality Award have been broadened to encompass business results. It is now necessary to show not only that one is 'doing quality' and a 'true believer', but also that the activity involved is actually contributing to company performance.

QUALITY PRIORITIES

The participants in the *Quality: The Next Steps* survey[4] were also asked to indicate the priority they felt would be placed upon certain areas of quality over the next five years. The overall ranking of the quality priorities in terms of 'higher priority' replies is given in Table 9.4.

The responses reflect the concerns that have been expressed about skills and attitudes. 'Quality of management' is considered to be the area of highest priority, demanding increased attention. Over eight out of ten of the respondents expect 'quality of management' and 'quality behaviour, attitudes and values' to be given a 'higher priority'. Those interviewed described the 'quality of management' they were seeking in terms of changes of attitude, values, beliefs, behaviour, perspective, approach and orientation, rather than technical or professional skills.

Table 9.4 *Quality Priorities*
Ranked in order of 'higher priority' replies (%)

Quality of management	85
Quality behaviour, attitudes and values	81
Vendor/supplier quality	73
External customers	73
Technical quality of products and services	65
Quality of information	63
Environmental quality	63
Quality implementation/change processes	61
Quality strategy	60
Internal customers	60
Quality of understanding	58
Incremental quality improvements	56
Speed of corporate action in response to challenges and opportunities	54
Quality along value chains	50
Fundamental quality steps	46

So far as expenditure of money is concerned, 'investment' in training is a clear priority. A consensus view emerged among interviewees that training represents an investment in the future. Motivation, commitment and implementation issues are the main priorities, from the point of view of the application of management time. The point was made in interviews that expenditure of itself will not lead to success unless there is management commitment, management motivation and quality of management.

Reference has already been made to deficiencies in 'communicating quality'. Participants in the *Flat Organisation* survey[5] were asked to rank in importance the management qualities which will enable organisations to implement the changes that are desired in order to respond more effectively to challenges and opportunities within the business environment. When these are ranked in order of 'very important' replies, the 'ability to communicate' comes top. Two-thirds of the respondents consider it to be 'very important'.

LEADING THE QUALITY TEAM

Who should be responsible for quality? A third of the respondents in the *Quality: The Next Steps* survey[4] consider it should be a responsibility of the chairman or CEO. Over two-thirds consider that responsibility for quality should be at director or board level.

The chairman or CEO can certainly be a blocker, if not an enabler. One director grumbled: 'Basically nothing is going to happen until the chairman and majority shareholder retires.'

The enthusiasm of the chief executive alone is unlikely to be sufficient to provide the top management commitment needed to implement total quality. A Cranfield survey suggests that corporate success is the consequence of having a strong and effective team that is able to achieve and sustain momentum, rather than a single charismatic leader.[10]

We saw in Chapter 3 that the effective board is composed of a united team of competent directors who share and can communicate a common vision. Is there an explicit commitment to improving the quality of management and quality of organisation?

Regardless of the allocation of quality responsibilities, the whole board needs to be committed to quality. All directors should feel responsible for quality. At the same time, it may make sense to give individual directors a facilitating or leadership role in respect of the implementation of certain aspects of the quality process.[11]

So far as quality is concerned, particular attention should be paid to the following factors when assessing the effectiveness of the board.

- Are opportunities in the business environment defined in terms of their potential for adding value to meet customer quality requirements?
- Has the board formulated and shared a clear and convincing quality vision?
- Do the words, deeds and role-model behaviour of the directors communicate a commitment to quality?
- Does the company attract, retain, motivate, empower, reward and develop quality people with quality attitudes?
- Is the board taking steps to develop a quality organisation, and a wider quality network?
- Has the board ensured that quality, and other management and business processes are in place to enable the full potential and capability of people and resources to be applied to the profitable exploitation of quality opportunities, and the delivery of the value sought by customers?

QUALITY THEMES

A number of themes emerge from the *Quality: The Next Steps* survey,[4] and from two other organisational surveys that have been cited,[5,6] that are consistent with messages emerging earlier in this book.

THE NETWORK ORGANISATION

Increasingly, companies are competing not so much on the basis of their products and services, as on their processes for: continuing learning, adaptation and change; and attracting, retaining, motivating and developing human talent.

Scale, where accompanied by bureaucracy, can be a burden when it does not allow a flexible and rapid response to changing customer requirements. As the focus shifts from product to process, managers are becoming catalysts and facilitators of continuing change. This implies responsibilities that are 'broader' or 'beyond' many of the 'traditional' concerns of quality practitioners.

Imposing too rigid a standard approach to quality can defeat one of the main purposes of seeking a network form of organisation, namely to achieve the flexibility to handle diversity, and respond differently to changing requirements and varying local circumstances.

According to one interviewee: 'Manuals and procedures smack of bureaucracy.' In a world of changing relationships people should not be tied down with the shackles of restrictive procedures and the dead weight of dating manuals. Once they know what they are about, they should be encouraged to be loose and free.

QUALITY IS THE RESPONSIBILITY OF EVERYONE

Everyone should add value for customers. Hence everyone needs to be involved in the change process. No single department or group can, by itself, 'deliver quality'. No one should be able to say: 'That's not mine – that's a matter for quality.'

This raises the question of the role of, and justification for, a quality specialism, as opposed to considering quality to be a part of the job of every manager and all employees. If quality specialists are to be retained, they may need to become more concerned with fundamental and strategic transformation issues, and with corporate change processes.

Given the many claims upon the time of the people of the 'flat organisation', they will need to be empowered and equipped to implement quality. Mintzberg's early work on how managers actually behave in the workplace revealed relatively chaotic days of frequent interruptions, with only enough time to keep balls in the air rather than do anything productive with them.[12] Quality should release and revive. In some companies it is the 'last straw'.

ATTITUDES, APPROACHES, PERSPECTIVES AND RELATIONSHIPS

As technical quality is increasingly assumed, the competitive focus is shifting to quality of process, quality of attitude, quality of understanding, quality of behaviour and quality of relationships. Experience is bringing about a change of quality perspective (Table 9.5).

Table 9.5 *Changing Quality Perspective*

Old focus	New focus
Product quality	Quality attitudes and values
Quality as distinct programme	Quality as integral process
Use of statistical tools	Focus on relationships
Quality as a cost	Quality as an investment
Quality a choice	Quality essential
Achieve quality standard	Move beyond quality to business excellence
Corporate focus	Supply chain focus

Both Juran and Deming were electrical engineers by training. Juran has acknowledged that certain approaches to quality, including that of Deming, have tended to be too mathematical, and he has stressed the people dimension.[13]

A company's relationship with its customers is critically important. We saw in Chapters 1 and 5 that the company is becoming more porous, more open to its environment. Customers are now regarded as a part of the quality network. They are colleagues and business partners rather than outsiders.[1]

QUALITY ALONG VALUE CHAINS

The emphasis appears to be shifting away from internal quality issues to relationships with other organisations. It is being realised that, in many sectors, the individual company cannot deliver the whole of the value added sought by customers, without working closely with other companies in the total supply chain.

Xerox recognises the need to build in quality along a supply chain. For example.

- since 1986 Xerox has offered its suppliers a specially developed quality programme with appropriate training;
- under a Continuous Supplier Involvement Programme Xerox suppliers are involved in the early stages of developing new products.

The inability of individual companies to deliver total value to customers gives an advantage to those who are able to work closely with a network of supply chain partners. Michael Porter has identified the synergistic advantages of 'clusters', or closely co-operating and mutually supporting enterprises, as a significant factor in international competitiveness.[14]

Many of those interviewed expect to devote more attention to joint quality approaches, working with business partners, and along value chains.[4] A natural progression is envisaged from quality product to quality organisation and then on to supply chain quality. The network organisation of Figure 1.1 becomes a quality network.

Implementation of quality within the quality network will depend even more upon relationships, the agreement of equal partners, rather than the 'traditional' approach of 'cascading down from above'. Network quality is a mutual and joint responsibility. Preoccupation with internal transformation should not be allowed to obscure the importance of network relationships.

QUALITY AND THE IMPACT OF ECONOMIC RECESSION

Economic slowdown and recession have increased the questioning of quality. In the words of one director: 'The recession is sorting out the men from the boys.' A polarisation is evident in the responses:

- The committed are digging in their heels. One managing director saw a chance: '..to steal a march on our competitors'.
- The half-hearted are cutting back their efforts, or slowing up implementation. One quality manager said ruefully: 'They were just waiting for this, and we didn't have much to defend ourselves with.'

The *Quality: The Next Steps* survey[4] stresses the consequences of economic recession:

'Organisations that have already been slimmed are having to be further cut. In many companies this is a painful process. The fat has long gone. It is muscle that is now being cut away, and nerves seem closer to the surface. Companies that recovered from previous recessions leaner and fitter expect in some cases to emerge from the current recession in a weakened state. Short-term action is prejudicing longer-term survival.'

The survey concludes: 'recession is clearly distinguishing the companies that are committed to quality from those that pay lip-service to it.'

Quality practitioners are not naïve. Many are battle hardened. Interviews suggest that most of the concerns of CEOs about quality which have emerged are understood by those closely involved with quality:[4]

- there is sympathy with requests for cost justification when significant commitments of management time are involved during a period of recession;
- in some companies, those responsible for quality programmes would welcome quality 'cost justification' arguments or tools that could be used to help put the case for protecting and increasing 'investment' in quality during a period of recession;
- it is understood that the argument 'quality is free' does not always appear to be convincing to those who are aware of the extent of management time being devoted to it;
- there is a positive desire for approaches to quality that can enhance 'managerial productivity' by better harnessing human talent, and improve the quality of management.

The point has already been made that a degree of concern and dissatisfaction is encouraging. Complacency can lead to stagnation. The need for improvement, refinement and change is easier to communicate when there is dissatisfaction with a current situation. A critical, questioning corporate environment appears to be generally regarded by those interviewed as healthy, and as a challenge, rather than as a threat.

CHANGING THE QUALITY PERSPECTIVE

The evidence we have considered provides some pointers as to what needs to be done to change 'the quality perspective'.

TAKE A BROADER VIEW OF QUALITY

Quality is thought to be a critical success factor and a source of competitive advantage. However, a broader and more comprehensive approach to quality is needed.

- Too narrow a view can lead a company up a blind alley to commodity product supplier status. Bernard Vanhecke of Bekaert agrees that a broader, 'more "holistic" approach may be needed, embracing the behavioural and managerial as well as the technical'.
- Quality of product has to be complemented by quality of process, quality of attitude and quality of behaviour. According to Sadayuki Kishi, managing director, NEC Semiconductors, Ireland Ltd, 'Quality has no limitations. Quality is not only quality of product, but also quality of management, service, technology and production control etc.'

The survey by A T Kearney also reveals the need for programmes to include a number of integrated elements and be sufficiently comprehensive to encompass all those involved in delivering value to customers. In addition to having clear and measurable objectives, successful programmes were those that focused on the customer, empowered people, used benchmarking, included support activities and had top management commitment[2].

RELATE QUALITY TO CORPORATE TRANSFORMATION

In too many companies, quality appears to be undertaken as a self-contained initiative, often managed by its own team, and unrelated to other corporate developments. It should be seen as an integral element of corporate transformation.

- Quality does not occur in a vacuum. Corporate transformation is occurring. Quality of process, attitude, understanding, behaviour, relationships and of management are required. Quality should not be limited, bounded and packaged. It has no limitations. It is open and ongoing.
- A company should be prepared to take large, as well as small, steps. The BIM *Beyond Quality* report[1] finds that 'in the main, quality improvement projects represent

adaptation to what already exists or is already done'. Japan's 'Kaizen' recognises that without small steps a supplier may fall behind. However, differentiation in the eyes of the customer may require that larger steps are taken. New alliances, for example, may need to be established.

It has been argued by Deal that in the absence of a crisis or other situation that results in a temporary loss of management control, it is not possible to bring about a major culture change as a result of regular management activity.[15] If the achievement of significant change is itself exceptional, it may require exceptional circumstances to bring it about.

Economic recession could be used as a catalyst. A number of interviewees saw the opportunities. According to one: 'These are not normal times... we've got to take quality ... by the scruff of the neck. If we don't do it now, we may never get the chance again.'

FOCUS ON THE CUSTOMER

The corporate quality programme must not become an end in itself. Customers do not wait on the sidelines while people wrestle with their quality humps. A company should never lose sight of the customer.

- Particular attention should be paid to those cross-functional processes that deliver the value that is sought by customers. It's not the rushing about or looking 'the right stuff' that counts, but what is being done to add value for customers.
- Corporate objectives should give priority to customer satisfaction. Does assessment and remuneration reflect value created for customers, or one's position in the organisation?
- Management should focus upon output rather than input. We saw in the last chapter that management by output should be management according to customer related outputs (MACRO management) rather than management by internal corporate related objectives (MICRO management).[16]

Customers buy from those who satisfy their needs. A commitment to quality and superb processes cuts little ice unless these result in benefits that are sought by customers. A review of experiences with quality in *The Economist* has found that 'many western firms have concentrated all their efforts on improving their quality processes, and lost sight of the customer on the way.'[17]

THINK THROUGH THE IMPLEMENTATION REQUIREMENTS

While 'rushing into activity' may be thought to demonstrate commitment, the people of the organisation might be more impressed with evidence that implementation requirements have been thought through and there is a degree of programme flexibility.

- Activity is no substitute for thought. Voluminous information does not necessarily lead to better understanding. Quality processes at a premium are those that achieve output objectives which both add value for customers, and develop the individuals and groups involved.
- A company should determine what it needs to do, and whether it has adequate resources to do what it wants to do, before rushing into hundreds of quality improvement projects. Otherwise, thousands of people may work harder to do more effectively things which they shouldn't be doing in the first place. This is the difference between doing the right thing and doing things right.
- An organisation should periodically reassess its approach to quality. Interview discussions suggest that quality may have outgrown its pioneers. Certainly it is more complex and subtle than many had first thought. Quality techniques should only be taken from the 'tool box' when relevant in the context of the company concerned.

BEWARE OF STANDARD SOLUTIONS

Each company should develop its own path to quality. We will consider the role of consultants in Chapter 14. General solutions can be dangerous.

- Off-the-shelf solutions and the generalisations of quality gurus should be taken with a pinch of salt. Kees van Ham, secretary-general of the European Foundation for Quality Management, insists 'there is no universal, standard path which leads in all organisations to progress, and, finally, to leadership in the market. Organisations differ in terms of history, markets, style of leadership and cultural environment.'
- Each organisation needs to formulate, and refine in the light of experience and changes of circumstance, its own approach to quality. This will reflect many considerations, such as marketplace factors, leadership style, corporate culture, and the contributions of suppliers and customers.

SEE IT THROUGH

The commitment to quality needs to be sustained if barriers to full implementation are to be identified and overcome.

- Change may need to be driven through internal organisational barriers. The *Beyond Quality* report[1] finds that some tenacity may be needed to introduce greater responsiveness, flexibility and speed of action, into many corporate bureaucracies.
- Successful communication of the quality vision requires integrity and a relationship of trust, and new approaches to team building and communication. Everyone needs to be involved in the change process.
- Like products and services, quality innovations can be copied. In a turbulent marketplace continuing vigilance and processes for ongoing adaptation, learning and change are needed. George H Labovitz, president of ODI concludes: 'The common element among winning companies is that they view continuous improvement as a never-ending journey.'

A short-term impact may be both unobtainable and undesirable. One study of change in UK companies undertaken by a team from Warwick University has cautioned against the longer-term value of what might appear to be a short-term turnaround.[18] A sustained commitment is needed for lasting success, and at all stages there should be openness and a willingness to challenge cherished views and existing practices.

BUILD QUALITY NETWORKS

For many companies, the key to continuing quality improvement and differentiation from competitors lies in their relationships with customers, suppliers and business partners. Tapping greater added-value opportunities may require a more holistic view, and closer relationships with both suppliers and customers.

As electronic and other collaborative links are established forward into customers, backwards to suppliers and sideways into business partners, the quality organisation is becoming the quality network. General progress towards the creation of the network organisation, and its associated attitudes and relationships, can be a powerful enabler of the development of quality along supply chains.

LEARNING FROM BEST PRACTICE

Finally, a company should always be on the alert for opportunities to learn from best practice. In Chapter 18 we will examine what can be learned from the experience of a role-model company, in this case Rank Xerox.

Rank Xerox is one example of a company which has obtained British Standard 5750 and is now is taking a broader view of quality. Around the world Rank Xerox and Xerox have chalked up several national awards for quality including the Malcolm Baldrige National Quality Award in the USA. In the UK Rank Xerox factories at both Welwyn Garden City and Micheldene have also won national quality awards.

Rank Xerox market and attitude surveys revealed that its customers assumed excellence of product, and therefore differentiated between competing suppliers and brands of copiers on the basis of customer service. In response, the company introduced a 'Total Satisfaction Guarantee'. Customers have been given a right to decide for themselves whether equipment is performing to their satisfaction. If not, at their request, Rank Xerox will replace the equipment with an identical or similar machine and pay all the costs associated with the replacement.

Although an innovatory step within its marketplace, Vern Zelmer, managing director of Rank Xerox (UK) Limited, sees the new guarantee as the 'next logical step' given the company's approach to quality. The aim is to 'fully meet customer requirements, whatever the size of step involved. We measure our success by one standard – customer satisfaction.'

CHECKLIST

▶ Does your company have a total quality management programme?

▶ Is it taking root or running out of steam?

▶ In what ways is the 'quality hump' impacting upon the programme?

▶ How does the programme relate to the central purpose of your company, and to its vision, goals and values?

▶ Are all the members of the board and the senior management team committed to it?

▶ Who is responsible for the programme?

▶ Is everyone involved?

▶ Is your company's total quality management programme tailored to its own particular situation and circumstances?

▶ Is the quality programme an integral part of your company's management and business processes?

▶ Does the programme embrace other members of the supply chain, whether customers, suppliers or business partners?

▶ Is there a gap between internal and external expectations, and what has been delivered?

▶ How much emphasis is attached to the 'softer' elements of quality, such as the building of quality relationships?

▶ Is the programme influencing attitudes and behaviour?

▶ Is top management behaviour, and are board decisions, consistent with the quality vision?

▶ Is the output of quality improvement groups and other teams focused upon key customer-related activities?

▶ Is the reward and remuneration system supportive of quality goals?

▶ From time to time does your company reassess its approach to quality?

REFERENCES

1 Coulson-Thomas, C and Brown, R (1990) *Beyond Quality, Managing the Relationship with the Customer*, BIM, Corby.

2   Cottrell, J (1992) 'Favourable Recipe' *The TQM Magazine*, vol 4, no 1, February, pp 17–20.
3   Graveling, M (1992) '"Management fads" show high rate of failure', letter to the editor, *Financial Times*, 10 March.
4   Coulson-Thomas, C and Coulson-Thomas, S (1991) *Quality: The Next Steps,* an Adaptation Survey for ODI International, Adaptation, London and (Executive Summary) ODI, Wimbledon, London.
5   Coulson-Thomas, C and Coe, T (1991) *The Flat Organisation: Philosophy and Practice*, BIM, Corby.
6   Coulson-Thomas, C and Coulson-Thomas, S (1991) *Communicating for Change*, an Adaptation Survey for Granada Business Services, London.
7   Coulson-Thomas, C and Brown, R (1989) *The Responsive Organisation, People Management: the Challenge of the 1990s*, BIM, Corby.
8   Beer, M (1980) *Organisational Change and Development: A Systems View*, Goodyear and Scott Foresman, Glencove, Ill; and Walton, R E (1987) *Innovating to Compete*, Jossey-Bass, San Francisco.
9   Deming, W E (1986) *Out of Crisis*, The MIT Centre for Advanced Engineering Study, Massachusetts.
10 Kakabadse, A (1991) *The Wealth Creators: Top People, Top Teams and Executive Best Practice*, Kogan Page, London.
11 Coulson-Thomas, C and Wakelam, A (1991) *The Effective Board, Current Practice, Myths and Realities*, an Institute of Directors discussion document, London.
12 Mintzberg, H (1973) *The Nature of Managerial Work*, Harper & Row, New York.
13 Juran, J M (1988) *Juran on Planning for Quality*, Free Press, New York.
14 Porter, M E (1990) *The Competitive Advantage of Nations*, Macmillan, London.
15 Deal, T E (1985) 'Cultural Change: Opportunity, Silent Killer, or Metamorphosis?', in Kilmann, R H, Saxon, M J and Serpa, R (eds), *Gaining Control of the Corporate Culture*, Jossey-Bass, San Francisco and London.
16 Coulson-Thomas, C and Coulson-Thomas, S (1990) *Implementing a Telecommuting Programme: a Rank Xerox guide for those considering the implementation of a telecommuting programme*, Adaptation Ltd, London.
17 'The Cracks in Quality', Business, *The Economist*, 18 April 1992, pp 85–6.
18 Pettigrew, A and Whipp, R (1991) *Managing Change for Competitive Success*, Basil Blackwell, Oxford.

10

ENVIRONMENTAL MYTHS AND REALITIES

THE PHYSICAL DIMENSION

Environmental problems are not new. Early Spanish explorers found the basin of what is now Los Angeles polluted with the smoke of Indian camp fires. What has changed is 'attitudes towards' and 'tolerance of'.

According to a contributing editor of *Newsweek*: 'By now, everyone is an environmentalist. But the label is increasingly meaningless, because not all environmental problems are equally serious and even the serious ones need to be balanced against other concerns. Environmentalism should hold the hype. It should inform us more and frighten us less.'[1]

In earlier chapters we have examined the quality of internal relationships, of working life, and of the goods and services provided to customers. In this chapter we turn our attention to corporate action in relation to the quality of the external and physical environment.

THE ENVIRONMENT AND THE NETWORK ORGANISATION

In June 1992 over 100 world leaders, and some 30,000 experts, advisers, advocates, activists and other interested parties assembled in Rio de Janeiro for an Earth Summit concerning the environment. This unprecedented public expression of concern reveals the extent to which the international network organisation needs to confront the environment as an issue.

- Attitudes and behaviour concerning the environment are of growing significance for the internal and external relationships between the network and its various members, such as employees, customers, suppliers and business partners; and the different stakeholders in a company.
- Just as at the Earth Summit differences emerged between the approaches and priorities of various groups, so within the network the views of different members may differ. For example, network members from underdeveloped countries may have different views from those from the developed world, and this could introduce an element of strain into relationships.
- The international spread of the network organisation will bring it into contact with the regulatory activities of governments, and numerous governmental and non-governmental bodies with interests and activities relating to the environment.

The extent to which the environment has emerged as an international issue is evidenced in the contents pages of the international relations textbooks. The latest edition of one popular text, *International Politics*, contains a separate chapter on the bases and forms of international collaboration to deal with environmental and social issues.[2] In earlier editions the environment did not merit a mention.

THE QUESTIONS

The visible attention being devoted to environmental issues raises a number of questions, as follows.

- How much of the concern expressed is deeply rooted, or is likely to prove transitory? How much is empty rhetoric and hype?
- How real are corporate concerns? Are environmental issues assuming greater importance on boardroom agendas, just as in public debates?
- How aware are companies of the likely impacts of environmental issues upon their own activities and operations? What are the implications for different functions in public and private organisations?
- How well thought out are corporate reactions? Have clear goals been set and measurable objectives established?
- Who is, or should be, responsible for environmental policy, and what environmental policies are organisations planning to have?
- What are companies actually doing, and what should they do, to achieve their goals, objectives and policies? Are there gaps between rhetoric and reality? Are they making it happen?

THE EVIDENCE

To answer these and other questions the *Managing the Relationship with the Environment* survey[3] was undertaken by Adaptation Ltd. The survey covered 104 UK public and private organisations, with a combined turnover of some £260 billion and employing over 2.3 million employees. The survey was sponsored by Rank Xerox (UK) Ltd as a result of the company's continuing interest in monitoring best practice.

ENVIRONMENTAL ISSUES

How concerned are people with the environment? The participants in the *Managing the Relationship with the Environment* survey[3] attach varying degrees of importance to different environmental issues. However, there is some consensus concerning those which are most and least important.

The overall ranking of environmental issues in terms of 'very important' replies is given in Table 10.1. Companies appear able to exhibit an overall concern for the environment, and at the same time discriminate between particular environmental issues.

The priority issue in terms of 'very important' replies is 'industrial pollution', followed by 'energy conservation'. Over eight out of ten respondents considered 'industrial pollution' to be 'very important' as an environmental issue, and about three-quarters felt 'energy conservation' to be very important. Two related 'atmospheric' issues were joint third – 'the greenhouse effect' and 'ozone depletion'.

This result is consistent with other findings. For example, according to a 'Eurobarometer' survey,[4] the proportion of people who believe that 'protecting the environment and the fight against pollution' is 'an immediate and urgent problem' has increased between 1986 and 1992 from 72 per cent to 85 per cent. The top-ranked concern is 'the destruction of the ozone layer', and the most important reason for considering environmental problems to be serious is that 'damages done to the environment today may have irreversible consequences for future generations'.

Table 10.1 *Environmental Issues in Order of 'Very Important' Replies (%)*

Industrial pollution	83
Energy conservation	74
'Greenhouse' effect	60
Ozone depletion	60
Waste disposal	57
Cutting out waste	55
Recycling of materials	39
State regulation and control	37
Quality of design	32
Congestion	32
Environmentally friendly purchasing	18
Improved working environment	17
Use of recycled paper	15
Noise reduction	14
Consumer lobbies	12
VDU screens	3

The pattern of responses in Table 10.1 suggests that priorities are changing.

- Significantly greater importance is attached to the 'external' physical environment rather than to the 'internal' working environment. Some companies appear to be overlooking internal opportunities directly to improve working conditions as a result of a new-found, and less tangible, preoccupation with the external environment.
- 'Direct' impacts of organisations' own activities upon the physical environment appear to rank ahead of the 'indirect' issue of pressures from consumer lobbies. As one manager put it: 'We used to feel hassled by external critics [and] we were very defensive. Now the pressure is internal ... we want to do something.'

The issue of 'VDU screens' is at the bottom of the environmental issues list, and by a large margin. Over six out of ten respondents consider this issue to be either 'not very important' or 'unimportant'. In some parts of the world, for example Scandinavia, 'VDU screens' have been an issue of public concern. The international network organisation should be aware of different national emphases and priorities.

Overall, the participants in the *Managing the Relationship with the Environment* survey[3] attach considerable importance to environmental issues. If one adds together the 'very important' and 'important' replies, some two-thirds or more of the respondents consider all but 1 of 16 issues to be either 'important' or 'very important'. Eleven of the 16 issues are thought by over 8 out of 10 respondents to be either 'important' or 'very important'.

ENVIRONMENTAL ATTITUDES

People can think something is important without being overly concerned about it. There is also the 'groupthink factor' to consider. One US chairman confided: 'No one would dare say global warming is a good thing, but I love it. The garden grows and we save on heating costs.'

In order to assess environmental attitudes, the participants in the *Managing the Relationship with the Environment* survey[3] were presented with a series of statements and asked to indicate to what extent they agreed or disagreed with them. Table 10.2 sets out the responses in order of 'strongly agree' replies.

Table 10.2 *Environmental Statements*
Ranked in order of 'strongly agree' replies (%)

All organisations should have an environment policy	47
Quality of life is a key issue of the 1990s	38
Environmental action should have a scientific base	34
Organisations should only buy from 'environmentally sound' suppliers	31
Environmental issues should be seen as an opportunity rather than as a problem	29
A specific director should be given responsibility for environmental issues	28
All organisations should undertake an environmental impact audit	28
Organisations should monitor the environmental impact of the use of their goods and services by customers	19
Organisations should investigate the environmental impact of goods and services they use	17
Environmental pressures will increase costs	14
Companies are jumping onto the environment 'bandwagon'	11
Environmental concern is the 'flavour of the month'	10
The environment debate is too emotive and irrational	5

The environmental statement most agreed with by survey participants is that 'all organisations should have an environment policy', followed by 'quality of life is a key issue of the 1990s', 'environmental action should have a scientific base' and 'organisations should only buy from environmentally sound suppliers'.

Only about one in ten of the respondents strongly agree with the statements 'companies are jumping on to the environment "bandwagon"' and 'environmental concern is the "flavour of the month"'. Less than 1 in 20 agree with the statement that 'the environment debate is too emotive and irrational'.

Let us look in more detail at the corporate reponses.

- When the 'strongly agree' and 'agree' responses are added together, the top issue for corporations becomes 'environmental action should have a scientific base', followed by 'all organisations should have an environment policy'.
- Companies feel even more strongly than public bodies that 'all organisations should have an environment policy'. Approaching nine out of ten corporate respondents 'agree' or 'strongly agree' with this statement.
- While two-thirds of the corporate respondents 'agree' or 'strongly agree' with the statement 'environmental pressures will increase costs', over eight out of ten 'agree' or 'strongly agree' that 'environmental issues should be seen as an opportunity rather than a problem'.
- Six out of ten of the corporate respondents 'agree' or 'strongly agree' that 'all organisations should undertake an environmental impact audit', and that 'a specific director should be given responsibility for environmental issues'.
- Over two-thirds of corporate respondents 'agree' or 'strongly agree' that 'organisations should monitor the environmental impact of the use of their goods and services by customers', and that 'organisations should only buy from "environmentally sound" suppliers'.
- Three-quarters of the corporate respondents 'agree' or 'strongly agree' with the statement that 'organisations should investigate the environmental impact of goods and services they use'.

THE CHALLENGE

The *Managing the Relationship with the Environment* survey[3] reveals an overwhelming consensus that quality of life is a key issue of the 1990s and all organisations should have an environmental policy. If companies are able to translate their own environmental rhetoric into operational action, suppliers that do not satisfy the environmental criteria being established by their customers face the prospect of going out of business. This should concentrate the mind.

The key question for many companies becomes: 'Is it for real?' As one interviewee put it: 'If our customers really did match their words with action, we would be in trouble.'

Gambling on the degree of non-performance of others may be a realistic strategy in some sectors, but for a limited time. In general, it is negative and could be fatal. David Thompson, chairman of Rank Xerox UK, believes that 'positive concern, followed by environmental action, is becoming a necessary requirement for business survival'. He concludes as follows.[3]

> *The implication is clear. Commercial suppliers who do not satisfy the new criteria will lose their customers. The acid test of the value and effectiveness of an organisation is the extent to which it meets its customer requirements. These requirements will increasingly include an environmental element.*

THE THREAT

In the arena of environmental concerns, the large corporation can appear remarkably vulnerable. Driving a 'corporate line' or 'position statement' through an organisation should not blind managers to the fact that in the marketplace there will be those with other views. In one David and Goliath struggle, the case of supersonic passenger transport in the USA, a vociferous lobby put a brake on one path along which the technology of a world-class and national champion industry might have evolved.[5]

If a company is to respond to threats and seize opportunities, it needs to monitor environmental issues in the business environment, think through their implications, and determine appropriate responses. One chairman pointed out: 'Once an environmental issue passes to the business decision maker it tends to become general. We are in danger of becoming so general and unfocused that I cannot see any practical or workable solutions emerging.'

The bureaucratic corporation with its hard shell invites confrontation in the face of environmental threats. The more open network organisation might view a challenge as an opportunity to enter into a new form of relationship. If that sounds glib, when in 1990 McDonald's Corporation was faced with a boycott, its response was one of mediation rather than conflict. A joint task force was set up with the Environmental Defense Fund to examine the issues.[6]

THE OPPORTUNITY

The macro problem can also be a macro opportunity. A UK survey of the North American motor industry has suggested that environment and safety regulations could impose an extra $40 billion of cost annually upon the industry, or $5000 per vehicle, by the late 1990s. However, these additional costs represent new opportunities for suppliers of components and materials that will allow the new requirements to be satisfied.[7]

One managing director was emphatic: 'There are things we have to do ... the regulators will see to it. The fastest with the solution will get the business. We're not interested in how wonderful the products are, [we] just want it fixed.'

Speed and flexibility of response may be needed to react to sudden changes in consumer sensitivity to environmental issues. A change in the general climate of opinion which results in the independent decisions of thousands of consumers not to buy aerosols with CFCs, or goods with excessive packaging, can have a devastating impact upon the company which is unprepared.[8] These are issues with which an issue monitoring system ought to be concerned.

Identified business opportunities rarely become business realities. If a company is to secure commercial benefit from environmental concern, it needs to be aware of the environmental concerns, and priorities of actual and potential customers. As one director pointed out: 'Why should the environment be any different or any more difficult? The technologies we use every day are complex enough. It's a question of listening, learning and flexible response.'

THE CHANGING BUSINESS ENVIRONMENT

The survey evidence we have examined[3] suggests that UK organisations have a positive attitude towards the environment:

- we have seen that over eight out of ten believe that environmental issues should be seen as an opportunity rather than a problem;
- there is little, if any, evidence from the corporate responses of cost or resource constraints standing in the way of environmental policy.

The findings also suggest that the UK marketplace is itself acting to cause suppliers to become more environmentally responsible. We have seen that:

- over eight out of ten believe that organisations should investigate the environmental impact of goods and services they use;
- over seven out of ten believe organisations should only buy from environmentally sound suppliers; and
- overall a high degree of concern is felt about the impact of activities upon the physical environment.

So what needs to be done in response? If anything is to happen, environmental attitudes need to be shared. They need to be incorporated into company goals, visions and values, and these need to be communicated if corporate thinking and behaviour is to be influenced.

TO IMPLEMENT OR NOT TO IMPLEMENT?

Moving from aspiration to achievement results in implementation problems similar to those we have encountered in other areas. Here are some examples.

- There are communication problems. One manager with environmental responsibilities complained: ' Why doesn't someone tell the purchasers about environmental policies? Why are they left off the distribution list? They carry on as before.'
- There is the question of credibility. One manager put a pointed question: 'Cutting down trees does not harm the forest. That's the message we put, but do you know anyone who would believe it?'
- Commitment is questioned. Are people just paying lip-service to environmental concerns? One marketing director explained: 'Most of our customers have environmental policies. Many have environmental guidelines. [Yet] ... we obtain virtually all our contracts on the basis of the lowest price tender.'
- Following initial and public enthusiasm, it slowly dawns upon people that they are in for a long haul. A manager confided: 'Our first reaction was to run some photos of exotic locations in the annual report. When we got down to work we found it was not so easy. Some alternatives that solve today's public concerns may store up worse trouble for the future.'

ENVIRONMENTAL FUNCTIONS AND RESPONSIBILITIES

Companies are also becoming aware of the wide range of impacts that environmental issues can have. They do not recognise departmental or functional boundaries. Some may have an impact upon the corporate organism as a whole.

According to the corporate respondents in the *Managing the Relationship with the Environment* survey.[3]

- The chief executive and production functions are those for which environmental issues are thought to be the most significant. Over seven out of ten respondents consider environmental issues to be either 'significant' or 'very significant' for these functions.
- A majority of the respondents also think that environmental issues are either 'significant' or 'very significant' for the marketing, sales, service, quality and personnel functions (the exceptions are the IT and finance functions).
- Some six out of ten respondents believe environmental issues to be either 'significant' or 'very significant' for line management. In the network organisation these are the people in the front line.

In five years' time, chief executives, the production, marketing, quality and sales functions, and line management are all expected by corporate respondents to be devoting more time to environmental issues. A majority of the respondents think that the personnel, service, finance and IT functions will be spending about the same amount of time on environmental issues.

A finding that regularly recurs across the author's various surveys is that 'people will be spending more time on it'. This is bad news for struggling and stressed managers who are already working longer hours than their predecessors of a generation ago, and against a background of static or declining white-collar productivity.

An 'environmental' manager, when asked about the incremental burdens being placed upon managers, replied: 'This one could really do it ... it could push our people over the top.' It would seem that the sanity of many people may depend upon ensuring that rhetoric is not followed through into implementation.

ENVIRONMENTAL POLICIES

How much of the evident 'environmental concern' is being expressed in the form of corporate policies? The *Managing the Relationship with the Environment* survey[3] suggests that many organisations are not waiting for government intervention prior to establishing policies and taking action.

- A majority of the respondents' organisations currently have a formal policy concerning environmental mission, environmental impact, own use of certain materials, working environment and compliance with law/controls (Table 10.3(a)).
- Over nine out of ten have formal policies concerning compliance with law/controls. Just under half have formal policies relating to waste products and recycling, which are ranked in the top half of environmental issues in terms of their importance.
- Over six out of ten respondents do not currently have a formal policy concerning sources of purchasing, and over seven out of ten do not have a formal policy relating to customer use of own products. However, within five years there is only one area, 'customer use of own products', in which respondents' organisations are not expected to have a formal policy. In all other areas some three-quarters or more of the organisations covered by the survey are expected to have a formal policy.

Significantly for suppliers, the areas in which the biggest increase in the number of organisations having a formal policy is expected to occur is 'sources of purchasing'.

Other areas in which a significant increase in the number of organisations with a formal policy is expected to occur are environmental impact, waste products and the working environment.

So far as the corporate respondents are concerned (Table 10.3(b)):

- a majority of the corporate respondents currently have formal policies covering all areas except 'customer use of own products', 'waste products', 'recycling' and 'sources of purchasing';
- within five years a majority of the corporate respondents expect their organisations will have formal policies covering all areas except 'customer use of own products'.

Table 10.3 *Organisations with a Formal Environment Policy*

(a) **All Respondents**

Area	(1) Currently have a formal policy		(2) Will have a formal policy within five years	
	Yes	**No**	**Yes**	**No**
Environmental mission	56	48	83	21
Environmental impact	52	52	87	17
Own use of certain materials	54	50	76	28
Customer use of own products	29	75	48	56
Waste products	47	57	80	24
Recycling	46	58	78	26
Working environment	62	42	93	11
Sources of purchasing	38	66	80	24
Compliance with law/controls	90	14	98	6
Others (please specify): Environmental Strategy		1	1	

(b) **Corporate Respondents**

Area	(1) Currently have a formal policy		(2) Will have a formal policy within five years	
	Yes	**No**	**Yes**	**No**
Environmental mission	44	39	64	19
Environmental impact	42	41	66	17
Own use of certain materials	38	45	57	26
Customer use of own products	23	60	39	44
Waste products	33	50	60	23
Recycling	33	50	57	26
Working environment	49	34	73	10
Sources of purchasing	25	58	79	4
Compliance with law/controls	72	11	79	4

As one participant said on learning of the results: 'This is strong stuff!' However, as we will see later, there may be 'good reasons' for wishing to give the appearance of action. Also, if the establishment of policies is to lead to action, measurable objectives need to be set, responsibilities and tasks allocated, and the necessary empowerments put in place and appropriate support provided.

THE GAP BETWEEN RHETORIC AND REALITY

So what is happening in terms of 'making it happen', or turning aspiration into achievement?

Commitment to action would appear to be less than the wording found in some annual reports might suggest. In particular, the associated interviewing programme reveals the following.

- Few companies have a clear quality of life, or quality of the environment, vision that has been agreed by the board, and communicated and shared generally within the corporate organisation.
- Objectives derived from such visions tend not be expressed in such a way as to enable the extent of their implementation to be easily measured.
- Policies to achieve quality of life and environmental objectives tend not to be deployed to appropriate decision makers throughout the organisation.
- Implementation in many companies appears to be in the hands of technical specialists rather than line managers. Some of them appear to be having a limited impact upon the wider corporate organisation.
- In very few companies have the cross-functional processes and inter-departmental linkages necessary to deliver appropriate corporate responses been established. In many sectors joint action is needed if significant external impacts are to occur.
- Environmental action is often regarded as desirable rather than essential. Related measures rarely appear on 'vital few' lists, and tend not to be the subject of any form of barrier analysis.
- For many companies, the 'external' communication of corporate concern appears to have a higher priority than the 'internal' implementation of appropriate corporate responses.
- Neither reward and remuneration, nor training policies, are being used to support quality of life and environmental objectives.

One study of references to environmental policies and action in the published reports of UK companies has concluded that the information provided tends to be limited to what is thought to have public relations value, and to be insufficient to justify claims that the organisations concerned are environmentally friendly or responsible.[9] Surely a company that managed to turn its rhetoric into reality would want to tell its stakeholders about it?

One Achilles' heel is those who buy. While the attitudes and behaviour of the purchasing community are crucial to the implementation of both environmental and quality policy along supply chains, purchasing professionals generally rank towards the bottom of the remuneration and standing league table.[10]

The problems of departmentalism, and the failure to turn well-meaning sentiments into practical programmes, are not confined to environmental initiatives. A 1991 survey of community initiatives found that the programmes of many companies had not been thought through and lacked clear objectives.[11]

ENVIRONMENTAL SCHIZOPHRENIA

People do not necessarily want to implement all aspects of corporate policies, just as there are laws which are not always enforced. They look good on the books. They may be fine, but 'not for us, here and now'.

A survey of regional businesses in the UK has revealed that many chairmen and CEOs are concerned that hasty environmental regulation at the national and regional level could pose a threat to their commercial prospects.[12]

Many senior executives appear to be schizophrenic in relation to environmental issues:

- As citizens they may be generally concerned about what they perceive as major threats to the world environment. They may be aware of the damage done by their own industry, and of the extent to which pollution can transcend national borders to become a global problem.
- However, as managers, their responsibilities may be limited to a particular operation within one country. While the external impact of any action they might take may be uncertain, and the benefits diffuse and shared, the internal costs can be real and particular to the individual company.

The existence of environmental schizophrenia makes it difficult for some boards and management teams to portray a united front that is positively committed to the achievement of carefully thought-out and clearly-defined objectives.

There are also some dangers in driving a common approach to environmental issues throughout an international corporate organisation to the extent that local differences are overlooked. Attitudes and governmental policies on a particular environmental issue can vary greatly between countries.[13]

RESPONSIBILITY FOR ENVIRONMENTAL POLICY

Confusion seems to reign so far as environmental roles and responsibilities are concerned. In the *Managing the Relationship with the Environment* survey,[3] 60 different responses were obtained to the question of who should be responsible for environmental policy.

Environmental issues appear to be handled at a senior level in most organisations. It is thought that a holistic approach and top-level commitment is needed:

- more than a third of respondents believe environmental policy should be a chief executive responsibility;
- some six out of ten believe it should be a responsibility of either the chief executive or the board, and about three-quarters consider the responsibility should be at director level.

Sustained top management commitment is essential if an environmental vision is to be translated into reality. The environmental words of the board must be matched by visible environmental action if the board is to be perceived as committed and credible.

The various comments submitted in the course of the *Managing the Relationship with the Environment* survey[3] suggest that environmental issues are expected to be of long-term and growing significance – so much so that they are expected to become an integral part of management thinking and planning, rather than largely the particular concern of technical specialists.

ATTITUDES TOWARDS REGULATION

Given the picture that has been painted so far, to what extent is government action desirable? The most appropriate role for government must depend upon how environmentally responsible public and private organisations are.

Those in business should not feel that they have been especially negligent in failing to bridge the gap between aspiration and achievement. Some variation between the promises of politicians on the election hustings and their performance in government is not unknown.

Misguided, even well-meaning, public initiatives can lead to unintended consequences. Regulatory measures concerning the environment highlight the gulf that can exist between rhetoric and reality. In some cases, its extent suggests that a conscious attempt may have been made to avoid reality.[14]

Milton Friedman has been a long-time exponent of the view that those in business within a market framework that allows voluntary transactions best discharge their social responsibility by focusing upon profitably satisfying their customers.[15] This suggests a concentration upon 'delivery', or turning customer aspiration into achievement, within a market context.

One market-based solution would be to tax a 'negative consequence', for example, a source of pollution according to the cost of cleaning it up.[16] Thus, an external cost would become internalised. This approach could be applied along an internal corporate process that crosses discrete units, or a supply chain among members of a network. An internal market could be created within the network organisation

In general, business appears to be in favour of commercial activities that are consistent with sustainable development, but opposed to any interference from government in terms of specific measures, or the imposition of a timetable to bring about a desired state.[17] The extent to which appropriate responses can be left to the free interplay of market forces will depend upon whether a critical mass of companies are able to translate aspiration into achievement.

To respond to particular public proposals, a company needs to identify its own environmental 'hot spots', and assess the impacts of proposed measures upon its operations and activities. Likely obstacles and barriers to implementation should be identified and examined. The preference of many legislators and regulators for 'workable solutions' means that corporate factors can sometimes be taken account of in the drafting of regulations, if they are notified early enough.

THE LURE OF THE SIMPLE

The action team, competing on speed, and focusing upon the 'vital few' priorities, loves simplicity. Objectives that are complicated and interrelated may be difficult to express as a few bullets points on a slide. Yet, many environmental issues are comparatively complex. Rapid progress may be difficult to measure in terms of quantifiable outputs.

The following views are typical of others which suggest that, in common with quality and general transformation initiatives, a 'wall' or 'hump' is often reached with the onset of the realisation that the issue may be more complex than was first thought:

'The initial enthusiasm turned to disinterest when we became aware of some of the practical problems. Recycling can actually be more damaging environmentally than disposal. Do you react to today's clamour, or tomorrow's realisation?'

'We were looking for something to report on in the next annual report. There are initiatives to demonstrate concern that we could publicise. But as for results, you can't change an industrial process overnight. We don't want to be accused of staging stunts.'

'I'm being pressured for results, but we are only a link in the chain. The public associates us strongly with the product, but the real environmental damage is done upstream. It takes time to build the relationships to tackle the problem, and when other companies are involved that's not something I can do at my level.'

In order to ensure that the complexity of what needs to be done is fully understood, a company should identify both the cross-functional and inter-organisational processes that deliver the company's negative environmental impacts, and those which will be needed to achieve significant improvements.

THE DRIVE FOR SPEED

The 'time culture' can impose unrealistic deadlines upon those who are charged with the responsibility of delivering improvements. When a supply chain is involved, the single company may be no more able to achieve a tangible impact upon the external environment than it can deliver all the value that is sought by a final customer. When others are involved, there is likely to be bargaining and negotiation.

Environmental initiatives should not result in the pressure for speed or 'response' driving out the long-term thinking that is required. Assuming 'results' are required, these might best be achieved as a result of flexibility within the framework of a longer-term relationship.

Today's craze can be tomorrow's memory. Too many managers assume that trends will continue longer than subsequently turns out to be the case. With many environmental policies taking many years to have a significant impact, companies face a dilemma similar to that encountered by those seeking to change attitudes and behaviour. By the time the outcomes initially sought have been achieved, the requirement may have changed.

In the USA, the state of California was one of the first to introduce a range of environmental measures. Today, there is something of a backlash against their consequences.[18] People are beginning to count the cost in terms of jobs and inconvenience. Also, after a time they become bored. Will environmentalism go the way of the skateboard and the Rubik's cube as people become more aware of the lack of achievement in relation to fundamental environmental problems?

Speed may be elusive if people are not empowered and equipped to respond. For example:

- perhaps cross-functional environmental task forces and teams should be established with clear accountabilities for action;
- techniques such as helps and hinders analysis could be used to identify enablers and barriers, and set 'vital few' priorities;
- the value of appropriate reward and remuneration signals should not be overlooked if people are to be motivated to respond.

BENCHMARK CORPORATE EXPERIENCE

Attempts to deal with 'isms' can open a Pandora's box of dashed hopes and unfulfilled expectations, especially when initiatives are not thought through. Enough noise may be raised to alarm some, while not enough is done to appease or deliver to others. Companies should beware of cosmetic programmes.

If properly implemented, environmental action can be compatible with other corporate objectives and priorities.

- 3M committed itself to a comprehensive programme to reduce the adverse environmental impact of its manaufacturing operations, and the implementation of this has occurred during a period of increased profitability.
- Rank Xerox has managed to gain market share in key sectors while implementing a demanding environmental improvement programme that aims to match or better the highest requirements.

In general, companies appear slow to learn from benchmark experience. Overall, while some companies are undertaking selected initiatives of a high technical quality, many are finding it difficult to achieve significant progress:

- they are not putting together a comprehensive, complementary and co-ordinated set of initiatives, embracing all the parties involved, that are likely to have a significant impact upon the environment;
- they are not achieving significant changes of attitude or behaviour, because all the various change elements that are necessary to achieve them have not been put in place.

CARROTS AND STICKS

There are incentives to encourage the laggards to close the gap with benchmark companies. First among these should be customer opportunity, but other stakeholders may become more interested in environmental performance, as opposed to environmental rhetoric.

The National Westminster Bank now examines the environmental policies and achievements of business customers prior to making loans. In certain cases loan applicants have been asked to undertake an environmental audit in order to provide the bank with the information it needs to make a decision for or against providing financial support. When bankers start worrying about it, perhaps some of the 'bean-counting' companies will begin to sit up.

In the background lurks the prospect of public intervention. Within the market environment, individual companies that are genuinely concerned about environmental issues can respond quickly and flexibly, tailoring their policies and actions to their particular situation. In comparison, action by government can be tardy, cumbersome and indiscriminate.

More convincing corporate performance could enable governments to establish broader frameworks, supplemented by specific action only where it is needed. Rather than be subjected to detailed regulation and intervention across the board, companies would be left to respond to the changing needs of their environmentally aware customers.

Progress towards the flexible network organisation can result in the framework and attitudes that are likely to increase the prospects of corporate success.

CHECKLIST

▶ Does your company monitor quality of life and environmental issues in the business environment continuously?

▶ Does it have a quality of life or environmental vision, and related goals and values?

▶ Has the vision been communicated and shared?

▶ Is your company aware of the views of customers, employees, suppliers, business partners and other 'stakeholders' on key quality of life and environmental issues?

▶ Has your company carried out any form of SWOT analysis to examine strengths, weaknesses, opportunities and threats?

▶ Has it determined how these will impact upon its operations and activities?

▶ What does your company plan to do in response?

▶ Have clear and measurable objectives been derived from the quality of life or environmental vision, goals and values, and is there an agreed strategy for their implementation?

▶ Are there clear quality of life or environmental roles and responsibilities?

▶ Have 'vital few' priorities been established, and have likely barriers and obstacles been identified?

▶ Have people been equipped and empowered to take the necessary actions?

▶ Are they motivated to respond and deliver?

▶ Have the cross-functional processes and the inter-departmental linkages necessary to deliver appropriate corporate responses been identified?

REFERENCES

1 Samuelson, R J (1992) 'The End Is Not at Hand' *Newsweek*, 1 June, p 32.
2 Holsti, K J (1992) *International Politics: A Framework for Analysis*, 6th edn, Prentice-Hall International, Hemel Hempstead, Herts.
3 Coulson-Thomas, C and Coulson-Thomas, S (1990) *Managing the Relationship with the Environment*, a survey sponsored by Rank Xerox (UK) Ltd, Adaptation Ltd, London.
4 Commission of the European Communities (1992) *The European and their Environment in 1992*, Press Release on Standard Eurobarometer Survey 37, IP (92) 457, Brussels, 4 June.
5 Horwitch, M (1982) *Clipped Wings*, The MIT Press, Cambridge, Mass.
6 Miller, A, Friday, C, Annin, P, and Barrett, T (1992) 'Do Boycotts Work?' *Newsweek*, 6 July, pp 42–4.
7 Knibb Gormezano and Partners (1992) *Opportunities in the North American Automotive Original Equipment and Aftermarket*, Department of Trade and Industry, London.
8 Cairncross, F (1991) *Costing the Earth*, Business Books, London.
9 Kirkman, P and Hope, C (1992) *Environmental Disclosure in UK Company Annual Reports*, Management Studies Group, University of Cambridge, Cambridge.
10 British Institute of Management (BIM) and Remuneration Economics (1992) *The 1992 National Management Salary Survey*, BIM, Corby.
11 Fogarty, M and Christie, I (1991) *Companies and Communities: Promoting Business Involvement in the Community*, Policy Studies Institute, London.
12 Tighe, C (1992) 'Green Rules Alarm Companies' *Financial Times*, 15 May, p 9.
13 Berkhout, F (1991) *Radioactive Waste: Politics and Technology*, Routledge, London.
14 Freeman, A M III and Haveman, R H (1972) 'Clean Rhetoric and Dirty Water' *The Public Interest*, no 28, Summer p 65.
15 Friedman, M (1962) *Capitalism and Freedom*, University of Chicago Press, Chicago.
16 Pearce, D, Turner, K and Bresson, I (1992) *Packaging Waste and the Polluter Pays Principle: A Taxation Solution*, Centre for Social and Economic Research on the Global Environment, University College, London.
17 Schmidheiny, S and the Business Council for Sustainable Development (1992) *Changing Course*, The MIT Press, Boston.
18 Kehoe, L (1992) 'Backlash in Golden State', Business and the Environment, *Financial Times*, 22 April, p 15.

11

INTERNATIONALISATION: MYTHS AND REALITIES

THE OPPORTUNITY

International opportunities abound for the network organisation with a global ambition. Companies are widening their perspectives to encompass the globe. The vision of BT is simply 'to become the most successful worldwide telecommunications group'.

The spread of privatisation, and the impact of a general slowdown in growth and particular national economic recessions is presenting the acquisitive with a flow of new opportunities, while barriers continue to fall as a result of deregulation and market forces. The global integration of manufacturing and other activities within international companies has now reached such a point that 'internal' trade within international network organisations accounts for a very significant and growing proportion of cross-border trade.

THE GLOBAL PERSPECTIVE

More people are developing a global perspective. Thinking global is the first step towards acting global.

All over the world, attitudes and perceptions are being influenced by the pervasiveness of certain media. While a younger generation may share a similar taste in popular music, their professional and executive parents may turn to Cable News Network (CNN). During the 1991 Gulf War, protagonists on both sides of the conflict could share the same images of unfolding events through the global news service CNN.

According to David Thompson, chairman of Rank Xerox UK: 'An increasing number of organisations are facing international competition. The image of the world as a global village has found reality in global communications and the global market.'[1]

Scratch what is perceived as a national institution, and an international organisation may be found underneath. For example, the Compagnie de Saint-Gobain may appear to be quintessentially French. It was established on the initiative of Louis XIV in an age of mirrors and chandeliers, when glass-making was regarded as a strategic industry. Yet today, two-thirds of the company's 100,000 employees are non-French.

In Ohmae's concept of 'the borderless world' such notions as home and overseas, or domestic and foreign markets, need to be replaced by a perspective of the corporation as equidistant from, and equally accessible to, all its customers.[2] This could be the view from any point within the network organisation.

THE CHALLENGE

While the opportunities are alluring, internationalisation is also bringing companies into contact with new areas of challenge, risk and uncertainty. Here are some examples:

- Wars, disorders, revolutions, disasters, and crises are a distressingly frequent feature of the international business environment. From a global perspective, they are no longer 'somewhere else', and as one director put it: 'When they happen they are big.'

- There are various states, and a variety of governmental and non-governmental organisations to contend with. Companies in the international arena cannot assume that 'the institutions' are 'on their side', or even on their wavelength.
- There are forces of both regionalisation and fragmentation at work. While western Europe attempts to unite, eastern Europe desolves into nationalism.
- In addition to customer and supplier risks, there are cultural and currency risks. New arenas of confrontation can arise for those unable to cope with a greater diversity of interests and perspectives.
- A network of cross-border links and relationships may need to be formed in order to meet the needs of global customers and markets. Communication within the network has to overcome barriers of distance, culture and time.
- The globalisation of the marketplace has given rise to a growing requirement for the internationalisation of management, and the capacity to access and harness relevant skill, regardless of location and nationality.

To operate effectively in the international business environment, a company needs to be open and receptive. There are relevant political, economic, social, technological and market developments at national, regional (eg EC) and international levels, to be monitored. Without the nourishment that comes from awareness, openness and external relationships, the closed corporation finds it difficult to develop the capability to respond appropriately.

Information on national and market differences needs to be up to date. In Japan, for example, there is now greater mobility of technical and professional staff in some sectors. The concept of lifetime employment is being challenged. As with customers, it is important to listen to people on the ground. Learning is more of a necessity and less of a luxury.

Dealing with foreign governments, as well as overseas customers, may be a new experience for some companies. The multinational company (MNC), at both the local and the strategic level, may have to reconcile the competing demands of responding to both global competitive threats and opportunities, and 'host' government requirements.[3]

THE EVIDENCE

The initial sources of evidence for this chapter are a 1990 Adaptation survey carried out for Surrey European Management School (SEMS),[1] and interviews undertaken by the author on behalf of Manpower plc as principal author and co-presenter of the 'employment and training' module of the CBI 'Initiative 1992', and in preparation for other of the surveys listed in Appendix 1.

The SEMS survey[1] specifically concerns 'human resource development for international operation'. It involved 92 organisations employing over $2\frac{1}{2}$ million people and with a combined turnover in excess of £300 billion.

Subsequently, a further programme of interviews with senior MNC and transnational company executives was undertaken in preparation for the book, *Creating the Global Company*.[4] This develops at greater length the various themes that are touched upon in this chapter.

THE GAP BETWEEN ASPIRATION AND ACHIEVEMENT

For many companies 'internationalisation' remains an elusive goal. For some, reality extends no further than the paragraphs in the annual report which refer to international ambitions. A typical view is: 'Internationalisation sounds nice, but what does it actually mean?'

At all levels, there appear to be problems in internationalising the people of those companies with international visions and ambitions. To take some examples:

- The membership of the main boards of most companies is made up exclusively of directors having the nationality of the 'home country'. While the situation is changing, very few companies have international boards.
- Efforts to build a more balanced international management team are frustrated by the fact that managers of different countries vary greatly in the extent to which they are prepared to be mobile. In the bureaucratic form of organisation many 'non-nationals' would 'rule themselves out' of consideration for head office positions, even if they were approached.
- The column inches devoted to international and 'Euro' recruitment drives are rarely matched by the number of young people taking up appointments. Most graduate intakes appear to be largely made up of 'nationals'.[5]

Too often, groups of people of a particular nationality are locked into territorial and departmental ghettos. The bureaucratic limits that have been placed upon their ambitions and prospects make them slaves rather than citizens of the MNC.

THE ROOTS OF FRUSTRATION

The internationalisation of management teams is more talked about than practised. Intention is not being translated into achievement for a variety of reasons, as follows.

- Many organisations are not thinking through what internationalisation means for them. In some sectors, such as shipbuilding, it may be possible to generate a high proportion of overseas turnover, while employing few foreign nationals. In services industries the reverse may be the case.
- While there are surface manifestations of internationalism, such as international travel and the ability to speak foreign languages, few managers appear to have developed an international perspective.
- While articulating the need for international managers, many companies do little to develop and retain their local managers. A disproportionate amount of many training budgets is devoted to expatriates, while 'non-nationals', believing their future career prospects are limited, are lured away by local competitors.
- At a time when some companies are seeking to develop a cadre of mobile international managers, a growing proportion of their managers appear to be reluctant to move abroad. The 'dual-career' family, and the desire to allow children to complete their education without interruption, become location anchors.
- There is a widespread mismatch between the efforts devoted to encouraging, preparing and locating managers abroad, and the attention given to the problem of repatriation at the conclusion of an overseas assignment. Many expatriates experience severe problems in reintegrating back into the domestic corporate organisation.
- Although greater use is being made of international project groups and teams as a means of internationalisation, relatively few managers are being specifically equipped with project management skills.
- Those with project management skills tend to see their future prospects as lying in such traditional areas as construction or IT project management, rather than the 'mainstream' management of multifunction, multilocation and multinational teams.[6]

- The concept of multinational team working may remain as no more than an element of the 'vision', unless people are equipped to become aware of the impact of their own culture and those of colleagues upon attitudes and behaviour within a multicultural group.
- Activities are rooted territorially, rather than spread around the network. Thus, many companies talk internationalisation while retaining all the key decision-making capacity and core activities such as R & D in the 'home' country.

Major multinational companies are recognising that a cosmetic commitment to 'Europe' or international customers is no longer enough. According to Paul Allaire, chairman and CEO of Xerox Corporation: 'Our commitment to Europe is not just rhetoric. We are investing heavily in the critical areas .... research, development and high-tech manufacturing.'

MYTH, HYPE AND REALITY

Because some markets are becoming global, it does not follow that all are. Assumption should never be allowed to take the place of observation. Every company needs to think through what internationalisation means for its own activities and prospects.

Honda came unstuck with its vision of the global car. For a period, the lure of the economies of scale of global production blinded the company to the realities of local market differences and a desire for customisation.

There is much misunderstanding concerning the requirements for, and indicators of, successful internationalisation. To take two examples.

- Big companies are not necessarily the most international in terms of the geographical distribution of their business. Siemens employs 350,000 people, but almost half of its turnover occurs in Germany, and some three-quarters of sales arise in western Europe.
- In some sectors it is possible to develop a significant international business while employing relatively few people abroad. In 1990, only some 4 per cent of the employees of the Celsius Group of Sweden were working on an Australian project, the total value of which was expected to amount to over $2\frac{1}{2}$ times the group turnover for the year.

Even when a company's employees are 'spread around the globe', it does not follow that more than a small minority of them may have an international perspective. As one interviewee pointed out: 'Having offices around the world does not make you international. Most of our people are imprisoned in national operating companies. We can't use them to satisfy a customer anywhere else.'

INTERNATIONAL AWARENESS

True internationalisation is of attitude, awareness, approach and perspective. It is evidenced by openness, tolerance and active encouragement of cultural and national diversity. Asea Brown Boveri, British Gas, The Netherlands company DSM, ICL and Nissan have all recognised the need for managers to have an international awareness and perspective. Drucker has recognised the need for the perspective of the manager to embrace global developments.[7]

According to one director: 'You don't have to fill airport lounges to be international, or train everyone in foreign languages. That may enrich their lives. You probably do need to broaden their perspective, and to focus them on understanding ... customers wherever they may be.' Mobility and travel *per se* may reinforce prejudices, and build bigots.

People can be internationalised in many ways, from visits, exchanges, job swaps to joining international project groups, task forces and teams. Here are two examples:

- 3M broadens the perspective of its managers by giving them parallel home and international responsibilities. Companies adopting this approach need to take care not to so overload executives that they experience a conflict of priorities between different roles. If additional responsibilities are given, other aspects of workload may need to be reassessed.
- L M Ericsson has sought to embed the qualities needed for effective international operation into the corporate culture. Moving roles around the organisation and managers through various international projects and teams helps to build a multiple perspective. Opportunities to come together across traditional divides expose many individuals to a diversity of viewpoints.

Companies that have thought it through use a combination of approaches, rather than the 'single solution'. Internationalisation is also integrated into mainstream processes, rather than regarded as a 'bolt-on for those who need it'.

MOBILITY AND INTERNATIONALISATION

Mobility may, or may not, be an indicator of internationalisation, according to its purpose. The appearance of internationalisation in the form of the jet-setting executive could conceal the reality of a lack of localisation. More local involvement might obviate the need for so much travel. The acid test should be the extent to which customer requirements are met.

The flexibility of the network organisation can allow major corporations to create internal labour and information markets to overcome the imperfections of external markets. The network can grow or contract organically, according to market opportunities and economic circumstances, without the dramas of starting up or closing local operations associated with the bureaucratic form of organisation.

Mobility has its costs. For example, after an initial 'honeymoon period', an adverse reaction may set in, with 'the vision of mountains, sea and sand being replaced by the reality of crime, disease and telephones that do not work'.[4] Mobility can be expensive, and may create tensions between expatriates and local managers. On the other hand, staff travelling overseas may obtain opportunities to work with and learn from customers.

Mobility is widely perceived as a means of equipping managers with an international perspective. In reality, it may provide them with some insight into particular countries and cultures, without developing a broader international awareness. Ford takes the view that an international perspective should precede the assumption of international responsibilities, rather than be left to arise as a consequence of them.

THE IMPORTANCE OF INTERNATIONALISATION

We have seen that a variety of changes are occurring within corporate organisations as a consequence of the transition from bureaucratic to responsive network organisation. There is a widespread preoccupation with quality, culture change and other corporate programmes. How important is internationalisation in comparison with other human resource issues and objectives?

The results of recent surveys suggest it is not among the top human resource priorities, particularly in the case of UK companies. However, if other priorities are achieved, the form of more flexible organisation that results will facilitate internationalisation. Let us consider the evidence.

- For the participants in the 1990 *Beyond Quality* survey[8] '1992 and the 'Single Market' emerges as 12th of 16 'customer issues'. 'Serving the international customer', however, ranks 7th among the issues, and 'global competition' 10th. The issue of 'global versus local market' was ranked as 15th out of 16 issues.
- This result is consistent with the findings of the 1989 BIM report, *The Responsive Organisation*.[9] The 1992 Single European Market ranks 10th in terms of the number of 'very important' replies, and 9th in terms of overall importance among the top human resource priorities.
- The 1990 SEMS survey[1] confirms that 'Europeanisation' and 'internationalisation' are not perceived as being the top priority issues. 'Internationalisation : Preparation for the globalisation of business' is ranked 6th, and 'Europeanisation : Preparation for 1992' is ranked 10th out of 12 human resource issues (Table 1.1).
- In a survey undertaken by Adaptation Ltd for the Institute of Directors[10] 'Europeanisation: Preparation for 1992' and 'Internationalisation; Preparation for the globalisation of business' came bottom of a list of 9 boardroom issues when 'important' and 'very important' replies were added together.

Follow-up interviews suggest that internationalisation is of considerable significance to particular companies. It could also be of absolute importance, while the higher ranking of certain other factors might be due in part because these are regarded as conducive of internationalisation.

THE IMPORTANCE OF QUALITIES ASSOCIATED WITH INTERNATIONALISATION

Another perspective on the relative significance of internationalisation is the importance attached to qualities and capabilities relating to it, in comparison with other management skills. The evidence suggests a low positioning.

- In the SEMS survey,[1] capabilities relating to 'European', 'international' and 'transnational' operation, including language skills, rank at the bottom of a list of qualities UK companies seek in members of their senior management teams.
- When the replies of non-UK European and international companies are also included, the ranking of qualities is as shown in Table 11.1. 'Strategic awareness' and 'customer focus' head the list of qualities that are sought. These may relate to internationalisation, but are not specific to it. An Ashridge survey has also found 'strategic awareness' to be top of a list of characteristics needed by international managers.[11]
- In a study undertaken by Adaptation with Exeter University, not one respondent mentioned the possession of a working knowledge of, or fluency in, a foreign language as a criterion used in selecting members for a board.[12] Over a third of the respondents in an earlier Exeter University survey of directors had a working knowledge of a foreign language, and over one in seven claimed fluency in at least one foreign language.[13]

The qualities being developed by many companies appear not to be specifically related to internationalisation. One human resource director explained: 'We have not really thought through what becoming an international company means. ... We go for the obvious qualities that are always valuable. ... But [with internationalisation] we are back to changing attitudes ... and also preferences in terms of who you work with. ... It's not easy to do.'

Table 11.1 *Senior Management Team Qualities*
Ranked in order of 'very important' replies (%)

Strategic awareness	76
Customer focus	61
Individual responsibility	59
Communication skills	52
Creativity	43
Perspective	40
Team player	35
Objectivity	34
Self-discipline	34
International awareness and perspective	28
Breadth	28
Transnational confidence and effectiveness	21
European awareness and perspective	18
Language ability	1

Source: Human Resource Development for International Operation, 1990

THE GOAL OF THE NETWORK ORGANISATION

Over time, as the volume of 'overseas', 'foreign' or 'international' business grows, companies appear to evolve through a series of identifiable stages.[4] Initially, foreign orders are treated as exceptions. Then, as more of them are received, an export department may be set up. This may grow into an international division, as arrangements for various 'territories' have to be established and managed.

In time, the establishment of local operating companies may be justified, and the multinational company may come into existence. This could evolve into a complex, if not confused, matrix of internal functional and geographic reporting relationships. Honeywell Europe is an example of a company that operates as a matrix, with both business units and national operating companies having profit responsibilities.

The next stage in the process of evolution is to move from multinational matrix to international network. The concept of the network organisation is particularly suited to internationalisation:

- the resources of traditional multinational companies are imprisoned in the 'mini bureaucracies' of self-contained national operating companies;
- the global network offers the prospect of being able to overcome the barriers of nationality, distance and time in order to bring together teams composed of the best people in order to address the needs of individual customers, wherever they may be.

As one chairman put it: 'The international network organisation must be the end point of corporate transformation.' The coming together of *ad hoc* groups and multinational and cross-border teams to tackle specific problems was envisaged by Mintzberg's categorisation of the 'adhocracy'.[14]

NCR, Procter and Gamble, and Unilever operate as transnationals. International headquarters functions, relating to significant areas of the business, are located outside of the country of ultimate incorporation. Global responsibilities may be spread between a network of locations in different countries, rather than concentrated at a single point.

THE NETWORK SOLUTION

We have seen that the company is becoming a network, as 'electronic' links are developed with customers, suppliers and business partners. Experts and specialists should aim to become facilitators, harnessing relevant expertise by all available means in such a way that it can be applied to add value for customers. As networks become global, much effort will be put into articulating or propounding a distinct and compelling mission that can transcend national boundaries.

Whether the customer is becoming European or international, or both European and international, a company intent on supplying its requirements will need to find a means of communicating rapidly across national boundaries. The network organisation must itself become European and international.

The corporate network should be sufficiently flexible to allow resources to be accessed and activity undertaken at local, regional or global level according to requirements and comparative advantage. The aim of management should be to minimise the costs of co-ordination or barriers to communication and interaction that might otherwise distort the location or focus of activity.

As chairmen and CEOs seek to build more flexible and international network organisations, the BIM *Beyond Quality* report[8] suggests that the drive towards 'internationalisation' of managers is perceived as a means to an end, defined in terms of customer satisfaction, rather than as an objective in its own right. If this is the case, 'internationalisation' might best be achieved by focusing upon its contribution to the satisfaction of customer requirements.

CUSTOMERS – THE PURPOSE OF INTERNATIONALISATION

Customers should determine the nature of the 'international' responses that are required. For example, as MNCs increasingly demand 'European' and 'international' solutions to regional or global problems, so their suppliers are having to establish European and international project groups, teams and task forces in order to respond.

The teams that result are likely to be increasingly multifunctional, multilocation and multinational.[8,9] Team members will need to be able to work with those of other cultures and nationalities.

Hawker Siddeley is using an international management programme to bring groups together to focus upon market sectors that cross national borders. It is hoped that programme participants will gain both an international and a customer-focused perspective.

Prior to establishing a mission, objectives, strategy, organisation and management processes, a basic question needs to be asked – who is the customer? Can the customer be defined and understood in terms of attitudes and values, location, age, sex, nationality or other attributes?

As we move into the 1990s, values and lifestyle preferences may become more significant in customer categorisation.[8] Organisations will increasingly define themselves in terms of their customers. The interaction of supplier and customer may help to shape the attitudes and values of each, according to the depth of the relationship.

MATCHING CORPORATE AND CUSTOMER CULTURE

A conscious effort should be made to match international corporate and customer cultures (Figure 11.1). Here are two examples:

- Where both corporate and customer culture is differentiated, diversity should result as efforts are made to tailor and match at the local level. When both are undifferentiated, a common global approach can be adopted. A matching of cultures allows the company to build upon its strengths.

- When corporate and customer culture do not match, help may be needed to achieve cultural adaptation. Where customer culture is differentiated, while that of the company is undifferentiated, local partners may be needed to tailor locally. When the customer culture is undifferentiated, while that of the company is differentiated, help may be needed to build global brand image and awareness.

International Corporate Culture

International Customer Culture	Differentiated	Undifferentiated/ Common
Differentiated	Encourage diversity, tailoring and matching at the local level [Build on 'strength']	Build links with local partners able to tailor locally [Need help]
Undifferentiated/ Common	Build global awareness/brand through use of international agencies [Need help]	Encourage common global approach [Build on 'strength']

Figure 11.1 *Matching Corporate and Customer Culture*

The long-term customer could be a more significant 'network member' than the peripheral or marginal employee. Some network companies may list their major customers and collaborators alongside or, in some cases, instead of their key employees in their profiles, brochures and annual reports. The portfolio of customers represents the essence, purpose and drive of the flexible network organisation .

In a global, and increasingly inter-dependent, marketplace, a company should view the world in terms of concentrations of actual and potential customers. These may, or may not, match state borders. In different locations, there will be cores of greatest opportunity surrounded by concentric rings of prioritised prospects.

Suppliers and customers should work together to meet customer requirements.[8] Joint teams could be set up with agreed objectives. The 'sale' may become a project to be managed. Awareness is growing of the margin and profitability benefits of emphasising higher added-value considerations and breaking out of the 'commodity products trap'.

In some sectors, this can involve working with customers to develop their understanding of what can be achieved and enhance their expectations. Within such a relationship, the gap between stimulated expectation and delivered achievement will be painfully apparent. As one manager put it: 'At least in the bureaucracy, few customers know how really bad you are.' Within some corporate bureaucracies, the functional barriers are such that 'the people next door don't know'.

THE AGE OF NETWORKS AND NETWORK RELATIONSHIPS

International networks of alliances, consortia, co-operative ventures and other arrangements are being forged as companies are coming together in various forms of co-operative activity to cope with the scale of international challenges and opportunities.

In a sector such as telecommunications there could at any one time be a kaleidoscopic pattern of parallel negotiations, as major players consider which grouping to join. For example, consider the situation at the beginning of 1992.

- Deutsche Telekom, and Nippon Telegraph and Telephone (NTT) could join consortia led by either BT of the UK, or France Telecom and AT&T and MCI of the USA.
- New players such as the Orion satellite consortium involving British Aerospace, Com Dev of Canada, General Dynamics, the Japanese trading group Nissho Iwai, Kingston Communications, Matra of France and Stet of Italy were planning to enter the growing market opportunity created by the desire of companies to create global networks.
- Companies with global networks were exploring ways in which these could be used by other companies. General Electric Information Services is an example of a company set up to offer a range of business services across an established corporate network.
- International groupings were also coming together to meet the international network needs of particular sectors. An example is the Financial Network Association which includes MCI, Mercury Communications and France Telecom.

In the early 1960s, growing awareness of the activities of multinational companies in international society, and the emergence of a network of links between them, and increased functional co-operation between governmental and non-governmental organisations, caused Haas to question the extent to which the nation state would continue to exist in its current form.[15]

There are still corporations that appear to ignore the emerging reality of a network of links and relationships when equipping young people for a 'career with the company'. Few companies are addressing adequately the need for network venture and relationship management skills. As one director put it: 'We are back to throwing people in at the deep end, and there are more drownings than there should be.'

NAÏVE EXPECTATIONS

A corporation can be naïve as well as negligent. Many companies are not thinking though the consequences of their drive for internationalisation. They are 'innocents abroad'.

Table 11.2 sets out selected enablers of the transition from multinational to international network organisation. The impacts are felt, and the requirements make demands, in many areas. The attitudes that help the transition are those associated with the open and organic network, while the 'hinders' are likely to be the closed attitudes and debilitating prejudices associated with the self-contained, bureaucratic form of organisation.

Each form of organisation presents its own management problems, as follows.

- The transition from multinational to international network organisation may result in the potential for controllable travel costs being replaced by the reality of uncontrollable telecommunications costs.

Table 11.2 *The Transition from Multinational to International Network Organisation*

Encourage international networking and cross-border all channel communication	Involve international participation in planning and issue monitoring, and management exercises
Create opportunities for informal international contact	Encourage shared and joint use of resources and facilities on a regional or international basis
Recruit to secure most relevant skills on an international basis	
Replace national procedures with international project groups, task forces and teams	Build interfaces between national IT networks, and develop a global computing and telecommunications network
Strengthen functional, business and sector units, and customer account groups, at the expense of national geographic units	Encourage organic growth and the shift of power and resources away from historic centres of bureaucratic influence and strength, and to areas of greatest customer opportunity.
Create mutual respect for, and build understanding of, cultural differences and variety	

Source: Creating the Global Company, 1992

- Along with an enhanced capability, may come a greater vulnerability to sabotage or commercial espionage on a global scale.
- Interface, funding and management problems may follow in the wake of technologies that are developed more rapidly than they can be applied.
- Insufficient thought may be given to the behavioural aspects. An interviewee commented: 'Just assume that ... behavioural problems will be there.'
- It may not be easy to establish a basis for allocating the cost of the network between its various members. Inevitably, costs will be compared with the benefits.

The people in the spotlight may be the gung-ho managers who are rushing about the world, signing up international joint ventures and arrangements. Those whose commitment to internationalisation appears to be in doubt may actually be the cooler heads, addressing such questions as: 'Who is going to manage this?' or 'What about the infrastructure requirements?'

One director of business development raised a telling point: 'How many of these [arrangements] can we handle without confusing the customers, ourselves and just about everyone else?' Some companies ought to pose the question: 'What would we look like if it all actually happened?' Again, one encounters the phenomenon of companies being saved from chaos by their own inability to implement.

JOINT VENTURE MANAGEMENT

The wise person has every reason to be cautious. A high proportion of joint ventures fail. While strategists assess the relative merits of different options for arrangements and joint ventures, their management colleagues 'bite their nails'.

- Those in human resources worry about where the people will come from to run a joint venture, when few, if any, existing managers may have had experience of operating within a joint venture framework.
- The marketing team may worry about whether proposed 'partners' share assumptions, and have a similar understanding regarding customer attitudes, values and motivations. Will there be empathy between a prospective 'partner' and existing customers?
- The engineers will be concerned about the extent to which there could be a mismatch between the technologies of partner organisations. Their IT colleagues

may have similar concerns about the compatibility of systems where IT may have been acquired from different suppliers, and 'the boxes may not talk to each other'.

- A range of people from general managers to corporate communicators may face the challenge of accommodating and sharing visions, values, goals and objectives that have derived from different cultural contexts with those of further nationalities and cultures.

The gap between aspiration and reality could be the result of external political factors rather than commercial logic. Arrangement negotiations, such as those between BT and IBM, or involving AT&T and Cable and Wireless, may be stopped or reviewed as a result of national political considerations. Awareness and sensitivity can be especially important in the international dimension.

JOINT VENTURE EXPLOITATION

Too many advocates of 'relationship management' appear to believe in the inherent 'goodness' of relationships, independently of degree of commitment or shared vision and values. In a significant proportion of joint ventures, one party 'rips off' the other.

Traditionally, if anything is retained in the host country it is research and development. Companies and nations jealously guard their intellectual capital. Yet, international co-operation in research and development is bringing many companies into partnership relationships, and governments are more encouraging of such links. For example:

- in the IT sector new pairings announced in 1992 within the space of a few months included Apple and Sharp, Apple and Sony, AT&T and NEC, Hewlett-Packard and Oki Electric, Hewlett-Packard and Samsung, IBM and Bull, IBM and Thomson-CSF, and Motorola and Alps Electric.
- in the UK the government's advisory body Acost (Advisory Committee on Science and Technology) has recommended that a higher proportion of R & D spending should be devoted to European and international research projects.[16]

Partners should be chosen with care. One director warned: 'You need to keep your wits about you.' In view of the relatively high number of strategic alliances and joint ventures that fail, a more flexible approach is to establish links and relationships on a project-by-project basis.

CORPORATE TRANSFORMATION — THE BENEFITS

Shared goals, common values, a distinct corporate culture and pervasive tools, techniques and approaches can help to hold an international network together. There are operational advantages. For example:

- those who are internationally mobile, or who work with others across national borders, may 'know what to expect' when they join a new group or team, and find it easier to become integrated;
- similarly, mobile customers, or those in segments that transcend national borders, or who buy at the regional (eg European) or international level, may be able to develop certain consistent expectations as to the standards of quality they may receive at various locations;
- the creation of a distinct and international corporate culture makes it easier for people to come together in *ad hoc* groups and teams. They will have certain expectations concerning the way colleagues think and the tools, techniques and approaches they are likely to adopt to tackle problems.

At the same time, as Kenichi Ohmae points out[17], successful internationalisation in a particular market sector may require that a corporation becomes an 'insider' in each of the indigenous business communities making up his concept of the 'triad'. This demands a degree of local flexibility.

We have also seen that corporate culture should be compatible with customer culture (Figure 11.1). Hoechst has recognised the need for diversity by allowing each element of the business to organise in a way that is most appropriate in terms of its own situation and circumstances.

CORPORATE TRANSFORMATION — THE DANGERS

Corporate transformation can cut across internationalisation. Several interviewees were involved in international initiatives to cascade or spread one or more change programmes such as 'quality' throughout a corporate organisation. A number of concerns were apparent.

- Exposing corporate initiatives to those from a different national and cultural background sometimes reveals the extent to which they are 'culture bound'. The universal panacea may turn out to be very much the product of a 'home country' or 'head office' culture, and unintended consequences can arise at the local level.
- The imposition of norms and standards may be in conflict with the desire to build greater tolerance for cultural diversity. The international organisation may wish to accommodate a mixture of cultures in order that some do not feel excluded, and all are encouraged to give of their best.
- An international company may need to establish working relations with many governments. This requires the flexibility to respond to a range of industrial policies, quite different approaches to the regulation of business, and attitudes to what are perceived as non-national companies that vary from the inviting to the paranoiac.

Multicultural awareness should not be sacrificed upon an altar of monolithic corporate culture. Closer 'positive sum' relationships with 'international' customers require effective cross-cultural communication. International segmentation, prioritisation and differentiation require an understanding of the relevance and significance of similarities and differences across national boundaries.

INTERNATIONAL EMPOWERMENT

An important element of a corporate transformation programme may encounter unexpected problems when applied internationally. Consider, for example, empowerment.

- An empowerment strategy may present particular difficulties for the company that has traditionally been reluctant to devolve management discretion to the locally recruited and foreign employees who run overseas subsidiaries. These may be little more than distribution outlets, with the key decisions regarding what is sold, and at what price, being taken many thousands of miles away at a head office.
- The company that is relatively self-contained at home may have local joint venture partners in overseas operations. The implementation of an empowerment strategy overseas might be perceived as a new departure, the sharing of power with other enterprises.

One manager cautioned: 'Some concepts travel better than others. The "OK" guy from the country you met at business school knows the score ... back home people think differently.' Something that seems second nature to one culture can bewilder or appear meaningless in a different cultural context.

QUALITY AND DIVERSITY

In spite of the hype of advertisers and their cronies, all the trends are not pointing in the direction of the undifferentiated global brand. There are people out there who think, feel and dream in a billion different ways. They are individual human beings, not a line on a graph.

We saw in Chapter 9 that technical or product quality of itself is becoming less of a differentiator between suppliers. Quality in terms of reliability and delivery is increasingly assumed, and by itself may not secure competitive advantage.[8]

More demanding customers may switch their attention to tailoring to particular circumstances, or less tangible factors, as they seek to become comfortable with what is offered. As a consequence, national differences may become more, rather than less, significant.

Tailoring and the satisfaction of softer requirements are likely to require a closer relationship between customer and supplier. In some cases the boundary between the two may become more difficult to discern. Again, joint teams or project groups, involving both customer and supplier staff, may be set up to explore and meet particular requirements. Members of such teams will be out there with the people. They will need sensitivity, intuition and cross-cultural awareness rather than media schedules.

LANGUAGE SKILLS

When among people, it helps if what they are saying can be understood. We have seen that little importance is attached to language skills for their own sake.[1,11] However, according to the BIM *Beyond Quality* survey:[8]

- establishing longer-term relationships with customers, and determining what represents 'value' to them are regarded as priority 'management' issues;
- respondents believe that, in particular, more attention needs to be devoted to communications *from* the customer. To be heard, they must be able to penetrate the corporate shell.

The open company understands incoming messages. Language training should reflect the requirements of customers, and the need for effective communication with them. Switchboard operators, receptionists and secretaries may be the first point of contact with customers.

Which languages should be learned will depend upon the requirements of existing customers, and which markets are being targeted. For example:

- if the aim is to become an international rather than a European company, Spanish and Portuguese may need to assume a higher priority;
- even in fields such as computing and electronics, where a high proportion of the documentation may be in English, service and retail staff in direct contact with customers may need local language skills.

A language audit should be undertaken of the availability of language skills, and the language requirements of establishing relationships with customers and delivering value to them. A distinction should be made between reading, writing, listening and speaking skills.

RECONCILING UNITY WITH DIVERSITY

While propagating the rhetoric of internationalisation, the head offices of many companies with extensive international operations appear to be the exclusive preserve of nationals from the 'home country'. This need not be so. For one director: 'Our vision is international, that is the important thing. Our people and resources can be almost anywhere so long as you can get hold of them.'

Matsushita, in responding to the need to increase international awareness and mutual understanding between operating units and the centre, decided to bring 200 foreign managers into its head office in Osaka. The company also ensures that there is an input from subsidiary companies into its key management processes.

The imposition of a standard corporate culture can prevent a company from obtaining the full benefits of diversity within international teams. A coming together of distinct values, viewpoints and approaches within a group can be a source of creativity. Xerox and Rank Xerox have recognised the importance and positive benefits of diversity in both a domestic and international context.

'[B]uilding and sustaining a healthy, empowered work team necessitates the recognition and optimisation of diversity within the team. Each team is characterised by a unique array of talents, experiences and backgrounds. These individual qualities should be blended harmoniously, rather than toned down and homogenised.

Managing diversity is one of our greatest potential advantages over [competitors who] are unified in their culture, history, and race. As superb as they are, this is a limiting factor. By contrast, we represent a cross-section of the richest mix of ethnic groups and races. The richer the mix, the broader the perspectives and the greater the creativity. Each ... manager is faced with the challenge of developing the real potential of our fantastic mix of people, thus capitalising on the competitive opportunity offered by employee diversity.

Corporate transformation can be compatible with both the desire for a global unity of purpose in terms of vision and goals, and diversity in response to local market conditions. Thus the technology of the organisation could be used to achieve what has been termed 'the computer integrated company',[19] while empowerment could be a means of achieving local diversity. Success demands that these distinct change elements be in harmony rather than in conflict.

INTERNATIONALISATION IN PRACTICE

Companies in general are not finding it easy to increase the international awareness of their managers. Those with a high proportion of their staff based in the 'home country' may lack opportunities to give rising executives experience of working abroad. The SEMS survey[1] throws some light on what steps major European companies are taking to 'internationalise' their managers:

- Over four out of ten respondents develop a 'European and/or international awareness and perspective', and 'capacity for transnational effectiveness' in senior managers by means of international work secondments, exchanges, transfers or assignments.
- Three out of ten cited work, or work-related, participation in international secondments, job rotations, exchanges, projects or task forces, or participation in international activities, including conferences and meetings, as a means of building international awareness.
- A similar number referred to the use of specific courses. Internal courses were cited more than twice as often as external courses. There is a strong preference for developing the qualities sought by integrating working and learning, by means of company-specific programmes and projects at the place of work.

The SEMS survey[1] contained an open question concerning how the process of internationalisation of senior management might be improved. A wide range of responses were received.

- Over a half of the participants felt that some improvement could be made. The responses suggest that, in the main, what is being sought is incremental improvement to current practice.
- There is little, if any, perception of a new or different 'external' solution that might be employed to better equip managers for international operation. While initiating the rhetoric of internationalisation, companies are generally reactive when it comes to action.

Interviews suggest that some enthusiasm is giving way to caution. Encouragingly, many of the practical steps which are being taken to internationalise managers result from organisational responses to the changing needs of customers.

EVOLUTIONARY EXPLORATION

While other corporate initiatives 'proceed at the gallop', many companies are cautiously 'feeling their way' with 'internationalisation'. The evidence we have examined suggests the following.

- Internationalisation tends not to be sought for its own sake, but only in so far as it relates to building more satisfactory long-term relationships with customers. The key human resource priority is creating a more flexible and responsive organisation.
- Few organisations appear to feel that anything approaching the whole of their management teams need to be 'internationalised'.[1] The ability to operate across national frontiers is not perceived as a key quality to be built and sought in all managers.

It is encouraging that some companies are recognising that their approach to 'internationalisation' must take into account a multiplicity of differing requirements. There is a requirement for flexibility and tailoring rather than the imposition of standard corporate programmes.[1]

On the other hand, few companies appear to have thought through the people consequences and requirements of becoming a genuinely international organisation. Also, the leisurely pace of implementation, and a relatively low priority in relation to other corporate initiatives, may result in a failure to adjust in time to cope with the full rigours of the more competitive international marketplace that is opening up.

LEARNING FROM OTHERS

Companies should be more prepared to learn from others. For example:

- Euro-benchmarking could be used, managers could be encouraged to compare notes with those with similar responsibilities and problems in non-competing companies;
- the board and senior management team might benefit from a greater range of international experience. Perhaps more non-nationals should be brought on to the board as non-executive directors.

Many companies devote much time and effort to external benchmarking, while doing little to learn from other parts of the same organisation. In an international context, different national subsidiaries or joint venture partners could learn from each other:

- the Swedish chemical company Perstorp moves staff between divisions and business units as part of its international management programme;
- following an exchange of shareholdings in 1990, Renault and Volvo have exchanged staff. This both develops the individuals concerned and helps the companies to learn from each other.

A company could also actively learn from its international customers.

EUROPEANISATION V INTERNATIONALISATION

For many of those interviewed, internationalisation to meet the demands of a global market rather than Europeanisation is regarded as the more significant issue, particularly by CEOs.

The significance of the emergence of the 'Single Market' depends upon its impact upon customers. The outward-looking company will not focus exclusively upon the 'direct' impact of '1992'. It will also be aware of the 'indirect' impacts that result from the direct impact of '1992' upon its customers and competitors. Focusing upon the changing needs of real customers is preferable to hypothetical speculation about the possible consequences of falling barriers.

Some companies have already signalled their intentions to become Euro-enterprises. Rather than deal with separate operating companies in each Member State, the Euro-company may wish to focus a purchase negotiation at a single point. European solutions may be sought to European problems. The network organisation needs to be able to access its capability and apply it at such locations. Too many companies still operate almost exclusively through national subsidiaries.

CONCERNS AND REALISATIONS

Many companies wish to be European, but within the context of a carefully thought-out international business strategy. Within Europe itself, they may see both threats and opportunities in the move towards a Single Market. Here are some examples.

- The full benefits of diversity may not be found within a single region. An organisation based in the EC might feel that corporations in the USA or Japan might be more complementary business partners than companies in Europe with similar strengths and weaknesses.
- The benefits to consumers of greater variety and choice, and lower prices, that result from a lowering of trade barriers can come straight off the bottom lines of producers. Euro-purchasing can erode price differentials and further reduce profit margins.
- The desire for flexibility may need to be tempered with accommodation to national restrictions relating to recruitment and new patterns of work. This may inhibit what would otherwise allow each business unit or account group to respond best to customer needs and opportunities.

One CEO looking for wider opportunities, said: 'I don't want all my eggs in one basket, however attractive it looks.'

The impact of 1992 is likely to be greatest for those companies which are currently facing high non-tariff barriers. The extent to which an individual firm will benefit from a lowering of barriers will depend upon their comparative advantage and relative productivity.

CRACKS AND FISSURES

The challenge for many national champion companies is how best to evolve into European and international organisations in order to meet the changing requirements of customers in the global marketplace better. The need to change can shake the foundations of traditional arrangements.

Cracks are beginning to appear in the façade of the MNC model of operation. National operating companies, like individual employees, are seeking greater discretion:

- aware of local preferences and needs, eager to generate local added value in meeting local customer requirements, they are demanding greater freedom from central control;
- many are no longer content just to be local distributors of a product designed and produced overseas within a strategy set by a board whose view of the world is limited to that of a group of similar people largely drawn from one company.

Desperate companies are advocating diversity while seeking to export panaceas, slogans, standard solutions and simplistic models in their eager search for corporate transformation. Their efforts are being resisted. Some programmes are foundering upon the rocks of the very diversity that is being heralded.

The natives, whipped up by the talk of involvement, empowerment and customer focus, are becoming restive. Gaps between actions and words have made them fidgety. They have waited too long for achievements to come through. When the damp night of recession gives way to the dawn of recovery, they may rise up and challenge the centre.

CHECKLIST

▶ Does your company have an international vision?

▶ How international is the perspective of the 'key players'?

▶ How tolerant are they of cultural diversity?

▶ Is the membership of the board drawn from a mix of nationalities?

▶ What does your company do to understand, and respond to, developments in the international business environment?

▶ Who are the key global competitors?

▶ Does it have a nationality, or is it an international actor?

▶ Whose cultural values predominate throughout the organisation?

▶ Are the resources of the organisation equally accessible from any point?

▶ What is done to allow the total resources of your company to be harnessed to deliver value to the individual customer?

▶ How easy is it for the people of the company to work together in groups and teams across the barriers of function, distance, nationality and time?

▶ Is it realistic for staff at various locations around the world to aspire to senior management positions?

▶ Are 'head office' functions concentrated at a single point, or dispersed around the international corporate network?

REFERENCES

1. Coulson-Thomas, C (1990) *Human Resource Development for International Operation*, a Survey sponsored by Surrey European Management School, Adaptation, London.
2. Ohmae, K (1990) *The Borderless World*, Harper Business, New York and Collins, London.
3. Doz, Y L, Bartlett, C and Prahalad, C K (1981) 'Global Competitive Pressures and Host Country Demands: Managing Tensions in MNCs' *California Management Review*, Spring vol XXIII, no 3, pp 63–74.
4. Coulson-Thomas, C (1992) *Creating the Global Company, Successful Internationalisation*, McGraw-Hill, London.

5   Pearson, R (1991) *Recruiting Graduates in Europe: What is happening?*, Institute of Personnel Management, Wimbledon.

6   Coulson-Thomas, C (1990) *The Role and Status of Project Management*, an Adaptation Survey for the Association of Project Managers, London.

7   Drucker, P F (1989) *The New Realities*, Heinemann Professional Publishing, London.

8   Coulson-Thomas, C and Brown, R (1990) *Beyond Quality, Managing the Relationship with the Customer*, BIM, Corby.

9   Coulson-Thomas, C and Brown, R (1989) *The Responsive Organisation, People Management: the Challenge of the 1990s*, BIM, Corby.

10 Coulson-Thomas, C (1990) *Professional Development of and for the Board*, an Adaptation Survey for Institute of Directors (IOD), a summary has been published: London, February.

11 Barham, K and Devine, M (1990) *The Quest for the International Manager: A survey of Global Human Resource Strategies*, The Economist Intelligence Unit, London.

12 Coulson-Thomas, C and Wakelam, A (1991) *The Effective Board, Current Practice, Myths and Realities*, an Institute of Directors discussion document, London.

13 Wakelam, A (1989) *The Training and Development of Company Directors*, a survey undertaken by the Management Centre of Exeter University for The Training Agency, Exeter, December.

14 Mintzberg, H (1979) *The Structuring of Organisations*, Prentice-Hall, New Jersey and (1983) *Structures in Fives: Designing Effective Organisations*, Prentice-Hall, New Jersey.

15 Haas, E B (1964) *Beyond the Nation State, Functionalism and International Organisation*, Stanford University Press, Stanford, Calif.

16 Advisory Committee on Science and Technology (Acost) (1991) *Science and Technology Issues: A Review by Acost*, HMSO, London.

17 Ohmae, K (1985) *Triad Power: The Coming Shape of Global Competition*, The Free Press, New York.

18 *Results Through Empowerment and The Role of the Manager* (1991) internal Xerox Corporation document, February.

19 Johnson, T and Chappell, C (1990) *The Computer Integrated Company, Market Driver for the 90s*, Ovum, London.

12

ARENAS OF CONFRONTATION

Fundamental change can open a Pandora's box of problems and conflicts, many of which may have been suppressed under the constraints of bureaucracy. Just as the Soviet Union fragmented into the Commonwealth of Independent States once the fetters were loosened, so enterprises can fragment also. The process of disintegration or disaggregation might be encouraged and helped by the lure of 'hiving off', the temptation to stage a management buy-out, or the attractions of network membership.

When the rate of change speeds up, new ways may need to be found to handle disagreement and confrontation. Where these enable latent and hidden conflicts to be brought to the surface and resolved, pent-up frustration may turn to advocacy of the change process. Even some dissidents may be willing to move ahead in the confidence that a means exists by which concerns can be raised and subsequently addressed. If they are not handled, when the 'going gets rough' group promotion may turn to self-protection.

SCOPE FOR CONFLICT

Changes, especially of organisation structure, may be resisted where people do not see their relevance to familiar situations. The redesign of an organisation could even be seen as a distraction from more important tasks.

Many individual components of a corporate transformation may give a new impetus to old debates. For example, the need for training could initiate a fresh round of discussion on the relative benefits which the company and the individual derive from expenditure on training and development.

It would be naïve to assume a company could ever be peopled by those who are entirely satisfied. Maslow has pointed out that the satisfaction of some requirements gives rise to others.[1] The satisfied employee, like the satisfied customer, can become a moving target.

There is more scope for conflict in some organisations than in others. Within the diversified conglomerate some units may have little in common with others. Those initiating corporate change programmes should reflect upon the extent of diversity within a large business or group context (Figure 12.1):

- In the case of relatively homogeneous business units, it may be possible to use a standard transformation plan, subject to a modest amount of refinement and tailoring of the implementation to suit each unit. There could be scope for engaging in process simplification, on a universal basis, across the organisation.
- Where business units are relatively diverse, it may not be possible to use a transformation plan without some review and modification of the plan itself. More fundamental exercises, such as process re-engineering, may need to be undertaken on a unit-by-unit basis.

Degree of Diversity

	Homogeneous Units	Diverse Units
Universal approach	Little modification of transformation plan. Corporate process simplification	Review applicability of transformation plan
Particular approach	Tailor implementation of transformation plan	Process re-engineering on unit basis

*(Left axis label: **Degree of Applicability of Corporate Programmes**)*

Figure 12.1 *Transforming the Diversified Business*

Within a diversified business, there may be some entities that need to be run quite differently from others. This was recognised by Christopher Hogg and the senior management team at Courtaulds which split itself into two separate businesses. Control Data has decided that its traditional computer products business is sufficiently distinctive from its computer services businesses to justify a split into two separate entities, Control Data Systems and Ceridian Corporation.[2]

ASPIRATION AND ACHIEVEMENT

When there is a gap between rhetoric and reality, a change programme may annoy all the interests involved.

- The 'haves' with a vested interest in the *status quo* may feel threatened by the prospect of change. As one interviewee put it: 'The rhetoric winds them up.'
- The 'have nots', the 'revisionists' who hope to benefit from change, may in return be disappointed by the lack of achievement.
- When the rhetoric continues, those in favour of the '*status quo*' may view the lack of results as no more than a 'temporary relief', or a 'calm before the storm'.
- The disappointment of the 'have nots' can turn to disillusion, despair and even a sense of betrayal, where the rhetoric has raised expectations beyond the prospects of delivery.

Douglas McGregor pointed out that the behaviour of managers within organisations reflects their beliefs.[3] Managers have a tendency to follow their beliefs rather than the words. Burying your head in the sand may enable you, for a time, to avoid contemplating awkward realities. Understanding what people really believe gives you some idea of what you may be in for.

Some managers may just not believe that it is going to happen. For example, one manager complained: 'I've been asked to bring together skill sets into teams, but the skills do not exist. You can't just drop people into teams without preparing them.'

ACKNOWLEDGING CONFLICT

Too many managers conceal problems rather than solve them. Many of those interviewed in the course of the surveys upon which this book is based (see Appendix 1) acknowledged that a range of tensions and conflicts existed within their organisations. The variety of these is illustrated by the following selection of comments.

'We just accept the differences of viewpoint and perspective without trying to do much about them.'

'Our chairman has solved the internal differences problem. When people ask about our differences, the latest line is to claim our cultural style is to encourage debate and internal competition as this benefits our customers.'

'A pyramid which narrows at the top encourages confrontation. Managers have a vested interest in rubbishing colleagues if they want to get ahead.'

'There was so much focus upon getting it right for the customer that we drove our people into the ground.'

'I can read and hear. I see their reports and I can hear what they are saying. ... It is what they are thinking that I would really like to know.'

The realities underlying confrontation need to be addressed. Beneath the symptoms, a latent conflict may be lurking. The drive to impose a change of culture, or a standard approach throughout a corporation, can bring issues to the surface. Under the pressures and demands of corporate transformation, the cracks may widen until the organisational structure blows apart.

TENSIONS BETWEEN DIRECTORS AND MANAGERS

Let us examine some examples of potential arenas of confrontation. In Chapter 4 we challenged a 'traditional' view that directors focus on the external business environment, and are concerned with long-term questions of strategy and policy, while the great mass of employees just concentrate upon short-term questions of implementation and the administrative requirements of the bureaucratic corporate 'machine' (Figure 4.1).

In one survey of company chairmen[4] not a single respondent referred to understanding, assessing or interpreting the external business environment as a function of the board. The latter was largely described in terms of the company and its activities, rather than the business context within which it operates. Even when establishing strategies, objectives and policies, the main consideration is the survival and development of the company, rather than the nature of external challenges and opportunities, and how the company might respond.

In practice, and at a time of economic recession, the focus of many directors is internal, while horizons have become noticeably short term (Figure 4.2).

- Directors are realising that, in order to respond effectively to challenges and opportunities in the business environment, their organisations need to be more flexible and responsive.[5] Many are turning their attention to creating a slimmer, flatter and more adaptable organisation.
- At the same time, boards of public companies feel under increasing pressure from analysts to improve short-term performance. They are giving greater attention to short-term actions to improve ratios such as return on net assets, and the impact of corporate activities and policies upon share price.

One chairman confided: 'We are in a bind ... we really are.'

The dilemma, while exacerbated by recent circumstances, is not new. Back in the 1940s Drucker recognised the challenge of maintaining a balance between a long term strategy focused upon the core purpose and capability of a corporation, and the maintenance of satisfactory levels of short-term performance.[6]

What is new is the extent to which managers are now focusing externally and thinking longer term. The BIM *Flat Organisation* report[7] found that 'understanding the business environment' is the only management quality that was considered important on every questionnaire received prior to the cut-off date.

Managers are being asked to devote more attention to external customers and supply chain relationships.[8] Quality programmes are encouraging all employees to 'focus on the customer'. The preference of chairmen and CEOs for linking remuneration to customer satisfaction[8] reflects their desire to prevent managers taking short-term actions for good 'internal' reasons, but at the expense of satisfactory long-term relationships with customers.

The shift of emphasis is causing more people to question board and senior management decisions that appear to be in conflict with stated long-term aims. Pragmatism and 'accommodating' may appear out of step with corporate values. When short-term actions impact upon customer and employee satisfaction, unease can develop into annoyance and hostility. As one manager put it: 'Screwing up our relationships with customers goes against everything we have been expected to believe in.'

In many companies, as we saw in Chapter 4, success in sharing visions and values has resulted in a slide in senior management credibility. A breakdown of trust is a likely consequence of promises running ahead of delivery. Having raised expectations, many boards have been caught 'on the hop'.

We saw in Chapter 7 that actions and symbols can communicate more than words. Table 12.1 lists a few of the areas in which there is sometimes a difference between what the board says and what the board does. If these persist, then the board itself is not acting as a role model.

Table 12.1 *The Board as a Role Model*

The board says	The board does
Satisfy customers	Set RONA* targets
Build relationships	Reorganises and disrupts relationships
Encourage teamwork	Divides and rules
Exercise restraint	Awards itself large increase in remuneration
Invest in people	Reduces training budget
Delegate and empower	Still takes the decisions
Calls for long-term commitment	Overreacts to short-term pressures

*Return on net assets

The view that actions can often lead to consequences that are different from those intended is not new. Chris Argyris has recognised that managers are frequently faced with contradictory pressures, and are in receipt of messages that may appear to be in conflict. In response they may adopt 'defensive routines', which may best be tackled by matching the speed of change to the rate at which people and groups can learn, and the benefits of incremental developments become apparent.[9]

APPORTIONING THE BLAME

In Chapter 9 we saw that the lack of 'top management commitment' is perceived as the major barrier to total quality (Table 9.3). When things go well, everyone wants to take the credit. Unintended consequences, however, are always someone else's fault. When things do not work out as planned, people start to point the finger.

Let us examine the 'source' of the lack of top management commitment as revealed by interviews for the *Quality: The Next Steps* survey.[10]

- Broadly, CEOs and directors believe the 'top management barrier' is the first couple of layers of senior management below the board. CEOs reported support for their messages further down the organisation, but felt, as one CEO put it, that too many managers, 'assess changes in terms of the impacts upon their own roles and standing in the corporate bureaucracy'.
- Interviews with CEOs suggest they associate 'vested interests', 'organisational politics' and 'cynicism' (see Table 9.3) with senior rather than junior managers. These are the people who are thought to have the greatest stake in the '*status quo*', or to have most to gain from it. One interviewee observed: 'They are doing OK thank you ... [they] just assume they will be worse off.'
- Overall, managers have a different perspective on the source of the 'commitment barrier'. To them, 'top management' represents the people 'above' them, and especially the board. Instances were given of directors thought to be sceptical, while many boards are not perceived to be committed.

According to one CEO who was interviewed following a change of job:

'Looking back I realise some of my colleagues in the boardroom were just playing with words. They would nod agreement, and then do nothing in their divisions. When people say things like 'If you say so' or 'You're the boss', you know you are in trouble. We should have kept at it until they were all committed. ... If I had my time over again, I would have been tougher on one or two of them.'

THE HEAD OFFICE — BUSINESS UNIT DIVIDE

An expectation gap, or the failure of the main board to deliver, can poison the relationship between head office and business unit. Head offices and business units may also have conflicting views and perspectives on the steps needed to implement a vision.

In the rhetoric, the management teams of business units may have been encouraged to act as 'independent businesses'. However, the reality of a 'different viewpoint' can be the cause of resentment. Often, the 'thinking teams' are labelled as troublemakers, rather than listened to. They may be avoided just when there is the greatest need for dialogue.

The pace of transformation can become an issue. A business unit, determined to achieve significant change, may be confronted with a corporate head office that is content to move at a slower pace. In one documented case, an innovative group within General Foods came into conflict with central management to such an extent as to result in resignations and transfers elsewhere within the group.[11]

The *Quality: The Next Steps* survey[10] identified 'short-termism' as a source of 'division' between a head office and business units. One director of quality explained: 'Business units are confused. We ... have asked them to put everyone through quality training. Some of them are now quite committed. But at the moment we have frozen headcounts and new consultancy contracts so they can't do the training.'

Reference has been made at a number of points in this book to the need for performance indicators to match business objectives. The use of financial measures to assess business unit performance, when corporate goals stress 'customer satisfaction', appears to be the source of much frustration at the business unit level.

One divisional director complained: 'I bought into quality, and the vision, as did my team. Everyone talks about quality, but I'm measured by the same old ratios. Quality is great, and we all know it's important, but numbers are real. The ratios decide my next move, not how many quality improvement projects I've got.'

A director of quality expressed some frustration at frequent requests to review and cost-justify what had been thought to be a long-term commitment: '[I am] on a quest for the Holy Grail. I won't get there, but I'm obsessive. I feel, but I can't always prove, that I'm doing the right thing.'

The criteria used to recover central or overhead costs are also a 'bone of contention'. One business unit general manager complained: 'I'm supposed to buy and hand out corporate videos on the vision, but our prices and margins are being squeezed, and I'm being squeezed. I get memos from head office to reduce headcount and cut costs, while my reallocated overheads have increased.'

In many companies, the most that can be learned from the relative bottom line performance of business units is something about the basis of group, or head office, overhead allocation.

RELATIONSHIPS BETWEEN HOLDING, SUBSIDIARY AND OPERATING COMPANIES

Differences of perspective and emphasis are particularly evident in the relationships between holding companies, and their subsidiary and operating companies. Relations between group boards and those of national operating companies may be distorted by misunderstandings that might result from differences of nationality and culture.

The *Quality: The Next Steps* survey[10] found that the desire of some companies to achieve a consistent implementation of a quality programme across a group made up of diverse units has resulted in the imposition of approaches to quality which are not thought to be appropriate in a local context. We saw in Chapter 11 that an initiative that is understood in one culture may appear meaningless in another.

According to one international director with personnel responsibilities for Central and South America: 'Many of my colleagues never think about how much our strategic vision is bound up with our own culture. [People] don't relate to it in South America. ... It's not their vision – it's our vision. We're telling them about it, not sharing it with them.'

Delayering and headcount reduction programmes appear to have exacerbated tensions. Many operating companies appear resigned to the prospect of 'absorbing' an unfair proportion of 'cutbacks', as corporate organisations are slimmed down. According to one subsidiary director: 'You always cut someone else. ... When group [makes] cuts, it's us [who feel the impact]'.

Perhaps corporate power should be redefined in terms of the ability to reduce someone else's headcount. A subsidiary managing director explained: 'Who gets the misery depends upon power, and there's still a lot of it at the centre. We worry about long-term vision and the investments it requires, but we make the cuts. Yet the headcount at holding company level hasn't really changed. What on earth do they all do?'

THE BURDEN OF THE CORPORATE SPECIALISTS

Many of those at the corporate centre appear adept at protecting their own interests. Surveys already cited in this chapter,[5,8,10] and others undertaken by the author,[12,13] have revealed a gap of perspective and understanding between CEOs and the heads of specialist functions, which often extends to a lack of mutual respect. Yet, in some companies, new staff positions and specialist roles appear to spring up as rapidly as others are cut out.

One frustrated CEO exclaimed: 'It's like wrestling with a multiheaded beast. We cut off heads, but new ones spring up. ... [Because of this] we have to resort to crude tactics like imposing headcount reductions. ... This drives out the good with the bad.'

The perception that there are protected positions 'at the top' causes resentment elsewhere in the corporate organisation. When new people are taken on board there are accusations of 'empire building'.

The EC Single Market or '1992' was cited by one national operating company director as an opportunity for the central bureaucrats: 'We had announced a run-down of central overheads, and along comes 1992. The head office politicians jumped at the opportunity to create another layer of bureaucracy at the regional level. Just when I need to cut prices to survive in a more competitive market I'm having to fund the staffing up of a European headquarters.'

CONFLICT WITHIN THE NETWORK

There are many sources of tension and arenas of conflict within corporate organisations. In the case of the network organisation, the scope for internal conflict or 'family quarrels' extends to the relationships between the core team and various project groups, and those with the customer, supplier and business partner members of the network.

One arena of conflict that could 'divide' members of the network is that between producers and consumers. Many EC governments have sought to promote the interests of domestic producers by encouraging their consolidation into national champions. However, Porter's analysis suggests that tough domestic competition leads to the edge needed for international success, while its absence can lead to complacency.[14] Some internal pressures may need to be generated to keep network members on their toes.

The degree of dissent could be an indicator of the extent to which progress is being made in transitioning away from the bureaucratic organisation. It is difficult to envisage situations that could lead to a revolt breaking out in the midst of the bureaucratic corporation. This is not so in the case of the network organisation in which all share common values and an understanding of what needs to be done.

One can imagine circumstances in which a province might rebel against the empire, a divisional team accusing a head office of breaking faith with the vision and values, and appealing to stakeholders for support. Insecure senior executives of the future may need to put down the 'quick reads' on how to achieve harmony and light in five easy stages, and dust off some tomes on why people rebel and revolt.[15]

DIFFERING NATIONAL PERSPECTIVES

Within the international network there is further potential for misunderstanding and conflict. These could be of a fundamental kind. An international company may find that managers in different countries vary in the priority they attach to customer-related objectives. For example:

- a UK manager may retain attachment to financial measures of performance, and focus upon profitability;
- a German colleague might stress turnover growth, and attach more importance to the employees or 'social partners';
- the Japanese equivalent might be more receptive to corporate values concerning the customer that are portrayed as a 'philosophy of business'.

When an attempt is made to reconcile these distinct perspectives through discussion there could well be scope for protracted debate. If a particular priority is imposed, then not all are likely to be equally committed.

Clashes of corporate culture can arise in the cases of joint ventures and acquisitions. Differences of corporate culture have been apparent in joint ventures, such as that between Apple and IBM in the systems software area. They were also apparent following the acquisition of Columbia Pictures by Sony.

Cultural differences should not be 'swept under the carpet'. The Japanese Travel Bureau has used a series of workshops across Europe to bring out into the open what appeared to be a lack of empathy between Japanese managers and local staff.[16] At the end of the exercise those involved had a better understanding of the differences of culture and perspective between members of workgroups drawn from different national backgrounds.

CULTURE AND CORPORATE TRANSFORMATION

The implementation of elements of a corporate transformation programme could also be affected by national and cultural differences. For example, there are significant differences in national approaches to involvement.

- Senior executives in US companies tend to decide first and then seek involvement in implementation. There is often a reluctance to trust people with major decisions. These are seen as the prerogative of corporate leaders. Many senior managers consider they would be earning their salary by fraud if they spent too long listening to other people, as opposed to taking decisions.
- In Japanese companies it is not unusual for initiatives for change to arise at a number of points and levels within the corporate organisation. Suggestions travel around and through the organisation, gaining support and being refined according to various contributions from those likely to be affected. By the time a proposal reaches a senior management level many of the implementation issues will have been addressed, and a favourable consensus may already have been assembled.

Clearly, how an empowerment programme is implemented would need to reflect these and other differences. Over-generalisation should be avoided, and it may be necessary to strip away a cloak of mythology. We saw in Chapter 11 that diversity can be a source of corporate creativity and strength.

THE DESIRABILITY OF CONFLICT

Pascale has argued that a degree of contention and creative tension is healthy and desirable if it encourages debate and the challenge of shared assumptions.[17] As part of its global issue monitoring and management process Xerox consciously sets out to obtain external 'inputs' that challenge its view of the world.

Invisible or hidden barriers cannot be tackled. Opposition, particularly when self interested or malevolent, is better out in the open than concealed in the recesses of bureaucracy where it can carp and corrupt. Without moving the stone it may not be possible to disturb the reptiles and creepy-crawlies lurking beneath it.

Change tends to impose strains and can exacerbate differences. Role-model behaviour must include a tolerance for uncertainty and diversity, and the ability to recognise, confront and resolve differences. A common vision or a shared focus on, or commitment to, the customer can act as a reference point, or a kind of cement that holds the corporate organisation together.

Some of those who are sceptical may be opinion formers. Their very caution, and a reputation for thoughtfulness, may cause them to be respected by various people across a corporate network. Their attitudes and responses to change may be watched by others. Their views need to be obtained and considered, and their concerns addressed. Because of their informal or political influence, they should not be ignored on the grounds of their role in the formal hierarchy.

DRIVING OR LISTENING

Many managers have a tendency to draw the wrong conclusions from their analyses of situations. For example, because top management commitment is important is does not follow that there should be an excessive, if not exclusive, focus upon the driving and cascading of a change programme through an organisation. Commitment at other levels is important as well, and this may be reduced rather than encouraged by the 'top down' approach.

Senge has warned of the dangers of imposing rather than sharing a mission.[18] Imposition tends to result in compliance rather than commitment, and discourages people from questioning and learning.

MECHANISMS FOR AVOIDING CONFLICTS

Some companies have recognised the potential for arenas of conflict to arise, and have created mechanisms to deal with them. Given goodwill and trust, latent conflicts can be brought into the open.

Specific means of diffusing potential conflict areas include the following.

- Giving local operating units greater autonomy. Japanese companies such as Honda have recognised the need to give local staff greater discretion to respond to local circumstances.
- A 'ring fence' could be put around a newly acquired company to reduce the risk of culture clash, and maintain valued cultural characteristics. Fujitsu has sought to maintain the European identity and special character of ICL following its acquisition.
- Allowing greater involvement of operating and business units in corporate issue monitoring and management exercises. Remember that cosmetic involvement can rebound and should be avoided.
- Representatives of operating and business units could be invited to attend board and management meetings for those items that directly concern them, and in respect of which they are known to have strong views.
- At the cost of some delay, every attempt should be made to secure operating and business unit involvement in the formulation of corporate visions, values and missions. This may allow early identification of issues that might arise in respect of certain countries and cultures.
- Local operating companies should be involved in the formulation and implementation of the various host country strategies developed by an international company. In cases where there is a clear conflict between global and national interest, at least local management will be made aware of the global viewpoint.

HANDLING CONFLICTS

A company may need to establish fora in which debate and the exchange of views can take place. To take two examples.

- General Electric of the USA has established a corporate executive council to bring together board members and those heading the corporation's various business units. This creates a forum for the discussion of issues of concern.
- L M Ericsson uses subsidiary boards and inter-unit teams to resolve differences. Participants are encouraged to build up their understanding of the distinct perspectives of various parts of the organisation by spending periods on assignment and working in cross-functional and multinational teams.

During the transition process from bureaucratic to flexible network organisation, there must be a means of authoritatively handling differences of opinion that might arise in such a way that outcomes are accepted as legitimate by those involved. The degree to which people actively participate in a process reflects the extent to which it is thought to be legitimate.[19] Senior managers are more likely to regard a change process as legitimate if their concerns can be developed and openly expressed, and they are subsequently evaluated and assessed.

Critiques that arise within the corporate organisation should be well informed, and criticisms should be justified. It is difficult to manage on the basis of opinion, and in the absence of argument and appropriate data, differences of opinion can be difficult to reconcile. Xerox encourages 'fact-based management', while Intel expects its managers to question, but on the basis of rigorous analysis and supporting information.

Conflict can be functional or dysfunctional. A culture that encourages challenge and debate does not want an excess of negative criticism. Hence, people should be encouraged to relate their points to the achievement of corporate goals.

The commitment of various groups may be better harnessed by encouraging them to focus upon customer problems that are significant to their particular business units or areas of activity. People could discover for themselves what the key barriers to delivering value to customers are. Top management could concentrate upon helping them with whatever tools and approaches are relevant to the solution of these problems. In the process, it might emerge that there is a need for greater cross-functional co-operation, in which case a degree of reorganisation might follow the thoughts of those involved.

IDENTIFYING COMMON GROUND

In order to reconcile conflicts concerning corporate transformation, it is necessary to determine the extent of agreement, and the source of disagreement. For example, it would be advisable to assess whether the conflict concerns any of the following.

- The factors influencing the change requirement. According to perspective, the pressures could be seen as motivating or overwhelming. Very different views could be taken of strengths, weaknesses, opportunities and threats.
- The need for change. Opinions might vary on how much freedom of action a company has. Even where a storm strikes, some may suggest seeking temporary shelter, while others favour riding it out.
- The timing of change. Does it need to be rushed, or could it be carefully planned and introduced at a leisurely pace?
- The nature or extent of change. Is a fundamental transformation required, or some incremental adjustment to what is? Does the need extend to the whole company, or is it confined to particular divisions?
- The process of change. One person might favour a more democratic route of involving and sharing in order to 'win hearts and minds', while another individual could view such an approach as 'a luxury that cannot be afforded'. In the time available, it may be felt that changes should be forced through.
- The use of change techniques. Even though agreement may have been reached to re-engineer a process, and to do this by splitting it into sections, views may vary on where the split should occur.
- The desired or achievable speed of change. Some members of a transformation team are likely to have more faith than others concerning the capacity of people, processes, organisations and systems to cope with the speed of change.
- The impacts or implications of change. Views may differ on how to assess and weigh consequences. Change can be unequal in its impacts and the burdens of readjustment it imposes.

- What has been achieved in terms of change. While some may be concerned at the lack of progress, others may argue that enough has been done, or even that some aspects of change have gone too far.
- Why change is occurring. Some way into a change programme, people can lose sight of the original reasons for change. A case could be put for reassessment in the light of changed circumstances and what has been achieved, while others might stress the need to 'stay true and see it through'.

To achieve a successful transition, a mixture of consensus and coercion may be needed, and the nature and extent of each will vary from company to company according to circumstances and the required speed of change. The mix may need to be varied according to the make-up of individual elements of the network organisations. An examination of revolutionary change in wider society suggests that continuing insistence that an organisation be regarded and treated as an integrated whole can lead to policy failures.[20]

THE INVISIBLE DIMENSION

What needs to be changed may not be visible. Look around your office. The people hard at work, the activity you see, and all the procedures and technology that support it may not be the problem. They may not be perfect, but rather than squeeze small incremental improvements out of what is already relatively effective, you should probably look elsewhere.

From the customer's point of view, the major sources of delay may lie in the invisible dimension for which no one is responsible (Table 12.2). Having been worked upon with diligence and speed, documents processed in minutes may wait for days in in-trays as they pass through the limbo land between departments and functions. And at each cross-over point they may be ranked differently in priority. At certain stages in the journey the priority may be low indeed.

Table 12.2 *Visible and Invisible Dimensions*

Visible	Invisible
Activity	Delay
Work time	Waiting time
'In play'	'Off the court'
Departmental responsibility	Lack of overall responsibility
Formal structure	Informal consultation
Processing cost	Cost of delay
Investment in information technology	Lack of investment in document management
Problem of justification	Customer dissatisfaction

As much as 90 per cent or more of the elapsed time through an order to delivery cycle may be spent 'waiting' at cross-over points that fall between functional responsibilities. This invisible dimension does not appear on lists of roles and responsibilities. The cost of delays is a general source of competitive disadvantage for the whole company rather than an item on a particular departmental account.

When the consequences of delay result in investigations and enquiries, blame and recrimination may have a field day. Departments and functions may be at each other's throats as they try to pass the buck. The functional boundary is the source of many of the most virulent and debilitating conflicts that can arise within corporate organisations.

FROM VERTICAL TO HORIZONTAL VIEW

In the bureaucratic corporation, the 'vertical' divisions between functions and departments, such as those shown in Figure 12.2, act as a series of barriers between customer requirement and customer satisfaction. The results of delays may result in informal consultation. Some well-meaning people may struggle to resolve the inevitable consequences of inherent defects in the organisation.

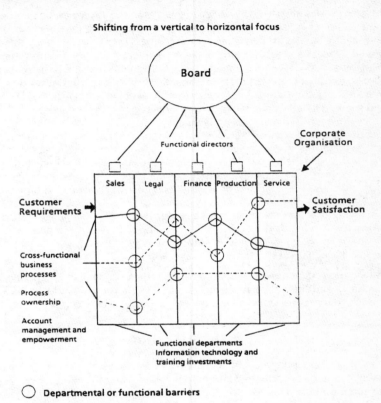

Figure 12.2 *The Board and Cross-functional Business Processes*

Conflicts that arise at the 'hot spots' between departments may also end up as disputes which are taken to the board by the heads of the functions concerned. When not brought into the open, the simmering issue can poison the atmosphere in the boardroom.

The transforming organisation reviews and simplifies or re-engineers its cross-functional business processes. These are the 'horizontal' processes that deliver the value that is sought by customers. When directors are given process, as opposed to departmental, responsibilities they tend to take a more holistic and customer-focused view of the enterprise.

INTEGRATING THROUGH PROCESSES

Cross-functional processes, such as those shown diagrammatically in Figure 12.2, can also encourage co-operation and act as an 'integrator', creating a lattice work of horizontal linkages. The result can be a sense of unity and shared purpose in place of former departmental rivalries.

At the same time, there is a risk that processes might be identified and re-engineered more quickly than the attitudes to operate them effectively can be firmly established. Processes need to be managed to deliver the value sought by customers. Herein may lie the source of new arenas of conflict.

- Process owners need to be identified to take responsibility for the people, assets and information associated with each process, and to ensure they operate effectively and evolve to meet changing requirements. These people may display the possessiveness and territoriality of the departmental form of organisation.
- While eventually a company might become organised on the basis of 'horizontal' processes rather than 'vertical' departments, during a long interim period a mixture, or matrix, of joint responsibilities may exist. This could result in a level of confusion, and some individuals might experience a degree of conflict between their roles as process owners and departmental managers.
- Identifying and re-engineering a first process such as the 'customer order to product delivery lifecycle' may be greeted as a novelty. Some of those involved may welcome the challenge of the new, and may just be able to cope with the confusion that tends to be uncovered when most key processes are traced through organisations. When further processes are tackled, or a number of processes are tackled simultaneously, the task can become overwhelmingly complex.
- Displaying a process diagrammatically can be a major challenge. When further processes are identified, a degree of overlapping and crossover is almost inevitable. The diagrammatic representation of the processes of the network organisation can appear like a plate of spaghetti.

Ultimately, the process organisation could become as confusing and political as the bureaucracy, with 'boundary problems', and conflicts of view and priority between processes and those responsible for them replacing those between departments.

BENCHMARKING

The use of benchmarking can be a potent tool for focusing people externally, and distracting them from debilitating internal squabbles. The subject of analysis is another organisation, whether a competitor or 'the best'. People can identify what needs to be changed and why, without their own sensitivities and defensiveness being involved.

The 'enemy' is outside in the street rather than down the corridor, or in the next department. Speculation and assumption concerning what might be is replaced by the consideration of what is, and what can be learned from it. Awareness of the scale of an external challenge can act as a catalyst in bringing about the internal unity and resolve to confront it.

Benchmarking also enables a company to identify what needs to be done. It allows an assessment to be made of the scale and pace of change, and it may also be possible to estimate resource requirements, and identify drawbacks and 'side effects'.

Securing internal support is helped by the fact that people are being asked to match or better something that has already been achieved by a competitor for a particular purpose. This tends to be less divisive than a change or cutback for a vague or undisclosed reason which can appear arbitrary, uncertain and obscure.

CHECKLIST

▶ Have the supporters and opponents of change been identified in your company?

▶ What is being done to understand the viewpoints of those who appear to be opposed to change?

▶ Do members of the board and senior management team have the capacity to listen?

▶ How tolerant are they of diversity?

▶ Is open and vigorous debate encouraged?

▶ Do the company's key players have the respect of people throughout the organisation?

▶ Do they themselves always behave as role models?

▶ Why should anyone believe the company's messages?

▶ Who cares if they are believed?

▶ What will be lost if they are not believed?

▶ Is the business and change strategy of your company credible?

▶ What evidence is there of senior management commitment to it?

▶ Where does it rank in the list of their priorities?

▶ Is day-to-day action consistent with the 'words'?

▶ What can be learned from those who appear to lack commitment?

▶ Are managers able to distinguish between a healthy level of questioning and disruptive opposition?

REFERENCES

1 Maslow, A H (1970) *Motivation and Personality*, Harper & Row, New York.
2 Kehoe, L (1992) 'Spin-off to Split Control Data in Two', International Companies and Finance, *Financial Times*, 28 May, p 28.
3 McGregor, D (1960) *The Human Side of Enterprise*, McGraw-Hill, New York.
4 Coulson-Thomas, C and Wakelam, A (1991) *The Effective Board, Current Practice, Myths and Realities*, an Institute of Directors discussion document, London.
5 Coulson-Thomas, C and Brown, R (1989) *The Responsive Organisation, People Management: the Challenge of the 1990s*, BIM, Corby.
6 Drucker, P F (1946) *Concept of the Corporation*, John Day, New York.
7 Coulson-Thomas, C and Coe, T (1991) *The Flat Organisation: Philosophy and Practice*, BIM, Corby.
8 Coulson-Thomas, C and Brown, R (1990) *Beyond Quality, Managing the Relationship with the Customer*, BIM, Corby.
9 Argyris, C (1985) *Strategy, Change and Defensive Routines*, Pitman, London.
10 Coulson-Thomas, C and Coulson-Thomas, S (1991) *Quality: The Next Steps*, an Adaptation Survey for ODI International, Adaptation, London and (Executive Summary) ODI, Wimbledon, London.
11 Walton, R E (1977) 'Work Innovations at Topeka: After Six Years', *Journal of Applied Behavioral Science*, 13, pp 422–33.
12 Coulson-Thomas, C (1991) *The Role and Development of the Personnel Director*, a questionnaire and interview survey undertaken by Adaptation Ltd in conjunction with the Institute of Personnel Management Research Group.
13 Coulson-Thomas, C (1990) *Developing IT Directors*, an Adaptation Ltd Report to the Department of Computing Science, Surrey University.
14 Porter, M E (1990) *The Competitive Advantage of Nations*, Macmillan, London.
15 Davies, J C (Ed) (1971) *When Men Revolt and Why*, The Free Press, New York; and Gurr, T R (1970) *Why Men Rebel*, Princeton University Press, Princeton, NJ.

16 Fitzgerald, J (1991) 'A Japanese Lesson in European Togetherness', *Personnel Management*, September, pp 45–7.

17 Pascale, R T (1990) *Managing On the Edge*, Simon & Schuster, New York, and Viking, London.

18 Senge, P (1990) *The Fifth Discipline: The Art and Practice of the Learning Organisation*, Doubleday/Currency, New York.

19 Easton, D and Dennis, J (1969) *Children in the Political System: Origins of Political Legitimacy*, McGraw-Hill, New York.

20 Johnson, C (1966) *Revolutionary Change*, Little, Brown & Company, Boston, Mass.

13

INTEGRATING LEARNING AND WORKING

DESTROYING THE DRIVE TO LEARN

All of us are born with an innate desire and drive to learn. We come into the world restless and curious to explore, and to experience. We search and investigate, open and receptive, eager for the stimuli that will expand our awareness and understanding. At the same time, we are fed, winded and largely left to our own devices.

Later in life, as children, we are confined for several hours a day, during many of our most receptive years, in institutions of education. Ostensibly, a central purpose of schools is the pursuit of learning. And, yet, for most people, the efforts of many thousands of well-meaning and committed teachers over a period of years destroys this desire to learn.

The educational system fails most people. They learn what they are not good at according to one approach to the development of understanding. As the 21st century beckons, most of us will approach the grave bereft of any real appreciation of our individual learning capability. We can peer into space and speculate about the origins of the universe while much of what happens within our own heads is unexplored territory. The 'non-academic' majority go through life without ever knowing how they might most effectively learn.

THE HIGH COST OF LIMITING POTENTIAL

To achieve this is expensive. Some £25 billion per annum is spent on education in the UK alone to produce a majority who are functionally illiterate in maths, science and IT. Another £25 billion or so is spent on training, much of which is devoted to remedying the deficiencies of the educational system.

The USA is more aware of the failure of the current approach to education. It spends some $600 billion on education and training, some 40 per cent of this being in the corporate sector. One in four people are receiving or delivering some form of education or training. The sector represents over 12 per cent of the US GNP. And yet, most young Americans lack a range of basic competences.

Why? Because the US educational system, like others, is based upon an inadequate understanding of the learning process. While our understanding is so limited, further investments in education could be said to be building upon foundations of sand.

A dramatic example in the education field of the need to distinguish between symptoms and underlying causes, and address the sources of problems, was provided by the 1992 resignation of Benno Schmidt as president of Yale University in order to head up a project to establish a network of 1000 private schools across the USA that would confront the deficiencies of traditional education.[1]

We will return to the question of learning in Chapter 17. Without it, the corporation acts like a zombie. Education, training and development should light the touch-paper, not suffocate the spark.

THE CORPORATE CHALLENGE

We cannot afford to continue with our current system which is so clearly failing the great majority of the people. In a global marketplace in which the knowledge worker is becoming the critical and limiting resource, the corporation or society that first and whole-heartedly adopts new approaches to learning that allow individuals to tap more of their potential will reap an enormous competitive advantage.

Is training and development a 'help' or a 'hinder'? How does one build a learning company that must operate within countries which are not learning societies? What are the preferred approaches to learning of major European companies? Where should learning be located, and how should it be related to work?

THE EVIDENCE

These and other questions were asked during the course of a wider 1990 survey[2] of how best to prepare managers for effective international operation. This was undertaken by Adaptation Ltd for Surrey European Management School (SEMS). In total the survey covered organisations with a combined turnover of some £320 billion, and over 2.7 million employees. Over a million people are individual members of the professional associations participating in the survey.

The responses reveal a clear preference for the integration of learning and working. The place of work is the preferred location of learning, and the most relevant approaches are thought to be tailored company-specific programmes with a project component.

We will also draw upon the results of organisational studies undertaken for the BIM.[3,4] Details of these, and other of the surveys that are cited, can be found in Appendix 1.

RHETORIC AND REALITY

The SEMS survey,[2] and especially its interviews, supports other findings. In particular, it provides further evidence of the importance attached to harnessing the talents of people.[3] Human resource is now perceived as a critical success factor, and there is an evident desire for more work to be undertaken by project groups and teams with clear output objectives.

A commitment to the development of people is a core element of the business philosophy of some companies. According to Hiroshi Hamada, president of the Japanese company Ricoh: 'realising the full potential of every company member is the company's most important aim.'

As more people become aware of the extent to which their companies are competing on the basis of their ability to learn and apply what has been learned, greater interest is being shown in the concept of the 'learning organisation'. Christopher Lorenz of the *Financial Times* has warned that: 'The notion is potentially extremely powerful, although its ambitious nature increases the chance that, like most management fads, companies will rush to adopt it in a half-baked way.'[5]

Most major companies appear to have committed the importance they attach to developing the skills of their people to print or the video-tape. Yet, many of the managers encountered stress in the divergence between rhetoric and reality. For example:

- while the critical importance of identifying, attracting, developing, motivating, tapping and retaining human talent appears to have become an article of faith, many training and related budgets have been cut back;[3,4]

- it is thought that many companies are not investing enough to equip staff for the new forms of group and team working they are being asked to adopt, and the extra responsibilities they are required to assume;[4]
- in most organisations training and development activity is undertaken on a departmental basis. The expenditure is not focused upon the activities and processes that add value for customers, and the skills being imparted are not specifically relevant to the achievement of corporate goals and objectives.

David Thompson, chairman of Rank Xerox UK is of the view that: 'Too many people still see training as an internal cost, to be cut back when times are hard. 'Whether training is a 'help' or a 'hinder' depends upon its nature and purpose.

Many companies find it difficult to decide how much to spend on training. The 'heart' wants to believe that training is a 'good thing', while the 'head' suggests that the results of training efforts are difficult to determine. The reality of 'what is' often differs greatly from the vision of 'what ought to be'. The intention may have been to 'invest', but the results of training can be disappointing, and in some cases positively harmful.

TRAINING AND CORPORATE TRANSFORMATION

How does training and development activity relate to the transition from bureaucracy to the flat and flexible network organisation? The BIM *Flat Organisation* report[4] reveals the following.

- 'Harnessing human potential emerges as perhaps the major "internal" management challenge, yet few companies appear to be satisfied with the extent to which they are tapping the talents of their people'.
- While companies desire corporate transformation, there is 'insufficient commitment to action to equip managers to cope with the new realities'.
- Organisations are becoming slimmer and flatter, and more work is being undertaken in teams. Yet 'few managers are being equipped with team working skills'.
- While 74 per cent of respondents strongly agree that human resource is a critical success factor, only 26 per cent rate 'a commitment to ongoing learning' as a very important management quality.
- 'Some companies still consider expenditure on the development of people as a discretionary cost rather than as a necessary investment. The "gap" between vision and conduct, and rhetoric and reality, suggests a lack of top management commitment in many companies'.

The report concludes: 'These results are disturbing. If human resource is to be the key to success, organisations need a highly skilled and adaptable workforce, which is in receipt of continual updating and training, in order to be able to respond to the ever faster pace of change'.[4]

According to one chairman: 'We are turning the organisation upside down ... [and] ... assuming people will be able to cope. ... So much of it is new to them ... [yet] most of our training continues as before.' Other work has confirmed that few major UK companies are equipping their managers to operate in the delayered organisation.[6]

Paradoxically, because of a failure to implement, some of those companies that have 'taken a lead' in trying to equip people for team work in the context of a flexible organisation have developed skills that cannot be effectively practised. Management qualities such as flexibility and adaptability need to be matched by a similar development in corporate capability.

According to the BIM *Flat Organisation* report:[4] 'Developing people in isolation can widen the gap between awareness of the need for action and the perceived ability to respond. The result can be a sense of powerlessness and disillusion.'

CHALLENGING THE CONVENTIONAL WISDOM

The value of much training and development activity is being questioned. Have companies 'invested' in training, or have they just spent money preparing people for a world they are now turning their backs on? Consider the following selection of comments:

'Lots of people have gone on courses, but attitudes and behaviour have not changed.'

'We think it is nice for people to learn things, whether or not they are of any relevance. We do not relate training to specific tasks.'

'Most training is departmental. People train with their function. Yet most of the key processes that generate value for customers are cross-functional.'

'If you are into debates about measuring the effectiveness of training, you are probably into the wrong training, ... or consider it as a cost. If you know what adds value for customers [and] have clear customer objectives ... expressed in output terms, you just do what is necessary.'

Overall, training and development should no longer be automatically assumed to be a 'good thing'. In many companies, including those in sectors that have made major investments in training, managerial productivity has actually fallen. As the author has concluded elsewhere:[7]

Training is not necessarily desirable; it depends both upon the training and the trainer. Many trainers continue to teach out-of-date ideas or jump aboard the latest bandwagon without thinking through the consequences for an individual company. Many of the notions that can appear the most compelling on the trainer's slide, and are delivered with the panache and confidence that come from frequent repetition, have limited application in the work context.

At a number of points in this book we have encountered the disturbing consequences of a widespread lack of key competences.

- In Chapter 2 we found little satisfaction with the effectiveness of boards, yet little is being done to develop directorial skills and competences.[8] Often deficiencies are not recognised, and when they are, people doubt that 'what is on offer' can remedy them.
- We saw in Chapter 7 that the ability of managers to communicate is often inversely related to the amount of communication skills training they have received. The problem is one of awareness, attitudes and approaches, rather than of communication skills.[9]
- The evidence reviewed in Chapter 9 suggests that in spite of an enormous investment in quality training, the overwhelming majority of quality programmes are failing to achieve significant breakthroughs.

A key question is the extent to which the skills that are developed, and the process of development itself, encourage the attitudes and approaches required by the network organisation. For example, does the Japanese emphasis upon rote learning and team work inhibit individual creativity?[10]

UNINTENDED CONSEQUENCES

Management education and development should reflect the requirements of the emerging network organisation. Initiatives such as the UK's Management Charter Initiative, with its succession of stages from supervisory, through junior and middle, to senior management, could help to entrench the hierarchical view of organisations, just at a time when within network organisations the need is to equip people to move between project teams and roles, rather than to climb functional ladders.

So many people appear to be working so hard to frustrate those CEOs who are trying to break free of past practices. They are sometimes imprisoned by their own prejudices and misunderstood preferences.

Many general trends in management education and development can have unintended consequences, as people uncritically apply whatever happens to be the latest craze. To take two examples:

- The definition of standard competences can result in great effort being devoted to the development of qualities that may not be relevant to the situation and circumstances of a particular company. Rather than think through what is required in a particular context, the trainer 'plays safe' and builds some general competence which may not relate to key priorities, or quite specific current transformation requirements.
- The transferability of skills can be dangerous when people move between organisations that are very different in structure or culture, or at different stages in the process of transformation. Whereas the practice might have been to address a requirement in a way that met the needs of the company, instead a tick is made in the 'skill checklist' that it was obtained elsewhere.

When unique people and particular companies are involved, and the requirement may change during a transition process, trainers who 'go automatic' can be dangerous. Too many glib experts appear to have answers up their sleeves that turn out to achieve little.

- One director complained: 'Even before I've finished speaking they've reached for the jargon. We may not have done it before ... [but] out come the words.'
- Another interviewee questioned: 'Why can't they just go away and think about it for a few days? I hope I'll still be here.'

We encountered in Chapter 4 the dangers of allowing rationality and prescription to drive out sensitivity and intuition. There are atmospheres to experience, relationships to understand, considerations to digest, situations to sense and feel, and people to listen to, before recommendations are put together. The rational solution might not be applicable in what Charles Handy has termed the 'age of unreason'.[11]

Technique and the mechanical are no substitute for inspiration and flair. Paul McCartney may not read or write a word of music, but that hasn't stopped him writing a record number of hit songs, or securing more gold and platinum records than any other artist.[12]

LEARNING ABOUT LEARNING

That we have such a limited understanding of how people learn should not come as a surprise. The Institute for Research on Learning (IRL) has calculated that in the USA R&D on learning is 0.025 per cent of expenditure on education.[13] This compares with health and business R&D of 1.5 per cent and 1.6 per cent respectively of expenditure, while high-tech businesses can spend 10 per cent or more of their turnover on R&D. IRL has concluded:[13]

'... any business that spent such a minuscule portion of total expenditure on fundamental research as education is spending, particularly at a time of rapid increase in demand and a revolutionary change in available technology, would inevitably be facing just the sort of monumental crisis that education is now perceived to be in.'

Far too few educationalists have bothered to ask fundamental questions about how people learn. The teachers and advocates of learning have themselves been reluctant to observe, reflect and learn.

For many people, the traditional classroom is among the least effective of learning environments. IRL suggests they feel 'cut off' and do not relate to the abstract symbols that are used in such subjects as maths and science. The SEMS survey[2] confirms these concerns. Relevance and purpose are often not perceived when learning is artificially separated from living and working.

DEVELOPMENT AND CORPORATE OBJECTIVES

A decade ago, one UK survey by Harbridge House revealed that only a third of respondents actually believed there should be a link between training and corporate objectives, while even fewer used training in a proactive way to help bring about corporate objectives.[14] A fifth actually argued against the desirability of a link between training and corporate objectives.

Development activities ought to reflect the situation and circumstances of a company, its business objectives and its key priorities. For example, there is little point in a company that has 'discovered empowerment' building hypothetical 'team skills' without addressing the following.

- The role of groups and teams in the management of change. The management culture and management style must be supportive.
- The clarity of the goals given to teams, and the relevance of their priorities to business objectives. People need to understand the broad boundaries within which they operate in terms of goals and priorities.
- The discretion given to teams, and the extent to which people are given the required freedom to act.
- The commitment of senior management to team work, and especially cross-functional team work. They must be dedicated to ensuring that decisions are taken as close to the customer as possible, and people are enabled to do what is necessary to add value for customers.
- Prevailing attitudes, such as the extent to which people feel part of teams. Empowered team work should be pervasive, rather than the isolated experiment.
- The management cadre. Managers should counsel and coach, value diversity, and foster and encourage teamwork, collaborative activities, self-development and group learning.
- How open people are, and the degree of trust and confidence they have. People need to feel they are able to take initiatives without being paralysed by fear of the consequences.
- Existing performance within teams, the tools shared within teams, and the approaches and support in terms of technology and process available to them. For example, there should be relatively open access to relevant information.
- Reward and remuneration. This should be supportive of, and should recognise, team work, the acquisition of team skills and the exhibiting of role-model behaviour.

Rank Xerox consciously plans to use its training resources to support business objectives and, wherever possible, learning is integrated with working. Training is but one element of a comprehensive empowerment programme which addresses all the issues just listed.

In Rank Xerox, much of the learning takes place within workgroups using a Learn-Use-Teach-Inspect process. This 'LUTI' process was used to cascade quality through the organisation. People learned themselves by using quality tools, and then taught others how to use them and inspected their use, assisted by a small team of facilitators.

SUPPORTING CORPORATE TRANSFORMATION

For many companies, the use of training and management development activity to support corporate transformation is a relatively new concept. When other transformation building blocks, such as specific and measurable objectives, are in place, the contribution of training to 'making it happen' can become apparent.

As one personnel director put it: 'Training is not something you have to believe in any more. It doesn't have to work hard to justify itself. Either there is a place for it, or there isn't ... people now know what they have to do. ...They come forward with specific development requirements.'

Changes of behaviour do not occur just because the board believes it is a good idea. For example, managers do not become coaches and facilitators without themselves receiving coaching and facilitation.

As one manager put it: 'It took the board five years to understand what a process is, and they have been talking about facilitation for three years. When they finally get there, why should they expect us to do it overnight?'

Transformation and learning ought to be natural bedfellows. Both should be a continuing process.

- Bennis and Nanus have stressed the importance of sustaining an ongoing commitment to learning;[15]
- Deming has stressed the need for top management to encourage everyone to commit to continuing self-improvement.[16]

Over the last few years, companies such as General Foods, ICL and Motorola have given the training role a central place in their corporate change programmes. Evidence on both sides of the Atlantic suggests that some companies are relating management development activity to the achievement of specific business objectives, but that others appear slow or reluctant to learn from their experience.[17]

LEARNING IN A DYNAMIC ENVIRONMENT

Corporate transformation is a process of transition from one form of organisation and associated activities, attitudes and values, to another. It is not a discrete event that just happens. It cannot be obtained 'off the shelf'.

It is particularly important that managers think in dynamic terms, and focus upon trends rather than static pictures. Reality is dynamic. The world is changing while we think about it. As we describe what we have seen, or what we feel is happening, events and circumstances are making our description more or less valid.

People without prior experience will need to be equipped to operate in unfamiliar ways, for example in a self-managed workgroup. The process of preparation may continue over a period of time, as new areas of responsibility are phased in.

Fundamental transformation changes do not occur 'on the first of the month'. Independence may come at midnight when one flag is lowered and another run up, but empowerment may be a gradual process. Those who claim there is a gap between rhetoric and reality could be describing the particular stage that has been reached, with the expectation that further progress ought to have been made.

Some will be satisfied earlier than others. For example, many advocates of empowerment are reluctant to allow groups of people to allocate their own remuneration. At a certain point they decide 'enough is enough', and draw a line in the sand.

CLOSING THE GAPS

Within the transforming organisation, learning should be related particularly to the gaps which emerge between expectations and outcomes. How have they come about, and what can be done to put transformation back on track?

If appropriate action is to be taken, the issue to focus upon may not be that a gap exists between aspiration and achievement, but whether it is closing or widening. Is the company on track, or are matters getting out of control? If the existence or direction of a trend is not identified, corrective action may make matters worse rather than better.

People need to probe and question. Reporting a trend does not allow appropriate action to be taken, if the reasons for it are not understood. Why has the gap occurred? Why is the gap wider in some areas and locations than in others? There are lessons in gaps and trends, and these need to be teased out.

THE PROCESS VIEW

An effective process should free people from the continual disruptions of fire fighting. The efforts of different groups are integrated towards a common purpose. When processes cross-function, many of the perils of departmentalism we examined in the last chapter can be avoided. Empowered people should be involved in process review and improvement, and in the choice of technology and tools to support processes.

A focus upon processes is unlikely to lead to a process view of an organisation, still less to seamless processes that speed actions and requirements through and between organisations, without a degree of development. A certain number of people will almost certainly need to be equipped with the skills to simplify and re-engineer processes.

Empowerment does not just happen. Processes need to be put in place to enable power and authority to be delegated, and people need to be equipped to use these and other processes to deliver what is required. The rate at which actual authority is devolved and delegated should match the rate at which the capability is developed to use the additional discretion in the desired ways.

A number of the requirements for successful corporate transformation are inter-dependent. For example, the implementation of process re-engineering is critically dependent upon the empowerment of people. Without the discretion to act, the time that has traditionally been spent seeking authorisation cannot be saved.

Whereas much of the benefit of process simplification can be obtained through empowerment, process re-engineering is more radical, involving fundamental or 'frame-breaking' change. More than empowerment is required, as successful execution requires an examination of the interaction of people, process and technology. Management development is but one element; the development of compatible and mutually supportive processes and technology is also required.

THE LEARNING PROCESS

Learning itself should be a process of exploration and discovery. It should continue throughout life, as capabilities are developed and matched to changing opportunities and requirements.

The traditional approach to education tends to assume that we all learn in a similar way. In fact people learn in a variety of ways. Those who perform best in approaches that require logic and structure may not be so effective in approaches that require sensitivity to links and patterns. The former may lead to academic honours. The latter may be what is needed to exploit the full potential of an artificial intelligence environment.

Our approach to learning is deep-rooted. Since the 12th century, logic has held sway with its emphasis upon categorisation and procedure, moving forward in incremental steps from current positions. There has been little emphasis upon the more process-based relational approach, which has been the source of many 'scientific revolutions'.

This is more concerned with links, patterns and relationships involving things which have not been logically related.

What is needed today is self-awareness and self-confidence, communication and team working skills, adaptability and flexibility and a commitment to lifetime learning. All of these are qualities which can be built by new approaches to learning, and yet are too often stifled by existing approaches.

DESTRUCTIVE TENDENCIES

Some disturbing aspects of many corporate transformation programmes are inhibiting the development of the required attitudes and approaches:

- the pressure of work, compounded by the reallocation of the tasks of those who have 'left' the flattening and slimming organisation, is squeezing out what little time many managers have for thinking;
- the effort to communicate goals and values, and the desire of many employees during an era of 'headcount reduction programmes' to demonstrate their allegiance and commitment, is discouraging critical comment;
- the concentration on a 'vital few' programmes, and the allocation of ever more specific responsibilities and objectives is causing many people to narrow their focus at a time when coping with internal change and a turbulent business environment, and the desire to tap greater value-added opportunities in relationships with customers is demanding a 'broader view';
- the lives of many managers, as a consequence of long hours and heavy workloads, appear to be becoming more unbalanced at a time when handling competing pressures and the uncertainties of transformation require a sense of proportion.

While listening to talk of empowerment, release and liberation, people are being labelled, confined and crushed. Too many are still treated like pawns in the game of corporate reorganisation. Having been given an overview of the whole board they find themselves stuck fast to one square. To think and learn, people need the emotional space to 'breathe'.

DEVELOPMENT PRIORITITES

Among the questions posed in the SEMS survey[2] was one concerning the importance of education and development at various levels of formal qualification. The traditional MBA type programme did not emerge as a priority.

- Executive programmes were ranked more highly by respondents than degree programmes. The greatest importance is attached to executive programmes for senior management and directors. Their role in relation to corporate transformation was stressed by several interviewees.
- More importance is placed upon certificate and diploma programmes for junior and middle managers, respectively, than upon master's degree programmes for senior management. As one interviewee put it: 'The reactions and performance of the intermediate levels will determine whether or not we get bogged down.'

The European and international respondents appear to attach greater importance to all forms of education and development than those from UK companies. The difference is noticeable in diploma level programmes for middle management, and at the master's degree level for senior management, as well as at the executive programme level.

In reality, the categorisation of people into levels can impede rather than assist progress towards the network organisation. To create the network, the challenge is to change attitudes and share values.

The training implications of corporate transformation can extend through and beyond the ranks of management. A recent CBI report suggests that the training of supervisors remains unsatisfactory and does not reflect the change of emphasis from controller and inspector to facilitator and coach.[18] The very term 'supervisor' is evocative of a set of values that represent the past.

In today's turbulent and changing world (see Table 1.2) we need people who can think. Decisions can no longer be left to 'the few'. Having established the framework, they are likely to be too far away and uninvolved to know what needs to be done in particular cases.

Customers increasingly require tailored products and services. They, and not the organisation, are the centre of their worlds, and they are demanding personal attention. Processes for continual adaptation and learning, and individualised responses, are replacing standard procedures. Everyone needs to be involved in the development and delivery of added value.

Empowerment happens not when people are trained, but when customers feel that those they meet from the company can do things for them. It is alive when the people of the organisation believe they can 'make it happen' for their customer.

ESTABLISHING LINKS AND RELATIONSHIPS

Creating opportunities to add value is often a question of establishing links and relationships. Within the network organisation, there is a need to develop relational approaches to problem solving.

Learning foundations and a commitment to continual learning ought to be established in school. If more people could themselves adapt to changing situations and opportunities, billions spent by industry and commerce on 'inducting', 'relearning' etc, could be saved. In the meantime, companies must act.

So what is needed? Essential first steps are as follows.

- A commitment to helping every individual to become aware of how he or she can learn most effectively. Everyone is good at something. Let us help people to discover what they can do best and most enjoy doing.
- Whatever is available for a person's education or development should first be used to help them uncover something of their own potential. A person requires self-awareness and self-knowledge to know how best to contribute to a group or team. There are too many people in companies who 'play back' slogans and 'go along with things' without really knowing who they are.
- To recognise that knowledge itself is becoming a commodity. It is increasingly there on the database, accessible by a terminal at home or on the manager's desk. While the data sit on the mainframe, customers may be going elsewhere, and the company may be folding.
- The value of data arises when it helps to improve understanding, and this is used to add value for a customer or further a specific objective. Machines store data. People use information and understanding for useful purposes. Working with it, discussing it, refining it and applying it are important, not just knowing it.
- Teachers and trainers, rather than pouring facts into the heads of people, should become facilitators of learning, able to guide, assist, counsel and complement each individual. The skill set required is that of the coaching and counselling manager, rather than the instructional approach of the traditional educator.

How people are approached and developed should reflect the values of the corporation. If the rhetoric refers to them as 'partners' and 'colleagues', they should not be treated as an 'audience' or as 'development fodder'. People can, and do, recognise inconsistencies between corporate words and training deeds.

TYPES OF PROGRAMME AND MODES OF STUDY

So how relevant are various types of programme and modes of study thought to be? The responses of the participants in the SEMS survey[2] to this question are shown in Table 13.1, ordered according to 'very relevant' responses.

Table 13.1 *Relevance of Various Types of Programme and Modes of Study In order of 'very relevant' replies (%)*

Tailored company-specific programmes	52
Project component	36
In-company delivery	30
Open programmes	24
Modular programme	23
Self-managed	21
Issue-based	21
Part-time day release	20
Evening	19
Distance learning	18
Portability of credits/qualifications within UK	14
Mutual recognition of qualifications within EC	14
Joint programme/joint validation	13
Residential element	13
Period of study in another EC country	13
Full time	13
Study visit abroad	11
Discipline-centred	11
Industry-specific programmes	11
Block release	3

Source: Human Resource Development for International Operation, 1990

Overall, taking account of both 'very relevant' and 'relevant' replies, the responses were as follows.

- The most relevant programmes are thought to be 'tailored company-specific programmes', with a 'project component' and 'in-company delivery'. 'Issue-based', 'modular' and 'open' programmes are also thought to be relevant.
- A 'period of study in another EC country', a 'study visit abroad' and 'block release' are not thought to be very relevant. Full-time study is ranked last in order of relevance when the 'very relevant' and 'relevant' replies are combined.

The importance of in-company delivery was further evidenced in a later question concerning the location of learning. The university is not always considered an appropriate place at which to offer management education and development programmes. The most appropriate location for learning is thought to be at a 'place of work', followed by a 'country house or specialist executive centre'.

Companies such as Apple, Ford, McDonald's, Motorola, Johnson & Johnson, SAS, TRW and Xerox run their own corporate colleges. This enables them to ensure that development activity matches their particular requirements, and can give them greater freedom to use the services of those individuals with skills that are especially relevant.

TRAINING MEMBERS OF THE NETWORK

Development and awareness-building activity can be opened to customers. This enables a company to build closer relationships with its key customers. The IBM Institute is an example of this approach.

According to David Thompson, chairman of Rank Xerox UK:

'The training vision needs to embrace the customer, and customer training is an essential element of adding value. Training people to use technology is not an "add on", but an integral part of the product.

'The customer is not an outsider, but a colleague and a partner in training. Customers should be directly involved in training and other activities that add value for them. The customer is part of the business. Suppliers should share their understanding with customers, work with them and learn from them. This is what joint, relationship, or supply chain training is all about.

'The perspective and vision of trainers needs to be broadened beyond the company. It needs to embrace all those who add value for customers. These include suppliers, business partners and the customers themselves.' [19]

Rank Xerox offers a range of customer education workshops designed to help users obtain better value from technology. These are designed alongside the products to which they relate. They are not an afterthought, introduced when problems arise.

WORKPLACE LEARNING

Effective learning comes from doing things and observing the outcomes. Group and team learning can be particularly beneficial in this respect.

The interviews carried out in the course of the SEMS survey[2] confirmed a strong preference for workplace learning, and a desire to integrate learning and working. It is thought that learning and working should not be separated, and that learning is more successful when its purpose and relevance to the work context are perceived.

The nature of the workplace is changing. The fixation of much of management education with competing, negotiating and winning has meant that many senior managers have had to discover for themselves that companies have common interests, and while competing in some areas they may usefully co-operate in others.

NEW SOURCES OF INSIGHT

Blood cannot be squeezed from a stone. So insights relating to the world of flexible network organisations may not always be obtainable from people and institutions whose experience, competence and literature have derived from the bureaucratic environment. More relevant sources of insight may need to be tapped, in relation to conflict and co-operation as follows.

- Political scientists have long realised that nation states have interests in common, and that these give rise to opportunities for functional co-operation. A functional theory of politics has been developed, and many managers concerned with improving co-operation along suppply chains would benefit from examining how inter-state collaboration has grown and developed.[20]
- Managers need to come to terms with the extent to which, in a marketplace of network organisations, there is competition on the basis of attitudes and values. When these are in conflict, there are often problems of perception to address. The literature of international relations yields a rich heritage of material concerning competition between value systems, and how attitudes and values influence perception.[21]
- Those seeking to understand the continuing global struggle between Coca-Cola and Pepsi might gain more insights from a history of the Punic Wars, or a study of the

global struggle between capitalism and communism, than from a management textbook.

We will return to this theme in a moment, and in the next chapter which looks specifically at the role of business schools and consultants in relation to corporate transformation.

DEATH BY CLONING

One apparent inconsistency between the findings of the SEMS survey[2] and those of other surveys[4,22] concerns the importance attached to tailored in-company programmes, given the acknowledged dangers of the 'identikit' or 'clone' manager. The interviewees admitted to being 'pulled in different directions'.

- They are aware of the dangers of 'introversion' and 'groupthink' that can result from company-specific programmes. They also understood the value of benchmarking and learning from others.
- At the same time, they acknowledge that as their companies were endeavouring to formulate distinct visions, and develop attitudes and processes that would distinguish them from the approaches of competitors, it was becoming more difficult to absorb 'general inputs' or 'standard solutions' from outside.

In Chapter 11 we saw that a common perspective can help to hold the international network organisation together. ICL acknowledges that its international management development programme 'reinforces the company's global values and beliefs'.

However, a common culture should not be allowed to become a straitjacket. Exposure to different cultures and ways of doing things may enable people to see 'outside of the square'.[23]

Management development that is too prescribed can encourage people to reproduce a standard response, or move forward in small incremental steps. What may also be needed is the corporate environment that enables people to link up and establish relationships between factors that were previously thought to be unrelated. The caterpillar moves incrementally, the kangaroo bounds ahead.

An international network organisation should do more than tolerate diversity, it should actively encourage it. The author's view is as follows.[24]

> Greater diversity and variety can and should be sought among those who share the vision as learning and change are more likely to occur where views are continually challenged and there is tension between alternative viewpoints. Debate can be more important than a consensus that is based upon uncritical acceptance. ...
> Different ways of doing things should be actively encouraged within an international network organisation, so that different elements of the network may learn from each other.

BROADENING AWARENESS AND PERSPECTIVE

A manager seeking to broaden his or her perspective should not expect to seek inspiration in the 'usual places', or from people whose expertise relates to a world from which companies are planning to escape. In other fields insights abound concerning the dilemmas faced by the transitioning corporate organisation. For example:

- the manager who feels some twinges of concern about the extent to which certain groups of staff appear to uncritically accept the mythology of the latest corporate panacea might wish to reflect upon the excesses of nationalism.[25]

- another manager seeking insights as to how to change the perspective of staff to embrace the growing interdependence of companies within supply chains could examine how a similar process among states led to a reassessment of a traditional competitive view of international relations.[26]

Reference has already been made to the literature of politics. This may be very relevant to the executive seeking to create an open culture in which people are encouraged to question, and the right to dissent is preserved. It could also yield valuable insights into how the various interests of a network might be held together against external pressures and divisive forces.

ACTIVE INVOLVEMENT

Involvement and participation are only of value if those who are to be involved and whose participation is sought are able to add value. To do this they must have the time and motivation to think.

Self-managed workgroups are pointless if people lack the capability to think for themselves. If they are not to draw upon a wide range of experiences, insights and perspectives, the benefits of giving responsibility to a group rather than to an individual will be lost.

Richard Pascale has emphasised that in a chaotic world people need to be equipped and encouraged to challenge prevailing organisational views.[27] To do this they may need to be focused on a problem or issue that is broader than their immediate responsibilities.

A group might secure some understanding of the network as a whole, and particularly of its dynamics and tensions, by charging it with a task of producing a strategy and programme for taking over or killing the network. The outputs from such a development exercise could be of considerable value to senior management in seeking to identify points of weakness and areas of vulnerability.

SHARING THE BENEFITS

During the SEMS survey[2] a requirement emerged for a range of services that effectively spans development and consultancy. Its source lies in dissatisfaction with much of what is currently on offer.

- Interviewees feel that much of traditional management education and development benefits individual students without offering corresponding gains for employing companies.
- A criticism of consultancy is that while corporate problems might be solved, little was usually done to increase the ability of internal staff to tackle related and similar problems at a later date.

Hence, there is a strong desire for project-based programmes which could be focused on significant workplace problems. Their solution in a development context might offer benefits to both student and employer.

LEARNING PARTNERSHIPS

The results of the SEMS survey[2] suggest that there are opportunities for external partners to work with companies in the identification and definition of workplace based projects that are both intrinsically important and offer development opportunities. The requirement can be met by the establishment of a learning partnership.

- The learning and development needs of the individuals or teams working upon the selected projects derive from their particular characteristics and requirements, and are facilitated by whatever means is thought most appropriate.
- The 'external' party involved provides a varying mix of services depending upon the portfolio of projects being undertaken at any moment in time.

As a number of learning partnerships are created, the network organisation metamorphoses into a learning network (Figure 13.1). When this becomes international, its members require sensitivity to cultural diversity.

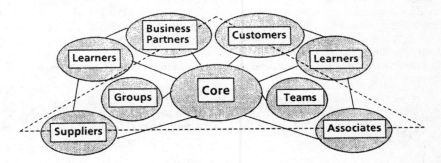

Figure 13.1 *The Learning Network*

Business schools have been criticised by Mintzberg for their excessive use of analytical tools and rational approaches, and inadequate attention to the encouragement of intuition.[28] Too often, students are encouraged to reach for their calculators and crunch the numbers, rather than observe and listen.

The members of the international learning network, as one interviewee put it: 'Have to be able to look and listen in different languages.'

BUILDING THE LEARNING NETWORK

Education and the technology that is used to support it should enable people to discover how they can best build their understanding. According to IRL, the traditional 'black box' that produces an outcome without revealing why this has occurred 'deskills', while 'transparent technology' that allows the learner to observe processes at work can increase understanding with each application.[13]

Experience of new approaches to education around the world is growing. There are school networks and 'electronic' universities that bring together learners and facilitators. Companies participate in the Danish Enterprise–University System. Henley has a functioning E-mail and computer conferencing network. At the European level there is the DELTA programme and Euro PACE encouragement of satellite and computer networks.

The educational institution itself needs to evolve into a learning network (Figure 13.1) that can participate in learning partnerships. Resources should be switched from the campus and its buildings, to the technology and processes of the network. International learning networks can bring together learners and facilitators from around the globe.

As we will see in Chapter 17, all the elements that are needed to turn the international network into the international learning network exist. The same, or compatible, processes and technology can support both learning and working across barriers of distance, function and time. They are available to those with the vision and will to use them.

BENCHMARKING

As an alternative to calling in expensive external expertise, a company should consider the extent to which people in different parts of the organisation might learn from each other. In the case of the larger company there may be scope for internal benchmarking to encourage different business units to learn from each other. Passing on experience and insights also enables centres of excellence to consolidate and internalise what they have learned.

When Unilever first started on the task of establishing a global network it found it had created a chaotic mess typical of that found in many multinational companies. As a first step towards co-ordination and consolidation, the central IT team set out to identify examples of best practice. An approach was found at Elida Gibbs–Fabergé, a French company within the group, that formed the basis of a system that was copied and made available throughout the corporation.

The experience of benchmark companies such as Rank Xerox suggests that:

- approaches, processes, tools and techniques have been developed that can enable more companies to achieve a better return from training expenditure;
- there are cost-effective and flexible ways of managing and delivering training, and focusing training effort upon core activities, key objectives and 'vital few' programmes.

THE KEY QUESTIONS

It is time that training and development activities were subjected to a critical review. There is a massive training and consultancy sector that has a vested interest in propagating the 'advantages' of training. Independent and objective advice can be difficult to find. From the point of view of the individual company there are two key questions that should be asked.

- If your company increased its expenditure on training by a factor of ten, would there be a significant improvement in customer satisfaction?
- If the people within your company spent half their time on training activities, would there be a significant change in their attitudes or behaviour?

Evidence suggests that, for most companies, the answers to both of these questions would be no. Few companies are equipping their people to bring about desired changes. Such training as is provided tends to be departmental and often has little, if any, impact on either external customer satisfaction or internal attitudes and behaviour.

In some areas, performance appears to be inversely related to the training that is provided. Development activity undertaken for the best of motives can be worse than neutral, it can turn out to be counter-productive.

It is essential that companies identify what constitutes value to their customers, and the processes, and particularly the cross-functional processes, that deliver this value. Relevant training is that which is focused upon those activities that generate satisfied customers.

Quality and other corporate programmes will continue to fail to achieve significant results until crucial missing pieces of the transformation jigsaw puzzle are put in place. Whatever is spent on training will do little other than increase frustration, until critical obstacles to change are identified and overcome.

CHECKLIST

▶ Is the culture of your organisation conducive of learning?

▶ Is there tolerance and the active encouragement of diversity?

▶ Do the members of the board and senior management team act as role models in terms of their commitment to learning?

▶ Are formal education and development programmes focused upon those processes and activities that add value for customers?

▶ Do these programmes embrace other members of the supply chain, such as customers, suppliers and business partners?

▶ What, if anything, does your company learn from customers and other supply chain partners?

▶ How willing is your company to refine and modify its objectives and processes?

▶ What is done to help the people of your company identify their learning potential?

▶ Are individuals encouraged to work and learn in ways that match their own preferences and potential?

▶ Are working and learning integrated?

▶ What does your company do to encourage informal learning?

▶ Is the reward and remuneration system, and are promotion decisions, conducive of learning?

REFERENCES

1 Prowse, M (1992) 'Yale Chief Quits to Build US Schools for Profit', *Financial Times*, 27 May, p 1.
2 Coulson-Thomas, C (1990) *Human Resource Development for International Operation*, a Survey sponsored by Surrey European Management School, Adaptation Ltd, London.
3 Coulson-Thomas, C and Brown, R (1989) *The Responsive Organisation, People Management: the Challenge of the 1990s*, BIM, Corby.
4 Coulson-Thomas, C and Coe, T (1991) *The Flat Organisation: Philosophy and Practice*, BIM, Corby.
5 Lorenz, C (1992) 'Bending Minds to a New Learning Circle', *Financial Times*, 17 February, p 11.
6 Tovey, L (1991) *Management Training and Development in Large UK Business Organisations*, Harbridge Consulting Group, London.
7 Coulson-Thomas, C (1992) *Creating the Global Company, Successful Internationalisation*, McGraw-Hill, London, p 331.
8 Coulson-Thomas, C (1990) *Professional Development of and for the Board*, Institute of Directors, London.
9 Coulson-Thomas, C and Coulson-Thomas S (1991) *Communicating for Change*, an Adaptation Survey for Granada Business Services, London.
10 Stephens, M D (1991) *Japan and Education*, Macmillan, London.
11 Handy, C (1989) *The Age of Unreason*, Business Books, London.
12 Booth, C (1992) 'Paul At Fifty', *Time*, 8 June, pp 50–2.
13 Institute for Research on Learning, (c1988) *The Advancement of Learning*, Institute for Research on Learning, Palo Alto, Calif, undated.
14 Ascher, K (1983) *Management Training in Large UK Business Organisations*, Harbridge House, London.
15 Bennis, W and Nanus, B (1985) *Leaders: the Strategies for Taking Charge*, Harper & Row, New York.
16 Neave, H (1990) *The Deming Dimension*, SPC Press, Knoxville, Tenn.
17 Hussey, D E (1988) *Management Training and Corporate Strategy*, Pergamon, Oxford; and Nilsson, W P (1987) *Achieving Strategic Goals Through Executive Development*, Addison Wesley, Reading, Mass.
18 CBI Education and Training Directorate (1992) *Focus on the First Line: the Role of the Supervisor*, CBI, London.

19   Thompson, D (1991) 'Wokefield Park Official Opening: Training, a Partnership with the Customer'; comments made at the official opening of the Rank Xerox UK national training centre at Wokefield Park, 23 September.
20   Mitrany, D (1975) *The Functional Theory of Politics*, Martin Robertson, London.
21   Jervis, R (1976) *Perception and Misperception in International Politics*, Princeton University Press, Princeton, NJ.
22   Coulson-Thomas, C and Brown, R (1990) *Beyond Quality, Managing the Relationship with the Customer*, BIM, Corby.
23   Ohmae, K (1982) *The Mind of the Strategist*, McGraw-Hill, New York.
24   Coulson-Thomas, C (1992) *Creating the Global Company, Successful Internationalisation*, McGraw-Hill, London, p 209.
25   Kedourie, E (1960) *Nationalism*, Hutchinson, London.
26   Keohane, R O and Nye, J S (1977) *Power and Interdependence: World Politics in Transition*, Little, Brown, Boston.
27   Pascale, R T (1990) *Managing On the Edge*, Simon & Schuster, New York and Viking, London.
28   Mintzberg, H (1989) *Mintzberg on Management*, The Free Press, New York and Collier Macmillan, London.

14

CONSULTANTS AND BUSINESS SCHOOLS: FACILITATORS OR PARASITES?

AN UNPRECEDENTED OPPORTUNITY

One senses urgency and desperation. Given the importance attached to corporate transformation, and the range of problems being experienced, consultants and business schools should be having a field day. Notwithstanding an economic recession or slow-down in key world economies, people running corporations need help.

Across a wide range of companies there is a requirement to equip people to cope with the demands of a turbulent business environment. There is also the desire of both public and private corporations, and other institutions, to become more flexible and responsive. There is now widespread agreement concerning the need for transition from machine bureaucracy to organic network. However, there is little confidence that the fundamental changes of attitude and perspective required to bring it about will be achieved.

As part of the transformation process, companies are also seeking to hive off and subcontract. As this trend gathers pace, it creates further opportunities for external providers of services.

In tackling the lucrative openings in the marketplace, consultancies have access to 'the brightest and the best'. When it comes to promotion, presentations and the production of glossy brochures, the services of the slickest and the smoothest are at their disposal. After reading just a few consultants' 'mailshots', it seems remarkable that many companies should have management problems at all.

THE BLIND LEADING THE BLIND

And yet, in general, those who have been interviewed in the course of the surveys upon which this book is based are far from satisfied with the quality of external services they receive. On occasion, their purveyors are perceived as parasites rather than facilitators. As one managing director put it: 'If you get it right, don't tell anyone. If you do, every consultant will be trying to get hold of your ideas. They seem desperate for anything that works.'

Although many business schools and consultancies have a public commitment to learning from, and sharing, best practice, this has not stopped some of them, and those who use their services, from jumping at techniques such as 'benchmarking' as if they represent a revelation. One director confided: 'We are into begging, stealing and borrowing like there is no tomorrow.'

Robert Camp has advocated corporate benchmarking programmes, or learning from the best, as a route to superior performance.[1] However, too many service organisations only compare themselves with average performers in their own particular sector. This can result in the spread of panaceas, hype and misunderstanding, and gives added momentum to the latest craze. While it may be good news for those who ride bandwagons, it is not so hot for those whose toes get in the way.

When external suppliers, such as consultants, do get hold of a best practice 'gem', their motivation is often to spread it around their client base as soon as possible. Thus the corporation's competitive edge can quickly become industry commonplace. One CEO of an innovative company mused: 'Sometimes I just feel as though we have been idea-stripped. We pay to be intellectually cleaned out.'

Some consultants receive as good as they give. Companies invite various consultants to pitch for business and then 'do it themselves', using the best of the various ideas they have picked up. The 'learning organisation' is a voracious and insatiable plunderer and consumer of intellectual capital. The wary choose their network partners with care.

PEOPLE AND CORPORATE TRANSFORMATION

In essence, corporate transformation is a service activity. Its achievement is dependent upon 'reaching', motivating, coaching and counselling people; involving, empowering and supporting them; equipping them with the skills they need; sharing values with them; helping them to build new forms of relationships; and changing their attitudes and perspectives.

Involving people in workplace activities that lead to desired outcomes encourages 'positive' attitude and behaviour changes.[2] Success leads to further success.

Coping with disappointment and failure can bring other qualities to the surface. It can lead to 'negative' behaviour such as concealment or the denial of reality, deception, deflection of the blame on to others, and the search for excuses and scapegoats. Hence the desire to close gaps between aspiration and achievement, and the need for help.

Collectively, consultants and business schools offer a wide range of programmes, including short courses and 'in-company' training. The faculties and staff of many individual suppliers represent significant concentrations of expertise. But how is this 'resource' perceived? Are organisations approaching consultants and business schools for advice on fundamental issues concerning corporate transformation, or to meet particular skill needs?

DOUBTS AND CONCERNS

There are clearly potential openings for the services of consultants, business schools, and of education and training generally. But several recent surveys[3–9] suggest that if this opportunity is to be seized, a fundamental rethink, and new attitudes and approaches may be necessary.

- In a number of key areas the advice of consultants, business schools and their staff is not perceived as either relevant or desirable.
- Traditional skills and services are no longer perceived as being sufficient to bring about the corporate transformations that are required. Changes of approach, attitude and perspective are sought, not knowledge *per se* or technical skills. Holistic programmes are needed, not discrete 'products'.
- Many companies have become wary, if not distrustful, of external sources of advice and services, and are instead relying upon their own internal resources.

THE ADVISER AS LEARNER

The smarter consultancies recognise that they have much to learn. We saw in Chapter 13 that a growing number of companies are seeking to integrate learning and working.

Consultants need access to these learning environments in order to become learning partners.

Within many consultancies and business schools people still learn and practise as individuals within a framework of functional departments. There is segregation by subject and specialism, rather than the cross-functional team. Buildings contain lecture and seminar rooms, rather than learning areas and atmospheres.

After many years of observation of workplace learning in group situations, Revans concluded that 'action learning' is preferable to solitary learning in the classroom situation.[10] Yet classroom learning persists, along with various devices from case studies, through simulation to the introduction of virtual reality to emulate and imitate learning situations that abound in far richer forms in most companies.

The desire of some consultants and academics to learn about new and alternative approaches has given rise to the accusation that they are 'learning from' rather than 'learning with'. The 'learning from' approach can cause much resentment, while the 'learning with' approach can command respect. According to one CEO:

> *'I would respect a guy who came in and said "Look, neither of us knows that much about this, but let's take a bite at it together". ... I can't stand those who try to con you when they haven't a clue. I would prefer to trust someone with their eyes open and a willingness to learn.'*

Consultants and business schools themselves face a transformation requirement. This chapter considers the challenge of changing their attitudes and perspective, and examines what selected surveys reveal about two basic questions

1   the perceived relevance of external advice and services; and
2   to whom corporate organisations are turning for advice.

THE NEED FOR NEW APPROACHES, AND CHANGES OF ATTITUDES AND PERSPECTIVE

One consistent finding of recent surveys[3-9] is the need for new approaches and changes of attitudes and perspective. We have observed the consequences and limitations of a narrow and mechanical approach to activities as varied as planning, communicating and problem solving, at a number of points in this book.

While many western business schools and consultants encourage the 'analysis of problems to the death', Kenichi Ohmae has drawn attention to the effectiveness of many of the more intuitive and pragmatic approaches of Japanese strategists.[11] They exude a positive commitment to finding practical solutions to real problems, rather than theoretical options and possibilities, or optimum outcomes.

THE EVIDENCE

Much of the evidence is persuasive, in that it is both unsolicited and partially unexpected. Let us first review some relevant findings which we have considered in earlier chapters. These are taken from three complementary survey reports published in 1991.[3,4,5]

MANAGING THE FLAT ORGANISATION

The BIM *Flat Organisation* report[3] reveals or concludes as follows.

- While every respondent agrees that human resource is a critical success factor, and harnessing human potential emerges as perhaps the major 'internal' management challenge, few companies appear to be satisfied with the extent to which they are tapping the talents of their people.

- There is uncertainty as to how qualities sought to manage change might be best developed, and there is insufficient commitment to action to equip managers to cope with the new realities. In particular, too few managers are being equipped with team-working skills.
- The 'gap' between vision and conduct, and rhetoric and reality, suggests a lack of top management commitment in many companies. What is needed is a new approach, a new perspective and new attitudes.

IMPLEMENTING TOTAL QUALITY

The *Quality: The Next Steps* survey[4] also suggests a need for both greater commitment and a change of attitudes.

- Over nine out of ten respondents consider 'top management commitment' to be a 'very significant' barrier to the implementation of a quality process.
- The 'quality of management' followed closely by 'quality behaviour, attitudes and values' are the top quality priorities. Over eight out of ten respondents expect to give them a 'higher priority' over the next five years.

COMMUNICATING FOR CHANGE

The findings of the *Communicating for Change* survey[5] again highlight the requirement for commitment, and the need to change attitudes rather than equip people with particular skills.

- There is widespread awareness of the need to change. However, a desire for significant change is rarely matched by a confident understanding of how to bring it about.
- Communication skills, followed by top management commitment, emerge as the most significant barriers to effective internal and external communication. The traditional 'technique-orientated' communications skills courses are thought to be inadequate when changes of attitude and approach are called for.
- Fundamental changes of attitudes, values, approach and perspective are needed, and these usually take a long time to achieve.

DIRECTORIAL ATTITUDES AND PERSPECTIVES

The questioning of top management commitment revealed by these surveys suggests that there may be a problem in the boardroom. As we saw in Chapters 3 and 4, other surveys completed in 1990 and 1991[6,7,8] reveal the need for development assistance at board level:

- nine out of ten directors did not receive any form of formal preparation prior to their appointment to the board;[6]
- six out of ten directors have not received any formal development since their appointment to the board;[7]
- three-quarters of chairmen are not satisfied with the performance of their boards;[8]
- awareness, attitudes and perspective feature strongly in the development needs of directors.[6,7,8]

All these 'director' surveys stress the importance of attitudes and perspective at all levels in organisations, up to and including the board. A further, and 1990, survey[9] has concluded that: equipping people for successful international operation is fundamentally a question of attitude and perspective.

THE SURVEYS AND THE SURVEY PARTICIPANTS

Are the views expressed in these surveys of significance, and should they concern the consultancy, education and training community? To answer this question, let us consider in more detail two of the 'management issue' surveys that highlight the need for changes of attitudes and perspectives, and one of the surveys dealing with development needs at board level.

- Half of the *Human Resource Development for International Operation* survey[9] respondents are at board level. Fifteen per cent are chairmen or CEOs.
- Approaching six out of ten of the participants in the *Quality: the Next Steps* survey[4] are at board level, and over a quarter of the responses are from chairmen or CEOs.
- Three-quarters of the *Professional Development of and for the Board* survey[6] responses were from those holding the job titles of 'chairman' or 'chairman and managing director'.

Overall, the seniority of the respondents, and the size of the organisations, participating in these surveys (see Appendix 1) are such that the views expressed about the relevance of various sources of advice and services concerning corporate transformation ought to be of interest to their external providers.

THE RELEVANCE OF EXTERNAL ADVICE AND SERVICES

So what relevance do survey participants attach to various internal and external sources of advice and support? Let us start by examining the question of the perceived relevance of business schools as a source of advice.

MANAGEMENT DEVELOPMENT

So far as advice on management development issues is concerned, the most commonly-cited sources for participants in the *HRD for International Operation* survey[9] are internal human resource, personnel or training specialists, followed by external consultants and advisers (Table 14.1).

Table 14.1 *Sources of authoritative advice and information on management development issues*

Source	No of Organisations
Internal HR/personnel/training specialists	41
External consultants/advisers	25
Business schools	16
Professional and national/international associations	8
Other educational institutions	6
Various/others	5

Source: Human Resource Development for International Operation, 1990

Two interview comments appear to sum up common views and concerns.

'If it's standard and structured, I know I can go out and get any number of different techniques. ... [They will be] documented, and the manuals will be available. But how do you get the people all around you to think in new ways ... to feel differently about things? That's tough for anyone else.'

'We used to buy things that were done to people ... they were equipped with this and that skill. It's you and and your colleagues who are [now] involved. ... Our relationships with people influence their attitudes ... the way they see problems. We have to work it out with them ourselves.'

IMPLEMENTING TOTAL QUALITY

The replies of participants in the *Quality: The Next Steps* survey[4] to a question concerning the importance given to various sources of advice and support on quality matters are summarised in Table 14.2, ranked in terms of both 'very important' replies at (a), and when one adds together the 'very important' and 'important' replies at (b):

- Business schools appear at the bottom of both tables. In spite of the overall importance they attach to training, not a single respondent considers the advice and support of business schools to be 'very important'.
- 'Internal/own quality specialists' are overwhelmingly the preferred source of quality advice and support. They are considered 'important' by over nine out of ten respondents, and 'very important' by six out of ten respondents.

Table 14.2 *Quality Advice and Support*

(a) Ranked in order of 'very important' replies (%)	
Internal/own quality specialists	60
Specialist quality consultants	14
Individual quality 'gurus'	9
Professional institutes and associations	6
Management consultants	5
Business schools	0

(b) Ranked in order of 'very important' and 'important' replies combined (%)	
Internal/own quality specialists	94
Specialist quality consultants	60
Professional institutes and associations	58
Individual quality 'gurus'	42
Management consultants	40
Business schools	13

Source: Quality: The Next Steps, 1991

We saw in the last chapter that because of a lack of faith in external providers, some companies have established their own colleges. Both Motorola and Xerox have used internal training and development as an integral and important element of their drives for total quality. Activity is related directly to the achievement of business objectives.

All those interviewed expressed a strong preference for internal sources of expertise. However, it was acknowledged that the company committed to total quality could benefit from an independent perspective, given the dangers of a narrow corporate view emerging.

According to one quality manager: 'It's difficult to find an overview out there. Different people are good at different things. We have drawn bits and pieces from all over the place. ... You just can't go to a single source ... we encourage people to benchmark ... to get different views.'

DIRECTORS AND BOARDS

For respondents in the 'director' survey,[6] the main sources of advice on matters to do with both individual directors and the board as a whole are professional associations, including the IOD itself. The next most relevant sources of advice are the companies' professional advisers, particularly professional firms of lawyers and accountants.

The relevance respondents attach to services from various sources are given in Table 14.3, which presents the rankings if one adds together the 'very relevant' and 'relevant' replies.

- For services which concern the 'development of the competencies of individual directors', professional associations, whether the IOD or other functional associations, head the list. Individual academics rank last as a source of services.
- For services which concern the 'development of the competencies of the board as a whole', the IOD itself is regarded as the most relevant source. Again, individual academics rank last as a source of services.

Table 14.3 *Professional Development Services Ranking in Terms of 'Very Relevant' and 'Relevant'*

(a) Services for the Development of Individual Directors' Competencies (%)

Functional Professional Associations	70
Institute of Directors	63
Specialist Consultants	60
In-Company Trainers	57
Postgraduate Business Schools	52
Open/Distance Learning	41
Management Consultants	39
'Consortium' Participation	38
Individual Academics	33

(b) Services for the Development of Whole Board's Competencies (%)

Institute of Directors	58
Specialist Consultants	56
Functional Professional Associations	50
In-Company Trainers	40
Management Consultants	39
Postgraduate Business Schools	36
'Consortium' Participation	36
Open/Distance Learning	29
Individual Academics	28

Note: Some respondents considered more than one service to be of relevance
Source: Professional Development of and for the Board, 1990

So far as the board as a whole is concerned, the IOD ranks some way ahead of 'functional professional associations', and significantly ahead of 'management consultants' and 'postgraduate business schools'. 'Postgraduate business schools' and their services only just rank ahead of 'individual academics'.

The business schools do not appear to be regarded as a relevant source, so far as the development of the competencies of the board as a whole is concerned. Over half of the respondents considered 'postgraduate business schools' to be either 'not very relevant' or 'irrelevant' as a source of services.

THE PRIMACY OF INTERNAL ADVICE

Let us now consider the question of the relative standing of internal and external sources of advice.

The *Quality: The Next Steps* survey[4] is not the only one which reveals 'the main source of advice' to be internal. The importance which respondents in another 1991 survey, *Communicating for Change*[5], attach to a number of sources of information and advice is summarised in Table 14.4. This ranks the sources in order of both 'very important' responses at (a), and when the 'very important' and 'important' responses are added together at (b).

Table 14.4 *Sources of Information and Advice to improve the management of change*

(a) Ranked in order of 'very important' replies (%)

Internal change project managers	27
External change consultants	13
Software houses and systems integrators	4
Computer and telecommunications suppliers	4
Professional institutes and associations	0

(b) Ranked in order of 'very important' and 'important' replies (%)

Internal change project managers	79
External change consultants	50
Software houses and systems integrators	33
Computer and telecommunications suppliers	31
Professional institutes and associations	15

Source: Communicating for Change, 1991

In short, 'internal change project managers' are considered important to the management of change, while external professional institutes and associations are considered 'not very important'. In the main, management teams appear to consider the management of change to be an internal responsibility.

The degree of commitment required, and the involvement of all employees, makes it difficult for many managers to identify other than specific tasks which could be undertaken by an external party. Consider the following comments.

'Role-model conduct is your responsibility. ... You can't go out and get a "stand in" ... [and] you need feedback from the people around you.'

'How can you smell what's going on around here, if you are not breathing the air?'

'Giving authority, ... taking out inhibitors, setting the scene and values ... these all involve lots of different people. No outsider would have the clout.'

'The [change programme] is evolving. ... [Because] it's changing you need to be here to steer it. There is no value in handing over a blueprint and walking away.'

'Outsiders always have to explain who they are, and under what terms they are working. ... It takes time for people to assess where they are coming from.'

The most important external source of information and advice is the 'external change consultant'. All other external sources are ranked by the majority of respondents as 'not very important'. A perceived 'problem' for many professional institutes and associations is their functional focus. The management of change is regarded as a holistic or 'total' process involving all functions and departments.

Scepticism towards external advice may be well founded. A survey of total quality programmes undertaken by A T Kearney and *The TQM Magazine* has found that successful companies are those that 'retain ownership of the programme', rather than abdicating this responsibility to external consultants.[12]

THE LIMITATIONS OF EXTERNAL ADVICE

Why are people putting such emphasis upon internal rather than external advice? The most cited reason in the *Quality: The Next Steps* survey[4] for preferring the development and use of internal staff, rather than buying in external expertise, is the need to understand the distinct corporate culture of a company.

- It is thought to be difficult for a third party fully to understand the particular features of an internal corporate culture. Companies appear reluctant to hand over what are perceived as culture-specific problems to third parties.

- People also doubt that 'standard solutions and packages' are of much value. According to a managing director: 'Perhaps we do sometimes exaggerate what's different about us. But what was good down the road may not work around here.'
- A frequent complaint of interviewees relates to the apparent reluctance of consultants to 'get to grips' with the unique situation and circumstances of individual companies. Instead there is a tendency to go automatic. As one director put it: 'Whenever I see earnest young people working their way through manuals or diagnostic kits that are inches thick, I worry. Someone somewhere is not thinking or asking basic questions.'
- Companies are finding it difficult to recruit experienced and competent quality practitioners who are able to move effectively between corporate cultures. Too often 'experts' turn out to be technical specialists, when the main problems to be overcome are managerial and attitudinal.
- There is a perception that much of what is provided is over-elaborate. One managing director expressed the view: 'If it's esoteric and you don't understand it, it probably misses the point. Working back from the customer reveals that complexity is often the result of a desire to justify an activity that is not generating value for customers.'

External suppliers are thought to be too complacent. There are those who uncritically apply deeply ingrained approaches, and who still claim to be practising 'scientific management' and following in the tradition of Frederick Taylor.[13] Science advances as a result of testing and observation. A few moments spent observing the actual outcomes of much of what passes as 'scientific management' would reveal that it is not working.

A RELUCTANCE TO BECOME INVOLVED

Independence and objectivity can be extremely desirable qualities. However, in some cases, the maintenance of 'professional distance' can conceal a reluctance to become involved.

One cynical interviewee suggested: 'If you provide a bit of what's required, and then stand back, you can avoid blame when things go wrong.' The fault can be ascribed to the whole, and how the individual change elements were combined or used.

According to those interviewed in the course of the *Communicating for Change* survey.[5]

- Many people selling external services have an inadequate understanding of the internal context within which these could be used and applied. They 'push' their own services, rather than work with 'users or clients' to develop new approaches that confront marketplace realities and opportunities.
- Many suppliers still focus upon 'the short-term sale' rather than the building of longer-term relationships, even though there is widespread use of such pat phrases as 'in-company', 'tailoring' and 'finding solutions to customer problems'.

Overall, the approach is that of external supplier rather than network member. As one director put it: 'There is a premature packaging of the product. The proposal is in while we are still trying to get to grips with what the problem really is. They want to supply to us ... [but] they are not working with us.'

THE MIGRATION FROM EXTERNAL SUPPORT TO SELF-HELP

Companies attaching most weight to external advice and support appear to be those that are relatively new to a corporate initiative such as quality.[4] The role of the external consultant as an initial catalyst is acknowledged.

During the process of corporate transformation, many companies appear to rely increasingly upon their own resources. Consider the following selection of comments:

'We used external help to get off the starting block. But now we're implementing ourselves. Externals are an expensive way of getting the legwork done.'

'The key points came across in the various pitches and presentations. We ended up deciding to use our own people. You need to do it yourself, as this is the best way of learning and getting the attitude changes that you need.'

'I'm beginning to get an overview of how it all fits together. Our consultants are still focused on their individual offerings. They don't see the big picture.'

'I would prefer a longer term partnership, but we tend to quickly absorb what [consultants] have to offer, and move on. How come those who advise and counsel are so incapable of learning?'

In order to play a useful role in facilitating change, a process consultant needs persistance and a high degree of staying power.[14] Organisational transformation is not a business for those with a penchant for working mechanically through a standard set of techniques and tools, and greeting the unexpected with the cry: 'What now?'

THE NAÏVE AND THE INNOCENT

The management teams of companies that are starting out on the 'quality journey' are drawn like moths to a light to those who promise results. Having committed the organisation, they crave reassurance. They are anxious, and want to feel that they have done the right thing.

The focus of most consultants is almost entirely upon the lessons of success, and yet Bennis and Nanus have rightly drawn attention to the importance of learning from failure.[15] The leaders they studied, 'simply don't think about failure, don't even use the word, relying on such synonyms as "mistake", "glitch", "bungle", or countless others'; and they concluded that 'early success' is 'the worst problem in leadership'.

Suave and beguiling consultants flatter and serve up great dollops of what they know or imagine their clients want to hear. Some may not even realise they are doing it. They 'keep in' by offering the reassurance that is so desperately sought, 'maintaining accounts' by avoiding reality and selling deception. Their life at court is only disturbed when the CEO is fired. They then have a successor to 'size up and work on'.

Companies that have made some progress with quality appear more sophisticated.

- They are more aware of the unique nature and requirements of their own companies. By now they know that simplistic approaches do not work. As one manager put it: 'Those were the teenage years – now we've grown up.'
- Suspicion of generalised solutions and experience gained elsewhere grows as an approach to quality comes to be seen as an integral element of a unique corporate culture.
- Their internal capability may have grown to match or exceed that of the external supplier. These are the companies that focus upon 'adding value' and raise the question: 'What's in it for us?'

As organisations seek to differentiate themselves from competitors, and develop strong and unique corporate cultures, interviewees in the *Communicating for Change* survey[5] are also finding it increasingly difficult to absorb 'external inputs'. Consultants take time to adjust to the unique aspects of corporate culture, and there is criticism of the general nature of much of their advice.

CRITICISMS OF STANDARD SOLUTIONS

Several interviewees complained during the course of the *Quality: The Next Steps* survey[4] that they were regularly in receipt of promotional material from a wide range of organisations, including business schools, offering quality and training services. Much of this is described as of 'indifferent quality', 'simplistic', 'insufficiently focused' or 'too technique oriented'.

In general, those with a few years' experience of implementing quality within their organisations do not feel that the contribution of most external organisations would 'add much value'. More mature and holistic approaches are sought, which are substantially tailored to the needs of a particular corporate culture, and confront the need to change attitudes and perspective.

Among interviewees in the *Communicating for Change* survey[5] there also appears to be considerable suspicion of standard 'off the shelf' solutions. Many organisations are relying primarily upon their own internal resources because of growing awareness of the time it takes to achieve a significant change of attitudes.

Some seasoned campaigners avoid those with solutions, and seek out those with the problems. A 1990 study of project managers and project management undertaken by Adaptation Ltd for the Association of Project Managers found that the 'information' most sought by project managers was details of problems, and 'things that went badly wrong' with projects and how they were overcome.[16]

SUSPICION OF THE EXPERTS

Those intimately involved in corporate transformation may encounter, almost daily, a variety of situations for the first time. They journey through a changing landscape, and are deeply suspicious of experts with maps. Too many of the 'specialists', both internally and externally, are thought to be but one step ahead of those they advise.

Organisational change is very threatening to specialist groups that are reluctant to shift their focus and to put the emphasis upon 'working with' as a team member, rather than 'working for' as an expert adviser.

- Groups of experts in head office specialisms from personnel to IT are being slimmed down, with many central groups being wound up. As one CEO put it: 'Around here, if you don't take a holistic view, we're likely to take a holistic view of your job.'
- Specialist services are being contracted out, or delegated to business units where they are closer to customers, and it is easier to align professional priorities with commercial objectives.
- Those at the centre are expected to take a broader view, focusing upon strategies and policies, rather than operational matters. Many individuals appear reluctant to 'step up' to this challenge, their perspective remaining functional rather than extending to embrace the totality of the company.
- Services may now need to be sold, rather than costs allocated. This means building relationships with possible users and understanding their priorities.
- Some professionals find that their area of expertise is suddenly in demand and that the CEO has 'at last noticed'. Rather than respond by rushing out to claim their place in the sun, many professionals fail to rise to the occasion and lurk in the shadows instead.
- The reluctance of many professionals to venture beyond the confines of the narrowest definition of their skills means they watch from the sidelines while a succession of new groups claim centre stage.

Experts and specialists are a distinguishing feature of the machine bureaucracy. In the 'locust years' of cartels and 'barriers to entry' they could be afforded. The size of central staffs was a mark of status, rather like the number of cattle in the chief's kraal.

Years of service in bureaucratic organisations have given many professionals a reluctance to examine alternative approaches, or stray beyond the confines of job descriptions and procedure manuals. They are inhibited and constrained, prisoners of the familiar, and victims of the routines and standards they administer and police.

Professional values put great stress upon reliability and predictability. Surprises are unwelcome and uncertainties are avoided. Too many managers, and those who advise them, are afraid to take risks. Rosabeth Moss Kanter has found that the more adaptive and innovative companies are those which encourage their people to take risks.[17]

MANAGING WHAT ISN'T

Too much management attention is paid to modifying what is, rather than searching for what is missing. What is can be 'seen and suffered'. What is not there may appear to be something of an act of faith. Managers are often reluctant to devote time to pursuing what may turn out to be a mirage. Squeezing small, incremental improvements out of the familiar may appear to be a 'safer' option.

Similarly, much consultancy effort is devoted to the application of tried and tested tools and techniques to existing approaches and activities, rather than to identifying missing elements, and devising and adopting new approaches that may have greater relevance. Expertise, training and technology are devoted to what is, rather than bringing about what ought to be.

If the key processes that deliver the value sought by customers are cross-functional and inter-organisational, delays are hidden, and 'hinders' have not been explored, a company should expect relatively limited returns from departmental consultancy projects. A more holistic approach may be needed if more fundamental change is to be achieved.

A checklist along the lines of Figure 14.1 could be used to identify areas of external expertise that might be needed to support the introduction of a corporate transformation programme. Any external resource that is contracted should understand the contribution of its particular area of authority in relation to the programme as a whole.

Requirement	Own Capability	Develop Capability	Consultant on Network
Formulating vision			
Communicating/sharing vision			
Strategic planning			
Allocating objectives/Roles and responsibilites			
Empowerment			
Self-managed work groups			
Reward and recognition			
Process simplification			
Process re-engineering			
Document management			
Team working			
Project management			
Quality training			

Figure 14.1 *Consultants' Checklist*

When certain elements are implemented exceptionally well, and in the process demand and receive an excessive amount of attention, a programme as a whole can become unbalanced. Enthusiasts must know when to stop. Some areas may need to be reined back in the interests of balance, and so that complementary aspects can catch up.

DANGERS OF SELF-RELIANCE

In certain companies a suspicion of 'external' services in general has been taken to an extreme. A dislike of what are termed 'general' or 'standard' solutions, appears to be leading to an excessive and unhealthy reliance upon internal expertise. For example:

- some companies, while readily admitting their own lack of speed and progress in tackling the management barriers to quality, are drawing almost exclusively upon their own experience;[3,4]
- many companies acknowledge a reluctance to learn from others by, for instance, benchmarking themselves against non-competing companies.[4]

Self-help is most dangerous where there is complacency, and of greatest value where there is openness, trust and a willingness to learn.

According to Vern Zelmer, managing director of Rank Xerox UK, in commenting upon the 'glory years' at Xerox: 'The main problem was getting the cash truck to the bank each night. We became complacent, and developed the overheads to match.'

We will see in Chapter 18 that, more recently, Xerox and Rank Xerox have displayed a sustained commitment to learning from both outside and within. External benchmarking and internal self-help are practised as integral elements of a comprehensive corporate change programme.

LEARNING RELATIONSHIPS

Many companies would benefit from the establishment of a wider range of learning relationships, in order to share experiences of tackling similar problems. Learning partners might be found in a wide range of sectors and locations, and could become members of the network organisation. Directors and senior managers have expressed a desire for networks of colleague and peer relationships that enable people with similar problems to learn from each other.[18]

The global network form of organisation allows certain territorial barriers to be overcome. In some countries, such as Japan, it may not be possible or practical for foreign professionals to operate locally in order to offer certain services. Rather than operate within a country, the service could be provided from without by means of network access and delivery.

We saw in Chapter 9 how important it is for companies to:

- enter into closer relationships with both customers and suppliers, in order to jointly explore change and quality requirements, and establish collaborative activities;[3,4]
- understand that a variety of approaches to quality are possible.[4] An external review can enable an approach to be more closely tailored to a company's needs and situation. The right external party can contribute a broader perspective and an awareness of alternative approaches.

These are areas in which there could be scope for external facilitation. The larger companies, and those more 'secure' in their commitment to change and quality, appear more open to the value of benchmarking, and a diversity of approaches. While many smaller companies seem to have adopted one approach and 'stuck to it', certain larger corporations appear consciously to be seeking different and competing overviews, in order to 'challenge' or 'test' their management teams.

ROOTS OF INCOMPATIBILITY

Many consultancies and professional firms face particular problems when seeking to establish longer-term partnership relationships with corporate clients. To take some examples:

- Their relatively flat organisation, and the existence of many directors and partners, linked with consensus management and the reluctance to delegate power to managing roles, makes it difficult to agree a common vision and specific objectives.
- A high degree of specialism, and a departmental culture, makes it difficult for multidisciplinary teams to be brought together. The brochures might refer to the various areas of expertise, but in practice there is often a reluctance to bring them together, due to billing problems, or internal political and territorial issues.
- While corporate clients seek increasingly to link remuneration to the achievement of tangible outputs, many professional practices cling obstinately to a preference for charging on an input or time spent basis.
- In the case of partnership structures, there may be a resistance to significant investment in IT and other requirements of creating a network and global capability, as the monies required 'come out of the pockets' of the 'equity partners'.
- Many professionals are reluctant to stray from what they regard as their areas of expertise. Their focus is upon the accumulation of expert knowledge, when the client may be more concerned with its application in a particular and fleeting context, and the problems which arise may be difficult to 'pigeon-hole' in terms of professional specialisms.
- Professional practices also tend to maintain a 'hard shell', and are often reluctant to forge network links, especially with other firms in similar fields. In many professional firms there is enormous scope for cost savings, for example, through shared specialist services, as a result of network links. Because of professional values, codes of practice and familiarity with 'Chinese walls', professional firms ought to find it easier than many commercial enterprises to co-operate in some areas, while competing in others.

An example of an international professional network is the Pacific Rim Advisory Council. The various law firms constituting the network, and located in a number of countries around the Pacific Rim, are able to access each other's specialist skills as required.

BUSINESS SCHOOLS

Business schools also have their problems. In order to respond to the changing requirements of network organisations for partnership relationships, business schools may face an increasing tension in their own links with host universities. Already a number of schools have an 'uneasy' or strained connection with the wider organisational setting in which they find themselves.

In May of 1992 no fewer than 14 'commercial' members of the council of Manchester Business School resigned *en masse* and appealed to the Secretary of State to enquire into the affairs of the business school. The 'captains' of industry cited 'a mutual lack of confidence and trust' between the school and Manchester University, and 'a complete breakdown of the concept of partnership' on which the school had been founded as the reason for their appeal.[19]

Having once written a book to spread the gospel of business schools[20] and compiled an edition of what has become the standard UK guide to business schools,[21] the author does not lightly question the role of business schools.

The reality is that in place of the early vision of a few centres of excellence, the ranks of business schools have expanded to include institutions of diverse, and at times dubious, quality. It is now legitimate to question whether, in view of the many changes in the business environment we examined in Chapter 1, business school MBA and executive programmes are now obsolete.[22]

PREPARATION FOR A CHANGING WORLD

How many business school programmes give priority to coping with diversity, turbulence and surprise; encouraging sensitivity to feelings, attitudes and values; building a holistic perspective, and multicultural and international awareness; and bringing about revolutionary change and corporate transformation?

Business schools concentrate too much on preparing people for jobs that may soon no longer exist, and roles that are rapidly disappearing from transitioning organisations.

> Few of today's MBA graduates will become general managers, leading a team composed of heads of functional departments at the top of a corporate bureaucracy. As companies change to accommodate a more demanding and international business environment, new management skills and competencies are required.[23]

The BIM *Responsive Organisation* report[24] concluded that:

> individual managers will need to become broader and more mobile. An international outlook, a sense of proportion and perspective, a willingness to accept responsibility, teamwork, project management, and communication skills will be highly prized.

The corporation is today more vulnerable to competition and challenges beyond its control. Opportunities are fleeting. Understanding these changes requires political and cultural sensitivity, and an acute awareness of underlying concerns and values.

Many business schools still place an excessive emphasis upon the internal functions of the corporate machine, with separate courses in production, marketing, personnel, finance, accountancy etc, and over-stress rational approaches to decision making and optimisation. In the 'real world' of 'global commercial warfare', and joint ventures and arrangements, a subject such as international relations, with its emphasis upon decision making in situations of stress and incomplete information, international negotiation, cross-cultural communication, crisis management and the establishment and break up of alliances may be more relevant.[22]

The international network organisation requires processes for identifying and anticipating change in the global environment. Managers require an awareness of contemporary international political, economic, financial, trade, environmental and moral issues and risks. It is important to appreciate the limitations upon corporate power and influence, and potential vulnerability to changing values.

C K Prahalad has drawn up a list of issues concerning the management of international companies that would benefit from further investigation and has concluded as follows.[25]

> There is no dearth of issues that are complex and challenging. Managing is increasingly an intellectual activity. The surprise is that so little of the intellectual energy of the academic community, in business schools, is focused on them. ... It is no wonder that managers do not perceive academic output as 'relevant' to the task of managing.

DIVERSITY AND THE NETWORK

To prepare people for movement around the network organisation, they need awareness of different perspectives, and experience of various forms of relationship rather than functional skills. The packaged programme can encourage one way of looking at the world, and may deny an organisation the opportunities to capitalise upon the rich diversity of backgrounds and approaches that might exist across an international network.

Some companies 'spend millions' wiping out diversity in the interests of instilling a common approach. The result can be the robo-corporation, peopled with clones with identikit attitudes, approaches, tools and techniques.

Respect for diversity need not be incompatible with developing a shared perspective of corporate goals and priorities, and a common position on certain international issues.

- Companies such as Asea Brown Boveri and General Electric bring groups of managers together to participate with senior management in issue-based seminars. People are exposed to each other's viewpoints and perspectives.
- In the case of Asea Brown Boveri, Percy Barnevik, the president and CEO believes the purpose of such events is: 'To further internal cohesion and understanding [and] to communicate and build acceptance for a common set of values.' Tolerance and respect for diversity could become a shared value.

IMPLICATIONS

Many of those concerned with consultancy, training and development may challenge the validity of the perceptions of the 'external' supplier of advice and services which have been presented in this chapter. Yet the perceptions exist, and in the minds of a significant group of corporate decision makers.

Suppliers of external and development services need to recognise the following in many companies.

- The emphasis has shifted from equipping people with particular skills to achieving a more fundamental change of approach, attitude and perspective.
- There is considerable suspicion of external experts and consultants. They are perceived as offering short-term, simplistic and standard solutions, when the achievement of fundamental change is thought to require a sustained commitment that may be beyond the perspective of the management team, let alone the 'assignment mentality' of the external supplier.
- Considerable effort is being devoted to creating distinct corporate cultures. This can make external inputs, and experience that has been gained elsewhere, more difficult to absorb.
- Internal sources of advice are becoming more confident. It is no longer thought that there are external experts who 'have the answers'. Strains of battle-hardened warriors are emerging that are more resistant to hype.
- The achievement of corporate transformation is perceived as more complex and intractable than was thought at first. Quick-fix merchants are beginning to be turned away.

If the advice and services of consultants and business schools are to be perceived as more relevant to the achievement of attitude and perspective change, they will need to put more emphasis upon establishing and sustaining longer-term partnership arrangements with specific companies. They need to put away the presentations, roll up their sleeves and join the team.

They must also remember to focus upon what isn't – the key items that are missing from the change programme. Perhaps the parable of the 'lost sheep' is a prophetic and elegant appeal to search for the change element that will complete the corporate transformation jigsaw puzzle.

CHECKLIST

▶ Does your company learn from its consultants or vice versa?

▶ Does your company regard consultants as external suppliers, or as elements of the network organisation?

▶ Do the consultants which your company uses understand its vision, goals and values?

▶ How flexible and willing to learn are the people who advise your company?

▶ Do they listen?

▶ Do they have a holistic view of business problems, or are they 'functional' in approach?

▶ Do they apply standard tools and techniques, or are they selective in tailoring approaches to your particular problems?

▶ Do they describe and confront reality?

▶ Are their 'feet on the ground'?

▶ Are they 'telling it as it is', or saying what they believe you might wish to hear?

▶ How many of the things they talk about have been successfully implemented in *their* organisations?

▶ Are they as willing to come forward with 'lessons of failure' as they are with 'success case studies'?

▶ What value results from your company's relationships with business schools?

▶ What would be lost if business schools ceased to exist?

REFERENCES

1 Camp, R C (1989) *Benchmarking: The Search for Industry Best Practices that Lead to Superior Performance*, Quality Press, Milwaukee, Wis.
2 Bandura, A (1977) *Social Learning Theory*, Prentice-Hall, Englewood Cliffs, NJ.
3 Coulson-Thomas, C and Coe, T (1991) *The Flat Organisation: Philosophy and Practice*, BIM, Corby.
4 Coulson-Thomas, C and Coulson-Thomas, S (1991) *Quality: The Next Steps*, an Adaptation Survey for ODI International, Adaptation, London and (Executive Summary) ODI, Wimbledon, London.
5 Coulson-Thomas, C and Coulson-Thomas, S (1991) *Communicating for Change*, an Adaptation Survey for Granada Business Services, London.
6 Coulson-Thomas, C (1990) *Professional Development of and for the Board*, a questionnaire and interview survey undertaken by Adaptation Ltd of company chairmen. A summary has been published by the IOD, London, February.
7 Wakelam, A (1989) *The Training and Development of Company Directors*, a report on a questionnaire survey undertaken by the Centre for Management Studies, University of Exeter for the Training Agency, December.
8 Coulson-Thomas, C and Wakelam, A (1991) *The Effective Board, Current Practice, Myths and Realities*, an Institute of Directors discussion document, London.
9 Coulson-Thomas, C (1990) *Human Resource Development for International Operation*, a Survey sponsored by Surrey European Management School, Adaptation Ltd, London.
10 Revans, R W (1979) *Action Learning*, Blond and Briggs, London.
11 Ohmae, K (1982) *The Mind of the Strategist*, McGraw-Hill, New York.
12 Cottrell, J (1992) 'Favourable Recipe', *The TQM Magazine*, vol 4, no 1, February, pp 17–20.
13 Taylor, F W (1947) *Scientific Management*, Harper and Row, New York.
14 Schein, E H (1988) *Process Consultation*, Addison-Wesley, Reading, Mass.
15 Bennis, W and Nanus, B (1985) *Leaders: the Strategies for Taking Charge*, Harper & Row, New York.
16 Coulson-Thomas, C (1990) *The Role and Status of Project Management*, a Survey undertaken for the Association of Project Managers, Adaptation, London.

17 Kanter, R M (1983) *The Change Masters: Innovation and Entrepreneurship in the American Corporation*, Simon & Schuster, New York.

18 Coulson-Thomas, C (1991) *The Role and Development of the Personnel Director*, an interim survey undertaken by Adaptation Ltd in conjunction with the Research Group of the Institute of Personnel Management.

19 Fazey, I H and Adonis, A (1992), 'Industrialists Quit Business School in Row', *Financial Times*, 30/31 May, p4.

20 Coulson-Thomas, C (1975) *A Guide to Business Schools*, Hamish Hamilton/St Georges Press, London.

21 Coulson-Thomas, C (compiler) (1981) *BGA Guide to Business Schools*, (5th edn), Macdonald & Evans, Plymouth.

22 Coulson-Thomas, C (1988) 'Is the Traditional Executive Programme Obsolete?', in Paliwoda, S J and Harrison, A C (ed), *The Association of MBAs Guide to Business Schools*, (7th edn), Pitman Publishing, London, pp 94–101

23 Coulson-Thomas, C (1992) *Creating the Global Company, Successful Internationalisation*, McGraw-Hill, London, p 345.

24 Coulson-Thomas, C and Brown, R (1989) *The Responsive Organisation, People Management: the Challenge of the 1990s*, BIM, Corby.

25 Prahalad, C K (1990) 'Globalisation: The Intellectual and Managerial Challenges', *Human Resource Management*, Spring, vol 29, no 1, pp 27–37.

15

IT AND CORPORATE
TRANSFORMATION

THE NETWORK ORGANISATION

Corporate organisations are transitioning to more flexible and responsive forms. We have seen that networks are being established that embrace customers, suppliers and business partners. These use information and communications technologies to facilitate new ways of working and learning, and new forms of relationships.

At least this is the theory. In practice, the functioning global network can sometimes appear a long way away. The complexity is intimidating and difficult to understand, while the cost is daunting and may not be affordable.

A vivid illustration of the gap between vision and reality in the IT arena is provided by the bag of plugs which many users of laptop computers have to take with them when they travel abroad. The 'collection' is needed to accommodate the range of voltages, and different sizes and configurations of socket that may be encountered.

THE BOTTOMLESS PIT

For many companies the vision of office automation has become the reality of what appears to be a bottomless pit into which money is poured with little prospect of achieving the 'benefits' that were originally sought. The OECD has concluded that the returns from investment in IT are problematic.[1] The potion is turning those with aspirations to become princesses and fairies into frogs and goblins.

Much of past 'investment' in IT has been used to shore up the bureaucratic organisation. One chairman commented ruefully: 'We have used IT to set our organisation in concrete. We have worked hard and spent millions consolidating a bureaucratic form of organisation which we are now trying to break down.'

IT suppliers, with a mixture of cheek and bravado, are now in the business of offering solutions to the many problems which their own products have created. They suggest that this or that attachment may yet turn the lead boots they have supplied into winged slippers.

Paul Strassmann suggests that while, overall, the introduction of IT may have had little beneficial impact, it does appear to have widened the gap between the more and less efficient companies.[2] There are 'winners', but for many companies IT has been an 'honest mirror' that has confronted them with their own warts and wrinkles.

IT AND CORPORATE TRANSFORMATION

Corporate transformation is taking longer to achieve than was first thought. In many organisations we have seen that a wide gulf has emerged between expectation and achievement.

Machine bureaucracies are not easily laid to rest. The persistence of bureaucracy derives from its perceived advantages compared with other forms of organisation.

These were systematically identified by Max Weber in the early years of the 20th century.[3] Applying IT to what is, as opposed to what ought to be, can further entrench a bureaucracy and make it more difficult to change.

The struggle to change raises certain questions that will be examined in this and subsequent chapters:

- Why is IT so often part of the problem, a barrier to the effective operation of those cross-functional processes that really add value for customers?
- Do IT directors really have the ear of CEOs, or understand how they could make a strategic contribution?
- What is the role of IT in the achievement of corporate transformation?

This chapter, along with the two that follow, draws particularly upon a project undertaken by the author, which examined the contribution of IT to corporate change from the perspective of both the CEO and the IT director.[4] The findings have been supplemented by a more recent programme of interviews.

Drawing upon these and other survey results (see Appendix 1) the chapter puts IT strategy into the strategic corporate management context. It looks at the role of the IT director, and the need for approaches that can help to facilitate and support the transition to the organic network form of organisation.

THE MISAPPLICATION OF IT

While IT may have transformed factory productivity, it has hardly touched the office in terms of improving the quality of management. In the office environment, IT is pervasive and visible without necessarily being beneficial. Some of those interviewed suspect that the reasons for this lie not in the technology itself, but in its use and application. Consider the following comments.

'The processes that are important from a customer point of view tend to be cross-functional. Virtually all our IT is departmental.'

'Most IT expenditure is to do in one way or another with data processing, yet most of our administrative costs relate to supporting the document flow. We have made hardly any IT investments in this area.'

'IT around here pushes information upwards ... it is used for command and control purposes.'

'There is fragmentation ... people and departments do their own thing and hoard their information. [Information] is not shared, either in groups or acrosss departments. You don't see much empowerment in the way we use IT.'

'If we have applied IT to the wrong things, why should anyone expect a positive return?'

By using IT to support re-engineered business processes, a significant improvement in managerial productivity may be achieved. But this requires looking at work and processes from a holistic rather than IT function point of view. Narrowness, introversion and departmentalism are not conducive of a vision-led approach.

Table 15.1 sets out the main elements that distinguish process simplification from process re-engineering. IT of itself, and by itself, does not deliver the solution. Most of the benefits of simplification usually derive from changing the workflow and empowering people, so the challenge for IT may be relatively modest.

In the case of process re-engineering the contribution of IT could be more significant. But the inter-relationships between people, process and technology, within a particular goal and value framework, need to be understood. The IT person is likely to be but one member of the re-engineering team.

Table 15.1 *Process Simplification or Re-engineering*

Process Simplification	Process Re-engineering
Step change	Radical transformation
Process-led	Vision-led
Within existing framework	Review framework
Improve application of technology	Introduce new technology
Assume attitudes and behaviour	Change attitudes and behaviour
Management led	Director led
Various simultaneous projects	Limited number of corporate initiatives

IT can facilitate or frustrate the task of corporate transformation, according to how it is managed.[5] An error of strategy can imprison a whole organisation, tying people down with the chains of inappropriate technology. The flexibility of the network organisation gives it the potential to spread, grow and evolve. This process of organic evolution needs to be assisted and not constrained by IT.

ASPIRATION: THE VISION

This is a good point at which to recap. We have seen that there appears to be a genuine desire for change. The continuing importance attached to building more flexible and responsive forms of network organisation has been confirmed by a succession of questionnaire surveys carried out in 1989, 1990 and 1991.[6,7,8]

In response to multiple challenges and opportunities (Table 1.2), and both longer-term trends and short-term economic pressures, CEOs are seeking to create flatter and more adaptable organisations. Externally, priority is being given to building closer relationships with customers, while internally the focus is upon harnessing human talent. There is a strong desire to integrate working and learning.[7]

THE OPPORTUNITY FOR IT

The opportunity for IT derives from the fact that the technology that best supports new ways of working within network organisations is also often that which can facilitate new approaches to learning. If properly applied, IT can enable working and learning relationships to be built and sustained across barriers of function, distance, time and culture.

There is little interest in IT for its own sake. One CEO questioned: 'Why does everyone feel they need an IT strategy? IT strategies can develop a life of their own. I can understand a strategy focused on the customer that identifies where IT can make a contribution.'

IT is only perceived as relevant where it can contribute to organisational goals. Information technology should be used to facilitate change and support the processes that add value for customers. In some areas the potential benefits are considerable. For example, Peter Bartram considers that the use of IT to support process re-engineering amounts to 'reinventing the company'.[9]

IT AND NEW PATTERNS OF WORK

IT is being applied to support the development of international network organisations. The growth of international corporate networks is already changing working patterns.

- Computer and video-conferencing can allow more frequent contact between physical meetings. Jacobs Suchard uses a corporate network to maintain direct contact with its operating unit managers around the world.
- Tasks can be allocated on a global basis. Software development can be undertaken 'offshore' in the Caribbean or in India.
- International units can be brought together that operate as international networks. VEBA is finding that its research activities are internationalising to such an extent that a 'unit of research' is increasingly a network rather than a building.
- Information can be assembled and accessed on a global basis. The Ford global network links up some 20,000 engineers and designers, and can handle over half a million messages a day.
- Networks can be used to achieve a rapid dissemination of information. Federal Express uses a TV network for this purpose.
- Groupware such as Lotus's Notes can allow people who belong to departmental, multifunctional or multinational workgroups to share information, irrespective of their location.
- Customer service can be handled on a global basis. AEG operates a global customer service network, enabling the company to respond flexibly to customer requirements on an international basis.
- Northwest Airlines makes use of scanning and workstation technology to operate an electronic working environment that allows a 24-hour-a-day response to customer requirements.
- The worldwide legal function of Xerox Corporation has 'worked electronically' for many years. Members of the legal team have been able to become 'maternity networkers', raising children and maintaining contact with colleagues around the globe via a workstation at home.

While these and other examples illustrate the possibilities, in many companies progress is slow and expensive. The network is often little more than a basic 'one-to-one' electronic mail service. Information cannot be easily shared by people who need to work together but are based at different locations. Single and isolated applications are not building new co-operative and group-working cultures.

THE CONTRIBUTION OF IT

Potentially, IT can have a very significant impact upon patterns of work and the distribution of power within organisations.[10] This excites certain people to the same extent that it makes others wary. While some seek to gain a competitive edge, their colleagues may be concerned about the loss of personal advantage.

The contribution IT is allowed to make will depend upon the context, and especially will, motivation and values. Scarce information can be a potent source of personal power in the machine bureaucracy. Ubiquitous information is the birthright of all the citizen members of the organic network organisation.

IT decisions can be very revealing of the extent to which senior management really believes in the concept of the open organisation. One manager commented of a decision concerning whether or not to introduce groupware: 'This will test how real commitment to sharing information actually is. ... If we back off, empowerment will be seen to be a meaningless word.'

In the above, and other, areas the key questions should be the following.

- Can IT facilitate and support new 'network' relationships with customers, suppliers and business partners? Does it facilitate learning, adaptation and change, and the integration of learning and working?

- Are investments in IT 'setting an existing departmental organisation in concrete', or are they supporting those key cross-functional and inter-organisational processes that generate and deliver the value that is sought by customers?
- Does IT support new patterns of group and distance working? Does it allow information to be easily shared within workgroups?
- Could IT enable new approaches to learning to be adopted? Are the attitudes and patterns of behaviour that it encourages supportive or destructive of corporate transformation?

The leverage obtained from IT will depend upon how effectively its use is co-ordinated with that of other change elements. For example, processes could be simplified with minimal reference to the application of IT, although when used alongside empowerment and other factors, IT can make a significant contribution to the re-engineering of business processes.

THE NETWORK ORGANISATION

CEOs are beginning to define their organisations in network terms. We have seen that as fewer companies are able by themselves to deliver 'total value' to customers, increasingly they are creating networks of relationships, with electronic links forward into customers, backwards to suppliers and sideways to business partners (Figure 1.1).

As networks and supply chains become global, bringing together all those who share a common vision or a particular mission,[11] the formulation and implementation of IT strategy increasingly involves co-operation and collaboration across organisational and national boundaries.

Interest in rules and procedures is waning, but a desire for the identification of tasks, the establishment of teams, and new processes for generating value for customers, and achieving adaptation and change is growing. IT and other specialists should aim to become facilitators, harnessing relevant expertise by all available means in such a way that it can applied to add value for customers.

Richard Joyce, president of 3Com Europe, believes the 'global data network', or GDN, of 'the vision':

'offers a 'complete infrastructure' that allows data and information to flow transparently, from computer to computer, regardless of type and location. Such 'arterial information highways' permit flexibility, faster decision making, and greater responsiveness to customers and suppliers. They allow new ways of working and can change the role of managers. ... Whole functions could be geographically dispersed across the globe to take advantage of lower costs and proximity to customers.'

Warren Bennis envisaged a form of organisation termed 'adhocracy' in which tasks are accomplished by project groups and teams.[12] Many of the teams that come together in the network organisation have a requirement for access to appropriate technology 'on demand'. A particular technology is used according to the task, just as one's selection of clothes may depend upon the weather.

THE FAILURE TO MAKE IT HAPPEN

But what is happening in practice? How much has actually been achieved? If 'barriers' exist, what are they, and what needs to be done about them? So far, the results have been very disappointing.[13,14,15]

- In very few organisations are significant changes of attitude and behaviour occurring. In most they are unlikely to occur while crucial change elements are not in place. IT could be consciously used to influence attitudes and behaviour positively, but tends not to be.

- Few major organisations are able to identify the key cross-functional processes that generate and deliver the value that is sought by their customers (Figure 12.2). In most organisations no one is responsible for them. Most IT and training is departmental, and hence makes a minimal contribution to improving the effectiveness of cross-functional processes.

- While greater use is being made of project groups and teams, the departmental form of organisation persists. Only rarely do project groups have access to a software environment that is conducive to the free and open sharing of information within the team.

- A few organisations have developed new approaches and techniques which are resulting in substantial improvements in management performance. However, most companies cling to traditional approaches which have been shown to be wanting.

In many companies, managerial productivity is actually falling as people struggle to cope with extra responsibilities, and little is done to equip them to work in new ways. David Thompson, chairman of Rank Xerox UK believes:[16]

> 'The failure to reap the full benefit from investments in technology usually results from how it is applied. People are given the technology, but are not prepared or equipped to use it.'
>
> Training is the key to obtaining better value from technology. For Xerox how people learn, and how its technology is understood, is an integral part of the technology itself, and of the products that are derived from it.'

EMERGING PROBLEM AREAS

In many companies there has been a trend towards the devolution of discretion to operating units.[6] As a consequence, a degree of fragmentation has occurred. Certain divisions and departments may be pursuing IT strategies, and acquiring hardware and software, that differ significantly from that elsewhere in the corporate organisation. This can complicate the task of supporting cross-functional processes with appropriate technology.

One IT director described what appears to be a typical problem:

> 'We have an absolute mess ... every sort and kind of equipment, from every supplier you could think of. As part of the culture change, everyone has been encouraged to do their own thing. ... Any thought of gateways and interfaces has gone out of the window. ... Technology-wise we are now a collection of self-contained cells. ... It's horrible.'

A combination of devolution, delegation and empowerment has swept like a wave through many companies, leaving self-contained islands of technology in its wake. Now the enthusiasm for identifying and documenting processes is being confronted by the formidable challenge of linking up the apparently incompatible. In the words of an IT director: 'I watched it break up ... now I'm being asked to stitch it together again.'

Another IT director touched upon an issue that could be added to the arenas of confrontation of Chapter 12:

> 'A network needs some common infrastructure if flexibility is to be achieved. You can't cross functions [etc] if the equipment does not link up. But even raising the issue smacks of 'centralism' ... people want their freedom. They have tasted freedom and are not interested in group things anymore. ... They just don't want to know or pay.'

Individual business units may only be interested in funding applications of IT that enable them to achieve their own particular objectives. The relatively high proportion of total IT spend that may be required to establish and operate the core network can be perceived as 'central overhead'. Too much local discretion could result in a network infrastructure that is not able to support cross-functional processes adequately, or enable expertise to be accessed independently of location.

Information technology provides the nerves and arteries of the network organisation. Yet the very process of identifying the processes that deliver value to customers can result in battles for the allocation of the IT budget and the control of its people.

Computer networks that embrace a number of companies, including those that may co-operate in some areas and compete in others, have already attracted the interest of regulators. The European Commission has required one computer network that enabled eight US and European manufacturers of tractors to share UK market information to be discontinued or scaled down to a level that does not interfere with free competition in the marketplace.

IT AND THE 'NEW ÉLITE'

Having portrayed 'the vision' earlier in this chapter, Richard Joyce of 3Com describes a confused and muddled reality.

> 'Data networks today are being formed almost accidentally, in an unplanned and unstructured way. Personal computers are being connected to LANs [local area networks] at a furious pace. ... LANs are being interconnected with other LANs in a complex mesh structure that is proving almost impossible to design, install, manage, and more importantly 'take ownership of'.
>
> While these problems of complexity are vexing the minds of the network managers at the central corporate locations, hardly any work has been done at all to provide 'corporate' or 'HQ' levels of network access for the 'remote user' of the corporate network. ... In its current course and direction [the global data network] is not scalable and way too complex for it to succeed in having the profound impact it ought to have.'

While the rhetoric is of empowerment and involvement, the IT investment decisions of many companies are concentrating and excluding. New 'core' élites are emerging that have access to a wide range of network information and services that are denied to others. In the view of one director: 'If you are not "on the network" you might as well be dead.'

The members of the new élite gather together in their high-tech and air-conditioned offices rather like travellers on a hostile planet congregating at the 'moon base'. They peer into their screens, and browse through data 'in case they might miss something', rather than breathe fresh air and meet customers. Other people of the network organisation can feel 'disenfranchised' or 'second-class citizens'. The 'money runs out' before the 'benefits of civilisation' can be brought to the far-flung reaches.

IT: AN ENABLER OR A BARRIER?

Is IT entrenching traditional bureaucracy or facilitating transformation? The IT 'architectural' requirements of the organic network are different from those of the 'traditional' machine bureaucracy.[4] We will examine these in Chapter 16. However, few CEOs[6,15,17] identify the technology of IT as the sole, or even a major, constraint.

- Many companies are held back by past investments in architectures that have now been pushed to their limits in accommodating contemporary requirements. However, people recognise that other architectures exist, and have been around for some time, that could support what is desired.
- The 'historic' IT is often viewed as part of the overhead cost of bureaucracy. Efforts are being made to subcontract or otherwise reduce this 'cost'. The IT that is

appropriate to the requirements of the network organisation is more likely to be considered an 'investment'. As a CEO put it: 'If you know it's doing something for a customer, you don't quibble so much about the cost.'

- The focus is likely to shift, as companies emerge from economic recession, from 'saving costs' to transforming relationships with customers and suppliers, and the support of cross-functional and inter-organisational processes, and new ways of working and learning.

In the main, the concerns of CEOs relate to attitudes towards IT which inhibit its application to those activities and processes that are important from a business point of view. In particular, the IT community is not thought to have a holistic view of the role of IT in relation to other change elements in either the vision of the 'network organisation' or how it might be brought about.

CHANGING PERSPECTIVES

As we will see in Chapter 16, the reputation of early generations of IT has been sullied by their association with the automation of the administration of the machine bureaucracy. However, views have mellowed and a more balanced perspective on information technology is emerging.[6,15]

- Cynicism, resulting from early experiences with technology that did not deliver the hoped-for benefits, is giving way to a realisation that what is important is the use and application of technology, not the technology *per se*.
- Awareness is growing that, in the main, the major 'barriers' concern people, their skills and attitudes, and the management of technology, rather than the technology itself. Technology needs to be applied to support those key processes that generate the value sought by customers.
- Technology is seen not as an end in itself but as a set of tools to be used, where appropriate, to support the way managers prefer to work and think, and enable more of them to move closer to their full potential.
- IT needs to be democratised. There is a demand for a more 'universal' technology that is simple, reliable and cheap, and available to all members of the network wherever they may be. For one interviewee: 'Usable ... unobtrusive technology must be the right of everyone [and not] the privilege of the office-bound few.'

Technology is neutral. Its application reflects the richness or poverty of our vision, the clarity or confusion of our objectives, and the utility or stupidity of our choices. Virtual reality is a good example of a technology with the potential to be applied in a variety of ways.

- It could be used to open up an unprecedented range of learning opportunities and expose people to various experiences. Aspiration can, for a time, take on the appearance of reality. The dream can become the product.
- The same technology could be used to pander to a variety of unsocial instincts by enabling people to act out their wildest fantasies. Little wonder that Barrie Sherman and Phil Judkins entitle their book on this emerging area *Glimpses of Heaven – Visions of Hell*.[18]

Appropriate IT has its place among the change elements that make up a corporate transformation programme. How relevant and significant it is will depend upon the situation and circumstances.

IT DIRECTORS AND THE BOARDROOM

IT is of strategic importance to many companies, and there is no upper limit to the number of directors which a company may have. Yet many senior IT professionals only carry 'courtesy' director titles, being managers within, rather than directors of, their companies. This raises some questions.

- Why is it that IT professionals are not securing more positions on company boards? Do IT professionals lack the qualities that would enable them to gain entry to the boardroom?
- Does the vision of the typical large organisation IT function match that of the CEO and board? In what ways should the perspective of an IT director differ from that of an IT manager?
- What role does IT play in the context of the requirements for successful corporate transformation?

In many companies there is a 'communication gap' between the CEO and the IT community.[4] The IT specialists regard the CEO as a 'technological illiterate' who uses a workstation as 'office furniture' and does not know 'one end of a keyboard from another'. In return, the CEO perceives the IT community as 'into boxes' and, apparantly, unable to speak other than in 'technological gobbledegook'. The two groups appear to have an uneasy relationship.

Directors require personal and directorial qualities which many IT professionals appear to lack. They need to share the CEO vision of the responsive network organisation, and require a broad, strategic awareness and perspective.

We saw in Chapter 3 that there is no such thing as a standard board in terms of size and composition, or perceived roles and responsibilities.[19] However, all company board directors share certain legal duties and responsibilities.

An IT professional seeking a board level appointment needs to develop and demonstrate qualities that match the situation and circumstances of the company, and attributes that are compatible with, and complement, the qualities of the existing members of the board. The individual must be perceived to offer a capability that relates to the function of the board.

Discussions with company chairmen[19,20] suggest that in future more boards:

- will spend less time establishing and monitoring procedures, and will devote more time to initiating and facilitating processes for delivering customer value and satisfaction, and achieving ongoing adaptation and change;
- will devote significantly greater effort to 'making it happen', or ensuring that measurable objectives are both set and achieved. There is little point in crafting a superb strategy that remains as 'words on paper'.

IT professionals aspiring to board level positions should consider the extent to which their perspective, skills and experience would enable them to work effectively with others in response to this challenge.

The view of chairmen is that the head of a function such as IT should not automatically secure a seat in the boardroom.[20] Much will depend upon the extent to which the individual concerned acquires and displays directorial qualities. 'Hybrid managers' may or may not have the potential to become IT directors. IT directors require directorial qualities in addition to management competencies, and many senior IT professionals lack a strategic and 'external' perspective.

In addition to directorial competencies, an effective director, whether or not a 'director of IT', needs knowledge that is relevant to the function of the board.

- Directors need to understand the role of the board, and their legal duties and responsibilities. They also require an appreciation of financial and other accountabilities and requirements.
- Directors need an awareness of developments in the business environment, such as ethical and environmental considerations.

- There are also boardroom matters to consider such as the succession, assessment and remuneration of directors, the structure and operation of the board itself, and effective boardroom practice.

BARRIERS AND HINDERS

Should the IT professional have a key role as a member of the directorial team? The answer is 'Not necessarily'. The path to the boardroom of the 'IT person' is strewn with barriers and hinders. Consider the following areas of concern.

- Most of the key issues facing CEOs and their boards do not fit neatly within functional boundaries. Major challenges tend to be cross-functional or multifunctional in their impact. A growing number of IT professionals need to be equipped to work more effectively with members of other functions.
- Many company chairmen feel that within 'their' IT functions fundamental questions of a strategic nature are not being asked.[4] Too much attention is devoted to the support of what is, and too little to facilitating 'vital few' initiatives.
- Chairmen and CEOs[6,17] seriously question whether 'experts' in various functional fields are barriers to, or facilitators of, change. IT professionals are often perceived by CEOs as introverted, 'departmental' in their thinking, insecure and overly defensive of past practices and historic investments in IT.[4]
- One managing director summed up another concern: 'Those close to the action sometimes can't see the wood for the trees.' Hence 'outsiders' are brought in to head IT functions.
- IT professionals are perceived by many CEOs as more technical, prone to jargon and detail, and blinkered than managers in general, and lacking in 'people' skills. Some suggest that the IT function attracts those with an interest in 'things' rather than 'people'.[4]
- People skills are increasingly important as IT professionals are expected to work in multifunctional teams, and barriers to the successful implementation of IT 'solutions' are identified as behavioural and managerial rather than technical. As one director put it: 'If you don't understand learning or teamwork, how can you improve it with IT?'
- The IT community appears to be fragmenting into excessive specialisation.[4] The management challenge is to integrate, and encourage, mobility between these areas, and greater interaction with users and colleagues in other organisations. In order to add more value, IT people need to get closer to their customers.
- Directors need to retain their objectivity and independence, and a sense of balance and perspective. A criticism of some IT professionals is that they can appear on occasion to be 'in the pockets of IT suppliers'. Many CEOs would like their IT team to be 'more robust'.

Overall, many CEOs put a higher importance than IT practitioners upon 'management' aspects of IT, such as organisational and people issues. They are also more concerned with 'networking up organisations'. IT professionals, with their narrower perspective, tend to be preoccupied with the bewildering range of new products and services emanating from suppliers, recruiting and retaining staff with scarce skills, 'networking up departments and workgroups', and corporate demands for 'overhead' cost savings.

There does appear to be a shortage of those with the breadth of view, strategic awareness and other qualities required for board level appointments.[19] An additional complication is that IT appears to be increasingly regarded as a supporting and integral element of many other functions, rather than as one in its own right. The genie has escaped from the departmental bottle.

APPOINTING DIRECTORS

There are strategic opportunities for awake and aware IT professionals who can make the transition from defending and rationalising the past to confronting the future. We saw in Chapter 3 that many chairmen are 'supply constrained' when it comes to making new appointments to the board. When seeking new members of the boardroom team:

- the key requirement of chairmen and CEOs is for individuals who are able to develop a perspective of the organisation as a whole and facilitate change;
- there also needs to be an understanding of the distinguishing characteristics of the network organisation that are sought by chairmen and CEOs.

In theory, an IT professional concerned with the strategic use of IT ought to be well placed to develop a relatively broad perspective. The building of effective electronic links with customers, suppliers and business partners ought to extend awareness beyond the confines of one organisation.

As more facilitating directors are appointed to supplement or replace 'traditional' functional directors,[20] further opportunities may be created for those with an IT background. Such facilitating roles will be occupied by those who can manage change and work with others, those who understand how IT can best be applied to support key management and business processes, harness skills and build external relationships.

Facilitating directors tend to have longer-term responsibilities for reshaping the organisation to meet strategic business development opportunities while colleagues deliver current business objectives. IT professionals with directorial qualities could aspire to such facilitating roles in the boardroom. The network organisation can be good news for 'network people'.

CHECKLIST

▶ Do the IT specialists in your company understand its vision?

▶ Are their activities supportive of the changes that are sought?

▶ Have the key cross-functional and inter-organisational processes that add value for customers been identified?

▶ Have particular individuals been made responsible for these processes?

▶ Is IT applied to support them, or to departmental activities that may or may not be generating value for customers?

▶ How fragmented is the IT of your company?

▶ Are there actual or latent conflicts within your company between the 'core' IT team, and those in business units and divisions?

▶ Does the IT perspective and strategy of your company embrace other members of the supply chain?

▶ Does your organisation's IT network allow groups and teams to come together and work across barriers of function, distance, nationality and time?

▶ Does it support the way people naturally work and think, or do people have to distort their preferred behaviour in order to 'fit in' with the technology?

▶ Is it a learning network, able to integrate learning and working?

▶ Is it sufficiently flexible to allow various people to work in different ways, and at a variety of locations, according to personal preferences and changing task requirements?

REFERENCES

1   Organisation for Economic Co-operation and Development (OECD) (1988) *New Technology in the 1990s: A Socio-economic Strategy*, Paris.
2   Strassmann, P A (1985) *Information Payoff*, Macmillan, New York and London.
3   Weber, M (1947) *The Theory of Social and Economic Organisation*, (initial publication 1924, translated and edited by Henderson, A M and Parsons, T), The Free Press, New York.
4   Coulson-Thomas, C (1990) *Developing IT Directors*, an Interim Adaptation Ltd Report to the Department of Computing Science, Surrey University.
5   Scott Morton, M S (1990) *The Corporation of the 1990s: Information Technology and Organisational Transformation*, Oxford University Press, New York and Oxford.
6   Coulson-Thomas, C and Brown, R (1989) *The Responsive Organisation, People Management: the Challenge of the 1990s*, BIM, Corby.
7   Coulson-Thomas, C (1990) *Human Resource Development for International Operation*, a Survey sponsored by Surrey European Management School, Adaptation Ltd, London.
8   Coulson-Thomas, C (1991) *The Role and Development of the Personnel Director*, an interim Survey undertaken by Adaptation Ltd in conjunction with the Research Group of the Institute of Personnel Management.
9   Bartram, P (1992) *Reinventing the Company: The Use of IT to Re-engineer Corporate Processes*, Business Intelligence, Wimbledon.
10 Zuboff, S (1988) *In the Age of the Smart Machine, The Future of Work and Power*, Basic Books, New York.
11 Coulson-Thomas, C (1992) *Creating the Global Company: Successful Internationalisation*, McGraw-Hill, London.
12 Bennis, W (1968) *The Temporary Society*, Harper & Row, New York.
13 Coulson-Thomas, C and Coe, T (1991) *The Flat Organisation: Philosophy and Practice*, BIM, Corby.
14 Coulson-Thomas, C and Coulson-Thomas, S (1991) *Quality: The Next Steps*, an Adaptation survey for ODI International, Adaptation, London and (Executive Summary) ODI, Wimbledon, London.
15 Coulson-Thomas, C and Coulson-Thomas, S (1991) *Communicating for Change*, an Adaptation survey for Granada Business Services, Adaptation, London.
16 Thompson, D (1991) *Wokefield Park Official Opening: Training, the Key to Obtaining Value from Technology*, comments made at the official opening of the Rank Xerox UK national training centre at Wokefield Park, 23 September.
17 Coulson-Thomas, C and Brown, R (1990) *Beyond Quality, Managing the Relationship with the Customer*, BIM, Corby.
18 Sherman, B and Judkins, P (1992) *Glimpses of Heaven – Visions of Hell*, Hodder & Stoughton, London.
19 Coulson-Thomas, C and Wakelam, A (1991) *The Effective Board, Current Practice, Myths and Realities*, an Institute of Directors discussion document, London.
20 Coulson-Thomas, C (1993) *Creating Excellence in the Boardroom*, McGraw-Hill, London.

16

THE NETWORK ORGANISATION: SUPPORTING TECHNOLOGY

EMBRACING THE GLOBE

Where will it all end? The growth of the organic network is limited only by the bounds of the earth. Quite small companies have the potential to operate as international networks. The limiting factor is generally awareness, vision and perspective. Most companies stitch their own blinkers and forge their own chains.

Increasingly network organisations, especially when composed largely of knowledge workers, are distinguished by their supporting technology and the extent to which they are able to harness human talent. These are the areas we will explore in this, and the next, chapter.

THE FEAR OF SCALE

Brave souls sometimes become timid at the thought of international operation. And yet, we live in what Kenichi Ohmae has called a 'borderless world'.[1] As a CEO pointed out: 'You may have much more in common with someone on the other side of the world than with the next-door neighbour.'

It is easy to become awed by the scale and complexity of many international networks:

- By 1990 the global network of Digital Equipment, for example, linked 57,000 computer terminals in 498 locations in 31 countries.
- An extensive international network may be necessary to integrate the global operating units of a company. For example, at the start of the 1990s The VEBA Group comprised, in addition to VEBA AG, 393 domestic and 252 foreign companies.
- Club Méditerranée operates a 2000-terminal global network which allows 24-hour-a-day bookings to be made for accommodation at any of its holiday centres. The total resources of the international organisation are accessible from any single point.

Yet even the possession of a telephone opens up possibilities for direct contact with customers and suppliers throughout the world. It was possible in 1990 to direct dial 197 countries from the UK, and to thereby secure access to 99 per cent of the world's 700 million telephones.

The extent of internationalisation and interdependence, the pattern of economic activity, the location of interacting knowledge workers, or the degree of integration of particular countries into the global economy can all be monitored by examining the pattern of cross-border telephone calls.[2]

The focus of this chapter is not upon the technology itself, but upon how it has been, can be and ought to be used. The creative use of information technology focuses upon the search for competitive advantage and differentiation, changing internal and external relationships, overcoming barriers and transforming the nature of the marketplace. We need smart heads not smart suits.

THE VALUE OF THE INTERNATIONAL NETWORK

Does your IT pass the 'So what?' test? The use of any technology should be justified in terms of its impact upon creating value for external customers. In order to be responsive to the changing requirements of customers, companies need to enter into a dialogue with them.[3] To do this, and to facilitate a relationship based upon two-way communication, the customer needs to be incorporated into the network.

- Xerox has equipped many of its office products with a self-diagnostic capability to monitor their own performance. The ultimate in the concept of network contacts with customers and preventive maintenance is the built-in Remote Interactive Communications (RIC) system. This enables the machine in the customer's office to 'call' a Xerox or Rank Xerox technician when it senses that it needs attention. The supplier knows before the customer that the customer has a problem.
- The Bank of Scotland has pioneered direct customer access by terminal to account information. It has also developed an Edipay system that allows international companies to electronically exchange payments through the international automatic bank payment system, and remittance information through the global information system of General Electric.
- TNT, a major player in the express services sector, is constructing an integrated global network to allow customers to track the progress of their shipments around the world. Customers of TNT Express Europe already use a customer communication programme, EDIFAST, to monitor the physical status of shipments and obtain 'real time' status reports.
- For a credit-card company such as Visa International, a global telecommunications network represents the essence of its business. Marks & Spencer, the UK retailer, introduced a credit card and found that by linking up its network with its customer database it was able to identify opportunities for such network-based services as the buying and selling of shares.

For a smaller company, the cost of establishing such a network might appear prohibitive. However, where a network is operated on a co-operative basis, the development and operating costs can be shared.

The 'IT solution' may also be available to the 'one location' business that joins a network. A centralised reservation system is run by Consort Hotels Consortium which represents over 250 hotels in the UK. Most of the members of this consortium are single hotels. For them, access to, rather than ownership of, the network may be the key to marketplace success.

SPEED OF RESPONSE

Many companies are 'competing in time'.[4] In competitive markets, the technology that allows a faster and tailored response to customer requirements can be decisive.

- As some Japanese companies review the time it takes for their consensus approach to decisions to reach conclusions, National, a Japanese bicycle manufacturer, combines flexibility and speed of response, and can produce a made-to-order machine in about two weeks.
- The US insurance company Mutual Benefit Life considers each insurance application it receives to be a distinct project or case. These used to spend days travelling

between specialist departments. A computerised network now enables the individual case handler to cut across departmental barriers, and applications can be received and processed the same day.

- Arthur Andersen offices across Asia, Europe and North America are linked together by an international voice, data and video network. When assembling teams, and working on client problems, this professional practice is able quickly to access relevant expertise around the globe.
- The oil company Amoco operates an extensive electronic mail network. On the network in Europe are 32 'off-shore' platforms. When located in the North Sea, a document that is sent electronically can dramatically improve response times, as compared with the expensive alternative of delivery of a physical document by helicopter.
- BMW uses business television to communicate simultaneously and directly with its dealers. This enables customers to expect a consistency of understanding and approach across all locations covered by the broadcast service.

In the 1990s competition will increasingly be between networks or clusters of co-operating companies, rather than between individual enterprises.[5] Within these networks companies can be both customers and suppliers. In Jacobson's terms, these are 'networks of interdependence'.[6]

Many networks will be composed of companies with complementary resources that can be harnessed by compatible computing and telecommunications networks. Network partners may operate in different industry sectors. For example, members of a cluster composed of a financial institution, IT supplier and management consultancy could access each other's complementary resources.

Incompatible networks can put barriers between companies that would otherwise work together. In the UK, it was not possible in 1985 to complete a merger between the Woolwich and Nationwide building societies because the two companies had built networks with the products of different suppliers, and it would have been both difficult and expensive to link them up.

During a period of recession telecommunication costs are, for many companies, a significant inhibitor of the internationalisation of networks. The high cost of international telecommunications has been maintained by a cartel of national operators, many of whom have a monopoly on international calls in their countries. The European Commission, the UK's OFTEL, and the US Federal Communications Commission have all called for a substantial reduction in international call charges. An opening up of the international call market to greater competition would reduce charges and encourage greater cross-border communication.

USING TECHNOLOGY TO OBSCURE AND CONFUSE

The use of information technology is transforming old markets and creating new ones. However, much early investment in IT was devoted to supporting internal bureaucracies rather than changing the nature of external relationships with customers.[7] Many attitudes towards IT are the result of experience of this internal use.

The quantity of information available to business decision makers in many organisations has increased dramatically. Boards and senior executives appreciate the strategic value of relevant and timely information. Internationalisation can greatly expand the range of sources from which information can be drawn. In some business sectors it has become a commodity, accessible on demand.

However, too much information is neither relevant nor timely. It does not always flow easily between organisations and the systems of different suppliers. Nor does its content and presentation improve the quality of decision making. It may be impossible to work with it, or share it, in order to improve understanding. Consider the following comments.

'We are just swamped with information. No one has time to read it. ... You get to the meeting and more of it is handed out. You see people's eyes just glaze over. It's ridiculous ... people are killing themselves to produce this stuff [and] it's killing us.'

'It's too easy these days. People just press buttons, and out it all spews. We're inundated with print-out and can't see anything. ... It's driven thinking out of the conference rooms.'

'People used to come to meetings with piles of slides. Now we have a standard format. All we ask for is trends, root causes, comparisons and some options. ... We've got a grip on it and are managing the business again.'

Early investment in information technology did not always materially improve the information flow. In many cases it made matters worse, as insight and understanding were imprisoned in mainframe computers to be released only in the form of indigestible print-out. An OECD study has suggested that information technology is not associated with any overall increase in productivity.[8]

The IT of many companies has not had a significant impact upon the structure of their organisations, the quality of their management processes or the nature of their external network connections. It frustrates rather than facilitates learning. This often leads to cynicism concerning the potential value of IT, as deficiencies are ascribed to the technology itself, rather than to its application and use. Such cynicism may remain until applications are seen to improve understanding, and lead to better relationships with customers and suppliers.

INFORMATION AND UNDERSTANDING

Information of itself may be of little or no value. It is generally not sought for its own sake. In a business context, it is usually required for a purpose. The value of information ought to exceed its cost. IT, like information, is a means to an end and is rarely acquired as an end in itself. As a CEO put it: 'I'm beginning to think it's like castor oil ... we take it, thinking it's doing us some good.'

Those who circulate and receive information have a shared responsibility for ensuring that what is transmitted is relevant and understood. Information is of strategic value only when it increases understanding at the point at which important decisions are made. Information that is understood by experts and specialists, but not by management colleagues, or in the boardroom, is not of strategic value. It may be high quality bumf, but is useless as a decision aid.

A director summed up an interview theme: 'We still put our investment where the data is. We are still spending to churn out more data when we don't understand what we have already got. Yet we seem to spend next to nothing working with all this information to get it in a form that can be understood.'

Information technology can improve the generation and availability of information to such an extent as to cause an excess or 'overload' . It can do this without improving understanding. A gap can emerge between information generation and its accessibility, between availability and the extent to which it can be worked with and understood. One CEO said simply, and with understatement: 'It has not turned out as we expected.'

SOWING THE SEEDS

Why has such an imbalance between information and understanding arisen? Why are there so many glum faces, tired eyes and empty bank accounts? The answer lies in the history of the use of technology in the office.[7]

Initial applications of IT concentrated upon the relatively large amounts of routine or clerical work found in bureaucratic organisations, such as payroll and accounting applications. These took advantage of the particular strengths of early technology in processing large numbers of similar transactions.

The result was an increase in the amount of information generated, and a reduction in labour-intensive activities. Office work grew at the expense of non-office work. In the 'head office' environment, fewer employees were now engaged in routine, predictable and 'structured' clerical work. However, as senior management struggled to assimilate the growing amount of data, the prospects for knowledge workers brightened. These 'staffers' and professionals were concerned with less predictable and more varied 'unstructured activities'.

In 'structured' areas it is relatively easy for routines to be established and documented, and processes mechanised. Office automation has effectively taken routine activities and analysed them, programmes have been written, and computational power has been used to handle relatively standard transactions more cost-effectively than clerical labour.

The use of IT to automate 'structured tasks' influenced how people were viewed in the machine bureaucracy. Consider the following reflections.

> *'I guess the "standard transaction" showed what we thought of people. Our own people and our customers became numbers. They didn't have their own cards and files any more. They just appeared half-way down a page of print-out.'*

> *'In those days we deskilled our people ... we took away what little pride they had in their work. ... They became computer fodder.'*

Many people became extensions of the technology. As one interviewee put it: 'Today we would call them peripheral devices.' The exceptions that would have shown that the company was putting itself out for the individual employee or customer were discouraged when the technology found it difficult to handle them.

Many of the changes in the business environment (Table 1.2) could not be so easily ignored. Confronting them requires greater flexibility and the less tangible contributions of the knowledge worker. The effectiveness of such 'unstructured' activities as researching, analysing, thinking, challenging, conceptualising, learning, refining, planning, publishing, communicating, changing and adapting can depend critically upon the ease with which relevant information can be accessed, manipulated, assimilated and shared. These processes are not easy to document and mechanise in the bureaucracy; but they are the essence of the network organisation, of critical importance in the achievement of competitive advantage, and can be facilitated and supported by appropriate technology.

THE EVOLUTION OF TECHNOLOGY

In the 1950s and early 1960s the computational capability of computers in performing routine and structured work led to the emergence of data processing options that could not be accommodated manually. Early office automation was, on occasion, justified by the technical suitability of an application for automation. As one director put it: 'There were not too many questions about customers and business objectives in those days. We wandered around the building looking for things to automate.'

In the late 1960s and early 1970s this experience of basic data processing led to the identification of opportunities to employ programmes which could do more than calculate, namely handle and process transactions, and hence support certain areas of corporate operations. Information systems emerged as a specialism concerned with the application of computer technology and transaction processing software to operational needs.

These information systems are widely found in the national operating companies of major multinationals. The emphasis in justification shifted from the technical feasibility of a solution, to whether the potential cost savings would be sufficient to cover the cost of developing or acquiring a suitable transaction-processing system.

A command and control mentality was encouraged. The role of management became more directive, and in many companies greater power began to be accumulated at the centre. A CEO explained:

> 'It gave us a tremendous feeling of power, being able to demand this and that. We started to reach out and control things all over the place. ... Information was demanded because the management team knew it could be done. People were generating information for the management team, not working for customers.'

In the 1970s and 1980s, as the technology further developed, a new set of needs emerged relating to enhancing the strategic value of the increasing flow of information being generated by the earlier 'generations' of investment in office automation. Database and network technology provided a foundation for the manipulation and management of data. Electronic links between departments and organisations became more extensive.

'Decision support systems' emerged to enable easier and more appropriate access to data, and improve the way in which information is used by decision makers. The grounds for justification shifted from 'cost saving' to the extent to which the strategic value of information and the quality of decision making is enhanced.

CONTEMPORARY TECHNOLOGY

So where are we today? Computer and communications technologies (C&C) are converging, creating opportunities to build more integrated global networks.

- The Japanese company NEC has based its business philosophy upon the integration of computers and communications: 'NEC strives through "C&C" to help advance societies worldwide toward deepened mutual understanding and the fulfilment of human potential.'
- The US company Xerox has become 'the document company', as more of its products are 'network citizens'. The company's technology and services span the full range of activities involved in creating, communicating and using documents. Its focus has shifted from 'the box' to the understanding and support of the key business processes in client companies that add value for their customers.

More recent developments in information technology have particular application to international operation.

- Video-conferencing and conference calls are being increasingly used as an alternative to international travel, and to facilitate the work of international teams. NTT of Japan pioneered video-conferencing technology that allows groups in various locations to be linked together by a network that can handle video, text and data.
- Developments in personal communications and voice messaging can significantly reduce the proportion of calls that are not completed. People can be reached, even though they may be in a meeting, out or even asleep at the time of a call. Using a voice mailbox, messages can be sent and played back at any time of the day or night, reducing the problem of communication across international time zones.
- Putting a very small aperture terminal, or VSAT, on a building can allow it to join a network of satellite-borne communications and access services, such as business television and data transmission. Two-way or interactive services are available. The information company Knight-Ridder uses VSAT technology to deliver a real-time financial information service. In 1991 this network comprised over 3000 terminal dishes in the USA alone.

- Electronic funds transfer (EFT) systems and electronic document interchange (EDI) or trading is transforming supply chains into electronic networks. Such networks can expand across national borders wherever there is compatibility of technology and standards.
- Computerised translation environments are being built to enable multilingual groups to work together using their preferred languages. The European Commission is supporting the Eurotra project, a computerised translation system. An earlier machine translation system used by the Commission covers 11 language pairs. In 1990 some 600 members of the Commission's staff used this system to generate around 25,000 pages of text.
- Companies such as Hewlett-Packard and Rank Xerox and Xerox are developing and testing multimedia work environments. These will allow workgroups to interact with each other, and with workstations by speech, freehand drawing and other means. The greater flexibility and accessibility that is available can make it easier for people from a range of cultural backgrounds to contribute to the work of groups.
- The use of information technology can facilitate new approaches to learning.[9] Using emerging 'virtual reality' technology, people can experience a wide range of cultural, learning, operating and market environments without leaving their office. Advances in neural computing offer the prospect of Artificial Neural Networks which imitate the brain, by learning from actual examples how to produce a desired result. The technology that supports learning is itself able to learn.

In the early 1990s, research in such centres as Xerox PARK, and its offshoot Rank Xerox EuroPARC, is focusing upon human learning, effective team working and 'interaction', or the interface between person and machine. Office systems technology is becoming increasingly pervasive, user friendly and more unobtrusive. The technology is being adapted to the needs of teams and groups, and the requirements of individual users and learners.

Business decision makers need no longer be victims of whatever emerges from the corporate information system. They can become proactive, viewing the technology as a crucial enabler, rather than as a threat. The technology can support new ways of working, shopping and learning. It is changing the business environment, creating new competitive threats and fresh business opportunities.

The realisation is beginning to dawn. One interviewee exclaimed: 'I've been beaten around the head long enough with this stuff ... I can now see a way of doing something useful with it.' The light can be seen, but many companies still have to climb out of a deep pit and change attitudes in order to get to it.

Justification is shifting from decision support to the extent to which system capability and intelligence can complement and enhance human contribution in improving decision making and management processes, in order to cope with challenges such as internationalisation and corporate transformation. Justification is now concerned with the value delivered to customers, and the quality of relationships and of the learning that can be facilitated.

THE OPPORTUNITY FOR THE IT BUYER

The information technology buyer is in a relatively strong position. The problems of suppliers have created opportunities for customers.

1 Falling levels of profitability mean competitive prices. As the pace of technological advance continues, more can be obtained for less.
2 Suppliers are having to slim down and become more flexible and responsive in order to survive. This means the customer is not contributing so much to supplier overheads.

3   Considerable restructuring is occurring. The alliance relationships that are emerging are strengthening the capability of suppliers to meet customer requirements.

4   Within the new groupings that are emerging, the co-ordination and planning of operations, and the allocation of resources, are increasingly being undertaken at the global level. Global groupings are more able to supply and service the international customer.

5   There is greater commitment to open systems. This reduces the dependence of customers upon particular suppliers, and is making it easier to build and operate global networks.

6   Companies are finding it more difficult by themselves to supply total value to customers. This is encouraging co-operation between suppliers, and closer relationships with customers.

7   As suppliers focus on core activities, their customers secure advantages of greater specialisation.

A range of facilities management options are also open to users of information technology who wish to focus upon their core activities. The growth in the use of 'contracting out' is having an impact upon both customers and suppliers.

●   Companies such as Benetton in Italy, and BP and W H Smith in the UK, have contracted out the management of their networks.

●   Suppliers of facilities management services such as Hoskyns in computer services, or Rank Xerox and Xerox in document management, are having to integrate more closely their pan-European and international operations in order to meet the cross-border needs of their clients.

Although the buyer is in a relatively strong position, there is still a need to be cautious. The availability of accessible technology does not mean it will be sensibly used. Companies will still make mistakes in their search for competitive advantage and new market opportunities. Citicorp, for example, has invested in more than one computerised information service that has failed.

SUPPORTING RATHER THAN REPLACING PEOPLE

Many past investments in office technology were constrained by an architectural base geared to 'structured' activity. As the emphasis moved to the 'decision support' of senior management engaged primarily in 'unstructured' activity, many information systems found it difficult to respond. Throughout the 1970s and early 1980s there was a steady growth in demand for the services of specialist professionals and consultants.

The cost of knowledge workers tends to be higher than that of clerical workers, so there was a consequent impact upon head office and overhead costs. The challenge in the late 1980s for incremental office technology investment was to secure flexibility, responsiveness to customer requirements and competitive advantage, while containing and reducing the number of managers and professionals engaged in 'unstructured' activity.

The use of technology is very revealing of how people are perceived by senior management. It communicates attitudes and expectations. Management teams who regard people as components in a machine, and treat them as extensions of the technology, should not be surprised if some of them behave as alienated robots. The 'expendable', who feel they are hanging on to their jobs only until the 'right software package' comes along, tend to withhold commitment.

In the 1990s, companies are more aware that people are a critical success factor, and that there is latent human potential to tap.[10] The emphasis is shifting to the use of technology to attract, develop and update people and facilitate their value-added contribution. People and their supporting technology are viewed in the network organisation as an investment rather than a cost.

THE NEW FRONTIER

The flexible and adaptable network organisation is able to bring relevant information to bear at the point of executive decisions. Information is derived from a variety of internal and external databases. It is analysed, refined and communicated within and across the network to those with relevant expertise. Views and opinions are sought, and checked, inside and outside of the company.

All this activity takes place in a hectic environment of interruption, changing views and assumptions, and constant pressures of time.[11] Knowledge workers face unpredictable demands upon their time and expertise. In this environment work is inevitably 'unstructured'. IT must be able to cope with chaos and uncertainty, and improve the effectiveness of professionals and other knowledge workers engaged in creative activities.

The failure of yesterday's inflexible technology to deliver improvements in 'white-collar' productivity in bureaucratic organisations[8] creates opportunities for subsequent generations of technology to facilitate the building of network organisations. According to Paul Allaire, president of Xerox Corporation: 'The next frontier for real productivity is in the office. At Xerox we are harnessing technology to help our customers to capture the opportunities that this new frontier offers.'

THE NETWORK ORGANISATION VISION

In the network organisation, information is valued to the extent that it improves understanding, and contributes to business objectives and customer satisfaction. There is less emphasis upon processing standard transactions, and more emphasis upon manipulating and refining information to build and share understanding, allow a more flexible response to individual requirements, and support new ways of working and learning.

The IT 'architectural' requirements that distinguish the network organisation from the bureaucracy are presented in Table 16.1. These emerged from interviews undertaken for the *Developing IT Directors* report.[12] The technology the network organisation needs must itself be flexible and adaptable in allowing multifunctional, multilocation and multinational teams to work together.

Table 16.1 *Architectures: Distinguishing Features*

Bureaucratic Organisation	Network Organisation
Information	Understanding
Data Processing	Document Management
Automation	Facilitating Systems
Replace People	Add value to people
Procedure	Process
Standardise	Customise to individual
Structured/Rigid	Flexible/Adaptable
Individual and Fixed Roles	Participative/Team playing/Learning
Single organisation	Multiple organisations

Source: Developing IT Directors, 1990

The process of working effectively in a team involves more than just sharing data. It must also be possible to share thoughts, insights and concepts. The technology that is used should allow thoughts, insights and concepts to be refined and amended. It should facilitate learning and development, and should itself be capable of learning and development.

Full citizens of the network organisation should have access to all relevant information, both physical and electronic. To enhance understanding or add value, this information must be assimilated, shared and correct conclusions drawn. Subsequently, what has been achieved, learned or refined must be presented to decision makers or customers in a form to which they can relate. An effective international network is that which allows information to be acquired, understood and communicated on a global basis.

The network should also embrace key customers, business partners and important suppliers.[13] It should be capable of organic international expansion. Seamless access is required to relevant internal and external databases via communication gateways and appropriate interfaces.

MAKING THE VISION HAPPEN

Documents are the currency of the network organisation. They flow along business processes, making things happen for customers. Yet, they are taken for granted, lost and cursed. In comparison with heavy investments upon the processing and generation of data, most companies devote relatively small amounts to the management of the documents that give life and value to information.

According to one interviewee: 'Presenting information well is not just a nice idea when it concerns customers. The document is the leaflet they don't understand, or the manual that is out of date.' The document could also be the invoice that is a source of 'billing queries'. The order may have been lost because a particular document spent too long buried in someone's 'in-tray'.

Knowledge work is largely based upon documents. They can exist in physical and electronic forms. The effective network needs to be able to capture physical documents in electronic form, access, share and manipulate electronic documents, and enable them to be created and managed. The technology needs to embrace scanning, creation, storage and document management.

The commissioning, assembly, structuring and external presentation of information are all stages of the publishing process. Traditional publishing can be slow, relatively expensive, remote from users and not easily controlled by them or responsive to their needs. The publishing process can now occur at the point at which needs and creative ideas originate. A publishing capability can be an integral part of today's network system.

The effective network allows combinations of text and graphics to be used. Understanding can be further enhanced through the use of a network not only to collect and organise information, but also to browse through what has been collected and discovered. Expert systems can enable relationships to be established and 'logic checks' made for coherence. Persuasive arguments to support a point of view may be constructed by using logical relationships discovered through the use of expert systems.

The enhancement of understanding is an interactive process. The output of one professional or knowledge worker is another's input. An effective office system allows information and understanding to be shared, circulated and refined, if need be across national borders. It empowers, develops and enables contributions to be received from many minds. The prospect of growing and sharing on a continuing basis encourages people to seek membership of the network.

THE SUPPORTING TECHNOLOGY

The technology of the network should be capable of capturing the sum total of available understanding and bringing it to bear at the point of decision or need. It should also allow this understanding to be communicated internally and externally. This encourages and builds team work. By allowing direct access, intermediaries, 'gatekeepers', and sources of confusion and distortion can be cut out.

Current office systems technology embraces data and document access, office publishing and document management. It allows the interaction and refinement that can increase understanding, and improves presentation and hence adds value to information. An example of a global document management environment is the Xerox GLOBALVIEW. This can run on a wide range of equipment, and enables documents to be created and published in over 40 languages.

It is now possible to integrate reprographic, word processing, electronic printing, document management, data processing and electronic publishing through integrated office systems that are built upon a suitable network architecture. Such an architecture can also allow access to knowledge-gaining tools and expert systems that further improve understanding.

Documents without electronic masters can be accessed by scanning devices that make use of image and character recognition technology. A priority for some vendors of technology is work on direct voice input to a network. The ideal network allows access to all available sources of relevant information.

MANAGEMENT ISSUES

There are certain issues which need to be addressed by companies that are seeking to become flexible and responsive network organisations.[5] In the case of the larger multinationals, many of the management problems listed in Table 16.2 are likely to feature on the IT director's agenda. The list is intended to be illustrative rather than definitive.

Table 16.2 *Management Problems on the IT Director's Agenda*

Transition to flat and flexible organisation
Multifunction and multilocation team working
EDI links with customers
Incorporating customers and suppliers into network organisation
Support of international project teams
Security and integration issues of pan-European and international operation
Systems for support of joint ventures
PTT standards and international expansion
Integration *vis-à-vis* mergers and acquisitions
Support of Research and Development
IT to support environmental monitoring and protection
IT to support business co-operation with eastern Europe
The facilitation of learning, and integration of learning and working
'Internationalisation' of senior IT (and other) management

Source: Developing IT Directors, 1990

A number of the issues listed in Table 16.2 are the result of a growing appreciation that individual companies cannot deliver 'total value' to customers without close co-operation with other organisations in the value chain, including the customers themselves.[13] Many people are spending more time working with their equivalents in other organisations.

The search for synergy across networks and along value chains, as well as within companies, is becoming a higher priority. The achievement of flexibility and how best to facilitate learning will replace such traditional IT management issues as 'centralisation versus decentralisation'.

As more international networks embrace customers and suppliers, compatibility of systems is likely to become a more significant issue. Incompatibility of systems is emerging as a major problem within the field of joint ventures, arrangements, mergers and acquisitions. It is also a significant 'barrier' for some companies who are contemplating geographic expansion into eastern Europe. The management of integration in the establishment of multifunctional, multilocation and multiorganisation networks would appear to be a common element of a number of the 'problem areas' identified in the course of interviews for this book.

It is likely that there will be an increasing trend towards the integration of office processes, as stand-alone solutions give way to integrated global networks. A networking capability, and compatibility with the equipment of a variety of vendors can be critical to achieving a higher return from past and current investments in technology. Compared with the scale of historic investments, relatively modest incremental expenditures on networking, gateways and workstations that are compatible with the equipment of more than one vendor, can significantly enhance network performance.

However, a word of caution should be issued. We saw in Chapter 15 that IT is but one of a number of key change elements that need to be brought together in order to effect corporate transformation. Little benefit will be obtained from applications of technology to activities and processes that do not relate to business objectives, or the delivery of value to customers.

The growth of global networks confronts governments with a profound regulatory challenge. According to John Redwood, the UK minister for corporate affairs:[14]

> *'World capitalism is moving to a global phase. Companies are developing more and more cross-border and international business. ... Cables and satellites are linking distant settlements as if they were but suburbs of a global city. Individual governments and regulators will not stop this process. They cannot disinvent the electronic switch or the digital highway. They cannot prevent new computer-based trading strategies and systems. All that a national or regional regulator can do is decide whether the market of his responsibility will plug into the new world market easily or not.'*

BUILDING INTERNATIONAL NETWORKS

Compatibility of systems and standards is an important issue for the network organisation.[15] Variations in national standards and the differing characteristics of national networks complicate the task of building global networks. Within Europe, since the establishment of the European Telecommunications Standards Institute in 1988, steady progress has been made towards the harmonisation of standards.

The task of building regional and global networks can be 'contracted out' to an external supplier. Unilever contracted Sprint of the USA to design and operate its pan-European data network. A variety of companies are opting for a facilities management route to the building and management of global networks. While some telecoms suppliers such as Cable & Wireless have a long-established global perspective, national PTTs have had to conclude a variety of arrangements and alliances in order to offer global network services.

Some hardware suppliers are finding it difficult to establish a reputation for independence and objectivity when advising clients. There is always the suspicion that behind the 'cover' of the initial consultancy lurks a desire to 'sell boxes'. Companies most likely to make the transition from 'box supplier' to 'global partner' are those such as Xerox and Rank Xerox, that focus on facilitating understanding and supporting business processes.

ASSESSMENT CRITERIA

Given that much past IT investment has been devoted to entrenching bureaucracy and the support of activities that are irrelevant in terms of business objectives and customer satisfaction, it is not surprising that many companies are seeking to 'regain control' of IT investments.[16] How should information technology investment proposals be assessed? Much will depend upon the situation and circumstances of the company. Key considerations that would apply to a community of relatively highly paid knowledge workers include the following.

- The extent to which a proposed system can cope with both 'structured' and 'unstructured' activity; access both electronic and physical documents; and allow refinement and integration.
- Whether its underlying architecture gives flexibility of use; and is simple and reliable; compatible with the equipment of multiple vendors; and allows adaptation and migration to the employment of expert systems.

Sophistication for the sake of it should be avoided. Given the importance of human skill as a critical success factor, a premium should be placed upon a supplier that recognises the importance of ease of access and interaction.

A commitment to the development and establishment of open standards, and compatibility with prevailing standards, will also be an advantage. The more open an office system, the more flexible and adaptable it will be in accommodating technological advances.

Particular attention should be paid to networking capability, and openness and ease of access. The aim should be to introduce cost-effective elements of technology employing a suitable architecture that may be compatible with past investments, and which may allow for adaptation and evolution towards a fully integrated global network.

If this advice sounds like 'techno-speak', consider supplementing it with some 'hard-nosed' first principle questions. The following approaches were used by interviewees to concentrate their minds.

'I always say to myself, what would I do if this were my business? Would I put my hand in my pocket?'

'We ask the people putting up the proposals how much they are going to contribute from their divisional or departmental budget. ... You see them melt away. The ones left in the room are those who think it will do them some good.'

'What does it all mean for customers? Is it about them, or about us and what we would like to have? That's the approach to take.'

'Stand back from it and reflect. If we do none of this, what would happen to customer satisfaction? What business objectives would suffer?'

To build flexible and international networks that meet a distinct set of requirements may require new forms of relationships between suppliers and users of IT. Rather than 'packaging' and marketing IT goods and services, more IT suppliers may seek to enter into strategic partnership relationships with major multinationals, making their underlying technology available and working in joint supplier–customer teams to customise both hardware and software to the requirements of particular networks.

Any process that is used to determine global network requirements should satisfy the criteria set out in Table 16.3. Independence and objectivity are particularly important when suppliers are involved. Often, it is the project management expertise which is the most critical, the ability to deliver what is required to budget and on time.

Table 16.3 *Suggested Evaluation Process*

A process to formulate and implement a global network should:

Understand the corporate vision and mission
Take account of business goals and objectives
Concentrate upon the activities and processes that generate and deliver value to customers
Be independent, objective and authoritative
Identify and confront barriers and obstacles
Focus on the application, use and management of technology
Involve customers, suppliers and business partners as required
Be representative of the various interests involved
Be sensitive to the diversity of requirements and perspectives
Access relevant research on learning
Tap best practice experience
Have the necessary commitment and support
Be empowered and equipped to deliver
Draw upon implementation experience
Allow for agreement in stages
Incorporate a 'learning loop' and quality review

COMPLETING THE TRANSFORMATION JIGSAW PUZZLE

It is worth repeating a key conclusion of Chapter 15, namely that barriers to the successful introduction of technology tend to be attitudinal and behavioural, rather than technical. How IT is introduced and used can influence both attitudes and behaviour. It could be applied for this purpose.

The correct application of IT also demonstrates commitment to people and to business objectives. Equipping people with the right technology can help turn the rhetoric of empowerment into a reality. People are involved and not excluded. They can access information and make their contribution. Objectives may not appear to be just 'words on paper' when the means to turn aspiration into achievement are visibly being put in place.

The most effective technology is often that which is relatively unobtrusive. For example, the basic telephone handset which appears to have changed little since the beginning of the century allows people to communicate quickly and effortlessly with friends and colleagues all over the world. This ease of use is the result of a complex switching and routing infrastructure which has undergone a technological revolution and yet remains hidden.

In time, the technology of the network organisation will merge into the background to become an accepted feature of the living environment. It should be as reassuring, and no more disturbing, than the crackling of a log on an inglenook fire.

CHECKLIST

▶ Does your company have an international information technology strategy, and how compatible is this with its international vision?

▶ How important are speed and access to your company's customers, and how might they be improved through the application of IT?

▶ Does your company's IT network facilitate multifunctional, multilocation, and multinational team working?

▶ Does it allow flexible access to all relevant external sources of skill?

▶ How might your company's relationships with its customers and suppliers be transformed through the use and application of IT?

▶ Does your company's IT network facilitate the building of understanding, as well as the acquisition of information?

▶ Is it supportive of communication, and the integration of working and learning?

▶ Is the technology of your company appropriate to its strategy, organisation, people and management processes?

▶ Is it supportive of continuing adaptation and change?

▶ How 'user friendly' is the technology of your company, ie is it compatible with, and supportive of, the way people naturally work and think, and conducive of 'interfaces' with, or links to, other networks?

▶ What are the main barriers to the more effective use of IT in your company and how might these be overcome?

REFERENCES

1 Ohmae, K (1990) *The Borderless World : Power and Strategy in the Interlinked Economy*, Collins, London.
2 IIC (1991) *The Global Telecommunications Traffic Report 1991*, International Institute of Communications, New York.
3 Coulson-Thomas, C (1991) 'Customers, Marketing and the Network Organisation', *Journal of Marketing Management*, 7, pp 237–55.
4 Keen, P G W (1986) *Competing in Time: Using Telecommunications for Competitive Advantage*, Ballinger, New York.
5 Coulson-Thomas, C (1991) 'Directors and IT, and IT Directors' *European Journal of Information Systems*, vol 1, no 1, pp 45–53; and (1991) 'IT Directors and IT Strategy' *Journal of Information Technology*, 6, pp 192–203.
6 Jacobson, H K (1984) *Networks of Interdependence*, (2nd edn), Alfred A Knopf, New York.
7 Coulson-Thomas, C (1989) 'Information Technology and the Responsive Organisation' *Information Technology and Public Policy*, vol 8, no 1, Winter, pp 29–30.
8 OECD (1988) *New Technology in the 1990s: A Socio-economic Strategy*, Paris.
9 Coulson-Thomas, C (1990) 'Breaking Through the Information Barrier: Management Development and IT' *International Journal of Technology Management*, vol 5, no 5, pp 618–23.
10 Coulson-Thomas, C and Brown, R (1989) *The Responsive Organisation, People Management: the Challenge of the 1990s*, BIM, Corby.
11 Mintzberg, H (1973) *The Nature of Managerial Work*, Harper & Row, New York.
12 Coulson-Thomas, C (1990) *Developing IT Directors*, an interim Adaptation Ltd report to the Department of Computing Science, Surrey University.
13 Coulson-Thomas, C and Brown, R (1990) *Beyond Quality, Managing the Relationship with the Customer*, BIM, Corby.
14 Redwood, J (1991) *One World, One Market*, speech to International Council of Securities Dealers and Self Regulating Associations, Department of Trade and Industry, London, 23 April.
15 Gray, P A (1991) *Open Systems: A Business Strategy for the 1990s*, McGraw-Hill, London.
16 Hochstrasser, B and Griffiths, C (1990) *Regaining Control of IT Investments, A Handbook for Senior UK Management*, Kobler Unit, Imperial College, London.

17

CREATING THE INTERNATIONAL LEARNING NETWORK

THE CREDO AND THE BACK ALLEY

A commitment to tapping more of the potential of people is an integral element of the credo of the new organisation. The rhetoric proclaims the central importance of empowered people who are counselled, mentored, supported and facilitated in building relationships with *their* customers, and delivering value to them.

The potential and the talents to encourage, nourish and build are not just the ones that are known about. They should include the latent capability that has been smothered and concealed, and the hidden strengths that people do not even know that they have. Beneath the job titles, and other labels and trappings, are attributes and qualities that should be brought to the surface.

We saw in Chapter 13 that the well-meaning efforts of many educationalists, trainers and developers destroy the innate drive of millions of people to explore and learn. Rather than being 'released', their ambitions and prospects are crushed in a vice of misunderstanding, mass deception and unintended consequences. Some accept their categorisation, 'settle down' and grumble about a humdrum existence, tinged with the occasional thought that they might have done better or glimpse of what might have been. Others rebel and seek an alternative route to peer recognition in the alley or the street.

BRINGING LEARNING INTO THE NETWORK

How can the reality of active and universal learning be brought into the network organisation? This chapter will examine new approaches to learning, and the creation of international networks to support both working and learning.

How should the technology supporting the international network be used to facilitate more effective approaches to learning, as well as new patterns of working? In the case of many educational applications of IT there has been too much emphasis upon the technology. In others, it has been used to 'automate' traditional approaches to learning that are of questionable value. The focus should be upon the nature of the learning process and how this can best be facilitated for individuals and groups, with or without IT.

LEARNING ISN'T WORKING

Internationally, people are concerned about learning. Around the world there is growing recognition that the relative performance of national economies can reflect the relevance and adaptability of skills.

- During his 1990 general election campaign, the prime minister of Australia, Bob Hawke, launched a 'clever country' initiative. Hawke acknowledged that more attention needed to be given to the educational system and scientific infrastructure in order to 'mobilise' the country's 'most valuable resource, the talents of the Australian people'. Under the initiative, a network of co-operative research centres was suggested.

- Singapore has made a sustained commitment to raising the levels of skills of its people. Considerable investment has also been made in the telecommunications and information technology infrastructure needed to support knowledge workers. As a consequence, the country has been able to attract and develop 'high-tech' industries.

- In the UK, prime minister John Major has acknowledged: 'The promotion of skills training is vital in the battle to make the UK more competitive in an increasingly competitive world. ... We are all engaged in a revolution ... in the way we stimulate enterprise, develop businesses and invest in our greatest asset – our people.'

Companies are recognising that with customers increasingly demanding tailored goods and services, and total quality becoming a necessary requirement for business success, they need to do more to harness the potential of all their people. In Europe, the prospect of an ageing workforce is creating a requirement to tap more of the potential of those who are older.[1]

CHALLENGES AND DEBATES

The roots of many learning limitations and inhibitions lie in early experiences at school. Traditional approaches to education are being challenged, there are 'great education debates'[2] and there is widespread concern that education is not 'reaching' many young people.

- In the USA, President George Bush has launched an America 2000 initiative to raise academic standards, while his vice-president struggles to spell the word 'potato'. There is widespread recognition of the continuing failure to develop the skills of what has become known as the 'bottom 70 per cent'. The need for more of a competence-based approach, and the concerns of employers, have been recognised with the appointment of David Kearns, a former president and chairman of Xerox Corporation, to the Bush administration's education team.

- In Japan, successive governments have given a high priority to education, and have understood its economic importance. However, there are those who question an educational system that has put great emphasis upon group orientation, rote learning and testing.[3] It is recognised that in a demanding and changing international marketplace, individual initiative and creativity need greater encouragement.

In the USA, the deficiencies of traditional education have led to an ambitious commercial plan to introduce a network of new learning environments that will use the latest technology, and a variety of innovatory approaches, to better meet the needs of learners and their parents.[4]

Some educational systems find it more difficult to respond to changing circumstances than others. The German 'dual system', for example, is deeply entrenched, and as a consequence is inflexible and relatively costly.

Internationalisation is encouraging cross-border comparisons. What was once uncritically accepted is now challeged. Returning to the German example, students question why they should spend year after year in overcrowded universities, while *en route* to their degrees, at an age when friends in other countries have already graduated and are moving 'up the ranks' in MNCs.

THE LEARNING PROCESS

How do people learn? In the past this was assumed rather than understood. For some years at a number of locations around the world, such as the Institute for Research on Learning (IRL) in California, relatively small and multidisciplinary groups have come together to examine how people learn – not just those who are academic, but all people.

The findings are consistent with many of the learning preferences of companies we considered in Chapter 13. In particular, there is a desire to integrate learning and working.[5]

The most effective learning is that which occurs in life generally, as a result of doing things and observing the outcomes. When left to themselves, people do not 'reserve' learning for certain hours and locations. The classroom is, for many people, one of the least effective learning environments. They feel cut off, estranged or distanced from normal life, and do not relate to many of the abstract symbols and concepts that are used.

Some of those interviewed talked of a 'fear of courses', an 'alien environment', 'formality' or 'uncertainty' associated with an unfamiliar environment. One manager summed up the misgivings: 'I like to be on my own ground, somewhere where I feel at home.' Learning at institutions, with teachers 'pouring knowledge into people', is unsatisfactory for the majority of people. The context is wrong, and relevance and purpose are not perceived.

There is a need for learning situations that enable the practical relevance of concepts and ideas to be more easily grasped. Too much emphasis has been given to the transmission of information. We saw in the last chapter that information of itself does not necessarily lead to better understanding.

DETERMINING CORPORATE REQUIREMENTS

The preference of major employers is for the building of skills and competencies that equip people to cope with work and life.[6] The nature of the work and life for which people need to be prepared will vary across countries, according to such factors as culture and stage of development. Learning materials developed at such North American business schools as Chicago, Harvard or Stanford may need to be different from those produced by the Asia Institute of Management at Manila in the Philippines, or Keio University at Yokahama in Japan, if they are to be relevant to local needs. The ability to communicate internationally should not obscure the need for local tailoring.

The importance of the context and relevance of learning has become better understood by some global competitors.

- In many Japanese companies the integration of working and learning is well established. Managers may spend between a fifth and a third of their time developing members of their teams.
- Ford Motor Company operates an Employee Development Assistance Programme which offers all employees the opportunity to undertake subsidised development activity that is tailored to their own needs and interests. This ensures that what is being learned is relevant to each person; and it has been found that the learning employee in one context can become more open minded and questioning in others.

We have noted how, increasingly, work within companies is being undertaken by groups and teams.[7] Team activity and group learning can be particularly effective, yet educational institutions generally require people to learn and be assessed upon an individual basis. Little attention is given to understanding group processes, supporting group learning or improving outputs from 'the team'.

KEY DEVELOPMENT QUESTIONS

Research at IRL reveals that not all of us learn in the same way. Each of us has a distinct potential as a learner. Education and training need to be able to respond flexibly to groups of people who may learn in a variety of ways. These findings suggest a hierarchy of questions which should be posed by those with people development responsibilities.

1   How should the development function become more flexible in securing access to scarce human resources and skills?
2   How can development be responsive to the learning and development needs of the individual, and of particular groups?
3   How should the role of facilitator of learning differ from that of subject teacher?
4   What are the implications of how different people learn for the roles of mentor and coach?
5   How should technology be used to facilitate team activity and group learning?
6   How could a learning network be used as a catalyst for the transformation of the corporate system as a whole?
7   How should a corporate learning network be developed to embrace both the EC–'1992' dimension, and the global learning environment?
8   How could collaborative partners and suppliers of technology be incorporated into the network?

The empowered person should be enabled to do more than harness the information and resources of the company on behalf of customers. People should be able to reach into their own minds and those of colleagues. The stimulation, release and application of learning potential is true empowerment.

LEARNING AND TECHNOLOGY

The results of research into how people learn have important implications for the use of IT to facilitate learning.[8] The traditional 'black box' that produces an outcome without revealing why this has occurred can 'deskill'. A more 'transparent technology' that allows the learner to observe processes at work can increase understanding with each application. This has been called 'glass-box' technology, and can assist the 'merging of learning and doing.'[9]

The ability of Japanese technology to blur the distinction between the real world and the electronic world could result in learning technologies becoming consumer products. Virtual reality technology offers the potential to create a wealth of learning environments that can adapt to the needs, interests and capabilities of the individual learner.[10]

IT that can facilitate interaction, team activity and group learning, is particularly valuable. The BIM *Flat Organisation* report[7], and interviews undertaken for the SEMS survey on 'human resource development for international operation',[5] both revealed that companies are doing little to equip their managers to work effectively in teams.

The strong desire of many companies to tap more of the potential of their staff is not always matched by the commitment to the investment in development and technology this can require. Consider the following comments.

'We had presentations in the boardroom, and saw the learning potential of the technology. By the time you go down two or three layers in the company, the vision gets lost. ... Our people went out and bought the cheapest boxes.'

'I have to focus on the immediate ... there are problems to be fixed. There are short term targets to be met. ... I just don't have time to think about the wider implications.'

'If people would pay for it and use it, I would go for the learning solution. ... But the benefits are not immediate. ... Other things are more immediate and get the priority.'

'Suppliers are the problem. We all agree on the concept ... [but] they go away and come back with whatever it is they want to sell. It's never what we want ... we cannot progress things.'

There are many benefits to be gained from networking up terminals and encouraging their use by groups. However, when a cost-saving approach to purchase decisions is taken, the 'commodity' technology that is acquired can sometimes fall short of what would most effectively facilitate team working.

SUPPORTING DIFFERENT APPROACHES TO LEARNING

So what is needed? A 'user-friendly' technology is required that does not distort too much the way people naturally learn. The technology that suits one group may be inappropriate for another that learns in a different way. There are different approaches that could be adopted according to learning aptitudes, styles and preferences. For example, we saw the following in Chapter 13.

- The traditional approach to learning tends to assume that we all learn in a similar way. It appears best suited to the 'academics', those who operate in a world of logic and structure, and who proceed by means of small incremental steps from an understood current position. The Japanese approach to quality is such a procedural approach.
- The breakthroughs and 'scientific revolutions' challenge the frameworks, the tidy boxes within which the academics are at work.[11] They occur when 'connections are made'. These 'other' approaches to learning are based upon the establishment of links, patterns and relationships. A process-based approach may release qualities in people hardly touched by the academic knowledge-based approach.

Creativity should not be 'something different', confined to those upon whom 'the gods have smiled'. It is too often treated as an exception or a surprise, rather than as part of everyday work. As one CEO put it: 'My customers demand creativity. ... I don't want to pay extra for creativity – I want to assume it.'

MISSING ELEMENTS

Creativity does not 'just happen'. Throughout this book, considerable stress has been put upon the importance of the attitudinal aspects of corporate culture. The technological environment can also be an important element of the 'learning culture'. Consider the following questions raised by interviewees.

'Can't we use technology to make everyone more creative? ... Isn't there software we can load on to our boxes?'

'There must be a way of magnifying people. Should we be using technology and 'know-how' to blow up their strengths?'

The artificial intelligence (AI) environment offers the prospect of a universal and affordable complement to human intelligence that can support both learning and working. However, just when the potential is within grasp attention has 'moved on'. Word has got around on the 'groupthink grapevine' that AI is 'over-rated' and 'hasn't delivered'. What it isn't should not blind us to what it is.

The AI environment suits those who are sensitive to potential links and relationships. The 'academic' who imposes assumptions and frameworks may cut himself or herself off from possibilities that the environment is suggesting. Those without formal academic qualifications, but who are receptive to patterns and possibilities, may, with an appropriate induction, outperform the graduate systems analyst.

An accessible AI environment may have sufficient flexibility to support different ways of learning. It could allow each individual to become aware of how he or she most effectively learns and, subsequently, could facilitate such learning. The aim should be to enable individuals to discover what their relative strengths as learners are, and how they might best build their understanding.

SELECTING THE TECHNOLOGY TO APPLY

Just as it is 'horses for courses', when it comes to facilitating the learning of individuals, so it is with making use of IT. Different technologies and their underlying architectures have distinct strengths and weaknesses. Use can be made of each, as appropriate, so long as interfaces exist.

The dilemma for companies is that they may need both the incremental or procedural, and the relational or process approach to learning, along with some others. For one director, the concept of the learning organisation presents a dilemma.

> 'The notion is attractive. ... It sounds good. When you think it through, all sorts of possibilities open up [but] the implications and potential costs can be intimidating. To get there means dramatic changes ... another revolution, when we have yet to accomplish the first. It's a question of how true you want to be to the vision.'

Given the diversity of people that may be found across the network organisation, the cost of a learning network could be astronomic, hence the need to focus the application of learning technology upon the key processes that deliver value to customers, 'vital few' programmes and critical barriers to the achievement of business objectives.

When considering the application of information technology to support new approaches to learning, a set of objectives should be established. An example of one such set is given in Table 17.1.

Table 17.1 *Objectives of a Learning Network*

Support key management and business processes
Faciltate learning rather than teaching
Focus on understanding, competence and capability
Allow individuals and groups to manage their own learning
Match learning need to appropriate learning activities and resources
Enable flexible access to relevant learning opportunities and environments
Overcome shortages of teachers and experts
Use specialists as facilitators and managers of learning
Integrate learning and working
Allow international access and expansion
Be integrated into the corporate and value chain network
Be 'open' to multivendor technology
Build on best practice
Prepare a migration path re future technologies
Be capable of organic growth and development

The facilitation of learning is most effective where there is access to architectures that are optimised for the building of understanding, rather than information processing *per se*. The aim is to add value to people rather than replace them. Facilitating processes are more important than the support of procedures. A technology that is sufficiently flexible and adaptable to support individual and participative approaches to learning is preferable to one that is structured and rigid, and offers a standard approach.

INTERNATIONAL LEARNING NETWORKS

The total market for learning and development services is expanding, as awareness spreads of the importance of human skill as a source of competitive advantage. In some dynamic markets, almost all employees have a continuing requirement for education and updating. For the international company this requirement can be a global one.

Information technology is overcoming the barriers of distance. The business school and the consultancy, like the user or client organisation, will increasingly resemble a network of electronic links, forward to customers, backwards to suppliers and sideways to business partners.

Developments in communications technology are supportive of the creation of joint working and learning networks. For example, satellite delivered services direct to the various geographically dispersed points of a corporate network could include broadcast television coverage of a conference or other corporate event, the delivery of courses by closed-user group TV, and the transfer of files by data transmission. Various language channels could be used. Satellite technology offers the prospect of two-way communication embracing voice, pictures and data where this is permitted by national regulation.

Broadcast technology can be used for both information and learning purposes:

- BMW of Germany uses a private television network to establish direct contact with its franchised dealers in the UK. By means of a dish and satellite link, a one-hour programme is broadcast each week to update the dealers on new product developments and other relevant information.
- Norwich Union of the UK has used the same technology to update its staff on budget changes. Corporate television can be used for a variety of purposes, including employee communications and the delivery of educational programmes.
- IBM has developed an Education Television Network that incorporates two-way video-conferencing. Classrooms at IBM offices in countries such as France, Germany and the UK are linked together, and significant savings in travel and hotel costs have been achieved.

The whole of western Europe can be within the footprint of a single satellite. As satellites broadcast at higher power, clear signals can be received by smaller and less expensive dishes and receivers. Satellite technology can allow rapid dissemination of information across a corporate network. Encryption of confidential information can occur and conditional access may be provided.

Companies such as British Aerospace and Granada Satellite Services have developed applications of satellite technology of particular value to learning networks. Future corporate and other users of interactive video may be able to receive via satellite, and record, interactive video programmes. Such programmes could be updated by satellite.

'ELECTRONIC' EDUCATION NETWORKS

A variety of electronic learning networks have come into existence.

- Pupils and teachers at schools in different EC Member States can talk directly to each other via live video conference links through the European Space Agency's Olympus satellite.
- In the USA, many corporations make use of distance-learning via satellite. In the UK, telelinked BT enquiries operators working from home can access colleagues and supervisors, and be updated, by video link.
- In Europe, a Joint Academic Network Using Satellites (JANUS) has been funded under the EC DELTA programme. This satellite-based network has been established

to enable European companies and universities to work together in the creation of educational software.

- Distance-learning students of Henley Management College are able to communicate with each other, and with tutors, using a variety of technologies. Tutoring techniques used include workgroup computer conferencing.
- Another IT-based network is the European Business and Language Learning Network. The network is composed of groups in the UK, France and Germany, and encourages the development of cross-cultural group-learning methodologies.
- Medical centres throughout the UK have been linked up by satellite. The network allows a degree of interaction between students and medical experts.

The extent to which a large number of sources of expertise can be accessed by means of a learning network was demonstrated in 1991 when, for one week, the UK's DTI linked with TV-am to offer a free helpline service concerning information on training, education, enterprise and employment to school leavers in receipt of their exam results. Over 1500 experts were on hand to respond to calls, and the helpline also had access to ECCTIS, a computerised database of university and polytechnic places.

A gradual switch of expenditure is likely from the 'campus' and its classrooms to the terminals of the 'enabling' electronic network, as 'learning' is taken to the 'learners'. Corporate networks and learning networks can be linked up and could converge. In certain 'knowledge industries' the quality of the 'network' embracing and linking learners and facilitators of the learning process may become the key competitive differentiator.

A corporate network along the lines advocated earlier in this chapter could itself become a learning network.[12] A possible development framework, or set of guidelines, is presented in Table 17.2.

Table 17.2 *Integrated Learning Environment Development Framework*

Articulation and agreement of common vision
Establish framework and guidelines
Set attainable objectives
Ensure compatibility with likely future developments
Reflect mixed technology environment of real world
Access relevant knowledge, competence and experience
Establish basis for seeking internal and external participation and support
Open to multivendor and sponsor involvement
Preserve international operation, growth and development options

THE GLOBAL CAMPUS

Electronic universities already exist, and have students in many countries who communicate with each other and contact their tutors via computer terminals. Classes made up of students in various locations can 'log' on at certain set times and interact with each other. The 'electronic' student can access relevant material, bounce ideas and drafts off others by electronic mail, and produce and deliver reports, essays and presentations using a terminal located at home or on an office desk. Such a learning environment can itself 'learn', as previous reading lists, other course material, and assignments can be accessed, updated and refined.

In the UK, ECCTIS and other video-text and database services are available to participants in the Campus 2000 schools network. This was established in 1989 by *The*

Times Network Systems, and within two years over 10,000 schools had joined the network. The wide range of international information services that are available are designed to be accessible by telephone as a result of a link between Prestel and Telecom Gold.

Campus 2000 is linked to the JANET academic and other networks. The contents of certain national newspapers are held on CD-ROM files and can be accessed by means of key words. Educational programmes delivered across Europe by various satellite TV channels are available. Business databases are included on the growing menu of available sources of information. Networks such as Campus 2000, supplemented by electronic mail and computer conferencing, can enable schools around the world to communicate with each other and establish joint projects.

The University of the World, based in California, uses a range of audio, video and computer based techniques to support learning across a network embracing schools, colleges and universities in a number of countries. Video is transmitted by satellite and cable, and learning material is also sent by facsimile and electronic mail. The University of the World makes use of the BITNET computer network which links institutions in Europe, North and South America, with those in Asia and Australasia. Individuals can learn through the network while moving between assignments and activities in a number of Asian countries.

Access to such a network is particularly beneficial for developing countries. Their young people are able to remain at home, rather than travel to the USA in order to study. This can reduce the extent of a local 'brain drain'.

MANAGING THE LEARNING NETWORK

The form in which learning opportunities and materials are presented can reflect the capabilities and interests of each student. Learner and facilitator become partners in the learning process. Each point of contact, or terminal, is able in theory to draw upon the resources of the whole network.

The technology can also be used to record contributions that are made, track progress, co-ordinate diaries, and monitor assignments, project groups and teams. It can determine who is 'living off the system', and who is putting most into the network. Geographic dispersion need not result in less awareness of what is going on.

One interviewee put a telling question: 'With all the talk of learning organisations, how many companies assess and reward learning?' The assessment of both work and learning could be based on demonstrated competencies and delivered output. Remuneration could then be linked to 'value-added', or tangible contribution, rather than position in a hierarchy. This would give an incentive to people to learn. Rewards of trainers could be linked more directly to the effective facilitation of learning. Learning environments can also be used to identify facilitator development needs.

In view of the great variety of requests for support which can be received, learning networks do not find it easy to retain a full-time staff with the range of experience and skills required. Instead a network of contacts could be built up of those with relevant facilitation skills which could be accessed as and when required.

A learning network could advertise its mission, or particular focus, and call for partners to work on individual projects, perhaps for named clients, rather than specific 'job' vacancies or opportunities. Similarly, those with particular skills or competencies may advertise them, and the sort of projects upon which they would like to work, and on what terms.

DEVELOPMENT REQUIREMENTS

So what should the objectives of a learning network be? As one director pointed out:

'Learning is great, and fun and all that, but I have business objectives ... concrete things that need to be worked upon.'

We cannot stop the clock, or put customers 'on hold', while we learn. Let us return to a theme introduced in Chapter 13, and which emerged from many interview discussions:

1   management consultancy tends to be directed at tackling discrete corporate problems, and even when concerned with systems and processes, does not do enough to develop the people involved (eg When the next problem comes along, will we be any better off?); while
2   management education and development focuses upon developing people, without, in the process, contributing significantly to tackling the problems which companies face (eg The course is fine for the people concerned, and may help them to get a better job, but why can't the company get a more immediate benefit?).

Both quality management consultancy, and quality management education and development, are becoming increasingly expensive. As a consequence, companies desire to get the best of each, namely personal and team development, and a value-added contribution to a corporate problem. In effect, what is sought is an option that is neither management consultancy nor management education and development, but a combination of the two.

The preferred option is the integration of learning and working. The requirement is for access to a flexible resource that can help to:

1   define corporate tasks in the form of projects which could be undertaken by individuals and groups in the working environment;
2   identify related development needs of the individuals and teams concerned; and
3   provide help and support, as required, to facilitate the acquisition of the required skills and competencies, and the successful completion of the project tasks.

Such a resource, with a specialisation upon facilitating processes and learning, could become part of an international network. The network organisation could be extended to incorporate international groups, whose learning and working is facilitated by specialist consultants and educational institutions (Figure 13.1). Specialism could be by learning process or barrier, rather than by subject or discipline.

ESTABLISHING A LEARNING NETWORK

A learning network could be established to facilitate the development of a particular set of competencies. A consortium of commercial, educational and other organisations could participate in such a development. One example of such a learning network is based in Salford, England. This collaborative network offers a degree in mathematics and computing, and places a particular emphasis upon helping individuals to identify and overcome barriers to learning.

Establishing a private global network can be a financial and management challenge for the company that opts to go it alone. As we saw in Chapter 16, international networks are increasingly being built on a co-operative basis. Strategic alliances among PTTs and telecommunications suppliers are improving their ability to meet the international communications needs of MNCs and transnational companies. To take two examples:

- Services such as video-conferencing are available on a global basis. Staff at a Mitsubishi research centre in the USA use this technology to 'electronically meet' colleagues in Japan.
- British Telecom runs a network management centre for global clients from San Jose in California. The implementation and management of an international network can now be contracted out to various specialist suppliers.

Many of the corporate networks being established for effective international communication could be used to support international distance learning. Electronic universities and colleges could participate, and interfaces built with learning networks that already exist. At the European level, the COMETT and DELTA programmes are designed in part to encourage such developments. The wider adoption of business television is also creating new learning opportunities.

International learning networks are being created on a collaborative basis. For example, several European high-tech companies have co-operated in the establishment of EuroPACE, an international educational network that is IT based and makes use of satellite communications. Students are able to interact with each other by telephone, telex or electronic mail.

In addition to global and regional networks, some local learning networks also exist into which a company might 'plug'. For example, in Denmark the Danish Enterprise University System (DEUS) brings together a number of companies, universities and other organisations to create an interactive learning network. A DEUS computer conferencing network exists which companies interested in securing access to it can join.

Table 17.3 sets out a suggested programme for the establishment of a collaborative learning network. A first step for many companies would be to link up their own internal training facilities and centres of expertise to form a corporate network which could then form links with a variety of external networks at local, regional and international levels.

Table 17.3 *Suggested International Learning Network Programme*

Establish purpose and focus
Identify possible collaborative partners
Explore needs and requirements
Share hopes and expectations
Agree common vision, values and goals
Set measurable objectives
Allocate roles and responsibilities
Contact relevant projects, research institutes, experts and authorities
Specify systems framework architectures and standards
Prepare guidelines on:

- acquisition and use of technology
- curriculum development
- training the 'facilitators'
- co-ordination and management of the network

Determine means of project management
Secure commitment of the core parties
Refine implementation plan
Articulate benefits of proposed learning environment to participants
Approach any external national, regional and international sources of support
Implement, trial and test
Review and refine

SKILL REQUIREMENTS

Information technology can make an important contribution to the development of network organisations. But without relevant skills, attitudes and learning partners, its role may represent an aspiration rather than a reality. Points made in earlier chapters about key skills should not be overlooked. For example:

- in the *Flat Organisation* survey[7] the 'ability to communicate' was considered (in order of 'very important' replies) the most important management quality that is needed in the flatter and more flexible network organisations that are emerging;
- in the *Communicating for Change* survey[13] 'communication skills' were regarded as the most significant barrier to both internal and external communication (eg Table 7.2). Communications technology *per se* is not considered significant as a barrier to communication.

The skills of facilitators of the learning process are likely to cross discipline boundaries. Their specialism could be in terms of learning approach or learning difficulty, rather than academic field. Their current ability to contribute to network processes is likely to be more important than previous job titles, or a past publications list.

An international learning network involves cross-national and cross-cultural communication. The key to turning the potential of the technology into the reality of its use, and the sharing of a learning vision and a common commitment to lifelong learning, lies in attitudes and approaches to cross-cultural communication. Technical skill has to be matched with awareness, empathy and sensitivity.

THE PROFESSIONS

Companies are having to forge relationships with new and unfamiliar 'learning partners'. Questions raised at interviews included: 'Who are these people?'; and 'Where are they coming from?'

The professions and educational institutions face a combination of pressures that are forcing them to reassess their roles and responsibilities.[14] What are the pressures, and how are they likely to respond? Let us start with the professions. Will the curse of professionalism be lifted?

First the challenges. A number of those we examined in Chapter 1 (see Table 1.2) relate to knowledge workers and appear in most developed countries; although it needs to be remembered that the 'chartered' professional body is a particularly British Commonwealth-USA phenomenon. Elsewhere in Europe, the status of the professional engineer, for example, may derive from a university department, or the company in which initial training was received, rather than membership of a chartered institution.

As new 'specialisms' emerge, and the demand for tailored programmes grows, both professional and educational institutions will be required to develop breadth, balance and perspective, while at the same time focusing upon the distinct imperatives of particular 'corporate' contexts. The contending pressures will not be easy to reconcile.

Then there are the 'new professionals' whose area of competence may not necessarily coincide with a traditional subject field.[14] People are likely to place less emphasis upon securing an initial 'qualification' for a lifetime career and to become more concerned with obtaining access to quality, relevant and competitive educational and professional development services, as and when needed at different stages of more flexible and multiple careers.

Companies that are internationalising are increasingly seeking regional and global professional development and learning services. In response to the requirements of companies examined in Chapter 13, management education and development is increasingly likely to be 'tailored', and delivered at the place of work or in the home.[5] Open and distance-learning provision could be via the terminal on a manager's desk.

EDUCATIONAL AND PROFESSIONAL NETWORKS

Educational institutions also face the prospect of transformation. The ivory towers could crumble. The narrowness and pettiness of departmentalism is being replaced by a broader, multidisciplinary and international perspective. The stultifying bigotry of 'political correctness' could give way to greater tolerance of a diversity of ideas and approaches.

With the increased use and application of learning technologies, institutions such as universities or polytechnics may also become 'networks,' embracing and linking learners and facilitators of the learning process.[12]

Professional associations are also linking together to form international networks. For example:

- in the field of project management, the activities of INTERNET are well supported by national associations;
- two major UK professional associations consider exchanges of staff between leading national associations, and participation in international networks, to be a more cost-effective method of learning about overseas developments than the maintenance of a full-time department devoted to international research and monitoring.

In Northern Ireland, the CLASS network illustrates the potential savings that can be achieved by educational and professional institutions that link together to share administrative resources. CLASS, a Computerised Local Administration System for Schools, embraces every post-primary school in the province.

IT AND THE PROFESSIONS

Along with telecommunications and computing technology, learning, research and working environments are likely to converge. The use of networks and expert systems will award an enhanced 'premium' to those who are professional and academic 'superstars' in comparison with their more 'average' colleagues. Learning environments may be used to monitor 'teacher' performance and training needs. Individual assessment will become the norm for knowledge workers. A qualification will not be expected to indicate any particular level of competence.

Information technology is likely to have a major impact upon the 'knowledge bases' of both the professions and academic disciplines, as well as upon patterns of work, the structure of organisations and the nature of management processes. Companies appear increasingly to stress the unique features of their cultures as they strive to differentiate. As a more 'situational' or 'contextual' view of the nature and relevance of knowledge and of expertise emerges, networks will need to become more tolerant of diversity.

EC INITIATIVES

People who are mobile across national borders can demand international learning services. The portability of professional qualifications across the EC has been encouraged by specific EC directives. There are also EC initiatives concerning the transferability of educational course credits. Both educational and professional institutions will need to 'match' the technology available in the work context if they are to become participants in international learning networks.

Within the EC, a number of programmes have been established by the European Commission to encourage the formation of networks of European exchanges, co-operation and collaboration. For example:

- the ERASMUS programme encourages the formation of certain partnerships between universities;
- in the 1990–1 academic year, the TEMPUS programme was launched to assist the countries of central and eastern Europe to adapt their educational systems in order to facilitate the establishment of co-operative links with EC educational institutions;

- Y-Net, an Esprit pilot OSI project, has been launched to establish a pan-European network that will link up all participants in Esprit and other EC R&D programmes;
- within the RACE programme there is an initiative to develop an EC-wide broadband communications network;
- IRIS is a pan-European network of over 300 programmes that focus specifically upon the training needs of women.

In its 1991 programme, the Commission of the European Communities gives a high priority to telecommunications initiatives and the establishment of Euro-networks. If the potential of the Single Market is to be reached, the people and institutions of the EC need to be linked up through appropriate networks.

STAFFING THE NETWORKS

Professional and educational institutions face severe shortages of certain categories of staff. Like companies, many are fishing in the same and, in future, a diminishing, pool for recruits. More of them may need to increase their recruitment from abroad. However, the international labour market in some fields is very competitive.

The various sources of vocational education are increasingly regarded by 'consumers' as not only complementary, but interchangeable. Individual suppliers of educational services may become more mobile between academic, professional and commercial organisations, as portfolios of 'contracts' are accumulated embracing all three 'sectors'.

More academics are likely to take advantage of flexible patterns of employment. Multiple part-time contracts can allow a number of institutions and learning networks to access a 'scarce resource'. Greater international mobility may occur. Commercial access to relevant skills might also be improved. Some individuals with talent could be attracted into 'subject shortage' areas, given the prospects to collect income from a number of organisations.

Institutions will have to compete to attract the 'stars'. Those who are mobile will be the people networks strive to attract and retain, while the 'inflexible' and 'low performers' cling like limpets to a diminishing set of tenured havens and secure job titles.

Traditional subject teachers are likely to become fewer in number, as demand grows for facilitators of the learning process whose skills cross discipline boundaries. Income levels of individual 'facilitators' will vary as remuneration is performance based, and greater use is made of contract workers or networkers to increase the level of skill that can be obtained for a given budget.

COLLABORATION AND COMPETITION

Some reallocation of roles and responsibilities may occur. Certain professional associations may pass responsibility for the creation of knowledge to academic institutions in order to concentrate more upon the definition of competencies, and their application in the workplace. Professional associations and educational institutions may increasingly view each other as potential collaborators rather than competitors. The focus of competition may switch to securing the leadership of projects, and focal roles within networks comprising educational, professional and commercial organisations.

In many ways, commercial, professional and academic institutions are complementary. For example:

- opportunities exist for the establishment of joint and common networks, and sharing the set-up costs of new distance and open-learning programmes, library and information services, and the introduction of new technology;

- co-operation is already occurring between academic, professional and commercial institutions in such areas as transfer arrangements and exemptions, encouraged by government programmes at the national and regional levels.

There is likely to be a growth in the number of development programmes leading to the award of combinations of 'educational' and 'professional', and possibly 'corporate' diplomas. In 1989 Motorola created its own 'Motorola University'. Motorola has established a working relationship with a leading business school in the USA, and universities in Europe and the Pacific Rim.

CHANGING INSTITUTIONAL ROLES

The formation of alumni associations that assume a responsibility for vocationally-oriented updating, could further blur the distinction between professional and academic qualifications. The differences between them are already being eroded as many academic programmes incorporate work experience and become more practical and relevant, while professional qualifications, in the absence of continuing education and professional updating, are perceived as having a definite 'shelf-life'.

Employers themselves appear more ready to determine the knowledge and competencies they feel professionals should have. Many now discuss their needs directly with the people concerned. They are prepared to 'second-guess' professional or educational bodies, in order to better secure their particular requirements.

Just when the professions are becoming reconciled to the sharing of responsibility for knowledge creation with the educational institution, both are having to adjust to the growing role, in a number of sectors, of the commercial organisation. Occupational control and graduate loyalty may also erode in favour of the corporate employer or international network.

MARKETPLACE PRESSURES

As their customers become more discerning, individual institutions and learning networks will need to demonstrate 'relevance' on a continuing basis, and establish a distinct focus and vision in order to differentiate themselves from other suppliers. Greater emphasis is being placed upon the continual refinement and updating of knowledge. Individuals, including professionals and academics, who do not make this commitment will experience a steady erosion of their relevance and value.

One CEO commented: 'We fight a continual battle to match the forces that erode our capabilities and skills.' This is why vision, values, attitudes and perspective are so important. They can survive storm and drought.

Networks of collaborating institutions will need to persuade those in their target marketplaces that their own grouping is able to enhance a skill, competence or quality to a greater extent than the alternatives available. Success will require greater emphasis upon competitor analysis, service packaging and tailoring, and more flexible access and delivery options. What constitutes value for 'customers' by sector or application area will need to be understood, along with the considerations influencing their purchases of learning services.

TRANSFORMING THE PROFESSIONAL ASSOCIATION

Professional associations and educational institutions need to adapt their strategies, people, technology, organisation and management processes to become more commercial and flexible in their approach. As they do so, they may experience a 'tension' between the imperatives of success in competitive markets, and 'constraints' deriving from their historic roles and constitutional status. Some will cling to rituals and symbols in order to differentiate. In certain parts of the world these will be recognised and valued, while in others they will not be understood and may be considered irrelevant.

A greater variety of organisational forms is likely to be encountered, due to a new willingness to enter into joint ventures and other arrangements. A large proportion of these are likely to involve commercial companies and overseas institutions. Collaborative ventures and participation in networks will spread development costs.

IT strategies will become more important. Certain institutions may face a 'dilemma of scale' through failure to reach the threshold of sufficient resources to maintain technological viability and compatibility. One interviewee made the point: 'There are far too many inadequately resourced bodies. If these organisations were companies, there would have been a shake out [and] amalgamations.'

The committee, or administrative, system of both the professional and the academic institution is likely to evolve to a 'model' closer to that of a commercial company, as management processes are introduced to allow resources and services to be quickly matched to shifting marketplace requirements. A less 'subject' and departmental, and more team or project, form of structure is likely to result. Campus and network-wide roles and responsibilities exercises are already occurring, along with quality programmes and project-focused profit centre accountability.

DIRECTORS OF LEARNING AND THINKING

In order to turn the rhetoric of the learning organisation into a working reality, companies are entering into new forms of relationships with learning partners. The international networks, structures and processes that are emerging need to be directed and managed. Companies, and their professional and educational partners, are becoming learning networks. Their *raison d'être* is tapping human talent through the facilitation of learning.

New breeds of executive could emerge with areas of expertise such as the integration of working and learning, or the management of international learning networks. They are likely to be driven by a desire for recognition through marketplace performance, rather than the academic or learned society award.

Preparation for a role in directing a network could involve a journey between and around customer, supplier, academic and professional organisations in order to gain experience of each of its elements.[15] Moving between significant roles within very different organisations, and bridging barriers of prejudice, misperception and misunderstanding, these managers and directors of learning or thinking will be both project leaders and diplomats.

Our leaders and champions of learning will not be easy to find. As when mining gold, it may be necessary to work through a ton of dross to obtain an ounce of what you want. However, if they succeed in their new roles we will have to reassess our views of what is dross, base metal and gold. A combination of learning culture, environment and network could yield an outcome more magical than that sought of the philosopher's stone.

CHECKLIST

▶ How committed is your company to harnessing human talent on an international basis?

▶ How critical is the concept of the learning network to the achievement of its vision?

▶ Does your company understand the learning process and how people learn?

▶ Who, within the company, is responsible for learning?

▶ What is being done to ensure that all members of the network discover their learning potential and how they as individuals might best build their understanding?

▶ If it has not already done so, should your company appoint a director of learning, understanding or thinking?

▶ How relevant is more appropriate technology to the facilitation of learning in your company?

▶ Should your company be more extensively linked up to national, regional and international learning networks?

▶ What needs to be done to ensure that the company itself takes on more of the attributes of a learning network?

▶ Does your company understand how the changing nature of educational and professional institutions, and the emerging requirements of the knowledge worker, will impact upon its own relationships with them?

▶ Have your company's managers and professionals been equipped to act as facilitators of learning?

▶ Are you prepared to act as a catalyst in encouraging the adoption of new forms of working and learning, and the integration of working and learning?

REFERENCES

1　Coulson-Thomas, C (1989) *Too Old at 40?*, BIM, Corby.

2　Gross, B and Gross, E (eds) (1985) *The Great School Debate*, Simon & Schuster, New York.

3　Stephens, M D (1991) *Japan and Education*, Macmillan, London.

4　Prowse, M (1992) 'Profitable Lessons for an Outdated School System', *Financial Times*, 4 June, p 25.

5　Coulson-Thomas, C J (1990) *Human Resource Development for International Operation*, a Survey sponsored by Surrey European Management School, Adaptation, London.

6　Secretary's Commission on Achieving Necessary Skills (1991) *What Work Requires of Schools*, US Department of Labor, Washington DC.

7　Coulson-Thomas, C and Coe, T (1991) *The Flat Organisation: Philosophy and Practice*, BIM, Corby.

8　Wenger, E (1987) *Artificial Intelligence Tutoring Systems*, Morgan Kaufman, San Pateo, Calif.

9　Wenger, E (1987) *Glass-box Technology: Merging learning and doing*, IRL Research Abstract 1, Institute for Research on Learning, Palo Alto, Calif.

10　Rheingold, H (1991) *Virtual Reality*, Secker & Warburg, London.

11　Kuhn, T S (1970) *The Structure of Scientific Revolutions*, University of Chicago Press, Chicago, Ill.

12　Coulson-Thomas, C (1990) 'Building Europe's Learning Foundations: The European Learning Network', *Europe IT Journal*, February, pp 14–19.

13　Coulson-Thomas, C and Coulson-Thomas, S (1991) *Communicating for Change*, an Adaptation Ltd Survey for Granada Business Services, Adaptation, London.

14　Coulson-Thomas, C (1988) *The New Professionals*, BIM, Corby; and 'Responsive professional and educational organisations' *International Journal of Manpower*, vol 10, no 6, pp 13–16.

15　Coulson-Thomas, C and Wakelam, A (1991) *The Effective Board, Current Practice, Myths and Realities*, an Institute of Directors discussion document, London.

18

SPRINGING THE TRAP

BREAKING OUT

Throughout this book we have shared the frank views of those who are struggling to 'make it happen'. There are others who, with varying degrees of confidence, believe that they are on the right track. There are enough 'real world' examples to suggest that dramatic breakthroughs in productivity and satisfaction can be achieved. These are occurring not just in 'quoted cases', such as Xerox, Kodak or General Electric, but in other companies that are jealously guarding their new-found sources of competitive advantage from external eyes, while 'going all out' within.

The champions of corporate transformation are organising around empowered and self-managed workgroups that operate and energise the key processes that deliver customer satisfaction. The information and technology needed to support these groups and processes define the network.

The organisation is fluid, change and learning occur naturally. What people learn, how people work, and the approaches, tools and technology, that are used by groups and teams depend upon customer requirements. The customer determines the evolution of the network. The people and members of the network are held together by shared vision, values and goals, and work harmoniously and co-operatively to the extent that human nature allows.

ALLURING PROSPECTS AND PERSISTENT UNCERTAINTIES

A rush of questions often precedes and heralds the dawn of a new age. People are thinking and forming conclusions. Consider the following selection of comments:

'We have created the "gap". We cannot lower expectations, so we must increase our capacity to deliver.'

'Why should achievement match aspiration, when people rarely think through the implementation barriers and requirements? Our priorities [now] derive from the barriers to change and customer satisfaction'

'There is no point in activity for its own sake. Do not start any major programme until all the elements needed for success are identified and lined up.'

'Try the "So what?" or "what is the point?" test. There is no point having the best of this or that if it does not add value for customers.'

'Everyone should know what he or she needs to do help the organisation achieve one or more quantified objectives. If they do not know, there is no point having them on board.'

'Why do we pay so much to be told what we already know, and then do so little about it? Our motivation and drive to "make things happen" derives from the customer.'

The results of the surveys upon which this book is based, and the experience of a 'benchmark' company such as Rank Xerox, suggest that significant progress toward the network organisation can be achieved, but it requires total commitment. A company that picks and chooses which survey lessons to apply, or which elements of 'benchmark' experience to adopt, will probably fail. The picture is not complete until every piece of the transformation jigsaw is in place. When many pieces are missing, and a likeness or guide is unavailable, the eventual image may be uncertain.

This chapter skims quickly, and in *aide-mémoire* fashion, over a small selection of the success requirements identified in the course of the book, before turning to a 'benchmark' example of a change programme. The purpose of this is to illustrate how a particular combination of change elements needs to be brought together to reflect the corporate context.

Corporate transformation is not a role for hermits in caves. The complexity of combination, and degree of effort needed to assemble certain change elements, demand the efforts of a group, and may involve many teams. Chester Barnard recognised in the 1930s both the need to 'make it happen', and the importance of shared values and co-operative activity in the achievement of business results.[1]

FORMAL MANAGEMENT OF CHANGE PROGRAMMES

Given both the hype and the rhetoric, and a genuine desire to change, one would have thought that by now most companies would have comprehensive transformation programmes in place. Not a bit of it. The *Communicating for Change* survey[2] reveals that 'in spite of widespread agreement concerning the need to change, and considerable commitment to change':

- 'Only a minority of four out of ten companies have formal management of change programmes.'
- 'Only some four out of ten management of change programmes are linked to the systems strategies of the organisations concerned. Hence only about one in six of the participating companies has a formal management of change programme that is linked to its systems strategy.'

The *Communicating for Change* survey[2] evidence suggests that almost all corporate change programmes are deficient to a significant degree. Enthusiasm or desperation is preventing many companies from taking a holistic and considered approach. The main findings of the survey report are as follows.

- There appears to be too much emphasis upon changes of structure such as 'reorganisation' or 'taking out management layers', and too little concern with processes, attitudes and values. Some companies are finding flexibility, adaptability and change relatively easy to describe at a superficial level, but very difficult to achieve in practice.
- Interviewees recognise that their change programmes need to embrace not only the attitudes, perspectives and approaches of people, but also management processes, and the supporting technology that can facilitate learning and adaptation. However, most lack the tools to move from concern to action.
- Some programmes are insufficiently focused upon better serving the needs of customers. 'The corporate organisation should not become an end in itself. Organisation is only relevant to the extent that it adds value for customers. Care needs to be taken not to disrupt service to customers while changes occur.'
- Many formal programmes are being inhibited by a lack of people with facilitation of change skills. 'Too many managers still take a narrow "departmental" view when a broader perspective is required. Too few people have sufficient understanding of the business environment.'

The *Communicating for Change* survey[2] suggests that changes of structure should follow, and not precede, reviews of roles and responsibilities. One interviewee admitted to 'putting the cart before the horse'. Such reviews should occur in the context of an agreed mission, and the activities and outputs that are required to add value for customers. Prioritisation and focus need to occur if effort is not to be wasted.

MATCHING STRATEGY AND CAPABILITY

The key to closing the gap between rhetoric and reality and aspiration and achievement is to match transformation capability with change strategy. Figure 18.1 illustrates some possible outcomes.

- When the strategy is right in relation to the situation and circumstances of the company, but the various change elements cannot be assembled in such a way as to 'make it happen', people experience frustration.
- When the capability to deliver is created, perhaps by assembling some missing pieces of the transformation jigsaw puzzle, frustration can turn to fulfilment.
- Nothing may save the company with the wrong strategy. The capability to deliver could actually bring about a quick termination rather than a slow decline. The efficiency with which erroneous objectives are pursued and mistaken policies are implemented brings management into contact with the destructive consequences of its decisions more quickly than might otherwise be the case.

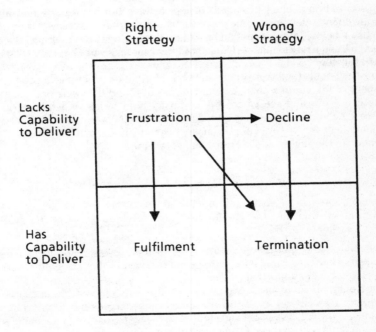

Figure 18.1 *Strategy and Capability*

For the frustrated, with a gap between aspiration and achievement, the right change strategy is clearly important, given that the prospects of decline or termination could well be perceived as less favourable than a current position.

MANAGING THE TRANSFORMATION PROCESS

There are a variety of individual change elements and requirements that a formal transformation programme could embrace. People need to be equipped, empowered and motivated to manage change. Changes of attitude, awareness, approach and perspective are generally required. Management and business processes will often need to be re-engineered, supported with appropriate technology, and facilitated by relevant competence.

Once all the pieces of the jigsaw puzzle, the various change elements, have been assembled, the change programme itself needs to be project managed. In general, there is insufficient recognition of the distinctive nature of project management competences, and of the important role project management can play in the achievement of corporate transformation.[3]

In the view of one chairman:

> 'We could do all of that ... specific objectives, roles and responsibilities, teams ... the lot. [But] we wouldn't have the project managers to run the projects. There's not much chance that we would deliver, given all the people from different areas that need to work together.'

Rank Xerox trains its managers specifically in project management. Major companies such as BT, Glaxo, IBM and Lloyds Bank are backing a certification programme that has been introduced by the Association of Project Managers. This provides a framework for the assessment and certification of project management competence.

Transformation project management can involve the sequencing and juggling of disparate change elements. Some pieces of the transformation jigsaw puzzle need to be put in place before later pieces can be added. To use another analogy, all the elements needed to build a house may be lying about in a builder's yard, but they still have to be brought together.

In the case of the Rank Xerox corporate transformation programme, progress to date in respect of the various change elements, is put up on the walls of a control room. People can go in and see where the company is in terms of achieving its change objectives. According to one manager: 'Just looking at the wall makes you feel good. You feel that collectively we are going to make it happen, because it is all there. ... We have thought of all the angles, and it's been pulled together.'

THE IMPORTANCE OF CLEAR VISION

If a new approach to managing organisations is needed to achieve corporate transformation, what are the key factors? Let us review some of the evidence we examined earlier in the book.

- The BIM *Flat Organisation* report[4] reveals that: 'Every respondent assessing it believes clear vision and mission to be important; and about three-quarters of them consider it "very important"' (Table 4.1).
- The *Communicating for Change* survey[2] finds that: 'Clear vision and strategy' and 'top management commitment' are jointly ranked as the most important requirements for the successful management of change. Approaching nine out of ten of the respondents ranked these as 'very important' (Table 7.1).

We saw in Chapter 4 that few companies have a clear, compelling, distinctive and memorable transformation vision. People sense the anxiety, see the disruption, and feel the pain, but they don't know what to do to help, or what it is all for. As the *Flat Organisation* report[4] puts it: 'While clear vision and mission are thought to be essential, in many companies both are regarded as just "words on paper", and they do not act as a guide to action.'

Until the various elements of a comprehensive change programme are put in place, those who trumpet visions are riding for a fall. They are raising expectations with little hope of delivery. Deming recognised that exhortation and over-management could be counter-productive, and advocated activities to break down barriers, empower, and instil a commitment to continuous learning and improvement.[5]

The impacts of corporate transformation activities are sometimes difficult to distinguish from those of other programmes such as a diversification strategy, or from the consequences of changes in the market and competitive environment. As the experience of BP has shown, commitment to corporate transformation will not result in commercial success if other policies and initiatives do not match the situation and circumstances of the company.[6]

MANAGEMENT REQUIREMENTS

Table 18.1 presents some of the attributes of bureaucratic and network organisations identified by interviewees. Only a selection of the many points of difference and various contrasts which emerged are given. Nevertheless, they illustrate the profound impact that corporate transformation can have upon the role of the manager.

Table 18.1 *Perceived Attributes of the Bureaucratic and Network Organisations*

Bureaucratic Organisation	Network Organisation
Managers	Leaders and facilitators
Decision makers	Counsellors and mentors
Departmental specialism and values	Shared vision and mission
Rivalry	Interdependence
Rules and procedures	Processes
Jobs and organisation charts	Roles and responsibilities
Hierarchy	Project teams
Status	Contribution
Homogeneous	Diverse
Privilege	Democracy
Committees	Taskforces and teams
Vertical communication	Horizontal and all-channel communication
Central direction	Individual initiative
Control	Empowerment and support
Narrow specialism	General awareness
Strong head office	Effective customer interface
Competition, office politics	Co-operation, mutual trust
Factions	Common interests
Continuity	Change
Loyalty	Participation
Generalisation and standardisation	Responsive to individual customers and employees
Automate	Support
Centralisation	Decentralisation and delegation
Closed and secretive	Open and transparent
Suspicion and monitoring	Trust and encouragement
Hoarding expertise	Sharing experience
Sophistication	Simplification
Inflexible and fixed	Responsive and dynamic
Teaching and talking	Learning and listening

What management qualities are required for the successful transformation from bureaucracy to network organisation? In the *Flat Organisation* survey,[4] the following was revealed.

- The one quality assessed as of importance on every questionnaire is 'understanding the business environment'. Corporate transformation does not occur in a vacuum and has to be related to the key requirements for business success. Some change programmes appear to be in pursuit of a concept or notion that is divorced from reality.
- Adaptability, the ability to communicate, flexibility and a balanced perspective are considered by almost all respondents to be important. Interviewees stressed the value of qualities associated with building relationships, mentoring, coaching and facilitating, which most companies appear to be talking about rather than developing.

To the above qualities, one should add intuition, sensitivity and a tolerance for diversity, if 'organic' rather than 'machine' managers are to be developed. What each of these should mean in practice will reflect circumstances and priorities. Every company is unique, and should define its own 'role-model' requirements.

REWARD AND REMUNERATION

There was overwhelming agreement among the *Flat Organisation* survey[4] participants that 'reward should reflect output and added value'. Over a half of them 'strongly agree' with this statement, and no one among them strongly agrees with the view that ' reward should reflect position and rank'.

Too much faith should not be put in reward and remuneration, or indeed in any single change element. But a supportive approach can help. Within General Electric there are people who are rewarded for learning. However, many companies actually encourage people, through the 'incentives' they provide, to act in ways that undermine the purposes and values of their transformation programmes.

People must believe that there is the prospect of a better life for themselves and for others. If not, why bother? The importance of encouraging and motivating people to act was recognised by one chairman at the 11th hour.

> 'It was all there and people said – "Yeah, great". ... It was interesting and probably right, but they were not that happy. There wasn't any incentive. ... We motivated them to do other things , but not to change how we operate.'

Schein has closely linked the exercise of corporate leadership to the achievement of culture change, and has suggested that reward and motivation strategies may need to change as a shift occurs in the attitudes of people within an organisation.[7] Key priorities and activities should be continuously reviewed, and may need to be adjusted during the course of a corporate change programme.

TOP MANAGEMENT COMMITMENT

People who 'really believe' can be so committed that it melts the rubber soles on their shoes. Reference has already been made to the importance of 'top management commitment' as a requirement for the successful management of change.[2] In BP and Xerox it appears to exist, but are these companies the exception?

How committed is top management to corporate transformation? We saw in Chapter 9 that 'top management commitment' is perceived as the main barrier to the successful implementation of a quality process. Over nine out of ten respondents consider it to be a 'very significant' barrier (Table 9.3). Most of those who are committed appear unable to communicate it, or to demonstrate it, in a convincing way.

The perceived 'commitment gap' is a serious problem. According to the *Communicating for Change* survey, the chairman, managing director or CEO is the person most likely to be responsible for the successful implementation of a formal management of change programme.[2] In two-thirds of the cases where a particular individual is responsible, the person concerned is at director level.

THE QUALITY OF CORPORATE LEADERSHIP

Top management commitment begins in the boardroom. We saw in Chapter 2 that there is little satisfaction with the quality of corporate leadership. It is badly and sadly inadequate. Three-quarters of chairmen believe the effectiveness of their companies' boards could be improved.[8] Composed of functional directors rather than process owners, most boards appear a crusty survival from the heyday of corporate bureaucracy.

The IOD's 'effective board' discussion document[9] suggests that, whatever the rhetoric, most boards recruit 'in their own image'. Routes to the board are 'closed' and hidden to all but a favoured few. Rather than 'break the mould' with appointments of front-line 'role models', too many boards 'play it safe', and turn to the head office and functional bureaucrats.

Too many boards lack vision, and are short-term oriented. They craft strategies that have little chance of implementation. The board itself is the source of much misunderstanding and distrust, and the cause of arenas of conflict in many companies. Corporate change programmes are generally incomplete and inadequately thought through. Some boards appear to be 'clutching at straws'.

Prahalad warned almost a decade ago of the dangers of 'fadism', suggesting that senior management should focus upon building the 'strategic capability ... to think and act strategically in a changing competitive environment rather than expend the energies of the organisation in pursuing current fads' or on 'seeking easy solutions'. [10]

Few boards have identified the key business processes that deliver customer satisfaction. In most organisations they have not been documented, and no one is specifically responsible for them or has been trained to operate them. IT, training and other investment are rarely applied to them, being largely devoted to departmental activities, which may or may not add value for customers. Process responsibilities must be brought into the boardroom.

CHANGE AND CONTROL

Many companies are over-managed and under-led. Several of those interviewed in the course of the surveys upon which this book is based loosely described the transition they were seeking in terms of movement away from a 'command and control model'. A typical view would be:

'In the past it was the command and control bureaucracy. The watchword of the flat and flexible organisation is empowerment. Self-managed workgroups control themselves. ... We have to give up control, and focus upon sharing and trusting.'

Control may still need to be exercised, but in new ways.[11] The challenge for senior management should not be whether or not to 'give up' control, but to determine more appropriate ways in which it could be exercised. The successful management of change may depend upon the extent to which chosen methods of control match what is required at each stage of the transition.

Measurable objectives need to be set, and roles and responsibilities allocated. Drucker recognised in the early 1950s that in order to realise corporate goals a company needs to establish and allocate specific objectives and related responsibility within the corporate organisation.[12]

COMMUNICATIONS SKILLS

The transformation vision must be shared, the purpose of change communicated, and employee involvement and commitment secured. We saw in Chapter 7 that, in general, managers are deficient in their approaches and attitudes to communication. Not one respondent in the *Communicating for Change* survey[2] considered 'communication skills' to be 'insignificant' as a communication barrier. As one chairman put it: 'Managers are lousy communicators.'

In the case of those at the top, their personal attitudes and actions, the symbols they protect, the prejudices they perpetuate, and the role-model conduct they display, often 'speaks volumes'. The combined effect of these, amplified by the leaks, rumour and gossip of the informal grapevine, 'drowns out' the anaemic, bland and sanitised prose of the hired scriptwriters and hacks.

In communicating the vision of the flat and flexible network organisation, considerable use is being made of images. The clear image, perhaps a simplified network diagram, can be a powerful aid to understanding.

At the same time, the power and persistence of an image, and how it might colour and distort perceptions, should not be overlooked. Boulding has stressed the influence of the image, and has pointed out the extent to which decision makers can be influenced by the representation of a problem on paper.[13] People should understand the thinking behind the portrayal of the concept, and the reasons why a particular form of organisation and operation is being sought.

CORPORATE CASE STUDY

The keys to corporate transformation are 'vision and communication',[2,4] 'top management commitment', a focus upon the customer, self-managed and self-motivated team work, the support of cross-functional and inter-organisational processes,[14] and a combination of further change elements to suit the context and situation. Let us now consider the example of a 'benchmark' company, in order to illustrate how a number of, by now, familiar themes have been brought together under the umbrella of a holistic approach to corporate transformation.

Picking a 'success story' means sticking your neck out. A CEO commented: 'You're just asking for it!' Hold success up in the light and it begins to fade. Nevertheless, among the participants in the *Quality: The Next Steps* survey[8] Rank Xerox stands out as a 'role-model' corporation.

The origins of Xerox Corporation lie in Chester Carlson's invention of the plain paper copying process in 1938. For many years, Carlson found it impossible to interest any established corporation in his discovery. It was not until 1959 that the first commercial copier, the 914, was introduced. Thereafter, growth was rapid and when Xerox reached an annual turnover of $1 billion, it had been the 'fastest' corporation to reach this figure.

Then, as a result of a combination of circumstances, a revolution occurred in the marketplace. In 1976 the Japanese entered the market at the 'low end', and they steadily increased market share during the 1980s. Arrows that had always aimed at the ceiling started pointing downwards on the graphs. Corporate profits almost halved between 1980 and 1981.

The Xerox 'fight back' has become a legend, a rare example of how to confront a concerted onslaught from a bevy of outstanding Japanese competitors and win back market share.[15] The recovery programme has passed through a number of phases from benchmarking, through quality and total quality, to the corporation's pioneering work with new approaches to process re-engineering.

The origins of quality lay in the New Xerox Movement started in 1976 within Fuji Xerox. The Leadership Through Quality programme of Xerox, embracing both quality principles and quality tools, was initiated in 1983.

CHANGING ATTITUDES AND BEHAVIOUR

The 'acid test' of the extent to which corporate transformation is taking place is the degree to which attitudes and behaviour have changed. In some companies, such as British Airways, ICL and Rank Xerox, the attitudes of many people do appear to be noticeably different, following the introduction of wide-ranging corporate programmes.

For most companies, ingrained attitudes have proved to be stubborn. Not only do they persist, but they resist reason and have a habit of bouncing back. In some companies, they must seep out of the walls, or enter the consciousness like bad spirits when people are asleep.

Alfred Sloan's 'federal decentralisation' of General Motors in the early 1920s shows that a fundamental restructuring of a corporation can be achieved.[16] However, the company's problems more recently demonstrate how much more difficult it is to change attitudes and values.

The following impressionistic comments from Xerox people highlight the scale of the challenge the corporation faced.

'People hated us. We had them over a barrel and sold on our terms. The moment they had a choice "they up't and went". It's surprising so many stayed with us.'

'We didn't sell in those days. If you were nice to us we gave you a good position on the waiting list.'

'The competition came at us out of the sun and swarmed all over us. Whatever we had was their starting point – they just seemed to do everything better. We really shouldn't exist now.'

'The Japanese were selling some products for less than we could make them. You don't solve that problem by going for volume.'

'Success breeds the worst kind of arrogance. Try to tell a salesman anything in those days, particularly an early stockholder, and they'd point to a picture of a yacht on the wall of their office and ask if you'd made a million.'

Rank Xerox and Xerox have achieved changes in attitudes and behaviour that surveys[2,4,8] suggest have eluded most other companies. Together, these companies have won nine national quality awards, including the Deming award in Japan and the Malcolm Baldrige award in the USA.

The tools and techniques that have been used are simple and straightforward. They could be considered common sense, but the 'litmus test' is performance. In the harsh reality of the global marketplace there is little requirement for 'cosmetic' programmes. Wishful thinking and 'make-believe' may fool some faithful retainers, but they do not keep the teeth of competitive wolves from flabby corporate flesh.

MOVING FROM RHETORIC TO REALITY

The management approach and style of Xerox and Rank Xerox is anchored in reality. The natural instinct is to probe until a bedrock of honesty and fact is reached.

The following selection of change elements has been found to work when combined in a particular corporate context. They illustrate the application within Xerox and Rank Xerox of some of the lessons which have emerged.

- A clear vision that is rooted in the customer is essential. The essence of the Rank Xerox strategic 'document company' vision lies in the 'real world' problems faced by the corporation's customers. It is not a creation of creative writers of copy.
- The customer should be regarded as a partner, colleague and network citizen. According to David Thompson, chairman of Rank Xerox UK: 'The quality vision needs to embrace the customer, and the quality of relationships is the key to adding value for the customer. ... The customer is a partner in quality.'[17] Rank Xerox works with, as well as for, its customers.
- Goals and objectives should be derived from the vision, shared, and roles and responsibilities allocated. A set of tools known collectively as 'policy deployment' is used to ensure that every Rank Xerox person knows what he or she needs to do to contribute to a business objective.
- Corporate organisation should reflect a focus upon the customer. Significant parts of Xerox have been reorganised on the basis of market-based units rather than functional departments. The Corporation's Vision 2000 sets out a model of a more flexible and responsive form of organisation towards which steady progress is being made.
- Top management commitment to quality and to change is crucial, and needs to be sustained and communicated if barriers and obstacles are to be identified and overcome. The Rank Xerox commitment is clear, and more than just words. Customer satisfaction is the company's number-one business goal.
- Obstacles and barriers should be assumed and tackled. People at all levels at Rank Xerox are equipped with problem-solving tools. 'Helps' and 'hinders' analysis is used to identify, assess and prioritise the 'things that get in the way'. 'Vital few' programmes are put in place to ensure they are overcome.
- Top management must be visibly committed in all that they say and do. Rank Xerox managers are expected to act as 'role models', and are assessed as such by their subordinates. Only those who have achieved and maintain 'role-model' status can aspire to senior positions in the corporation.
- The vision must be shared, the purpose of change communicated, and employee involvement and commitment secured. Employee involvement and commitment is the number-two Rank Xerox business goal. A comprehensive empowerment programme is under way. Self-managed workgroups have become the norm in certain areas.
- The ability to communicate and 'share' are essential management qualities. They require integrity and relationships of trust. These are emphasised by corporate values. Rank Xerox invests heavily in training to support its values and business objectives. Particular emphasis is placed upon the role of the manager in relation to communication, empowerment and the management of change. The company is intent upon becoming a learning organisation.
- More than vision, talk and targets may be required. People may need to be motivated to give priority to the requirements of customers. Reward and remuneration should reflect a strategic focus upon the customer. Within Rank Xerox, an increasingly important element of remuneration is linked to improvements in customer satisfaction. An employee satisfaction element is being introduced.
- Activity for its own sake is of little value if it does not add value for external customers. Motivation needs to be harnessed and applied to customer-related tasks. Rank Xerox has developed a family of techniques that can be used to allocate responsibilities and resources so that all employees focus upon negotiated outputs that contribute to customer satisfaction, and specific measures are used to enable progress to be monitored.

- People need to be equipped to satisfy customers and to cope with change. More effort needs to be devoted to implementation tools, and in particular those that can be used to identify and re-engineer the key management and business processes that generate value, and deliver it to external customers.
- A variety of approaches and techniques have been developed by Rank Xerox to identify, document, and re-engineer or simplify key management and business processes in order better to deliver customer satisfaction and tackle particular sources of customer dissatisfaction. Even within a slimmed-down organisation, dramatic savings in both resources and elapsed time have been achieved.
- Information technology needs to be focused upon those processes that deliver value for customers. Within Rank Xerox UK the key cross-functional processes have been identified and documented, and process-owner responsibilities have been allocated to individual directors. Processes have been brought into the boardroom.
- Appropriate technology can facilitate the transition towards the network organisation. Rank Xerox is a beneficiary of the Xerox PARC heritage. Xerox has been an early pioneer in the use of technology to support new ways of learning and working. Rank Xerox used its own AI environment to configure the technology of its international headquarters and network.
- The achievement of network quality demands closer and partnership relationships between departments and companies. Rank Xerox has introduced new approaches to account and business partner management. At the local level, staff in such functions as sales, service and administration work together in 'partnerships' across functional barriers in harnessing the resources of the company to meet the requirements of individual customers.
- Companies in general are not learning from those who have developed ways of breaking through many of the more common implementation barriers. Rank Xerox and its parent Xerox have been pioneers of 'benchmarking'. All managers are encouraged to learn from those with similar responsibilities in non-competing companies. The intention is to aspire beyond the standards of 'the best'.
- The various corporate activities and initiatives that are introduced to bring about fundamental change need to be co-ordinated. Rank Xerox adopts a holistic approach. The overall responsibility for corporate transformation and IT has been brought together under a facilitating director with a seat on the board. The total transformation process is regularly reviewed by the board as a whole.

One could go on, and tie in various other Rank Xerox programmes with further lessons that have arisen at different points in this book. The 'overall message' is that good initiatives of themselves may not be enough. Rank Xerox found, in common with the experience of most companies, that it was some time before a combination of initiatives started to have an effect. However, in due course enough pieces of the jigsaw puzzle were found to be in place to 'make it happen'.

With hindsight, the process of transformation could have been speeded up. Were the company able to 'start again', customer satisfaction would have been made the number-one business objective much earlier, and the reward and remuneration card would have been played sooner.

Rank Xerox has secured dramatic improvements in many areas of management productivity, and has strengthened its market positioning against formidable competitors in one of the world's most intense and challenging business sectors. Organisations should be more prepared to learn from the insights of those in 'real companies' who are successfully turning the vision of the network organisation into a reality. Other companies are now able to obtain access to, and use, many of the proprietory tools and approaches that have been developed within Rank Xerox UK to support its transformation programme.

COMPLETING THE TRANSFORMATION TOOLKIT

In addition to a range of quality tools, and its experience of benchmarking, Rank Xerox has more recently been using additional approaches to help bring about corporate transformation. These include the following.

POLICY DEPLOYMENT

Rank Xerox uses 'policy deployment' as a cascade mechanism to translate a corporate vision or strategic intent into a co-ordinated set of operational plans throughout the organisation. This is achieved by deriving action programmes from the company's business goals, and then formulating roles, responsibilities and objectives, preparing support plans, and subsequently identifying and allocating specific actions that need to be undertaken by specified individuals.

As a consequence of 'policy deployment', the vision, goals and objectives of the company are communicated throughout the corporate organisation. All functions and individuals are made aware of what they are expected to contribute to their achievement. By looking through a 'blue book' which is circulated to all managers, people can also see what all their colleagues are expected to do. This makes it clear to them that the actions and initiatives are in place to 'make it happen'.

MANAGEMENT PROCESS RE-ENGINEERING

In the Rank Xerox context, a management process is defined as a cycle of inter-related specific forums, held at specific frequencies, requiring specific inputs and outputs, that control and review business processes.

The re-engineering of management processes starts with the organisation's goals, objectives, roles and responsibilities, and key actions. Existing functional and cross-functional processes are then examined for gaps, overlaps, duplication and sources of unnecessary delay. The views of various users are sought, and the implications of alternatives and changes are assessed. Input and output requirements are related to what is necessary to achieve business results.

At the end of the review process, both functional and cross-functional processes will have been documented and a management calendar published. This will contain details, such as frequencies and attendees, and inputs and outputs, of the various meetings and other forums.

BUSINESS PROCESS RE-ENGINEERING

Rank Xerox has developed a range of proprietary process simplification and re-engineering techniques. Simplification involves the removal of non-value-added activities from a business process in order to reduce elapsed time and save on resource requirements.

Simplification involves such activities as identifying process owners, and examining and documenting what happens in relation to customer requirements at each stage of the process. Particular attention is paid to measurements, control points, and whatever empowerments are necessary to achieve the potential savings of time and resources that are identified.

Re-engineering involves a more radical approach (Table 15.1). It is vision led, and the interactions of processes, people, information and technology are assessed in order to achieve a fundamental rebuilding of business processes. Improvements in time and management productivity of the order of 1000 per cent or more have been achieved. The focus is always upon the generation and delivery of customer value and satisfaction.

EMPOWERMENT

Empowerment is a word that is widely and loosely used, including within companies that are doing little to make it a practical reality. Empowerment is defined within Rank Xerox as follows.

Empowerment consists of being energised, committed and enabled to autonomously achieve continuous quality improvement in work processes and outputs.

Rank Xerox has adopted a comprehensive approach to empowerment. People are given both the freedom and the capability to act.

- The vision is shared, and there is commitment to two-way communication and to equipping people with the skills they need to 'make it happen' for *their* customers. Investment is made in relevant training as required.
- The focus is upon the customer, and a shared understanding of processes, approaches, tools and techniques enables people to spend less time finding their way around the organisation and trying to 'get on each other's wavelength'. Instead, they can concentrate on the more creative task of adding value and satisfying customers.
- Work is increasingly undertaken in groups and self-managed teams. The self-managed teams are expected to assume accountability and ownership. They are nourished by ubiquitous information and supported by appropriate technology.
- A conscious effort is made to create an atmosphere and culture of trust, within which people are expected to assume responsibility. Risks can be taken, but people are expected to learn from failure.
- Managers are coaches and facilitators. They focus upon the release of energy, commitment and potential, and the support of people in 'the front line'. They help people to translate objectives into work processes, support individual performance, act as 'social architects' when building teams and provide cross-functional leadership.
- Managers are specifically equipped to support empowerment. Their development workshops include topics such as 'the learning organisation and learning styles', 'coaching', 'supporting team performance', and 'tearing down the walls'.

Empowerment is pervasive throughout the corporation. Empowerment methodologies have been developed, and competency centres have been established to provide world-class advice and support whenever they are required. Above all, a Xerox person reading this section would probably say: 'Yup, that's right.'

The consequences of empowerment, such as opportunity, challenge, development, participation, recognition, involvement and respect are increasingly sought by the more capable.[18] At the end of the day, companies need to match the changing expectations of their people. As Sir John Harvey-Jones puts it in a commentary to the BIM *Responsive Organisation* report: 'If organisations do not accommodate themselves to the wishes and aspirations of individuals, people will not join them.'[19]

BUILDING ON FIRM FOUNDATIONS

To close the gap between aspiration and achievement, some form of orderly progress is suggested (Figure 18.2), building upon firm foundations. A host of worthy initiatives should not be left to topple over because the essentials have not been attended to.

It is logical to start with the clarification of vision, goals and values, and then to establish measurable objectives. Subsequently, attention should be given to the various elements that need to be in place if objectives are to be achieved, the pace and direction of change maintained, and accomplishments consolidated.

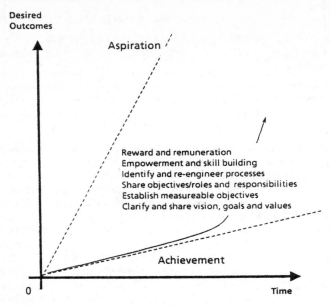

Figure 18.2 *Closing the Gap*

A well thought-out programme appears to be 'cumulative', as incremental elements both reinforce, and take advantage of, attitude shifts that are beginning to be achieved. A change element that jars, or does not seem to fit, may feel rough in the mouth. As a result of its introduction, it may be spat out and other elements may be 'thrown up'.

THE APPLICATION OF TECHNOLOGY

People have a tendency to exaggerate benefits, while failure is played down or concealed. After all, in the words of an interviewee: 'You don't sell ways of doing things less badly. ... You sell success.'

Paul Strassmann has shown that while the overall returns from investment in IT are problematic, some companies have done better than others.[20] A more recent study of selected case studies by the Kobler Unit has confirmed that while 'no correlation was found between the amount of money invested in IT and the general business performance of both leading and lagging companies',[21] benefits in some areas in certain companies appear to exist.

Self-contained departmental applications of IT are likely to be of dubious value, unless they happen to 'hit' a value-generating activity. However, applying technology to the work process can result in significant returns. For example, 'groupware' allows the members of project groups, task forces and other teams open access to a pool of common information. In 1992 Lotus Development Corporation examined 11 applications of its Notes 'groupware' at 8 customer sites. According to CEO, Jim Manzi:[22]

> 'What we found is that ... applications have had a significant impact on our customers' business. The return on investment has averaged well over 100 per cent, and often as much as 500 per cent or more. For one ... customer ... the return was over 2000 per cent.'

IT should be applied, where appropriate, to the support of those cross-functional and inter-organisational processes, that generate and deliver value and customer satisfaction, and contribute to the achievement of business objectives. These are the fields in which improvements of 1000 per cent or more on key measures, such as elapsed time, can be obtained.

The point was made in Chapters 15 and 16 that the 'boxes' are not 'out to get us'. If we misapply technology, it is our own fault. Areas of IT that may appear 'remote' to a lay person can have beneficial impacts when used on a 'horses for courses' basis. For example, AI-based techniques that can handle the confused and chaotic nature of the real world have been found to outperform conventional statistical techniques.[23]

STAY SHARP AND KEEP MOVING

Success can bring as many problems as failure. Complacency, slackness, arrogance, becoming sidetracked with trinkets and irrelevances, forgetting the customer, or just falling asleep are all towards the top of the list. People and companies tend to be their own worst enemies, and to come to the gallows with their own rope.

Programmes can 'lose their way' or 'go off the rails'. David Thompson, chairman of Rank Xerox UK cautions:[24]

'Winning quality awards demonstrates a company is still in the game, not that it has arrived. Relax for a moment in a competitive market and you are dead. ... We never stop looking for ways of increasing customer satisfaction.'

David Kearns, while president of Xerox, took the view that:

'Quality is a race without a finish line. A focus on quality has made Xerox a stronger company, but we know we'll never be as good as we can be because we'll always try to be better. We are on a mission of continuous quality improvement.'

PRESERVE DIVERSITY AND ENCOURAGE LEARNING

Clones and crawlers should be discouraged from joining the network organisation. The organic network thrives on argument and debate, and is made more vibrant by variety and diversity. Common and standard approaches should not be allowed to solidify the criss-cross pattern of communications into the bars of a prescribed cage.

In Chapters 13 and 17 the emphasis was upon the integration of working and learning. People should be encouraged to find themselves, and not forced to hide themselves, in the work environment. The author has pointed out that the most fulfilled individuals are often those who are self-aware and true to themselves.[25]

'Those who focus upon what they enjoy doing and do best, and are able to work at a location and time of their choice, find it easier to close the gap between actual personal performance and their maximum potential. Career development should be managed to build a personal combination of competencies, experiences and qualities with a market value. This is more easily achieved by those who understand how they as individuals learn most effectively, and consciously seek to draw lessons from their experience. ...Individuals likely to be in the greatest demand will be those who are open minded, flexible and adaptable, willing to learn, and who have something distinct to contribute.'

We saw in Chapter 13 that approaches to learning and development should be adapted to reflect the unique capability and potential, and the preferred learning style, of each individual. The 'learning conversation' that arises out of daily life enables people to enrich their lives and build upon their natural strengths.[26] The bringing together of people from a variety of cultural backgrounds into international groups and teams offers the opportunity to create a diversity of learning environments. Individuals can be encouraged to build up a personal network of learning relationships that match their own unique attributes, interests and preferences.

FOCUS ON REALITY

A consistent theme of most of the surveys undertaken in the course of preparing for this book is the difficulty that many companies have in assessing the effectiveness of such basic activities as communicating and training, and the consequences of major investments in information technology. Is what is being done inherently defective, even counter-productive? Alternatively, does some complementary activity need to be undertaken, or are efforts being applied in the wrong areas?

Within Rank Xerox, managers, as part of the process of 'self-empowerment', are encouraged to identify any mismatches that might exist between intended and actual impacts, and subsequently align them. Managers are expected, *inter alia*, to:

- translate expectations, goals and objectives into definable and documented work processes that will enable their team to bring about the reality of achievement;
- ensure that their teams are positioned to contribute to those cross-functional and inter-organisational processes that generate and deliver value for customers, and achieve business objectives.

The learning that occurs within Rank Xerox derives from 'concrete experience'. Certain aspects of the problem-solving processes used exhibit features of the Kolb learning cycle.[27] There is 'reflective observation' of reality, 'abstract conceptualisation' of various options, and varying amounts of 'active experimentation' to try out alternative solutions. In essence, a learning approach to problem solving is practised.

Too often, the single-minded pursuit of 'the concept' against opposition and caution results in passionate advocates of change losing touch with reality. For example, the 'learning network' and the 'learning partnership' may appeal as concepts, but they have to be thought through in order to assess their value in a particular context.

Setting up links and relationships does not automatically result in their use for learning purposes. Global alliances and joint ventures are viewed by Japanese companies as an opportunity to learn. This approach can provide them with greater benefits than their western partners.[28] Not all the members of the network organisation will be equally committed to learning from their network partners.

A health warning about the intellectual voraciousness of the 'learning organisation' was issued in Chapter 14. What to some is openness and receptiveness, can appear to others as mental banditry and the piracy of ideas. The naive and unguarded can quickly become the victims of plagiarising parasites.

We need new ways of putting a finger on what is going on. The signs that may reveal what is happening in the organic network organisation are likely to be different. For example:

- the BIM *Flat Organisation* report points out that: 'Changes are evidenced by the shifting pattern of communications rather than by the removal van';[4]
- progress will be marked by joining teams that are working on more complex and critical problems, rather than by job titles and the dimensions of an air-conditioned office.

CHANGES OF ATTITUDES AND BEHAVIOUR

Where behaviour is changed and is seen to be effective, attitudes may follow, even though they may have been initially hostile. Festinger has demonstrated that people are prepared to modify those of their attitudes which appear to be in conflict with a new situation.[29] How does one judge the extent of such changes?

More basically, are people for it, or going along with it? Duplicity and an eagerness to please combine to confuse our senses. The BIM *Flat Organisation* report warns that: 'Eagerness among managers to agree and conform, to appear supportive and a "team player", and to use the "right words" can make it difficult to judge the extent of internalisation or "real understanding".'[4]

In the case of Rank Xerox, changes of attitudes and values are measured by means of employee involvement surveys and role-model behaviour assessments. An employee satisfaction element is being introduced into management remuneration. People are assessed in terms of their 'role-model' behaviour, for example, whether they 'hoard' or 'share' information, or are committed to developing others.

When 'reward and remuneration' is employed to influence attitudes, like other change elements, its use needs to be appropriate to the context. A recent study by the Institute of Manpower Studies suggests that performance-related pay can affect attitudes, but not always in desired or expected ways.[30] Companies are failing to think through the likely consequences, and their initiatives are not always part of a coherent change programme.

REINFORCE SUCCESS

Success can encourage further success, if the overall culture is supportive of innovation and change (Figure 18.3). The favourable climate is an inducement to innovation within operating units. The success of these can reinforce a positive commitment at the centre, while appropriate 'reward and remuneration' can cause other units to follow in the path of what is seen as 'role-model' conduct.

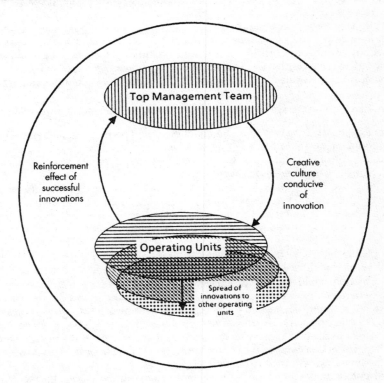

Figure 18.3 *The Innovative Culture*

It may be tempting to introduce change on a test basis into a part of an organisation. However, evidence suggests that the extent to which such 'experiments' are successful and spread within a corporation will reflect whether or not the culture of the company as a whole is conducive to, and supportive of, change.[31]

CONFRONT THE BARRIERS

The key to closing the gap between aspiration and achievement lies in 'helps and hinders' analysis, and identifying the missing elements of the transformation jigsaw puzzle by means of some form of corporate health check. Whatever form of checklist is used, it should focus on the critical factors, and be sufficiently flexible to reflect the situation and circumstances of the particular company.

Chalmers Johnson has concluded that a great many inter-related factors combined to bring about historical revolutions, and awareness of a gap between expectation and achievement is one such factor.[32] In this might lie the seeds of hope for those who may wish to stage a corporate coup at a certain stage in the transition to network organisation.

HOLD TRUE TO THE VISION

The coming together of a compelling vision, shared values and the capability to deliver is a potent combination. There is no limit to the sacrifice and commitment people will make for their deeply-held beliefs. No end of disappointment and disruption, or privation and pain, will be suffered if the imagination is captured, the purpose is right and the cause is just.

Innovations across a range of products and services have the potential to transform the daily lives, hopes and aspirations of millions of people. By enthusing and harnessing the capability of network organisations and the potential of their members, those who are alive and awake today have the means to achieve impact, at a speed and on a scale, that would dwarf the wildest imaginings of the most fertile imaginations of past ages.

COMPLETING THE JIGSAW PUZZLE

If you are fighting a war against entrenched interests and prejudices, blather, deception and hype you cannot afford to use one weapon at a time. The various barriers and obstacles need to be simultaneously overwhelmed with carefully selected combinations of 'change element' weapons in your armoury.

Some of those interviewed in the course of this book have been very hard on themselves. They should take heart if some pieces of the jigsaw puzzle have been put in place as a result of their efforts, even though enough elements have not been assembled to achieve a 'breakout'. By standing on the next brick they might, for the first time, be able to see over the top.

Some people have lost their jobs between first and second interviews which the author has undertaken, as a result of a perceived failure to deliver. Most of these 'victims of transformation' could not have produced the results that were sought for a variety of reasons. Generally, this was because some other piece of the jigsaw puzzle, for which they were not responsible, needed to be in place if their own efforts were to bear fruit.

Above all, every piece of the transformation jigsaw puzzle must be in place. People need to be able to see that all the change elements that are required to 'make it happen' are lined up. They must come to the conclusion: 'This is going to work.' This is when they become believers and committed converts.

The various elements that need to be brought together lie all around us in corporate organisations. In some cases, the programmes are already in place that could be managed to overcome what technical or financial barriers remain. For many people, all that lies between them and their dreams is their own reluctance to venture forth, and to think and feel, share and trust, and listen and learn.

The payoff from running the extra mile can be quite considerable. Today's caterpillar may become tomorrow's butterfly.

CHECKLIST

▶ Have you thought through what you are trying to achieve?

▶ Has it been expressed in terms of clear objectives?

▶ Are these agreed by all the key players?

▶ Are they committed to it?

▶ Is the commitment visible?

▶ Will the key players act as role models?

▶ Can the objectives be measured?

▶ Is someone responsible for their achievement?

▶ Have the 'vital few' tasks which need to be done been identified?

▶ Are roles and responsibilities relating to key tasks understood?

▶ Have the objectives been shared with all those who need to contribute to their achievement?

▶ Do each of them understand their individual contributions?

▶ Have these people been empowered to act?

▶ Are they motivated to act?

▶ Is their reward and remuneration consistent with what you are seeking to achieve?

▶ Have they been equipped with the skills to make it happen?

▶ Have the delivery processes been identified?

▶ What are the likely obstacles and barriers?

▶ What needs to be done about them and who is responsible?

REFERENCES

1 Barnard, C (1938) *The Functions of the Executive*, Harvard University Press, Cambridge, Mass.
2 Coulson-Thomas, C and Coulson-Thomas, S (1991) *Communicating for Change*, an Adaptation Survey for Granada Business Services, London.
3 Coulson-Thomas, C (1990) *The Role and Status of Project Management*, An Adaptation Ltd survey for The Association of Project Managers, London.
4 Coulson-Thomas, C and Coe, T (1991) *The Flat Organisation: Philosophy and Practice*, BIM, Corby.
5 Neave, H (1990) *The Deming Dimension*, SPC Press, Knoxville, Tenn.
6 Lynn, M and Ruddock, A (1992) 'BP All at Sea', Business Focus, *The Sunday Times*, 24 May, Section 3, p 3.
7 Schein, E H (1985) *Organisational Culture and Leadership*, Jossey-Bass, San Francisco.
8 Coulson-Thomas, C and Coulson-Thomas, S (1991) *Quality: The Next Steps*, an Adaptation Survey for ODI International, Adaptation, London and (Executive Summary) ODI, Wimbledon, London.
9 Coulson-Thomas, C and Wakelam, A (1991) *The Effective Board, Current Practice, Myths and Realities*, an Institute of Directors discussion document, London.
10 Prahalad, C K (1983) 'Developing Strategic Capability: An Agenda for Top Management' *Human Resource Management*, fall, vol 22, no 3, pp 237–54
11 Sites, P (1973) *Control: The Basis of Social Order*, Dunellan Publishing Company, New York; and Thomas, J and Bennis, W G (1972) *Management of Change and Conflict*, Penguin, Harmondsworth, Middlesex.
12 Drucker, P F (1954), *The Practice of Management*, Harper & Row, New York.
13 Boulding, K E (1956) *The Image*, University of Michigan Press, Ann Arbor, Mich.
14 Coulson-Thomas, C (1993) *Creating Excellence in the Boardroom*, McGraw-Hill, London.

15 Jacobson, G and Hillkirk, J (1986) *Xerox, American Samurai: The behind-the-scenes story of how a corporate giant beat the Japanese at their own game*, Macmillan, New York.

16 Sloan, A P (1963) *My Years With General Motors*, Doubleday, New York.

17 Thompson, D (1991) *Wokefield Park Official Opening: A Commitment to Quality*, comments made at the official opening of the Rank Xerox UK national training centre at Wokefield Park, 23 September, p1.

18 Coulson-Thomas, C (1988) *The New Professionals*, BIM, Corby.

19 Coulson-Thomas, C and Brown, R (1989) *The Responsive Organisation, People Management: the Challenge of the 1990s*, BIM, Corby.

20 Strassmann, P A (1985) *Information Payoff*, Macmillan, New York.

21 Hochstrasser, B and Griffiths, C (1990) *Regaining Control of IT Investments, A Handbook for Senior UK Management*, Kobler Unit, Imperial College, London, p 170.

22 Manzi, J (1992) summary of *Impact of Lotus Notes on Productivity: Evidence from Customers* Survey, AGM speech, Lotus Development Corporation, Cambridge, Mass, 8 June, p 6.

23 Treleaven, P and Goonatilake, S (1992) *Parallel Problem Solving from Nature*, Statistical Office of the European Communities, Brussels.

24 Thompson, D (1991) *Wokefield Park Official Opening: A Commitment to Quality*, comments made at the official opening of the Rank Xerox UK national training centre at Wokefield Park, 23 September, p2.

25 Coulson-Thomas, C (1989) *Too Old at 40?*, BIM, Corby.

26 Harri-Augstein, S and Thomas, L (1992) *Learning Conversations*, Routledge, London.

27 Kolb, D A (1984) *Experiential Learning: Experience as the Source of Learning and Development*, Prentice-Hall, Englewood Cliffs, NJ.

28 Lorenz, C (1992) 'When Friendship Proves to be All One Way', *Financial Times*, 12 June, p 13.

29 Festinger, L (1957) *A Theory of Cognitive Dissonance*, Stanford University Press, Stanford, Calif.

30 Thompson, M (1992) *Pay and Performance: The Employer Experience*, IMS Report 218, Institute of Manpower Studies, University of Sussex, Brighton.

31 Walton, R E (1987) *Innovating to Compete*, Jossey-Bass, San Francisco.

32 Johnson, C (1966) *Revolutionary Change*, Little, Brown & Co, Boston.

Sources of Information

The research programme

The following selection of reports from an ongoing programme of investigations of current issues and best practice represents the prime source of evidence used in the preparation of this book.

Coulson-Thomas, C (1988), *The New Professionals*, BIM, Corby.

Coulson-Thomas, C and Brown, R (1989) *The Responsive Organisation, People Management, the Challenge of the 1990s*, BIM, Corby.

Coulson-Thomas, C (1989) *Too Old at 40?*, BIM, Corby.

Coulson-Thomas, C and Brown, R (1990), *Beyond Quality, Managing the Relationship with the Customer*, BIM, Corby.

Coulson-Thomas, C (1990) *Human resource development for international operation*, an Adaptation Ltd Survey sponsored by Surrey European Management School, Adaptation, London.

Coulson-Thomas, C (1990) *Professional Development of and for the Board*, an Adaptation Ltd Survey for the Institute of Directors. A summary published by the IOD, London.

Coulson-Thomas, C (1990) *The Role and Status of Project Management*, an Adaptation Ltd Survey for the Association of Project Managers, London.

Coulson-Thomas, C (1990) *Developing IT Directors*, an interim Adaptation Ltd Report to the Department of Computing Science, Surrey University.

Coulson-Thomas, C and Coulson-Thomas, S (1990) *Managing the Relationship with the Environment*, an Adaptation Ltd Survey sponsored by Rank Xerox (UK) Ltd, London.

Coulson-Thomas, C and Coulson-Thomas, S (1990) *Implementing a Telecommuting Programme: A Rank Xerox guide for those considering the implementation of a telecommuting programme*, Adaptation, London.

Coulson-Thomas, C and Coulson-Thomas, S (1991) *Quality: The Next Steps*, an Adaptation Ltd Survey sponsored by ODI International, Adaptation & (Executive Summary) Wimbledon, London.

Coulson-Thomas, C and Coulson-Thomas, S (1991) *Communicating for Change*, an Adaptation Ltd Survey sponsored by Granada Business Services, London.

Coulson-Thomas, C and Coe, T (1991) *The Flat Organisation: Philosophy and Practice*. The initial questionnaire survey was entitled: 'Managing the Flat Organisation', BIM, Corby.

Coulson-Thomas, C (1991) *The Role and Development of the Personnel Director*, an interim Adaptation Ltd Survey undertaken in conjunction with the Institute of Personnel Management (IPM) Research Group, Wimbledon, London.

Coulson-Thomas, C and Wakelam, A (1991) *The Effective Board: Current Practice, Myths and Realities*, an Institute of Directors discussion document, London.

Survey participants

Table 1 provides a percentage breakdown by job title of the participants in eight of the above surveys. Overwhelmingly, the respondents were those with policy or implementation responsibility for the area in question.

Table 1 *Job Titles of Survey Participants (%)*

	The Responsive Organisation	Beyond Quality	HRD International Operation	Prof Dev of and for the Board	Managing the Relationship with the Environment	Quality, The Next Steps	Communicating for Change	The Flat Organisation
Chairmen and CEOs	62	44	15	87	25	26	33	61
Director	23	31	35	9	27	32	25	17
Manager	14	25	45	0	35	29	35	14
Other	1	0	5	4	13	13	7	8

Table 2 presents a percentage breakdown in terms of their main activities of the organisations covered by these surveys. Overall, the survey participants represent a broad mix of European, US, Japanese and international companies.

Table 2 *Main Activities of Survey Participants (%)*

	The Responsive Organisation	Beyond Quality	HRD International Operation	Prof Dev of and for the Board	Managing the Relationship with the Environment	Quality, The Next Steps	Communicating for Change	The Flat Organisation
Manufacturing/ Production	44	33	29.5	36	33	59	35	38
Leisure	3	4	0	7	3	3	6	2
Utilities	3	1	1	1.5	6	1	6	12
Financial Services	14	16	7.5	9	2	0	4	10
Retail/Distribution	11	6	7.5	15	10	12	23	5
Public Administration and Government	4	9	1	1.5	24	0	0	10
Construction/ Engineering	7	4	5.5	13	9	8	8	2
Educational body	0	1	1	3	1	0	0	0
Professional Scientific or Consultancy	0	6	29.5	14	1	1	0	0
Transport/ Communications	7	7	5.5	7	7	3	4	5
Others	7	13	12	14	4	12	14	12

Note: Some *Professional Development of and for the Board* respondents cited more than one main activity

Table 3 gives a percentage breakdown of the turnovers of the organisations covered by seven of the eight surveys. The participants in the *Professional Development of and for the Board* survey were not asked to disclose turnover information.

Table 3 *Turnover of Respondents' Organisations (£s in %)*

	The Responsive Organisation	Beyond Quality	HRD International Operation	Prof Dev of and for the Board	Managing the Relationship with the Environment	Quality, The Next Steps	Communicating for Change	The Flat Organisation
1b +	38	50	42		40	24	33	65
501m–1b	26	11	14		16	14	14	22
101–500m	23	21	21		31	46	45	7
51–100m	5	7	3		6	5	8	2
11–50m	7	7	8		5	7	0	0
0–10m	1	4	12		2	4	0	4

SURVEY PROFILES

There follow brief profiles of ten selected questionnaire and interview surveys.

The *Responsive Organisation* survey (Coulson-Thomas and Brown, 1989)

A questionnaire was sent to some 300 individuals. One hundred and thirty-six written replies, including 102 completed questionnaires, were received (of which 100 that arrived prior to the cutoff date were used). Forty-six per cent of the questionnaire respondents indicated they would be willing to be contacted to discuss their views regarding human resources management issues.

Some 38 per cent of the respondents were chairmen and over 60 per cent held the job titles of either chairman, chief executive or managing director.

The returned questionnaires covered in excess of 2.97 million employees. Almost half of the responses were from organisations employing in excess of 10,000 people.

Approaching two-thirds of the responses were from organisations with a turnover in excess of £500 million, while 38 per cent of responses were from organisations with a turnover in excess of £1 billion.

The *Beyond Quality* survey (Coulson-Thomas and Brown, 1990)

A questionnaire was sent to those most likely to have an overview of the relationships between an organisation and its customers. Sufficient questionnaires were distributed to obtain 100 replies. A response rate of over 34 per cent was achieved.

Of the respondents, 44 per cent were chairmen, chief executives or managing directors.

The participants represented predominantly large organisations. Forty-three per cent of the organisations employed in excess of 10,000 people. Over half employed more than 5000 people and 85 per cent more than 1000 people. Overall the survey covered more than 2 million employees.

The turnover of 60 per cent of the respondents' organisations exceeded £500 million. The turnover of about half of the organisations exceeded £1 billion, while the turnover of 17 of the 100 organisations participating in the survey exceeded £10 billion.

The *Human Resource for International Operation* survey
(Coulson-Thomas, 1990)

A questionnaire was sent to both 'continental' European and UK companies. Those surveyed were predominantly from large organisations, a number of professional associations and a selection of leading accounting firms. The survey was designed to seek the views of about 80 organisations. This number was thought appropriate in relation to the size of the total population of 'major professions', and of corporations with a turnover in excess of £1 billion. In the event a slightly higher number of responses was achieved (91), the response rate being 17 per cent.

Of the respondents, 38 per cent were chairmen, chief executives or managing directors.

Over a quarter of the companies returning questionnaires had in excess of 50,000 employees, and eight out of ten employed over 10,000 employees. In total the survey questionnaire covered over 2.7 million employees.

The turnover of four out of ten organisations represented by returned questionnaires exceeded £1 billion. Over seven out of ten had a turnover in excess of £500 million. In total the survey covered organisations with a combined turnover of some £320 billion.

The *Professional Development of and for the Board* survey
(Coulson-Thomas, 1990)

Two thousand seven hundred copies of a questionnaire were distributed to members of the IOD who were chairmen of the boards of companies. It is believed that the 'sample' group selected is representative of the distribution of company size in the UK. Consequently, the most common company size was represented by a turnover in the range of £1-10 million.

Two hundred and eighteen completed questionnaires were received, and 134 of these respondents indicated they would be willing to be contacted to discuss their views regarding professional development of and for the board.

Three-quarters of the responses were from those holding the job titles of chairman or chairman and managing director.

The *Role and Status of Project Management* survey (Coulson-Thomas, 1990)

A questionnaire was distributed to a random sample of members of the Association of Project Managers, and to companies that were major users of project management services. The questionnaire was sent out in batches of 50 until 100 usable responses had been achieved. The 100th returned questionnaire was received when some 500 questionnaires had been distributed.

The main activities of the respondents' organisations were 'construction/engineering' (31 per cent) and 'professional scientific or consultancy' (20 per cent). Two thirds of respondents indicated that they would be willing to be contacted to discuss their views regarding project management issues.

The *Managing the Relationship with the Environment* survey
(Coulson-Thomas and Coulson-Thomas, 1990)

Sufficient organisations were approached by questionnaire to secure around 100 participants. The 104 responses were split about 80/20 between corporate and local government organisations. The overall 'response rate' is about a quarter. Two-thirds of local government respondents, and approaching half of corporate respondents, were prepared to be contacted for further discussion of their views.

Over a quarter of the corporate responses are from the chairman or chief executive of the organisation concerned.

Four out of ten of the participating organisations have a turnover, or an income, in excess of £1billion. Over half of them have a turnover in excess of £500 million. In total the survey covers organisations with a combined turnover of some £260 billion.

In total the questionnaire survey covers over 2.3 million employees. About a quarter of the organisations participating in the survey employ over 20,000 people, and about a half have over 10,000 employees.

The *Quality: The Next Steps* survey
(Coulson-Thomas and Coulson-Thomas, 1991)

A questionnaire was sent to 681 large organisations, and follow-up and supplementary interviews were held. In total 105 organisations participated in the survey, a participation rate of some 15 per cent.

Over a quarter of the participants are chairmen or chief executives of their organisations, and approaching six out of ten are directors of their organisations.

In total, and only taking into account the employees of those organisations for which employment figures were supplied, the questionnaire survey covers over 1.6 million employees. About a third of the organisations participating in the survey employ over 5000 people.

The combined turnover of those organisations surveyed for which respondents provided turnover information, exceeds £84.6 billion. Thirty-six per cent of the participating organisations have a turnover in excess of £500 million. Some eight out of ten of them have a turnover in excess of £100 million.

The *Communicating for Change* survey
(Coulson-Thomas and Coulson-Thomas, 1991)

The survey involved a questionnaire and interview examination of 52 large organisations.

A third of the participants are either the chairman, chief executive or managing director of their organisation, and a further quarter are a director of their organisation.

In total the survey covers companies employing 1.2 million people. Some three out of ten of the participants' organisations employ in excess of 20,000 people.

In total the survey covers companies with a combined turnover of some £90 billion. Over four out of ten of the respondents' organisations have a turnover in excess of £500 million.

The *Flat Organisation: Philosophy and Practice* survey
(Coulson-Thomas and Coe, 1991)

A questionnaire was sent to 422 major organisations. A response rate of 15 per cent was achieved.

Over six out of ten of the respondents were the chairmen and/or chief executives of their organisations.

Approaching half of the organisations employed over 10,000. In total the survey covered organisations employing 1.3 million people.

The turnover of over six out of ten organisations represented by returned questionnaires exceeded £1 billion. Over eight out of ten of the companies returning questionnaires had a turnover in excess of £500 million. In total the survey covered organisations with a combined turnover of some £180 billion.

The *Effective Board: Current Practice, Myths and Realities* survey
(Coulson-Thomas and Wakelam, 1991)

In 1989 a survey, *The Training and Development of Company Directors*, was undertaken for the Training Agency by Alan Wakelam of the Management Centre of Exeter University. It is based upon an analysis of 373 of 390 responses to a questionnaire sent to 3266 directors. Approaching two-thirds of the respondents held the job titles of chairman or managing director. The most common turnover of the respondents' companies was represented by the band of £1–10 million, and this covered over four out of ten respondents.

In order to relate the findings of this 'Exeter' survey to the role and purpose of the board, the follow-on survey (*The Effective Board: Current Practice, Myths and Realities* (Coulson-Thomas and Wakelam, 1991) was carried out jointly by Exeter University and Adaptation Ltd.

The 'effective board' survey was specifically designed to obtain the views of chairmen and CEOs. One hundred and twenty-two questionnaires were distributed, and 56 replies received which covered 60 boards. Almost all those who replied expressed a willingness to be interviewed.

The largest single category of respondent is represented by 'manufacturing/ production'. Just under a third of the questionnaire respondents highlighted this as their organisation's main activity.

FURTHER INFORMATION

Further information on any of the surveys referred to in this Appendix can be obtained from Susan Coulson-Thomas, Managing Director, Adaptation Ltd, Rathgar House, 237 Baring Road, Grove Park, London SE12 0BE, England. Tel: 081-857 5907.

Details of the BIM publications cited, and of other related BIM surveys and reports, can be obtained from the Publications Department, British Institute of Management, Management House, Cottingham Road, Corby, Northants, NN17 1TT, England. Tel: 0536 204222

Selected Bibliography

Abe, E and Suzuki, Y (1991) *Changing Patterns of International Rivalry*, University of Tokyo Press, Tokyo.

Adair, J (1990) *Understanding Motivation*, Talbot Adair, Guildford.

Allison, G T (1971) *Essence of Decision*, Little, Brown, Boston.

Ansoff, H I (1984 and updated 1990) *Implanting Strategic Management*, Prentice-Hall, Englewood Cliffs, NJ.

Ansoff H I, Declerck, P and Hayes, R L (joint eds) (1976) *From Strategic Planning to Strategic Management*, John Wiley & Sons, London.

Apter, D (1968) *Some Conceptual Approaches to the Study of Modernisation*, Prentice-Hall, Englewood Cliffs, NJ.

Argyris, C (1985) *Strategy, Change and Defensive Routines*, Pitman, London.

Argyris, C and Schon, D (1978) *Organisational Learning: A Theory of Action Perspective*, Addison-Wesley, Wokingham.

Ascher, K (1983) *Management Training in Large UK Business Organisations*, Harbridge House, London.

Bachrach, P and Baratz, M (1962) 'Two Faces of Power', *American Political Science Review*, vol 56, pp 947-52.

Baldwin, D (1985) *Economic Statecraft*, Princeton University Press, Princeton, NJ.

Bandura, A (1977) *Social Learning Theory*, Prentice-Hall, Englewood Cliffs, NJ.

Barham, K and Devine, M (1990) *The Quest for the International Manager: A survey of Global Human Resource Strategies*, The Economist Intelligence Unit, London.

Barham, K and Oates, D (1991) *The International Manager*, Business Books, London.

Barnard, C (1938) *The Functions of the Executive*, Harvard University Press, Cambridge, Mass.

Bartlett, C A, Doz, Y and Hedlund, G (1990) *Managing the Global Firm*, Routledge, London.

Bartlett, C A and Goshal, S (1989) *Managing Across Borders*, Harvard Business School Press, Cambridge, Mass.

Bartram, P (1992) *Reinventing the Company: The Use of IT to Re-engineer Corporate Processes*, Business Intelligence, Wimbledon, London.

Bartram, P and Coulson-Thomas, C (1991) *The Complete Spokesperson, A workbook for managers who meet the media*, Kogan Page, London.

Beckhard, R and Harris, R T (1977) *Organisational Transitions: Managing Complex Change*, Addison-Wesley, Reading, Mass.

Beer, M and Walton, E (1987) 'Organisational Change and Development', in Rosenzweig, M and Porter, L (eds), *Annual Review of Psychology*, Annual Reviews, Palo Alto, Calif.

Beer, M (1980) *Organisational Change and Development: A Systems View*, Goodyear and Scott Foresman, Glencove, Ill.

Benjamin, R I and Scott Morton, M (1988) 'Information Technology, Integration, and Organisational Change', *Interfaces*, 18, May–June.

Bennis, W (1968) *The Temporary Society*, New York, Harper & Row.

Bennis, W (1976) *The Unconscious Conspiracy*, Amacon Press, New York.

Bennis, W and Nanus, B (1985) *Leaders: the Strategies for Taking Charge*, Harper & Row, New York.

Bennis, W, Benne, R and Chin, R (eds) (1970) *The Planning of Change*, Holt, Rinehart & Winston, New York.

Berkhout, F (1991) *Radioactive Waste: Politics and Technology*, Routledge, London.

Blau, P M (1964) *Exchange and Power in Social Life*, Wiley, New York.

Boss, W B (1983) 'Team Building and the Problem of Regression: The Personal Management Interview as an Intervention', *Journal of Applied Behavioral Science*, 19, pp 67–84.

Boulding, K E (1956) *The Image*, University of Michigan Press, Ann Arbor, Mich.

Bownas, G (1991) *Japan and the New Europe: Industrial Strategies and Options in the 1990s*, Special Report No 2072, The Economist Intelligence Unit, London.

Brooke, M Z (1984) *Centralisation and Autonomy: A study in organisation behaviour*, Holt, Rinehart & Winston, New York.

Bull, H and Watson, A (1984) *The Expansion of International Society*, Oxford University Press, Oxford.

Burgenmeier, B and Mucchielli, J-L (1991) *Multinationals and Europe 1992*, Routledge, London.

Burns, T and Stalker, G M (1961) *The Management of Innovation*, Tavistock, London.

Burton, J W (1968) *Systems, States, Diplomacy and Rules*, Cambridge University Press, Cambridge.

Burton, J W (1969) *Conflict and Communication*, Macmillan, London.

Burton, J W (1972) *World Society*, Cambridge University Press, Cambridge.

Burton, J (1979) *Deviance, Terrorism and War, The Process of Solving Unsolved Social and Political Problems*, Martin Robertson, Oxford.

Butler, R A (1971) *The Art of the Possible: The Memoirs of Lord Butler KG CH*, Hamish Hamilton, London.

Cairncross, F (1991) *Costing the Earth*, Business Books, London.

Camp, R C (1989) *Benchmarking: The Search for Industry Best Practices that Lead to Superior Performance*, Quality Press, Milwaukee, Wis.

Campbell, A and Yeung, S (1990) *Do You Need a Mission Statement?*, Special Report No 1208, The Economist Intelligence Unit, London.

Campbell, A, Devine M and Young, D (1990) *A Sense of Mission*, Hutchinson and *The Economist*, London.

Campbell, A and Tawadey, K (1990) *Mission and Business Philosophy*, Heinemann, Oxford.

CBI Education and Training Directorate (1992) *Focus on the First Line: the Role of the Supervisor*, CBI, London.

Chandler, A (1962) *Strategy and Structure*, The MIT Press, Mass.

Committee on The Financial Aspects of Corporate Governance (Chairman, Sir Adrian Cadbury), (1992) Draft Report issued for public comment, 27 May, London.

Connock, S (1991) *HR Vision: Managing a Quality Workforce*, Institute of Personnel Management, Wimbledon, London.

Cottrell, J (1992) 'Favourable Recipe', *The TQM Magazine*, vol 4, no 1, February, pp 17–20.

Coulson-Thomas, C (1975) *A Guide to Business Schools*, Hamish Hamilton/St Georges Press, London.

Coulson-Thomas, C (compiler) (1981) *BGA Guide to Business Schools*, (5th edn), Macdonald & Evans, Plymouth.

Coulson-Thomas, C (1990) 'Building Europe's Learning Foundations: The European Learning Network', *Europe IT Journal*, February, pp 14–19.

Coulson-Thomas, C (1992) 'Breaking Through the Information Barrier : Management Development and IT', *International Journal of Technology Management*, volume 5, no. 5, pp 618–23.

Coulson-Thomas, C (1991) 'Competent Directors: Boardroom Myths and Realities', *Journal of General Management*, vol 17, no 1, autumn, pp 1-26.

Coulson-Thomas, C (1992) *Creating Excellence in the Boardroom*, McGraw-Hill Europe, London.

Coulson-Thomas, C (1992) *Creating the Global Company: Successful Internationalisation*, McGraw-Hill, London.

Coulson-Thomas, C (1991) 'Customers, Marketing and the Network Organisation' *Journal of Marketing Management*, 7, pp 237–55.

Coulson-Thomas, C (1992) 'Developing Competent Directors and Effective Boards', *Journal of Management Development*, Vol 11, No 1, pp 39-49.

Coulson-Thomas, C (1990) 'Developing Directors', *European Management Journal*, vol 8, no 4, December, pp 488–99.

Coulson-Thomas, C (1993) 'Developing Directors: Creating an Effective Boardroom Team', McGraw-Hill, London.

Coulson-Thomas, C (1990) *Developing IT Directors*, an Adaptation Ltd Report to the Department of Computing Science, Surrey University, London.

Coulson-Thomas, C (1991) 'Developing Tomorrow's Professionals Today', *Journal of European Industrial Training*, vol 15, no 1, pp 3–11.

Coulson-Thomas, C (1991) 'Directors and IT, and IT Directors', *European Journal of Information Systems*, vol 1, no 1, pp 45–53.

Coulson-Thomas, C J (1990) *Human Resource Development for International Operation*, a Survey Report for Surrey European Management School, Adaptation Ltd, London.

Coulson-Thomas, C (1989) 'Information Technology and the Responsive Organisation', *Information Technology and Public Policy*, vol 8, no 1, winter, pp 29–30.

Coulson-Thomas, C (1991) IT and New Forms of Organisation for Knowledge Workers : Opportunity and Implementation', *Employee Relations*, vol 13, no 4, pp 22–32.

Coulson-Thomas, C (1991) 'IT Directors and IT Strategy', *Journal of Information Technology*, 6, pp 192–203.

Coulson-Thomas, C J (1978) 'New Product Development Checklist', *Accountants' Digest* No 60, Institute of Chartered Accountants in England and Wales, London.

Coulson-Thomas, C (1981) *Public Relations is Your Business: a guide for every manager*, Business Books, London.

Coulson-Thomas, C (1979) *Public Relations: A Practical Guide*, Macdonald & Evans, Plymouth.

Coulson-Thomas, C (1988) *The New Professionals*, British Institute of Management, Corby.

Coulson-Thomas, C (1983) *Marketing Communications*, Heinemann Professional Publishing, Oxford and London.

Coulson-Thomas, C (1990) *Professional Development of and for the Board*, Adaptation Survey for Institute of Directors, Summary published by IOD, London.

Coulson-Thomas, C (1990) 'Project Management, a necessary skill?', *Industrial Management and Data Systems*, no 6, pp 17–21.

Coulson-Thomas, C (1992) 'Quality: Where Do We Go From Here?', *International Journal of Quality and Reliability Management*, vol 9, no 1, pp 38–55.

Coulson-Thomas, C (1989) 'Responsive Professional and Educational Organisations', *International Journal of Manpower*, vol 10, no 6, pp 13–16.

Coulson-Thomas, C (1988) 'Status and Professional Association Councils', (unpublished PhD thesis), University of Aston in Birmingham, Birmingham, January.

Coulson-Thomas, C (1992) 'Strategic Vision or Strategic Con?: Rhetoric or Reality?' *Long Range Planning*, vol 25, no 1, pp 81–9.

Coulson-Thomas, C (1992) 'Surveying the Scene', *The TQM Magazine*, vol 4, no 1, February, pp 25–31.

Coulson-Thomas, C (1990) 'The Responsive Organisation', *Journal of General Management*, volume 15, no 4, summer, pp 21–31.

Coulson-Thomas, C (1991) *The Role and Development of the Personnel Director*, an Adaptation Ltd Interim Survey undertaken in conjunction with the Institute of Personnel Management (IPM) Research Group, Wimbledon, London.

Coulson-Thomas, C (1990) *The Role and Status of Project Management*, an Adaptation Survey for the Association of Project Managers, London.

Coulson-Thomas, C (1989) *Too Old at 40?*, BIM, Corby.

Coulson-Thomas, C & Brown, R (1989) *The Responsive Organisation, People Management: the Challenge of the 1990s*, BIM, Corby.

Coulson-Thomas, C and Brown, R (1990) *Beyond Quality, Managing the Relationship with the Customer*, BIM, Corby.

Coulson-Thomas, C and Didacticus Video Productions Ltd (1991) *The Change Makers, Vision and Communication*, booklet to accompany integrated audio and video-tape training programme by Sir John Harvey-Jones. Available from Video Arts, London.

Coulson-Thomas, C, (Metra Consulting and International Joint Ventures) (1980) *Brazil: Business Opportunities in the 1980s*, London.

Coulson-Thomas, C and Coulson-Thomas, S (1991) *Communicating for Change*, an Adaptation Ltd Survey for Granada Business Services, London.

Coulson-Thomas, C and Coulson-Thomas, S (1990) *Implementing a Telecommuting Programme*, A Rank Xerox guide for those considering the implementation of a telecommuting programme, Adaptation, London.

Coulson-Thomas, C and Coulson-Thomas, S (1991) *Quality: The Next Steps*, an Adaptation survey for ODI International, Adaptation, London, and (Executive Summary), ODI International, Wimbledon, London.

Coulson-Thomas, C and Coe, T (1991) *The Flat Organisation: Philosophy and Practice*, BIM, Corby.

Coulson-Thomas, C and Wakelam, A (1991) *The Effective Board, Current Practice, Myths and Realities*, an Institute of Directors discussion document, London.

Cox, R (1987) *Production, Power and World Order: Social Forces in the Making of History*, Columbia University Press, New York.

Dahrendorf, R (1959) *Class and Class Conflict in Industrial Society*, Routledge & Kegan Paul, London.

Daniels, C (1991) *The Management Challenge of Information Technology*, Economist Intelligence Unit, London.

Davies, J C (ed) (1971) *When Men Revolt and Why*, The Free Press, New York.

Deal, T E (1985) 'Cultural Change: Opportunity, Silent Killer, or Metamorphosis?', in Kilmann, R H, Saxon, M J and Serpa, R (eds), *Gaining Control of the Corporate Culture*, Jossey-Bass, San Francisco and London.

De Bono, E (1967) *The Use of Lateral Thinking*, McGraw-Hill, Maidenhead.

De Bono, E (1971) *Lateral Thinking for Management*, McGraw-Hill, Maidenhead.

Demb, A and Neubauer, F-F (1992) *The Corporate Board: Confronting The Paradoxes*, Oxford University Press, Oxford.

Deming, W E (1986) *Out of Crisis*, The MIT Centre for Advanced Engineering Study, Massachusetts.

Deutsch, K W (1978) *Analysis of International Relations* (2nd edn), Prentice-Hall, Englewood Cliffs, NJ.

Deutsch, K W (1963) *The Nerves of Government*, Free Press, New York.

Dicken, P (1986) *Global Shift*, Harper & Row, New York.

Dougherty, J E and Pfaltzgraff, R L (1971) *Contending Theories of International Relations*, Lippincott, Philadelphia.

Douglas, T (1990) *Basic Groupwork*, Routledge, London.

Downs, A (1967) *Inside Bureaucracy*, Little, Brown, Boston.

Doz, Y L, Bartlett, C and Prahalad, C K (1981) 'Global Competitive Pressures and Host Country Demands: Managing Tensions in MNCs', *California Management Review*, spring, vol XXIII, no 3, pp 63–74.

Drucker, P F (1946) *Concept of the Corporation*, John Day, New York.

Drucker, P F (1969) *The Age of Discontinuity*, Heinemann, London.

Drucker, P F (1989) *The New Realities*, Heinemann Professional Publishing, London.

Drucker, P F (1954) *The Practice of Management*, Harper & Row, New York.

Easton, D and Dennis, J (1969) *Children in the Political System: Origins of Political Legitimacy*, McGraw-Hill, New York.

Eckley, R S (1991) *Global Competition in Capital Goods*, Quorum Books, New York.

Eli, M (1990) *Japan Inc : Global Strategies of Japanese Trading Companies*, McGraw-Hill, London.

Evans, P, Doz, Y and Laurent, A (eds) (1989) *Human Resource Management in International Firms, Change, Globalization, Innovation*, Macmillan, New York.

Festinger, L (1957 and 1962) *A Theory of Cognitive Dissonance*, Stanford University Press, Stanford.

Fitzgerald, J (1991) 'A Japanese Lesson in European Togetherness', *Personnel Management*, September, pp 45–7.

Fogarty, M and Christie, I (1991) *Companies and Communities: Promoting Business Involvement in the Community*, Policy Studies Institute, London.

Freeman, A M III and Haveman, R H (1972), 'Clean Rhetoric and Dirty Water', *The Public Interest*, no 28, summer, p 65.

Friedman, M (1962) *Capitalism and Freedom*, University of Chicago Press, Chicago.

Geneen H S, (1984) 'Why Directors Can't Protect the Shareholders', *Fortune*, 17 September.

Gilpin, R (1987) *The Political Economy of International Relations*, Princeton University Press, Princeton, NJ.

Gilpin, R (1976) *US Power and the Multinational Corporation*, Macmillan, New York.

Gray, P A (1991) *Open Systems: A Business Strategy for the 1990s*, McGraw-Hill, London.

Gross, B and Gross, E (eds) (1985) *The Great School Debate*, Simon & Schuster, New York.

Gurr, T R (1970) *Why Men Rebel*, Princeton University Press, Princeton, NJ.

Guy, V and Mattock, J (1991) *The New International Manager*, Kogan Page, London.

Guzzo, R A, Jette, R D and Katzell, R A (1985) 'The Effects of Psychologically Based Intervention Programs on Worker Productivity: A Meta-analysis', *Personnel Psychology*, 38, pp 275–92.

Haas, E B (1964) *Beyond the Nation State, Functionalism and International Organisation*, Stanford University Press, Stanford, Calif.

Halperin, M H (1974) *Bureaucratic Politics and Foreign Policy*, Brookings Institution, Washington DC.

Hambrick, D and Mason, P (1984) 'Upper Echelons: The Organisation as a Reflection of Its Top Management', *Academy of Management Review*, vol 9, no 2.

Hampden-Turner, C (1990) *Charting the Corporate Mind: from dilemma to strategy*, Blackwell, Oxford.

Handler, S (1992) 'The Emphasis on Value-based Strategic Management in UK Companies', *Journal of Strategic Change*, vol 1, no 1, January–February.

Handy, C (1978) *Gods of Management, How they work and why they will fail*, Souvenir Press, London.

Handy, C (1984) *The Future of Work*, Basil Blackwell, Oxford.

Handy, C (1989) *The Age of Unreason*, Business Books, London.

Harri-Augstein, S and Thomas, L (1992) *Learning Conversations*, Routledge, London.

Harvey-Jones, Sir J (1988) *Making it Happen*, Collins, London.

Hermann, C F (1972) *International Crises: Insights from Behavioural Research*, Free Press, New York.

Hertzberg, F, Mausner, B and Snyderman, B (1959) *The Motivation to Work*, Wiley, New York.

Hochstrasser, B and Griffiths, C (1990) *Regaining Control of IT Investments, A Handbook for Senior UK Management*, Kobler Unit, Imperial College, London.

Holsti, K J (1992) *International Politics: A Framework for Analysis*, (6th edn), Prentice-Hall International, Hemel Hempstead, Herts.

Horwitch, M (1982) *Clipped Wings*, The MIT Press, Cambridge, Mass.

Humble, J (1971) *Management by Objectives*, McGraw-Hill, Maidenhead.

Hussey, D E (1988) *Management Training and Corporate Strategy*, Pergamon, Oxford.

IIC, (1991) *The Global Telecommunications Traffic Report 1991*, International Institute of Communications (IIC), New York.

Institute for Research on Learning (undated, c 1988) *The Advancement of Learning*, Institute for Research on Learning, Palo Alto, Calif.

Jacobson, G and Hillkirk, J (1986) *Xerox: American Samurai, the behind-the-scenes story of how a corporate giant beat the Japanese at their own game*, Macmillan Publishing Company, New York.

Jacobson, H K (1984) *Networks of Interdependence*, (2nd edn) Alfred A Knopf, New York.

Janis, I L (1972) *Victims of Groupthink*, Houghton-Mifflin, Boston.

Jaques, E (1951) *The Changing Culture of a Factory*, Tavistock, London; and (1956) *The Measurement of Responsibility*, Tavistock, London.

Jervis, R (1976) *Perception and Misperception in International Politics*, Princeton University Press, Princeton, NJ.

Johnson, C (1966) *Revolutionary Change*, Little, Brown, Boston.

Johnson, T and Chappell, C (1990) *The Computer Integrated Company, Market Driver for the 90s*, Ovum, London.

Jones, S (1991) *Working for the Japanese*, Macmillan, London.

Juran, J M (1988) *Juran on Planning for Quality*, Free Press, New York.

Kakabadse, A (1991) *The Wealth Creators: Top People, Top Teams and Executive Best Practice*, Kogan Page, London.

Kanter, R M (1983) *The Change Masters: Corporate Entrepreneurs at Work*, Simon & Schuster, New York.

Kanter, R M (1989) *When Giants Learn to Dance*, Simon & Schuster, London and New York.

Kanter, R M, Stein, B A and Jick, T D (1992) *The Challenge of Organisational Change: How People Experience It and Manage It*, The Free Press, New York.

Kedourie, E (1960) *Nationalism*, Hutchinson, London.

Keen, P G W (1986) *Competing in Time: Using Telecommunications for Competitive Advantage*, Ballinger, New York.

Kent, R C and Nielssen, G P (eds) (1980) *The Study and Teaching of International Relations, A Perspective on Mid-Career Education*, Frances Pinter, London.

Keohane, R O and Nye, J S (1970) *Transnational Relations and World Politics*, Harvard University Press, Boston.

Keohane, R O and Nye, J S (1977) *Power and Interdependence: World Politics in Transition*, Little, Brown, Boston.

Kirkman, P and Hope, C (1992) *Environmental Disclosure in UK Company Annual Reports*, Management Studies Group, University of Cambridge, Cambridge.

Knibb Gormezano and Partners (1992) *Opportunities in the North American Automotive Original Equipment and Aftermarket*, Department of Trade and Industry, London.

Kobayashi, K (1991) *The Rise of NEC*, Blackwell Publishers, Oxford.

Kolb, D A (1984) *Experiential Learning: Experience as the Source of Learning and Development*, Prentice-Hall, Englewood Cliffs, NJ.

Kornai, J (1990) *Vision and Reality, Market and State*, Harvester/Wheatsheaf, Hemel Hempstead, Herts.

Kotler, P (1983) *Principles of Marketing*, (2nd edn), Prentice-Hall, Englewood Cliffs, NJ.

Kotter, J P (1990) *A Force for Change, How Leadership Differs from Management*, The Free Press, New York.

Krasner (1985) *Structural Conflict*, University of California Press, Berkeley.

Kuhn, T S (1970) *The Structure of Scientific Revolutions*, University of Chicago Press, Chicago.

Laudon, K C and Turner, J (eds) (1989) *Information Technology and Management Strategy*, Prentice-Hall, Englewood Cliffs, NJ.

Lawrence, P R and Vlachoutsicos, C A (1991) *Behind The Factory Walls – Decision Making in Soviet and US Enterprises*, Harvard Business School Press, Boston.

Levitt, T (1962) *Innovation in Marketing*, McGraw-Hill, New York.

Levitt, T (1983) *The Marketing Imagination*, The Free Press, New York.

Likert, R (1961) *New Patterns of Management*, McGraw-Hill, New York.

Likert, R (1967) *The Human Organisation: Its Management and Value*, McGraw-Hill, New York.

Lindblom, C E (1977) *Politics and Markets, The World's Political–Economic Systems*, Basic Books, New York.

Little, R and Smith, S (1988) *Belief Systems and International Relations*, Basil Blackwell, Oxford.

Lorsch, J and MacIver, E (1989) *Pawns or Potentates: The Reality of America's Corporate Boards*, Harvard Business School Press, Boston.

Mace, M (1971) *Directors: Myth and Reality*, Division of Research, Graduate School of Business Administration, Harvard University, Boston.

Manpower plc (1990) *Employment and Training*, Mercury Books/CBI Initiative 1992, London.

Maslow, A H (1970) *Motivation and Personality*, New York, Harper & Row.

McDonald, O (1992) *The Future of Whitehall*, Weidenfeld & Nicolson, London.

McGowan, W G et al (*Harvard Business Review* collected articles) (1991) *Revolution in Real Time: Managing Information Technology in the 1990s*, Harvard Business School Press, Boston.

McGregor, D (1960) *The Human Side of Enterprise*, McGraw-Hill, New York.

Mintzberg, H (1989) *Mintzberg on Management, Inside our strange world of organisations*, The Free Press, New York.

Mintzberg, H (1979) *The Structuring of Organisations*, Prentice-Hall, Englewood Cliffs, NJ.

Mintzberg, H (1983) *Structures in Fives: Designing Effective Organisations*, Prentice-Hall, Englewood Cliffs, NJ.

Mintzberg, H (1973) *The Nature of Managerial Work*, Harper & Row, New York.

Mitrany, D (1975) *The Functional Theory of Politics*, Martin Robertson, London.

Monks, R and Minow, N (1991) *Power and Responsibility*, Harper Business Books, New York.

Moran, R T (1991) *Cultural Guide to Doing Business in Europe*, Butterworth/Heinemann, London.

Morgenthau, H J (1978) *Politics Among Nations, The Struggle for Power and Peace*, Alfred A Knopf, New York.

Neave, H (1990) *The Deming Dimension*, SPC Press, Knoxville, Tenn.

Nilsson, W P (1987) *Achieving Strategic Goals Through Executive Development*, Addison-Wesley, Reading, Mass.

Ohmae, K (1985) *Triad Power: The Coming Shape of Global Competition*, The Free Press, New York.

Ohmae, K (1990) *The Borderless World: Power and Strategy in the Interlinked Economy*, Collins, London.

Ohmae, K (1982) *The Mind of the Strategist*, McGraw-Hill, New York.

Olson, M (1982) *The Rise and Decline of Nations*, Yale University Press, Newhaven, Connecticut.

Organisation for Economic Co-operation and Development (OECD) (1988) *New Technology in the 1990s: A Socio-economic Strategy*, OECD, Paris.

Parsons, T (1969) *Politics and Social Structure*, The Free Press, New York.

Pascale, R T (1990) *Managing On the Edge*, Simon & Schuster, New York and Viking, London.

Passmore, W A (1982) 'Overcoming the Roadblocks in Work Restructuring Efforts', *Organizational Dynamics*, 10, pp 54–67.

Pearce, D, Turner, K and Bresson, I (1992) *Packaging Waste and the Polluter Pays Principle: A Taxation Solution*, Centre for Social and Economic Research on the Global Environment, University College, London.

Petersen, D and Hillkirk, J (1991) *Teamwork: New Management Ideas for the 90s*, Victor Gollancz, London.

Peters, T (1987) *Thriving on Chaos*, Alfred A Knopf, New York.

Pettigrew, A and Whipp, R (1991) *Managing Change for Competitive Success*, Basil Blackwell, Oxford.

Porter, M E (1980) *Competitive Strategy: Techniques for Analysing Industries and Competitors*, Free Press, New York.

Porter, M E (1985) *Competitive Advantage*, Free Press, New York.

Porter, M E (1990) *The Competitive Advantage of Nations*, Macmillan, London.

Prahalad, C K (1983) 'Developing Strategic Capability: An Agenda for Top Management', *Human Resource Management*, fall, vol 22, no 3, pp 237–54.

Prahalad, C K (1990) 'Globalisation: The Intellectual and Managerial Challenges', *Human Resource Management*, spring, vol 29, no 1, pp 27–37.

Price Waterhouse Cranfield Project on International Strategic Human Resource Management, *Annual Reports 1990 & 1991*, Price Waterhouse & Cranfield School of Management, Cranfield.

Quinn, B (1980) *Strategies for Change: Logical Incrementalism*, Richard D Irwin, Homewood, Ill.

Razvigorova, E and Wolf-Laudon, G (1991) *East-West Joint Ventures*, Blackwell Publishers, Oxford.

Raffia, H (1982) *The Art and Science of Negotiation*, Harvard University Press, Boston.

Reeser, C (1969) 'Some Potential Human Problems of the Project Form of Organisation', *Academy of Management Journal*, p 463.

Revans, R W (1979) *Action Learning*, Blond & Briggs, London.

Rheingold, H (1991) *Virtual Reality*, Secker & Warburg, London.

Rokeach, M (1960) *The Open and Closed Mind*, Basic Books, New York.

Scase, R and Goffee, R (1989) *Reluctant Managers: Their Work and Lifestyles*, Unwin Hyman, London.

Schein, E H (1988) *Process Consultation*, Addison-Wesley, Reading, Mass.

Schein, E H (1985) *Organisational Culture and Leadership*, Jossey-Bass, San Francisco.

Schelling, T C (1963) *The Strategy of Conflict*, Oxford University Press, New York.

Schlesinger, L A and Oshry, B (1984) 'Quality of Work Life and the Supervisor: Muddle in the Middle', *Organisational Dynamics*, 13, pp 4–20.

Schmidheiny, S and the Business Council for Sustainable Development (1992) *Changing Course*, The MIT Press, Boston.

Schon, D (1967) *Technology and Change*, New York, Delacorte Press.

Schonberger, R J (1990) *Building a Chain of Customers*, The Free Press, New York and Business Books, London.

Schumacher, E F (1973) *Small is Beautiful: A Study of Economics As if People Mattered*, Blond & Briggs, London.

Scott Morton, M S (1991) *The Corporation of the 1990s: Information Technology and Organisational Transformation*, Oxford University Press, New York and Oxford.

Scullian, H (1992) Attracting Management Globetrotters, *Personnel Management*, January, pp 28–32.

Secretary's Commission on Achieving Necessary Skills (1991) *What Work Requires of Schools*, US Department of Labor, Washington, DC.

Senge, P (1990) *The Fifth Discipline: The Art and Practice of the Learning Organisation*, Doubleday/Currency, New York, p 3.

Sherman, B and Judkins, P (1992) *Glimpses of Heaven – Visions of Hell*, Hodder & Stoughton, London.

Sites, P (1973) *Control: The Basis of Social Order*, Dunellan Publishing Company, New York.

Sloan, A P (1963) *My Years With General Motors*, Doubleday, New York.

Smith, P and Reinertsen, D (1991) *Developing Products in Half The Time*, Chapman & Hall, London.

Sobel R (1981) *IBM: Colossus in Transition*, Truman Talley Books–Times Books, New York, and (1984) Sidgwick & Jackson, London.

Steinbruner, J D (1974) *A Cybernetic Theory of Decision*, Princeton University Press, Princeton, NJ.

Stephens, M D (1991) *Japan and Education*, Macmillan, London.

Strange, S (1988) *States and Markets : An Introduction to International Political Economy*, Pinter, London.

Strassmann, P A (1985) *Information Payoff*, Macmillan, New York and London.

Taylor, F W (1947) *Scientific Management*, Harper & Row, New York.

Thomas, J and Bennis, W G (1972) *Management of Change and Conflict*, Penguin, Harmondsworth, Middlesex.

Thompson, M (1992) *Pay and Performance: The Employer Experience*, IMS Report 218, Institute of Manpower Studies, University of Sussex, Brighton.

Toffler, A (1970) *Future Shock*, The Bodley Head, London.

Tovey, L (1991) *Management Training and Development in Large UK Business Organisations*, Harbridge Consulting Group, London.

Treleaven, P and Goonatilake, S (1992) *Parallel Problem Solving from Nature*, Statistical Office of the European Communities, Brussels.

Tricker, R I (1978) *The Independent Director: A study of the non-executive director and of the audit committee*, Tolley Publishing Company Limited, Croydon.

Tushman, M L, Newman, W H and Nadler, D A (1988) 'Executive Leadership and Organisational Evolution: Managing Incremental and Discontinuous Change', in Kilman, R and Covey, T J (eds), *Corporate Transformation*, Jossey-Bass, San Francisco.

Von Hippel, E (1978) 'Successful Industrial Products from Customer Ideas', *Journal of Marketing*, vol 42, no 1, pp 39–46.

Wakelam, A (1989) *The Training and Development of Company Directors*, a Report on a questionnaire survey undertaken by the Centre for Management Studies, University of Exeter for the Training Agency, December.

Walton, R E (1977) 'Work Innovations at Topeka: After six years', *Journal of Applied Behavioral Science*, 13, pp 422–433.

Walton, R E (1987) *Innovating to Compete*, Jossey-Bass, San Francisco.

Waterman, R H, Jnr (1987) *The Renewal Factor*, Bantam, New York.

Weber, M (1947) *The Theory of Social and Economic Organisation*, (initial publication 1924, translated and edited by Henderson, A M and Parsons T), The Free Press, New York.

Wenger, E (1987) *Artificial Intelligence Tutoring Systems*, Morgan Kaufman, San Pateo, Calif.

Wenger, E, *Glass-box Technology: Merging learning and doing*, IRL Research Abstract 1, Institute for Research on Learning, Palo Alto, Calif.

Woolfe, R (1991) *Globalisation: The IT Challenge*, Amdahl Executive Institute, Hounslow.

Zuboff, S (1988) *In the Age of the Smart Machine, The Future of Work and Power*, New York, Basic Books.

INDEX